THE GREAT LEAP

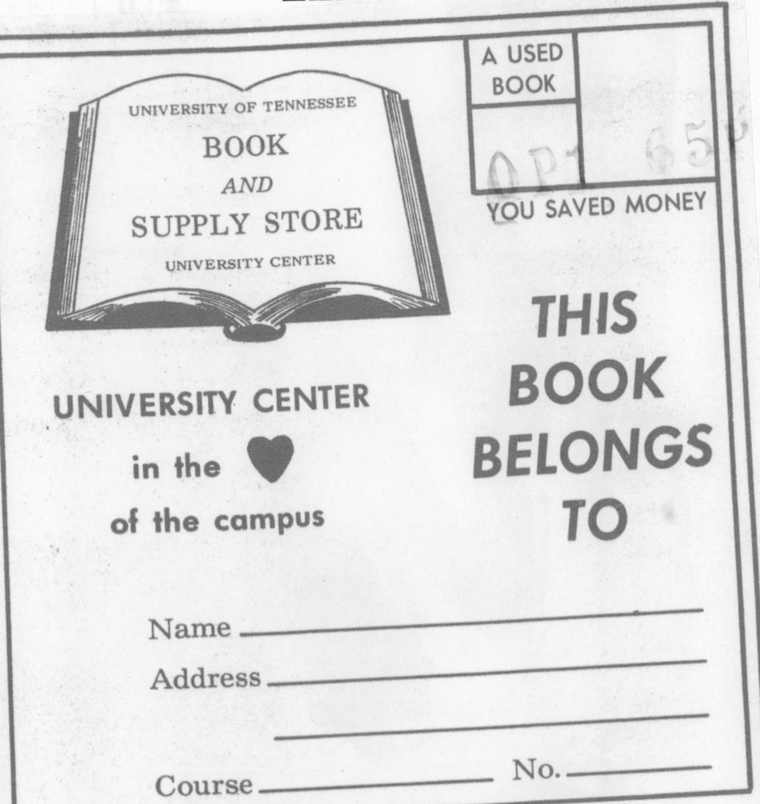

THE GREAT LEAP

The Past Twenty-five Years in America

JOHN BROOKS

HARPER COLOPHON BOOKS
HARPER & ROW, PUBLISHERS
New York and Evanston

Printed in the United States of America.

First HARPER COLOPHON edition published in 1968 by Harper & Row, Publishers, Incorporated, New York, N.Y. 10016.

Library of Congress Catalog Card Number: 66-20726.

For C. B. and J. A. B.

CONTENTS

ILLUSTRATIONS

The following are grouped in a separate section after page 190

I. BEFORE AND AFTER

1

In the United States of America not very long ago, a good many conditions prevailed that seem rather odd today. The birth rate was failing to keep up with the death rate, and demographers, looking to the far future, were gloomily predicting a more or less depopulated country. Not much less than half of all Americans lived outside cities, towns, and suburbs, and almost 40 percent, urban and rural, lived without a bathtub or shower, although less than one fifth had no radio to listen to. The average wage for production workers in manufacturing was sixty-three cents an hour, or $23.86 a week based on the average work week. The average annual earnings of doctors amounted to $4,229; of lawyers, $4,391; of college teachers, a bit under $3,000. The well-to-do white-collar suburbs of Madison and Summit, New Jersey, boasted average annual family incomes of $2,500. On the other hand, lunch at a good restaurant could be had for sixty-five cents, a summer suit at Gimbel's for $8, a silver fox coat at Bonwit Teller for $165, a new Ford sedan for $685, and a six-day cruise to Nassau for $55. The New York State Labor Department estimated that the annual income necessary for a woman living alone —to pay for rent, food, fuel, light, clothing, hospital and medical care, insurance, transporation, gifts, candy, cigarettes, cosmetics, leisure-time activities, and even contributions to charity—was $1,160.75. Income-tax exemptions and rates were such that the lawyer or doctor of average income, if he were married and had two children, had an annual tax bill of about $25, while a highly successful businessman in the same family situation whose net for the year was $16,000 owed the government less than a thousand dollars. The average industrial worker paid no income tax at all, and, indeed, only about one American in thirty-three paid any. A great howl went up when the President proposed a federal budget of about nine billion dollars, which sum was needed, among other purposes, to support an Army and Navy totaling about 300,000 men.

Nor was optimism about the nation's economic future in the air; experts were talking about how a formerly expanding economy had now been replaced by a "mature" one, and a well-known social philosopher was saying, "Today capitalism has reached a frontier. . . . We have arrived at the age of stability; our horizon has contracted." Other signs of the times were the facts that influenza and pneumonia had recently for the first time been surpassed by cancer as a national cause of death; that the average American had had just over eight years' schooling, or an elementary school education; that there was one telephone for every seven of us from coast to coast; that a quarter of all our housing units had no running water, 35 percent of them had no flush toilet, and all of them had no television. Cooking on wood- or coal-burning ranges was the rule in not much less than half our homes, and Sears, Roebuck was advertising—for $76.95, only $5 down—a handsome cast-iron coal range that the firm claimed to be "the favorite of young moderns" because "no other range achieves its brilliant styling." At the same time, there were some 26 million automobiles on the country's roads, and just about half of the Americans alive in 1965 were alive then.

If the country thus described now seems rather bleak, sparse, frugal, quaint, and faraway, it may seem even stranger when one knows that the year was 1939. But other aspects of the same time seem more reassuringly familiar. There were country clubs, evenings of bridge, traffic jams, and even a few devotees of the new fad of backyard cookery. Parents and teachers were debating whether or not sex education ought to be included in school curricula. Commencement speakers deplored godlessness and called for a return to traditional beliefs. The *New York Times* remarked on the mobs of "almost naked" people on resort beaches, although in the age of the bikini it is easy to see how little the *Times* understood the potentialities of the situation. Moralists deplored the purposelessness of youth (and youth happily took up the theme). In a state-of-the-Union issue of a weekly magazine, Dr. William H. Kilpatrick of Teachers College, Columbia University, wrote, "The term 'chaos' will not be too strong if we do not succeed in getting our working ethical theory off its old dogmatic taboo basis onto a new basis. Just now the old authoritarian morals have largely broken down and new morals . . . are still struggling to come into effective being." Dr. Kilpatrick, if he were still alive, would probably agree that the crisis for our working ethical theory remains much the same in the mid-1960s as it was in 1939.

2

Be that as it may, and granting that the seeds of many recent changes had been sown before 1939, the quarter-century since then has seen such rapid and far-reaching changes in many aspects of American life as are not only unprecedented in our own national experience, but may well be unprecedented in that of any nation other than those that have been suddenly transformed by the devastation of war or plague. Irving Kristol has written, "It is fair to say that 'our times' begin in 1945, with the end of World War II in Europe." I see 1939 as the watershed year between the older America and the newer one, partly because various technological developments that were to be of great importance happened, by one of those accidents that may not be accidental, to get started then; but, much more important, I see it as such because it marked the end of one era, that of the depression, and the beginning of the war that was to be the basis of our transformation. The depression was petering out anyway in 1939; boom and expansion were in the cards, even though the economists of the time could not see it. The war enormously accelerated the process, by creating the need for a vast military and war-production establishment that ended unemployment and sent national production zooming. The war, by making scientific and technological advance into matters of national life and death, became the forceps that brought the new age into being. It need scarcely be said that scientific and technological change, along with its direct and indirect effects on the bodies, minds, and souls of men, is the heart of the story of the postwar United States.

And change of all sorts is the heart of the story of the modern world—or is it? Let us pause to consider the question. Two traps, it would seem, lie in wait for the student of change. One is the tendency to look on the appearance of drastic change as an illusion arising from the inexperience, cultural egotism, and lack of perspective of the beholder—the attitude summed up in the phrase, *"Plus ça change, plus c'est la même chose."* It has all happened before; it seems new only because it has happened to us. The other is the habit of accepting change too uncritically: of building up a zephyr into a hurricane, of using a scare headline when eight-point type will do, of calling a fad a revolution, of accepting all change as permanent and significant and thereby forgetting the tendency of life to repeat itself and of human events, like natural ones, to move in cycles.

Obviously, the American temperament makes us more prone to fall into the second trap—pessimism, faith in permanence, and world-weariness have never been our style—but then the whole American experience has beyond much question done more than any other in history to make change its central fact. "The most salient fact about modern life, capitalist and communist, is the ideological commitment to social change," writes Daniel Bell, and he goes on to claim the ideology as an essentially American one: "The United States is probably the first large society in history to have change and innovation 'built into' its culture." Further, I believe that we are the first nation to worship change for its own sake. Our ally Great Britain recognizes with a certain reluctance the need for it—in 1965 Prime Minister Wilson warned his countrymen that resistance to change was a "prescription for national decline," yet one sensed the regret in his voice

—while on this side of the Atlantic we welcome it with open arms. The word "change" rang like a musical chord through President Johnson's inaugural address the same year:

> Ours is a time of change, rapid and fantastic change. . . . Change has given us new weapons. . . . Change and growth seem to tower beyond the control, and even the judgment, of men. . . . The American covenant called on us to help show the way for the liberation of man. . . . Change has brought new meaning to that old mission. . . . I do not believe that the Great Society is the ordered, changeless and sterile battalion of the ants. It is the excitement of becoming. . . .

And so on.

We are probably the first nation in which advocacy of things as they are is automatically and permanently a defensive position: we unhesitatingly equate change with progress. "We want change. We want progress . . . and we aim to get it," said President Johnson in a later 1965 speech, treating the two words as synonymous. We are forever announcing with satisfaction "the end of an era." At our most conservative, we allow ourselves to be rueful and resigned about change. I recall talking with a barber in Colorado Springs a couple of years ago about the impending destruction of the old Antlers Hotel, a wonderful pile of Victorian Romanesque straddling the town's main street, built by its founder, with a porch looking toward Pike's Peak. The Antlers was to be torn down, and nobody—or at least nobody in the barbershop—knew exactly why. "It's a shame," the barber said, and then added with a shrug, "but I guess that's progress." Even when we go in for pickling our past, as we have done more and more in recent years, there manages to be an aura of advance about the movement; anyone who has visited Colonial Williamsburg will have to admit that it is the damnedest, most up-to-date restoration of the past he ever saw. In the very act of combating change, we glorify it.

"Change is the biggest story in the world today, and we are not covering it adequately," James Reston of the *New York Times* said in an address at Columbia University in 1963. But change, from a strict journalistic point of view, is more than the biggest story; indeed, the word defines news, far more accurately, as well as more succinctly, than the famous "man bites dog." There is no story in permanence. "What's new?" we ask each other ritually, and there is generally a ready answer at hand. Journalism, with its vested interest in change, had become enormously more pervasive and influential in the nation over the past twenty-five years, mainly because of the rise of television, and perhaps this influence has been felt in the form of an increased national conviction that we are transforming ourselves in a way that has never happened before.

But sober historians and scholars have joined enthusiastic journalists in making the point. "The gulf separating 1965 from 1943 is as deep as the gulf that separated the men who became builders of cities from Stone Age men," writes the cultural anthropologist Margaret Mead. "The date that divides human history into two equal parts is well within living memory," writes Kenneth Boulding. ". . . In a very real sense the changes in the state of mankind since the date of my birth have been greater than the changes that took place in many thousands of years before this date." (Boulding was born in 1910.) And in 1962 the members of the American Historical Association listened to a paper delivered by their president, Carl Bridenbaugh, in which, as some of his hearers interpreted his words, he called into question the very relevance of past history to contemporary events, so drastic did he consider what he called "the great mutation" of this century.

Not surprisingly, such sweeping statements have evoked a counterattack. Some American historians insist that the past is still as relevant as it ever was; that change in our time differs only in degree and not in kind from change in the past; and that the fault lies in the change-intoxicated historians, who have themselves remained so inflexible in their thinking as to be unable to see the matter in perspective. "There is no seismograph with which to gauge the fissures between generations produced by the plagues, famines, population movements, wars, technological innovations and political revolutions of earlier eras," writes Elizabeth L. Eisenstein. ". . . We can only note that the fissures were sufficiently great to enable man to imagine an Armageddon long before we learned to make an atom bomb." "A sense of remoteness from a precious cultural heritage," Mrs. Eisen-

stein points out, has been a familiar emotion all through the ages, back to the lamentations of the Old Testament prophets; the late Roman Empire was as concerned about the possible extinction of its civilization as we are of ours; while "the recurrent sense of standing on the threshold of a new age" has marked each generation in turn since about 1800.

In our wild and dangerous times the thought that it is all basically *"la même chose"* is reassuring, and at the least it may serve as a corrective to overenthusiasm. Certainly the sheer weight of human population and of man's physical creations makes the modern world more resistant to change than the ancient one with its far fewer people and their far simpler artifacts; short of nuclear war, nothing can change modern America so much and so fast as, say, Greece was changed by Thermopylae, or medieval Europe by the decimations of the Black Death. (As Harry N. Rivlin of the City University of New York has remarked, "Undoubtedly Adam told Eve as they were leaving the Garden of Eden that 'This is a period of great social change.' ") The winds of change must blow more strongly now than in former times in order to move mankind off dead center.

But the evidence is overwhelming that they *do* blow more strongly, and that America in recent years has been a kind of Cave of the Winds.

3

What was 1939 really like in America?

For one thing, although the depression might be on its way out, its remnants were still to be seen everywhere. Unemployment had crept downward year by year from the catastrophic 1933 high of nearly thirteen million persons, or a quarter of the labor force; nevertheless, it still stood at nine and a half million, or 17 percent of the labor force, and wretched tar-paper shacks were still to be seen under bridges and on similar scraps of public land. One day that February, 239 women, ranging from recent college graduates to gray-haired matrons, showed up at the Armory on Fourteenth Street in New York

City in response to an ad for twelve laboratory helpers at $960 a year; the women were twenty-four hours early in arriving, and were fully prepared to wait in line on the sidewalk through a midwinter night, although a compassionate or worried management eventually let them move inside to wait. Works Progress Administration rolls varied during the year from 1.7 million to 2.9 million persons. Strikes accompanied by violence, such as had marked much of the decade of the Thirties, were still a familiar part of the national scene, and it was in 1939 that the city of Flint, Michigan, headquarters for Chevrolet, got around to passing an ordinance to protect workers from intimidation inside or outside local plants. The average farm family, which had an annual income of around a thousand dollars, kept expenses down through participation in one or more of the 10,700 farm cooperatives, which had membership of three and a third million persons and aggregate annual sales of two billion dollars. The plight of the sharecroppers of the South and West, which was brought home to the whole country that year with the publication of John Steinbeck's novel *The Grapes of Wrath,* was still acute; in New Madrid, Missouri, that January, a thousand tenant farmers deliberately encamped outdoors in the middle of winter, and remained there through a brutal snowstorm, to dramatize the issue of sharecropper poverty.

Others, of course, were doing a good deal better. In April the Treasury announced to Congress that for 1937, the most recent year for which income figures were available, Louis B. Mayer of Metro-Goldwyn-Mayer had been paid $1,161,753; Major Edward Bowes, impresario of the *Amateur Hour* on radio ("All right! All right!"), $427,817; Thomas J. Watson of International Business Machines, $419,398; and George Washington Hill of the American Tobacco Company, $380,976—all at low tax rates. It was the era of astronomical show-business salaries; on the list of the ten highest-paid persons in the country, theatrical people outnumbered industrialists.

The social and political attitudes that had arisen out of the depression were still firmly in control of the national mind. There were, as John Dos Passos had written, two Americas—the capitalistic one that saw the solution to its problems in low wages and repression of labor's demands, and the rising liberal and labor faction ever pressing for higher wages, better working conditions, and improved social legislation—but what the two had in common was that they were both reacting to the conditions of the depression. For the businessmen and factory hands alike in Middletown, the model Midwestern city about which Robert S. and H. M. Lynd wrote, "The experience [of the depression] had been more nearly universal than any prolonged recent emotional experience in the city's history; it had approached in its elemental shock the primary experiences of birth and death." Federal Social Security itself was still something new; it had existed in any form only since 1935, and up until 1939, when benefits were extended to include dependents, no one had been covered but the worker himself.

Politically, it was still the era of the Popular Front embracing Communism and liberalism—or was until August of 1939, when the Nazi-Soviet pact was to bring abrupt disillusionment to masses of American liberals, and open the chasm between them and Communism that has been there ever since. In 1939 college students in many parts of the country still sang "Peat-Bog Soldiers" and *"Freiheit"* in romantic tribute to an already lost cause, that of the Spanish Loyalists (Barcelona fell that January, and the Loyalists surrendered to Franco in March). Communists, albeit probably in rather small numbers, dominated certain large and powerful labor organizations like the National Maritime Union; some of Hollywood's leading writers were Communists, although, as Murray Kempton has pointed out, most of the scripts they turned out would have been found unexceptionable by the Daughters of the American Revolution; and there were Communists or fellow travelers employed in the federal government, probably mostly at its lower levels. (A friend of mine was working in a government agency in California in 1939, until one day he was abruptly fired after having expressed anti-Communist sentiments to his fellow employees. He learned later that the division he was working in was a Communist cell, and that the man who had hired him had done so in the mistaken belief that he was a Party member.) In 1939 a man then unknown to the public named Whittaker Chambers, who had broken with the Party the previous year, was living a furtive, hunted life because of his fear, real or imagined, of retribution by his former comrades; and that September he had a talk with A. A. Berle in which he made the first of the sensational charges about Communists in government that were to be a national *cause célèbre* a decade later, and the truth of which will probably remain in doubt permanently. Earl Browder, general secretary of the Communist Party in the United States, claimed in 1939 that his organization had 100,000 members, although other sources estimated the figure was much lower. At the other end of the political spectrum, Fritz Kuhn claimed that his Nazi-like German-American Bund had twenty thousand members.

In 1939 the American cities were already jammed with cars and the American landscape defaced with billboards, but in other ways things looked a good deal different from the way they look know. (For one thing, the cars themselves looked different; they were humpbacked and long-hooded, and to modern eyes they have something of the prehistoric look of an anteater.) New urban building, which had gone through a fantastic boom during the Twenties, had been at a virtual standstill for a decade; so the nation's cities had a certain air of faded splendor. Now, though, a small crop of new buildings was beginning to appear, many of them pioneering low-cost housing projects; with their unadorned rectilinear planes they anticipated the joyless boxes that were to be a feature of the postwar period. Some new buildings, like a high-rise apartment house under construction on New York City's Riverside Drive, represented the last gasp of the elegant past, with such elaborations as decorative towers, filigree in stone, perhaps even a gargoyle or two; but the tide had turned against elegance. In New York three more of the end-of-the-century merchant palaces on Fifth Avenue were about to go under the wrecker's hammer, and the brand-new Museum of Modern Art, designed by Philip L. Goodwin and Edward D. Stone, foretold the future in its simple lines and generous use of glass. The skyscraper—a phenomenon that had become a hallmark of America around the world—was definitely on the way out.

In the suburbs Tudor and Colonial houses were the fashion, many of them with fieldstone first floors; some of them cost under $10,000, and all but a few under $20,000. (The exceptions, though, could be spectacular. In Greenwich, Connecticut, Mr. and Mrs. Robert M. Hilles were building themselves something practically unheard of, a house that was air-conditioned from top to bottom, with a bowling alley in the basement; set on a six-acre site that was said to have cost $75,000, the house was expected to run to $200,000.) In little towns, the jukebox blared "Deep Purple" or "Jeepers Creepers" in the short-order joint, and the old hotel with the mansard roof, although looking a little forlorn, still stood near the railroad station. In the countryside, rows of tiny "tourist cabins," shedding paint and heated with kerosene stoves, were the forerunners of the Neronian motels of today.

In 1939 there were still Italian hand organs to be heard in the streets of American cities, and Yiddish-language movies were still made and shown here. The cities and even the towns, with their Little Italys and Little Dublins, had a certain European flavor that has been lost. The great waves of European immigration that had rolled westward across the Atlantic in the early years of the century were definitely over—during the Thirties the combined effects of earlier restrictive legislation and the depression had slowed immigration from a flood to a trickle and finally to a drip—but one in four of us was either foreign-born or of foreign parentage. Nevertheless, such an astute observer as Bruce Bliven could still affirm that the United States was firmly dominated by the Anglo-Saxon Protestant found most characteristically in the small towns of the Midwest, whose religious tolerance was such that he could get along with any man so long as that man *had* a religion—that is, wasn't an atheist—and whose political tolerance could be extended to any Republican or Democrat but less easily, if at all, to a Socialist or Communist.

This prototypical American of 1939 was probably a businessman; quite likely he belonged to one or more business clubs that sometimes had group singing as a feature of their luncheon meetings (Kiwanis alone had two thousand clubs with more than a hundred thousand members); he was a booster of his town and his country, but was beginning to have serious doubts about perpetual progress ("One senses a growing and disturbed feeling that perhaps, after all, everything is not going to be bigger and better forevermore," Bliven wrote); he had the traditional American passion for self-improvement; and, of course, he often had his business troubles (business failures that year ran at a rate of seventy per ten thousand concerns, the highest since 1933). He certainly felt contemptuous toward the European and metropolitan institution, Society—which, nevertheless, was still influential enough so that the Sunday editions of metropolitan papers devoted a separate section to it, and self-assured enough so that its debutantes and young matrons were often photographed on the front page of that section in bathing suits. The debutante of the year was the debutante of *any* year, the coy yet queenly Brenda Diana Duff Frazier.

It was the heyday of local summer theaters, generically called the straw-hat circuit; these cheerful institutions, in their barns and on their wharves, used local amateur talent for everything from acting to scene-building, not yet having been commercialized by the introduction into their casts of national celebrities from Broadway and Hollywood. That summer in the Eastern and Middle Atlantic states alone, some seventy-five summer theaters were in operation, putting on, among other things, *Our Town* at Lake Mahopac, New York; *Private Lives* at Pikesville, Maryland; *The Last of Mrs. Cheyney* at Boothbay, Maine; and *Shadow and Substance* at Hopatcong, New Jersey. Among books, the great critical and public success of the year was *The Grapes of Wrath,* which perhaps still stands as the culminating social record of the decade. Other best-sellers were Thomas Wolfe's *The Web and the Rock*, projecting the old American theme of the boy who goes from the provinces to the great city; Anne Morrow Lindbergh's *Listen! The Wind*; Daphne du Maurier's *Rebecca*; and Rachel Field's *All This and Heaven, Too.* Among the hits of the Broadway theater were *Abe Lincoln in Illinois, The Man Who Came to Dinner, The Philadelphia Story,* and *Hellzapoppin'*.

But the really big media of popular entertainment were, of course, radio and the movies, which, having not yet encountered their postwar nemesis, television, were having a golden age—in the financial sense, anyhow. The number of radio sets in use in the nation was one of the few statistics that had risen steadily and inexorably all through the depression; between 1929 and 1939 the number of

American families owning sets had gone from 10 million to 27.5 million, and the total number of sets in use had reached 45 million. In effect, all but those living in the direst poverty or possessed of the more heroic cultural perversity now had at least one radio to listen to. What was to be heard? Because of international events, 1939 was the year when radio news coverage really came into its own, and millions sat anxiously straining to understand broadcasts from Europe above the rush of static and interference; but the most popular programs were drama and variety shows. The most popular program of all was *The Chase and Sanborn* (Coffee) *Hour*. All over the country, even in the most remote farm areas, young and old alike tuned it in to keep up with that odd phenomenon, an invisible ventriloquist. Edgar Bergen's perky, irreverent puppet, Charlie McCarthy, was quite possibly the most widely known figure in American show business up to that time. Daytime radio programming was a simple matter—with few exceptions, it consisted of one soap opera after another. Serials took up 85 percent of network daytime time, as against 3.5 percent for news; it was clear enough that the millions of wives who kept the radio blaring while they cleaned house would rather keep up with Vic and Sade than with the fall of Europe. Gossipy, moralistic, slyly salacious, interminable, often dripping with blood and haunted by disease or the fear of it, the soapers have never been shown conclusively to have had any particular effect for good or bad on the behavior of their listeners. But they were there, and very much part of the scene, in 1939.

The year 1939 saw the appearance of what many people still consider the movie to end all movies, *Gone with the Wind,* but it saw a good deal else in the motion picture field. With an investment of two billion dollars and 282,000 persons regularly employed in it at the start of the year, the industry in 1939 turned out 530 feature films and more than seven hundred short subjects. People went to the local movie house on a set schedule so that they would never miss a show. Eighty-five million Americans, or 65 percent of the total population of all ages, went to the movies at least once a week. The movies formed the country's image, abroad and to a great extent at home. Everyone knows that it was a distorted image that did us harm in the world and probably continues to do us harm, but many of the movies of 1939, taken in their own terms, were remarkable achievements of popular entertainment. Some of the most popular of them were *Stagecoach, Wuthering Heights, Dark Victory, Good-bye, Mr. Chips, Ninotchka*, and *Juarez*, and the most popular performers were Shirley Temple, Clark Gable, Sonja Henie, Mickey Rooney, and Spencer Tracy. It was the year Barbara Stanwyck and Robert Taylor, and Carole Lombard and Clark Gable, thrilled their fans by getting married in real life. If anyone doubts the depth and breadth of the country's acceptance of the movies as a cultural asset in 1939, let him remember that it was the year when the Los Angeles Museum of History, Science and Art proudly accepted for its collection the sarong worn by Dorothy Lamour in *Her Jungle Love*. History, science, and art the movies were; they were also, for many, something not very far from religion.

What with cars and the beginnings—however rudimentary they look now—of mass industrialization and urbanization, the traditional basic American unit, the family, was showing signs of changing or breaking up. "With the authority of the home destroyed, with the stern parent of the past a discarded image and the new-type father and mother pathetically striving to be just good pals, responsibility rests with the young for their own behavior," a social commentator wrote. Concern for the delicate psyches of the young and permissiveness in the school and the home, notions to which the middle class of the Twenties had paid aggressive lip service but not much more, were now the rule in practice—and the first signs of a backlash were appearing. A nationwide survey of fourteen hundred husbands and wives made by the American Association of University Women resulted in the conclusion that children of middle-class families were more apt to suffer from their mothers' overconscientiousness than from neglect. The same survey showed that among the educated couples under consideration, 92 percent handled their money jointly, 80 percent took joint responsibility for the upbringing of their children, 60 percent of the husbands helped their wives with the dishes, and 40 percent of the husbands regularly took a hand in the cooking. Incidentally, two-thirds of the husbands in the survey earned under

$5,000 a year, and almost one-third of the families—presumably the other third—had full-time domestic help.

Meanwhile, the long-established American custom of discriminating against people on the basis of religion and race remained firmly entrenched. Anti-Semitism, as we shall see later, was at a kind of flood tide—and by no means just among members of organizations with foreign connections like Fritz Kuhn's Bund. As to discrimination against the country's twelve and a half million Negroes, it is startling now to realize that the whole humanitarian New Deal movement of the Thirties had left it virtually untouched. In February, 1939, the National Association for the Advancement of Colored People, of the very existence of which most white Americans were certainly unaware at the time, celebrated its thirtieth anniversary by holding dances in cities throughout the country. But there was little enough to dance about. Not a school in the Deep South was integrated; hardly an industrial plant anywhere in the country did not discriminate against Negroes, consciously or not, in one way or another; hardly a leading hotel or restaurant anywhere in the country did more than make a gesture toward nondiscrimination by occasionally admitting a Negro celebrity. It would be two more years before the federal government would take its first step since Reconstruction to correct inequities based on race. From Amos 'n' Andy on radio to the grinning waiters and fat maids in the movies, the old stereotype of the Negro was unabashedly shown in all the mirrors of national opinion and taste; he was amiable, obliging, musical, subservient, sometimes perhaps allowed to outwit his employer with his earthly, "native" shrewdness—but always stayed in his place.

In Middletown, the Lynds had written only two years earlier, the business class tolerated the comparatively small Negro population complacently as a convenient instrument for getting dirty work done at low wages; an official at a nearby automobile plant explained that the plant employed no Negroes because "it's degrading to a white man to have Negroes doing the same type of work." Nationally, more than 30 percent of all Negroes were on the federal relief rolls. Even in a thoroughly industrialized Northern state like New Jersey, a State Commission in 1939 could find Negroes discriminated against in all forms of skilled employment; in education, with schools in the state's southern reaches remaining completely segregated; in the terms of insurance policies; and even in employment with private health agencies, with the state, its countries, and its municipalities, and with the local projects of the Works Progress Administration. A Mrs. Roosevelt might be widely applauded for quitting the DAR because of its refusal of Constitution Hall in Washington to Marian Anderson for a concert, but that case involved the First Lady of the country and one of its leading artists. (Meanwhile, the President was having no success in getting an antilynching bill through Congress.) Ordinary people, even intelligent and high-principled ones, seldom felt more than an occasional twinge of guilt about America's treatment of its Negro minority. For one thing, they had economic troubles of their own arising out of the depression, and for another, all but a few still frankly believed in the Negro's inferiority.

In making this sketch of the country in 1939, I have avoided until now putting in the great shadow that lay across it—the shadow of war in Europe. To begin with, our attitude toward even our friends in Europe was still to a remarkable degree the suspicious, truculent, defensive one that Mrs. Trollope had remarked on a century earlier. In May, 1939, a prominent American living in London complained with a certain lack of grace that British clothes had waistlines too high, shirt tails too long, and socks too long; he was doing his best, he added, "to convince them that we have left behind the horse-and-buggy age and that we are now in the motor age." The prominent American's opinion gained weight from the fact that he was the Honorable Joseph P. Kennedy, United States Ambassador to Great Britain. (A month or so later, King George VI redressed the balance by coming to Hyde Park and gamely eating a hot dog with our President.) But now Europe was coming to be dominated by those who were clearly not our friends. The previous year, the Nazi conquest of Austria and the partition of Czechoslovakia had given a clue to Hitler's intentions, and now came one crushing blow after another: the dissolution of the Czech republic, the occupation of Bohemia and Moravia, the annexation of Memel, the threats to Danzig, the Nazi-Soviet nonaggression treaty. The spirit of the whole Western alliance in the months preceding September 1, 1939, when Germany marched on Poland and started the Second World War, was perhaps never better summed up than in a plea for peace addressed to the German government by eighteen noted Britishers in January: "A spirit of uneasiness broods over the world. Men and women in every country are uncertain what the next weeks and months may bring."

To be sure, war seemed a good deal further away to the United States, with three thousand miles of ocean separating it from Europe, than it did to Britain. We had our Neutrality Act to keep us out of foreign squabbles, and we had a young generation brought up on antiwar attitudes arising out of the First World War, and embodied in plays like *What Price Glory?* and novels like *Three Soldiers.* (Two years earlier, in 1937, an estimated half a million American students had taken part in a student strike against war and were said to be united in a pledge never to support any war declared by a United States government.) But the fact remains that the shadow of war in Europe did fall heavily over the country in 1939. It stifled optimism and shortened perspective; it discouraged a forward view. In May, real-estate men gathered in New York complained to each other that fear of war was "killing deals."

If David L. Cohn was right in his thesis that the year-by-year contents of the Sears, Roebuck catalogue faithfully reflect American moods, then a flourish or two may be added to the sketch of 1939 by taking a look into the editions of that year. Among many other things, the 1939 spring number shows beautiful new horse-drawn farm wagons ("ten hound braces, six front and four rear for extra strength"); a girl's bicycle "smart and distinctive as the newest Paris gown" ("Girls! Be modern—go cycling!"); windmills for $29.95 and up; a great number of objects called "refrigerators," although we would now call some of them iceboxes, since the ones in question were designed to use block ice and had no refrigeration equipment; and a number of washing machines run by gasoline. The boys shown in the catalogue are usually wearing knickers; the men are wearing suits with wide lapels, many of them double-breasted, and trousers so wide at the cuff that they now look ridiculous; and the heels of the women's shoes are so broad and low that they look as if they could actually be walked on without teetering, such was the practical wisdom of fashion in those primitive times. The fact that only about three-quarters of American dwellings, and only about one-quarter of farm dwellings, had electric service then is reflected in the comparatively few pages devoted to electrical equipment, and the great amount of space devoted to gadgets of all sorts driven by wood, coal, and kerosene. And, of course, the 1939 catalogue now seems striking for its omissions. Missing, for obvious reasons, are long-playing records and turntables with changers, drip-dry clothes, dishwashing machines, home air conditioners, DDT sprays, television sets and their accessories, car-top campers, tape recorders, riding lawn mowers (other than farm tractors), and Geiger counters.

Finally—not to slight entirely the transitory fads, fashions, and vexations of the movement—in 1939 skiing and ping-pong were rising fast in American popularity, while bowling was still considered almost as lower-class a pastime as pool, and miniature golf, the rage of the mid-depression years, was dying out, although its characteristic Lilliputian fairways with their tunnels and water traps were to be seen, often standing neglected and overgrown, on the outskirts of many towns. The most notorious manifestations of depression nerves, marathon dancing and flagpole sitting, still hung on. Bare-midriff dresses, snoods covering women's hair entirely as if they had just emerged from a shower, and knee socks for college girls were new, while "hats quieted down and were no longer silly," as the fashion authority Carmel Snow reported firmly. Gardeners all over the East, and even city-dwellers in New York and Philadelphia, were harassed by hordes of Japanese beetles, which had been multiplying unchecked ever since they had been accidentally introduced from the Orient two decades earlier and had not yet been brought under control by natural enemies and insecticides. It was the day of the big-name dance bands—Benny Goodman and Artie Shaw and a couple of dozen others—and of a national dancing craze; 1937's favorite dance, the Big Apple, was out of style, but "jitterbugging" went on full blast among those whose sacroiliacs could stand it, and a Cuban import, la conga, had just made an emphatic appearance. The threat, and then the reality, of war in Europe seemed to heighten the national passion for dancing. The world's first "danceteria," occupying three large floors devoted to dancing and short-order eating, made its appearance in the heart of Times Square in 1939, and the celebrated dancing master Arthur Murray commented that conditions in his trade "vividly recalled the dance craze which flourished before and immediately after the outbreak of the First World War." (Or, he might have added, during the Black Death in fifteenth-century England.) Also, 1939 was the year when college boys took up the fad of eating live goldfish in huge quantities, and it was the year when zippers became practically standard equipment on men's trousers; it was a year when women averaged five feet five inches in height (less than now) and 120 pounds in weight (more than now) and, at least in the view of Lois Long in *The New Yorker,* went in for hollow cheeks to create an effect of exoticism; and it was a year when people took leave of each other by saying "Good-bye now."

4

In retrospect, it is surprising how many developments that have made obvious marks on the country and the rest of the world since then had their beginnings in 1939.

To take the most spectacular example, it was late that January that the atomic age really began. As Henry DeWolf Smyth tells the story in *Atomic Energy for Military Purposes*:

> On January 16, 1939, Niels Bohr of Copenhagen, Denmark, arrived in this country to spend several months in Princeton, N. J. and was particularly anxious to discuss some abstract problems with Einstein. . . . Just before Bohr left Denmark two of his colleagues, O. R. Frisch and L. Meitner (both refugees from Germany), had told him their guess that the absorption of a neutron by a uranium nucleus sometimes caused that nucleus to split into approximately equal parts with the release of enormous quantities of energy. . . . Immediately on arrival in the United States Bohr communicated this idea to his former student J. A. Wheeler and others at Princeton, and from them the news spread by word of mouth to neighboring physicists including E. Fermi

at Columbia University. As a result of conversations among Fermi, J. R. Dunning, and G. B. Pegram, a search was undertaken at Columbia for the heavy pulses of ionization that would be expected from the flying fragments of the uranium nucleus. On January 26, 1939, there was a conference on theoretical physics at Washington, D. C. . . . Fermi left New York to attend this meeting before the Columbia fission experiments had been tried. At the meeting Bohr and Fermi discussed the problem of fission. . . . Before the meeting in Washington was over, several other experiments to confirm fission had been initiated, and positive experimental confirmation was reported from four laboratories . . . in the February 15, 1939, issue of the *Physical Review*. By this time Bohr had heard that similar experiments had been made in his laboratory in Copenhagen about January 15.

The news of this cornucopia of nearly simultaneous developments certainly did not stir up the uncomprehending public; the *New York Times'* report of them appeared on an inside page and went unnoticed by laymen. Smyth says that even physicists in the United States had little realization of the implications, and, to be sure, the production of atomic bombs was still a long way off; but the process leading to them had been started. The first approach of physicists to the United States government was made by Pegram that March, and during the summer Einstein wrote his famous letter to President Roosevelt explaining the desirability of encouraging work in the field of atomic fission. The President appointed an Advisory Committee on Uranium, and the committee, meeting in October, recommended as a first step the procurement of large quantities of graphite and uranium oxide to be used in further experiments. The first transfer of federal funds to carry out the recommendation was to be made early in 1940.

At the same time, the shrinking of the world that was to be brought about by international air travel was just getting under way. At the start of 1939 the United States had eighteen domestic air carrier companies using a total of 276 aircraft, and the annual number of airline passenger fares paid had just passed the million mark; financially, the carriers were beginning to show a slight profit after years of operating consistently in the red. There was no overseas service for either passengers or mail. But now the horizons of commercial aviation began to widen rapidly. In May the Yankee Clipper, a great, four-engine flying boat, absurdly slow and clumsy-looking by present-day standards but spectacularly advanced for 1939, successfully inaugurated the first regular North Atlantic air service, going from Port Washington, Long Island, to Lisbon in twenty-six and a half hours, with a stopover at the Azores; the Clipper carried a crew of fourteen and a shipment of mail, but no paying passengers. Passenger service was not long in coming, though; Pan American began it in June, on a once-a-week basis. One left Long Island at 3 P.M. on Wednesday, and could have dinner at Lisbon on Thursday evening, continuing on to Marseille the next morning. The fare was $375 one way New York to Marseille; the free baggage allowance was fifty-five pounds; and the inside of the plane, since interior design of aircraft was still in its infancy, looked a good deal like a musty old Pullman car. Within a matter of weeks, transatlantic passenger service came to be considered almost a routine thing. That fall aviation got a huge boost with the opening of the latest thing in airports, New York City's La Guardia Field.

Cars were in the process of transition from Tin Lizzies to what Lewis Mumford was later to call "insolent chariots." The new Lincoln Zephyr "coupé"—a word now long vanished from teen-agers' vocabularies—had a wonderful new appointment, a convertible top that could be raised or lowered at the touch of a button. The 1940 Oldsmobile, put on the market that fall, had as a $57 extra something called a hydraulic clutch, which was an early version of automatic transmission—something then brand-new on passenger cars, although it had previously been used on trucks. Synthetic plastics were in their infancy, and the possibilities for their use in a wide variety of household products were just beginning to be explored. Fluorescent lighting was introduced that year, and so were nylon stockings, although the latter were not to be in regular production until 1940. In the field of book publishing, the seeds were sown of a revolution that was to have a wide cultural impact when a new firm called Pocket Books began issuing paper-backed reprints of popular titles for twenty-five cents each. It was in 1939 that reports were published in the United States of an Argentinian researcher's discovery that he could produce cancer in rabbits by painting them with tobacco extracts. But hardly anyone paid the reports any attention.

And then there was television. The idea of "seeing by telegraph" had engrossed inventors for many years, and as early as 1884 a German named Paul Nipkow had taken out a patent on a method of television transmission. It did not work, and neither did many subsequent efforts, but during the Thirties, while radio was making millions, television was finally perfected in the laboratory. However, at the beginning of 1939 there was no such thing as public television. It was introduced that April 30 with a telecast by the National Broadcasting Company of the ceremonies opening the World's Fair at Flushing Meadow, in New York City, which was picked up by between one and two hundred experimental receivers set up in public places around New York, and was seen by an estimated one thousand viewers. The program was generally considered a success, despite the tiny pictures, which measured less than ten inches across.

As for the prospects for commercial television, informed views on the subject differed widely in 1939. Du Mont Television Receivers, Inc. said ebulliently in its advertisements for the Fair broadcast, "Sooner than you realize it, television will play a vital part in the life of the average American," but the more skeptical Television Committee of the Federal Communications Commission felt that the day when television would be commercially feasible might still be far in the future. Another authority, a Harvard professor of electrical engineering named Chester L. Dawes, was afraid that the conditions imposed on both viewer and performer by television's nature would tend to limit its popularity permanently. "Television viewing is limited to a few persons, it must take place in a semi-darkened room, and it demands continuous attention," Dawes wrote,

> whereas with sound alone [as in radio] a person can be doing other things while listening. Again, the program itself presents many technical difficulties such as arrangement of stage and actors, and requires in televising outdoors a high degree of skill, since there cannot be any time for planning. Also, the public has been educated to the high degree of perfection of sound broadcasting with its nationwide hookups. . . . The public has probably forgotten the experimental stage of radio when

crystal sets were in general use; and hence, the growth and the future of television is highly uncertain at this time.

In hindsight it would appear that Dawes, in his concern about the adaptability of actors to new kinds of stages and of audiences to semi-darkened rooms, underestimated the traditional ability of Americans to endure the hardships of pioneering.

5

I won't attempt right here to sum up the changes that have occurred since 1939—to set a sketch of "After" beside one of "Before"—since that will be largely the subject of the chapters that are to follow. But a selection of comparative statistics may serve to give some impression of the magnitude of the change. The percentage of Americans who live in places classified by the Census Bureau as urban went from 56 percent in 1940 to just under 70 percent in 1960, and it has approached the three-quarter mark since then. Clearly, we are fast on the way to becoming a nation of city-dwellers and suburbanites. Over the same period, housing units without bathtub or shower went down from roughly 40 percent to roughly 12 percent. Even so, we still have many more radios than bathtubs—only 8.5 percent of housing units were without radios at the time of the 1960 census—and the percentage without television sets at that time was almost exactly the same as the no-bathtub-or-shower figure. By 1964 the average weekly wage for production workers in manufacturing was just over $100 for slightly more than forty hours' work—more than a quadrupling of gross weekly income since 1939. (Over the same period the Labor Department's price index of all commodities went, in round numbers, from 42 to 100, meaning that what cost forty-two cents in 1939 now costs a dollar, and that in terms of buying power the production worker's raise over the quarter-century amounted only to a doubling.) The average net annual income of doctors passed the $10,000 mark in 1945, and of lawyers in 1954.

The tremendous advances in the treatment of bacterial disease are reflected in the fact that influenza and pneumonia, running practically neck and neck with cancer as a cause of death in 1939, in 1962 caused only one death per 4.7 for cancer and 18 for cardiovascular disease. The advances in public education are reflected in the fact that the average American has now completed twelve years of school rather than eight—which is to say, he is now a high school graduate rather than an elementary school graduate. The trend toward a universal middle class is dramatically shown by the facts that about 40 percent of American families now have annual incomes above $7,000 and that *more* than 40 percent of all American youngsters aged eighteen and nineteen are now attending college.

Only one in six of us is foreign-born or of foreign parentage now, and the distribution of the foreign-born has changed; Germany and Ireland are down since prewar days, while Italy, the Netherlands, Hungary, and Yugoslavia are up. Our median age has hardly changed at all—it was 29 years in 1940 and 29.5 in 1960—because increasing longevity has been balanced by a huge crop of postwar babies who pull the average down. It need hardly be said that the glum population predictions of 1939 have been proved spectacularly wrong; we now number around 195,000,000, or almost 50 percent more than in 1939, and are increasing our numbers at such a fast rate that demographers have adopted another sort of glumness. In 1940 births exceeded deaths, but only by a ratio of about eighteen to eleven; now the ratio is not far short of three to one. Meanwhile, the geographical center of our population has continued a long-established slow trek westward, retracing, with a curious statistical mimicry, the trek of the pioneers in the last century. From just east of Carlisle, Indiana, in 1940, in twenty years it pushed on some ninety miles to a point just east of Salem, Illinois, in 1960.

Unemployment has, of course, come down from the crisis level of 1939—though it remains among our most serious problems, for reasons related to new technological advances and rapid expansion of the working force; in the early Sixties it hovered stubbornly around 5 percent of the labor force, which was quite a drop from the 17 percent of 1939 but which still meant that more than four million Americans who wanted jobs didn't have them. Meanwhile, economic security from sources other than jobs made huge advances. Social welfare expenditures by the federal government, states, and localities went from $8.766 billion in 1940 to $66.5 billion in 1963. Life insurance in force in 1939 was at the seemingly fantastically high figure of $111 billion, having tripled in the preceding two decades; now it stands at about $700 billion. The number of individual owners of common stock has risen from three or four million in 1939 to more than twenty million today, and of those twenty million more than eight million are persons with annual incomes of less than $7,500; indeed, the idea of "people's capitalism" has become so popular that some commentators have recently been proposing universal stock ownership, to be made possible through federal credit, as an answer to the unemployment problem. If people can't find jobs with companies, maybe, it is suggested, they can make a living by owning them instead.

The $9 billion federal budget of 1939, as almost everyone knows, had grown by 1964 to $100 billion, give or take a few billion, and most of the money comes from personal and corporate income taxes, which between them brought in somewhat over $2 billion in 1939, and about $75 billion in 1963. (The number of taxpayers contributing to the federal take meanwhile rose from under four million in 1939 to over fifty million in 1963.) About half the money in 1964 went for national defense expenditures—that is, around $50 billion a year as against somewhat over $1 billion in 1939. The much-talked-of expansion of the federal government has been many times more modest in terms of manpower; we had 1,128,000 federal civilian employees in 1940 and 2,528,000 in 1963.

Economically, in short, we have become a different country.

Perhaps the reader can stand one more paragraph of statistical comparisons that may throw more oblique light on the nature of the change. The nation's top salaries are about what they were in 1939, but their recipients now are far more apt to be corporate officials than show-business celebrities, who now take their returns in capital gains when they can. As for the big businessmen, they too have to find ways of keeping as much of the money as possible out of Uncle Sam's hands—a concern that has siphoned off a good deal of our national energy and talent in recent years. The roll of American Communists has over the quarter-century apparently shrunk to near the vanishing point. The membership of Kiwanis has risen from 100,000 to 270,-000; the rate of business failures per ten thousand concerns, after dropping from 1939's seventy to a low of four in 1945, had climbed back to around sixty in the early Sixties, suggesting that business is still a gamble in the age of welfare; the number of persons engaged in distribution and service in the motion picture industry has dropped 70 percent in a little over a decade, while the number of television sets in use was rising from virtually none in 1945 to 56.4 million in 1963; and the sale of sports jackets nationally multiplied ten times between 1940 and 1955.

6

What view did the Americans of 1939 themselves have of our future as a nation?

I have already noted that they expected little further economic expansion; in fact, our gross national product and national income were to become almost seven times greater in the next quarter-century, while the price of all commodities was hardly more than doubling. I have already noted that they expected an end to national population growth; more specifically, in 1939 an officer of the Census Bureau itself predicted that our population would reach a peak of 136 million and then begin a long, gradual decline that would bring it down to 126 million by 1980. The 136 million was reached, all right, but it was no peak. Population growth was to continue through wartime, and to reach an unprecedented rate in the years immediately following; in 1964, assuming a continuation of the current birth rate, our estimated 1980 population would be 260 million, or somewhat more than twice as many Americans as were foreseen for that year by the Census Bureau man in 1939. It would be hard to imagine two predictions by qualified experts of basic matters being more flatly wrong.

Insight into the horizons of the 1939 American may perhaps be gained by looking at his view of the future of a favorite American artifact then as now—the automobile. At a meeting of the World Automotive Engineering Congress that spring in New York, a leading engineer, Edwin L. Allen, predicted that the American car of the future would be built in the shape of a teardrop, with the point at the rear. "In the not too distant future," Allen went on, "we will walk up to our car, push a button and the door will be open. We will have the impression of entering a commodious room. It will not be necessary to crawl over stationary seats and trip over humps and tunnels in the floor. The seats will be light, movable chairs and the floor will be wide and flat. A portion of the roof will be made of a curved translucent material which will admit the health-giving rays of the sun and at the same time remove glare." At the same congress another engineer confidently, and quite correctly, predicted that the running board was on the way out.

Does it all sound rather naïve? Could anyone be expected to know in 1939 that the teardrop shape, then all the rage because it had been proved aerodynamically satisfactory for aircraft wings, would remain permanently just as impractical for passenger cars as it was at that time? Could anyone be expected to know that a postwar vogue, almost totally irrational, for low cars would make a mockery of the dream of a "commodious room"? Could anyone be expected to know that within about fifteen years the manufacturers of automobiles would be making psychological studies of the symbolic meaning of cars to their owners, and that the designers would be aiming not so much to achieve maximum comfort, safety, or even speed as to project the right "image" in terms of sex and status? Seldom, perhaps, in the long history of crystal-gazing has it been shown so graphically to be an undertaking in which knowledge and logic are powerless.

The great clearinghouse for 1939 projections of the future was, of course, the New York World's Fair, the theme of which was "The World of Tomorrow." President Johnson, speaking at the opening ceremonies of the more recent New York World's Fair in April, 1964, commented on how the reality of change over the preceding quarter-century had outstripped the vision as it was embodied in the

1939 Fair, and pointed out in particular that there had been "no mention of outer space, or atomic power, or wonder drugs that could destroy disease." How, then, *did* the "World of Tomorrow" look to those who were trying to envisage it in 1939?

As a matter of fact, there were at the 1939 Fair certain portents, however dim, of the true shape of things to come. The Hall of Medical Science featured an exhibit designed to show that man was not helpless against infection, but its emphasis was on natural and acquired immunity rather than on the destruction of bacteria in the body by drugs. A mechanical heart, built by the versatile and unpredictable national hero, Colonel Charles A. Lindbergh, for Dr. Alexis Carrel, perhaps offered a faint hint of the coming development of a heart-lung machine such as now makes possible open-heart surgery. And there *was* mention of space, if not "outer" space; in the Theatre of Time and Space a motion picture showed an imaginary rocket-ship flight from New York to London via the "stratosphere," which, as every schoolboy knows now, is not really outer space at all but merely the upper regions of the earth's atmosphere.

Other exhibitors, their minds apparently a blank when confronted with the possibility of future technological advance, seemed to take refuge in sheer size as the way of the future. The National Cash Register Company displayed a cash register of conventional design but seven stories high. The business-systems pavilion featured not a computer but a typewriter, ordinary enough except for the fact that it was eighteen feet long and weighed fourteen tons. Still others seemed to be able to see nothing ahead but greater domestic convenience; a not particularly daring exhibit in the Home Furnishings Building showed a woman of the future ordering a house and furnishings by telephone—something she could, at least from the standpoint of technology, have done perfectly well in 1939.

The most graphic representation of the future, and the most popular exhibit at the Fair, was, of course, the General Motors Futurama. Designed by Norman Bel Geddes as his conception of the world of 1960, it was the largest animated scale model ever built, containing 35,000 square feet of miniature highways, cities, towns and farms, half a million miniature buildings, a million trees, and fifty thousand scale-model vehicles. Doubtless many of the 25 million persons who rode through the wonders of the Futurama exhibit on a moving platform either gaped in disbelief or considered the whole thing a pleasant fantasy. In fact, some of the Bel Geddes' predictions have come more or less literally true; some continue to seem unattainable, and some of these now seem undesirable as well; and a surprising number have been surpassed so decisively that they now seem almost absurdly timid. Here were the expressways cutting through cities that, in the years after 1939, were indeed to make cross-country travel so much faster; here was the expansion of suburban living that was indeed to take place on a vast scale; here were the interstate superhighways that were to ruin the railroads in the post-war period. The hundred-mile speed limits that the Futurama envisaged have not developed, nor have the 150-story skyscrapers, nor has the segregation of vehicular and pedestrian traffic to separate levels in cities; furthermore, most planners would agree that the Futurama's assumption of the desirability of rigidly dividing cities into residential, commercial, and industrial sections has still been emphatically reversed by recent experience. Still, in its version of the general tone of the future America—bigger, richer, more impersonal, more mechanized, more crowded—the Futurama was a remarkable essay in prophecy. Where it chiefly erred was not in overexuberance but, characteristically for 1939, in nearsightedness. "There are approximately 38 million motorcars in this America of 1960—almost a third more than 1940," the voice in the ears of the Futurama's visitors assured them in awe-struck tones. The figure for the real 1960, when it duly arrived, was 74 million.

So the prevision of 1939 was weakened by a depression just behind and shadowed by a war just ahead. But if some miraculous seer could have overcome these limitations, he would hardly have been acclaimed. If he had been able to show 1939 the real 1960, nobody would have believed it.

II. BIG BEYOND IMAGINING

1

At the end of the Thirties large corporations, which through the course of American history up to 1929 had generally been eulogized as among our most characteristic and laudable national creations, had been through a decade of public battering. They had been accused—all too often, with justice—of grinding down the working man and meeting with arrogance or violence his attempts to bargain with them on equal terms. They had been accused of building up great concentrations of economic power and using it for oligarchic and selfish purposes rather than in the public interest. The whole spirit of the New Deal was against them, and along with their bankers, known generically as "Wall Street," they were the New Deal's pet villains. If they had one characteristic upon which their detractors harped more than any other, it was their bigness. The general belief was that no matter how good their intentions might be—and their intentions were seldom thought to be good—their bigness per se worked against the public interest. Men like Supreme Court Justice Louis D. Brandeis wanted to break them up and return the nation to something like a handicraft economy.

By studying their annual reports, the brochures through which corporations present themselves in profile to their stockholders every spring, one can often derive a striking impression of what they are like at a given moment, both quantitatively and qualitatively. Let us consider the annual reports of some of the country's very largest corporations for the year 1939. United States Steel, almost the granddaddy of the modern corporate colossus ever since it had been put together by J. P. Morgan the Elder at the turn of the century, reported total sales of $857 million, and net income of $41 million—the latter figure being a most encouraging one inasmuch as the firm had had a net deficit for 1938. It had 217,386 stockholders and, on the average for the year, about 224,000 employees; the latter, it coolly reported, had worked an average of just over thirty-five hours per week and had been paid an average of just under ninety cents per hour, for an average annual wage of about $1,600. General Motors, which even then was able to boast of having a 42 percent share of the United States market in automobiles and trucks, reported sales of $1,376,828,227, net earnings of $183,290,222, and net working capital of $434,172,831. It had about 386,000 stockholders and 220,000 employees, who earned on the average about $1,500 for the year. The oldest American industrial dynasty, E. I. du Pont de Nemours, in 1939 had sales of $300 million, net income of $93 million, 77,000 stockholders, and 55,000 employees. General Electric had sales of $304 million, assets of $392 million, net profit of $41 million, 210,000 stockholders, and not quite 63,000 employees. Big enough figures all around, surely, to give substance to the attacks—especially when sales and earnings were set against wages.

Apart from figures, what do the reports show about these companies in 1939? Perhaps something can be learned from their style of presentation and from their reticences—from what they did *not* say. They were printed on rough paper, their pages were small—scarcely too big to fit into a legal-size envelope—and they were illustrated sparsely, in black and white, when they were illustrated at all. Their type was generally small and forbidding, and the prose that accompanied their charts and balance sheets was laconic and to the point. They assumed they need not woo the reader, since as a stockholder he already had a vital interest in the information they had to impart.

Moreover, they assumed they knew his point of view and the limit of his interest. Although labor disputes, some of them involving these companies, were front-page news during 1939, none of the reports more than mentioned them in passing. Implicitly, the reports assumed that the stockholder-reader had no interest in the corporation's morality or citizenship, its place in the society where it operated; they assumed that he was interested in profits and dividends, present and future, and that was that.

At the same time, the reports showed that the companies were aware of their problems regarding public and governmental attitudes toward them, and that they were reacting with a combination of arrogance and defensiveness. The General Motors report showed signs of ill temper on the subject of rising taxes; in two separate places it called attention to the fact that the company's tax bill for the year, which came to about $102 million, was almost double what it would have been at 1929 rates, with a consequent reduction in earnings and dividends. And the reports of both General Motors and General Electric included sections emphasizing that the companies were giving increasing concern to public relations in the interest of improving the general opinion of them. Yet the very form and content of the reports themselves—cold, brief, factual, take-it-or-leave-it—belied these words, and showed that public relations in the companies in question were still more a concept than a program. Reticence, sometimes aggressive reticence, was the keynote.

Nor were the 1939 annual reports of U.S. Steel, General Motors, du Pont, and General Electric especially atypical of the period. A survey made three years earlier by a Philadelphia advertising man had shown that out of a sample of 150 reports only forty contained anything besides statistical tables, only twenty included photographs or drawings, and only thirty-nine so much as mentioned their company's products. The annual reports of the time—and, perhaps to a marked extent, the operations of the companies they described—were aimed at stockholders, and most particularly large stockholders, *as* stockholders. The idea that stockholders might also be customers seems not to have occurred to the reports' authors.

Now let us glance through the annual reports of the same companies for 1964, a quarter-century later.

U.S. Steel reported sales of $4.13 billion, up almost five times from 1939, and net earnings of $236 million, up almost four times. It reported 368,000 stockholders, a modest increase since 1939, and 200,000 employees, a modest *de*crease—but the employees were paid on the average $4.08 per hour, or four and a half times what they had been paid in 1939.

General Motors reported sales just below the $17-billion mark, up more than twelve times since 1939, and net earnings of about one and three-quarters billion, up not quite tenfold. Its stockholder total and employee roll had each tripled, the former to well above the million mark, while the employees' average annual earnings were up four and two-thirds times. As for General Motors' net assets, over the twenty-five years to around $3.65 billion they had about octupled.

Du Pont had grown more modestly. That is to say, its sales had multiplied a mere 9.2 times, its earnings a mere 5 times, and its stockholder total 3.2 times, while its employee total had not quite doubled. As for General Electric, its sales were up sixteen times over those of 1939, its earnings almost six times, its net assets five times, its stockholders about two and a half times, its employees four times.

That was what had happened over a quarter-century to the terrifying giants of 1939.

But, as the nature of the reports containing these figures bears witness, the companies had changed in other respects. The most obvious new characteristic was a heightened anxiety to please the companies' customers, employees, even the general public—almost everybody except the stockholders *qua* stockholders. The 1964 General Motors report, far from being the chilly statistical tract that the 1939 one had been, was a magnificent brochure in which pages of facts and figures about company operations were judiciously mixed with brightly colored pictures clearly intended to sell more Chevrolets, Pontiacs, Buicks, and Cadillacs. Indeed, the report's chief feature was a four-page colored spread of General Motors cars, each one set against an appropriately uplifting setting—a ballet school, a steeplechase track, a college campus, a wooded picnic ground, a country inn. (The sign above the inn's door read "Lounge and Dining Room" rather than anything so blunt as "Bar and Dining Room," which presumably might have alienated teetotaling potential GM customers.) What GM had clearly discovered between 1939 and 1964 was that its stockholders had become so numerous, and so different from the old investor stereotype of the hard-bitten coupon clipper, as to be no longer distinguishable from its customers.

The 1964 General Electric report was *all* on shiny paper and had colored pictures on twenty-three of its thirty-two pages. Even though only about a quarter of the company's annual sales are of consumer goods, there were plenty of pictures showing highly photogenic consumers enjoying such GE products as portable television, toasters, and modern kitchens; alongside them, the text pointed out jubilantly that "family formations are beginning to climb as 'war babies' marry and start their own homes," resulting in still more consumer purchases of GE goods. GE also made much of its employees—"competitive people who give General Electric one of industry's finest creative and productive teams"—and it might have added that most of them were very likely GE stockholders, too. Eleven such competitive people's pictures, in full color and with their names included, occupied all of page 19; even the company's directors were not shown until page 30, where they appeared in a hazy group picture. As for the stockholder—the man, and the only man, to whom any company's annual report is nominally directed—he was scarcely even mentioned anywhere.

All this de-emphasis of ownership and emphasis on consumption and participation by employees in a big, happy family is part of the new blandness of huge corporations. "We believe that fairness and equity to our employees can be combined with fairness to the owners of the business," the president and chairman of General Motors wrote smoothly in their 1964 letter to stockholders. True, the blandness left room for small, barely detectable bits of evasion; GM for example, printed elaborate charts showing the average weekly earnings of hourly-rate employees throughout the United States in 1964, but did not print the average rate for GM employees—an oversight that may have been due to the fact that a strike against GM during 1964 might have made the precise figure appear in an unfavorable light. But, with a welter of gorgeous Chevrolets and Cadillacs to warm the ego and distract the eye, who would cavil over a small omission like that?

In general, though, the old reticence about facts and figures was gone from the reports along with the old defensiveness about corporate attitudes, and a new emphasis on salesmanship had been added. Capital and labor, the companies seemed to be saying, were getting to be almost the same fellow—and, in any case, the fellow was a potential customer. Even du Pont, a traditionally conservatively managed company, and one that for decades used to be singled out for criticism on the brevity and uninformativeness of its annual reports, had long since bent to the wind. True, its 1964 report had no full-color pictures, or any other kind of illustrations other than charts and small drawings. But this fifty-page booklet contained as much and as detailed financial information as any stockholder could hope for. It also included on page 20 the striking statement: "During 1964 . . . recruiting was conducted at predominantly Negro colleges with satisfactory results. Company locations were able to employ qualified applicants of minority groups for numerous assignments of increased responsibility." The fact that stockholders of du Pont were now presumed to be interested in something like that—clearly a matter of corporate citizenship rather than of how much next year's dividend would be—was a pretty good measure of how much things had changed.

What had happened, in sum, was that the giants of 1939 had grown so prodigiously since then as to make their former selves look almost like dwarfs. By a delicious stroke of irony, at the very moment in 1939 that they were being so energetically scolded for being giants, they were unwittingly on the verge of becoming supergiants. And, as a crowning irony, the growth was to transform their character in a way exactly opposite to what was expected. The big, coldly menacing grizzlies of 1939 were to become the superbig, smiling, approval-seeking pandas of 1964.

2

The growth of the giant corporations into supergiants, and the transformation of their character that accompanied it, seem to me to be the single economic change that has had the farthest-reaching effects over the past quarter-century. If it isn't the key to the whole transformation of American life—and I don't think it can be called that—it is, at any rate, a sort of master key capable of opening many rooms in our national house. "Since the end of the Second World War, the corporate form has emerged as the characteristic institution of American society," Andrew Hacker of Cornell wrote recently. True enough, and happily enough, it has not become the all-powerful and all-embracing institution on which everyone's livelihood depends. Even now, the one hundred largest corporations provide only about six million jobs, or less than one-tenth of the national total, and even the five hundred largest provide no more than ten million jobs. Economically, and probably culturally as well, small business, from the corner cigar store to the hi-fi or electronic-component firm set up in a loft by two or three brainy young Ph.D.s, is still close to the heart of our national life. But how many small businesses have huge corporations as their most important customers, or live by supplying goods or services to the employees of huge corporations, or otherwise depend upon them! To put it in terms of sheer economic power, about half of the productive assets of American manufacturing are held by about 150 corporations, and it has been estimated that about two-thirds of such assets, agriculture excluded, are held by not more than five hundred.

Consider, as an index, the fantastic growth of the national economy that was set off by, and in large measure accounted for by, the growth of big corporations. In 1964 we had disposable personal income—after taxes—of some $435 billion; for 1939 the figure was about $76 billion. Per capita, man, woman, and child, the figure rose from under $600 to well over $2,000. (It is interesting to note that national-income statistics themselves were comparatively new in the 1930s. The very machinery by which national economic growth is now measured was a recent invention.) Just the *interest* on our public debt is now about equal to the *total national budget* of the late 1930s. What all this means in terms of wages is that in June, 1963, the national average weekly earnings of factory workers for the first time ever passed the $100 mark—which in the 1930s had become almost the established figure denoting affluence. What it means in terms of easy living is that by 1964 more than 80 percent of American families owned at least one automobile, as against less than 60 percent in 1939; that sales of household appliances, many of which did not yet exist in 1939, were at near-record levels, and sales of all kinds of clothing were the highest ever; while services, ranging from motel rooms to laundromats and diaper services, were operating at levels undreamed of even a decade earlier. As a European diplomat said in 1964, "The American economy has become so big that it is beyond the imagination to comprehend. But now on top of size you are getting rapid growth as well. It is a situation of fundamental power unequaled in the history of the world."

Consider in detail one or two parts of the vast anatomy of that power. The directors of a corporation, let us say, decide to spend a million dollars—or ten million, or a hundred million, or a billion—on plant expansion. Is this simply a business gamble, a play on the free-enterprise roulette wheel, of interest chiefly to the gambler and the croupier? Indeed not. Such a decision, as Hacker points out,

> may well determine the quality of life for a substantial segment of society. Men and materials will move across continents; old communities will decay and new ones will prosper; tastes and habits will alter; new skills will be demanded, and the education of a nation will adjust itself accordingly; even government will fall into line, providing public services that corporate developments make necessary.

So it has been the past decade and more; the advent of a plant of IBM or General Electric or Corning Glass to some sleepy hamlet has time and again transformed it into a bustling small city, with new people and a new social structure and new ideas about life. If anyone doubts the economic muscle of the individual corporate investment decision, let him contemplate the fact that in 1964 General Motors alone spent about one billion on new construction. Yet even that fantastic figure is dwarfed by the $3.9 billion spent in 1965 by the largest company in the world, American Telephone and Telegraph.

It is startling to realize the number of ways in which the big companies have served as the magnets around which our national life has come to arrange itself in directed patterns. Urbanization, the flight from the farm and the hamlet to the city and the suburb, has been one of the most marked national trends in recent years. Corporations produced the equipment and the fertilizer that made the farm hand superfluous; corporations offered him the job that brought him to the city. Suburbia itself is the corporation's creation: the corporation needs a city to serve it, and the corporation employee needs a place to live. (Lately, some corporations have taken to setting up offices and even small factories *in* the suburbs, thereby changing them into cities.)

It is the giant corporation, far more than any single force, that has transformed America over the past quarter-century from a country in which several fairly distinct social and economic classes were still easily discernible, and usually acknowledged by their respective members, into a country in which a single group, the middle class, includes a majority of the whole population and seems to be heading toward becoming more or less universal. (I intend to take up the social consequences of this change in later chapters.) The giant corporation, in alliance with the most efficacious advertising medium ever invented, the television screen, has done more than anything else to establish our present habits of consumption and thus to a great extent set the style and pattern of our lives. And it has changed our relations with the rest of the world. Between 1940 and 1961 U.S. assets and investments abroad went from $12 billion to $80 billion. The increase, apart from its effect on the economies of other countries, and on that of our own, meant that hundreds of thousands more Americans were traveling to and living in foreign parts, not as tourists to be smirked at and fleeced, but as employees with the responsibility of earning a living—that is to say, not as objects but as people.

Sometimes such Americans have been liked, and sometimes they have been hated; in all cases, they have become better known.

Finally, the giant corporation, almost inadvertently, has tended to become a force against race discrimination at home. Its impartial and practical devotion to the idea of profit; the fact that its scope is national, with tentacles reaching into all parts of the country; and the fact that the federal government, by virtue of so often being among its biggest customers, is in a position to put direct economic pressure on it—all these factors have combined to make the typical national corporation's Southern plants become in many cases the quiet, and sometimes reluctant, leaders of local integration of races. The Southern-born and Southern-bred manager of the Atlanta branch of a national firm expressed the matter well in 1964. "We've already about put an end to what was left of the Old South," he said. "Doing business in national companies and competitive markets, the requirements of manufacturing technology, and, in a funny way, the impersonality of the big corporation that a lot of people complain about—they all spelled the end of the old way. I haven't had a mint julep in years."

How did the corporation explosion come about? Like so many postwar developments, it was set in motion by the war itself. With a war to be won and industrial production on an unprecedented scale needed to turn out weapons, it was no time for denunciations of bigness or sentimentality about handicrafts; the national heroes of wartime in the field of economics were not the idealistic New Dealers but the tough production bosses like William Knudsen and Donald Nelson. Gross national product more than doubled between 1940 and 1945, while the cost of government and government enterprises was more than quadrupling. But what would happen to the economy when the war ended, removing the need for war production and thus taking the props from under the artificial boom? Industrial managers and academic economists were, for once, in agreement: both groups expected a collapse. Nothing of the kind took place. The wartime props were summarily removed, all right—from the wartime peak of almost $100 billion in 1944 and 1945, government expenditures dropped off to only $33 billion in 1948—but so great was the public's appetite for automobiles and other items of consumer goods of which it had been deprived all through the war that the total output of the economy dropped hardly at all.

The appetite had to become sated eventually, of course, and there was some hard going for a couple of years—especially in 1948, which has been called the one real peacetime year in postwar history, when the federal budget reached its low point; but even then families were expanding at an unprecedented rate, wages were rising rapidly, demand for housing and all kinds of household equipment was at a high level, and the economy was holding its own. Then in 1950 came the Korean War, and the prop of high military spending was back, and, though no one could know it at the time, the modern era in American economic life was inaugurated. Military spending was to be a continuing major factor. By the time the Korean War ended in 1953, the Cold War was a well-established fact; soon technological developments like the thermonuclear bomb and rocketry made the waging of the Cold War incomparably more complex and more expensive, and in the early 1960s roughly half of the government's annual income was being spent on defense. Meanwhile, beginning with the end of the Korean War, the nation went on a consumer-goods-buying binge such as had never been seen before, and besides, as the population grew by leaps and bounds, the number of customers swelled proportionately. Thanks to the presence of two voracious customers—the government and the ordinary citizen—the corporations were sitting pretty.

It would be a mistake, though, to suggest that the big companies were merely beneficiaries of an expanding economy, and that postwar growth was just something nice that happened to them. On the contrary, they can take a good deal of the credit themselves. Even in the early postwar years, when economic pessimism was so prevalent, they were betting on their own and the country's future in a big way. Immediately before the war, American corporations were reinvesting about 40 percent of their profits after taxes in expansion of one sort or another; during the 1946–48 period the figure was up sharply to 62 percent. Thus when the fat years came in the middle 1950s, the corporations were in a position to exploit prosperity, and in so doing to increase it—something that they would have had a great deal of difficulty in doing if they had spent the late 1940s cautiously hoarding their profits in cash or passing them along to stockholders as dividends.

In part, this corporate foresightedness was undoubtedly adventitious, an incidental product of government tax policy; income-tax rates had soared so high during the war, and remained so high in the postwar period, that many stockholders in the higher brackets didn't particularly want big dividends on which they would have to pay top rates, and preferred to see profits on their money reinvested so that they could eventually take capital gains, on which they would be taxed at much lower rates. But undoubtedly there was a deeper reason, too. The old, innate, often naïve optimism of the American businessman, which went all the way back to the early nineteenth century, and which had suffered such a punishing series of setbacks during the depression that by 1939 it was practically eroded away, had now come back strong. The war was over, thought the men who made the corporate decisions; the country was growing again; the future was a shining promise; to hell with the pessimists! On this occasion, whether or not for the right reasons, the optimists were right.

And there was more to it than that. The whole climate of the postwar United States favored the further growth of big business. The reformist spirit of the Thirties had faded—or at least, most of its main tenets had seeped into the national mainstream, so that they no longer could be called reform. There was little public enthusiasm for antitrust activities; when the government's long-drawn-out antitrust cases against AT&T and the leading Wall Street investment bankers in the early 1950s were lost, most of those who cared one way or the other approved the decisions. Tired of both reform and war, the country seemed to want above everything both the consumer products and the comparatively secure jobs that only huge corporations could provide in profusion. The old hostility between big business and government from New Deal days became more or less perfunctory during President Harry S. Truman's Administration, and changed to warm friendship with the advent to the White House of

Dwight D. Eisenhower. It was a time when Americans wanted their leaders, institutions and men alike, to be bland, benign, fatherly—and big.

3

But which is the key word—"benign" or "big"? Where there is power, there is a need for responsibility; a professor at the Harvard Business School told me recently that the main thing he tries to impress on his students is that power has a moral dimension. If the American economy has recently developed a store of power unequaled in world history, and if that power resides chiefly in huge corporations, the question immediately arises: How well is the power being used? The answer, I am convinced, is that it is being used less well than it should be and a good deal less badly than it might be. Certainly it is being used in different, and generally far, far better, ways than anyone—New Deal economist or company executive—could have predicted in 1939. And no wonder, because, as the contrasting annual reports of 1939 and 1964 suggest, the change in corporations has been as much in kind as in size.

For one thing, in the process of increasing in quantity the corporate power has been diffused. It has become so great as to be almost invisible.

Everyone knew who wielded the power in the traditional American family-controlled corporation, which, though already losing ground, was still probably the characteristic American corporation at the end of the 1930s. The controlling family wielded it, and no bones made. In *Middletown in Transition* the Lynds describe how in Middletown in the Thirties the "X" family, through their corporation and its power, ran the town: not only could they choose the factory pay scale ($15 to $17 a week) and keep unions out; they could also choose the city's mayor, deprive a liberal minister of his pulpit, control the morning newspaper, and baronially shift the select residential area from one place to another according to whim. Everyone in Middletown knew who wielded the poker; the "X" family did. If not everyone knew who wielded the power in the Ford Motor Company, at least the choice was a narrow one; it might be old Henry Ford, the founder, or it might be his son Edsel—there was no question of its being any third party. But family capitalism was near the end of the road. Various postwar factors, probably the chief of which were the tax structure and the need for new capital for expansion, forced one company after another to "go public" by selling its shares on the open market, until in the late Fifties Daniel Bell could write that in two decades the Lynds' picture of the "X" family "has become a picture of the past rather than of contemporary society." Ford itself, one of the last holdouts among the giants, went public in 1956 by distributing over ten million shares to more than a quarter of a million investors for a sum in the neighborhood of $650 million, in what still stands as the most spectacular stock distribution on record.

Where did the power go? Theoretically, to the new owners, the stockholders; but in practice they are usually utterly unable to exercise it because there are so many of them. The degeneration of the stockholder from a real force in management to a mere receiver of dividends or putter-in-the-wastebasket of proxy statements has been commented on again and again over the past decade. It has been pointed out that there is a disturbing parallel between the "elections" held at corporate annual meetings and the political elections in Russia, since in each case the officially sponsored slate invariably gets at least 99 percent of the votes cast. As A. A. Berle writes, "When corporations were still small, the stockholder powerfully influenced the director, but today they are so far apart that the stockholder can hardly communicate with management even by megaphone. We go through the ancient forms . . . but everyone knows that a stockholders' meeting is a kind of ancient, meaningless ritual."

The directors who represent the stockholders more immediately control the power; but many boards of directors are made up largely of men from "outside" the company, without intimate knowledge of its myriad complicated affairs, who are compelled by sheer lack of acquaintance with detail to act as rubber stamps for the decisions of the day-to-day operating officers. Thus the power is apt to fall to that new breed, the trained, high-salaried professional managers who are often not substantial owners. Yet by the nature of their training and the dynamics of their situation, these men are inclined to make cautious, safe-and-sound "consensus" decisions that will not stir up the sleeping giants who might unseat them, the directors and stockholders.

Furthermore, so complex are the affairs of the supergiant corporations that even the professional managers, skilled and dedicated as they may be, cannot always know what is going on within their commands. A case very much in point is the electrical-industry conspiracy of the late Fifties—the biggest business scandal of the postwar years—in which executives of the leading manufacturers contrived, by an elaborate system involving secret telephone calls, hotel-room meetings, and codes, to defeat the free market by illegally fixing prices on billions of dollars' worth of equipment. When the conspiracy was uncovered, the guilty executives of General Electric, the biggest company involved, said they believed that in conspiring they had been acting on orders from their superiors. On the other hand, Ralph J. Cordiner, General Electric's chief executive officer, said that he had not even known about the conspiracy, far less ordered it. Many people understandably refused to believe that Cordiner was telling the truth. Yet the fact remains that it is entirely possible, in view of the confusion and misunderstanding that attends the bureaucratic operations of a supergiant corporation, that Cordiner *was* telling the truth. In that case, his men had been acting on orders that had originated—nowhere! By way of further contrast, imagine a family capitalist like old Henry Ford, or Mr. X of Middletown, excusing himself by pleading that he had not known what was going on in his command. It would have been unthinkable! But Cordiner could do it, to the satisfaction of his board of directors and a good portion of the business community, for a simple reason: they thought it perfectly natural that neither Cordiner nor anyone else had the power to oversee General Electric.

Headless as they sometimes seem to have become in the process of growing unthinkably big, the corporations have assumed the status almost of national states. And in many respects, ironically enough, the particular states they tend to resemble are socialized rather than free-enterprise ones. What is General Motors, an American economic analyst asked recently, but a vast planned economy, similar in many respects to the Polish economy, which happens to be not a great deal larger? The top officers of American Telephone and Telegraph are not being pretentious when they speak of their regular Monday morning gatherings in the company's board room in lower Manhattan as "cabinet meetings." Possessing economic power greater than most of the nations of the world, and political influence less great but still far from negligible, AT&T is quite worthy of having a cabinet.

In the past quarter-century the biggest corporations have gone a long way toward converting themselves into welfare states. The whole array of "fringe benefits"—medical plans, group insurance plans, pension trusts, and so on—have come to provide many corporate employees with something approaching cradle-to-grave security, and have attained such importance in the eyes of employees that they now often take precedence over wages and salaries in union negotiations and as inducements to executive talent. (The staggering sum of around $100 billion was owned by private pension funds of all types in 1965, as against $4 billion in 1940 and $15 billion as recently as 1955. By the nature of these trusts, the figure is increasing inexorably, year by year, and at least one such trust, that of Sears, Roebuck & Company's employees, now owns a controlling interest in the company. Thus, Sears, Roebuck has, in effect, socialized itself, and the list of companies in which the same thing happens is bound to grow rapidly as time goes on.)

At the same time, companies have shown the extent to which they have come to regard themselves as polities, with constituents to be wooed and even served rather than with mere employees to be compensated for work, by setting up all kinds of social facilities. They send their employees back to college, or set up entirely new colleges. IBM has its country clubs, Richfield Oil has its model homes, Reynolds Tobacco has its chaplains, RCA has its company neckties not in lieu of wages or to forestall labor troubles but to give employees a sense of belonging—to make them feel that the company is their community rather than merely their meal ticket. As Andrew Hacker has written, "The national government, as socialists throughout the world have discovered, is too large and unwieldy to provide satisfaction [of people's need for a sense of community]; and local governments are too weak and ineffectual to cater to such deep-seated needs." Small wonder that du Pont and Eastman Kodak are far from being the only companies that have available for employee consultation their own staffs of psychiatrists.

And along with their growing sense of responsibility for conditions and needs within their own organizations, the corporations, by and large, have come to look upon themselves as citizens with duties toward their local communities. In a very important respect, this is something entirely new since 1939. The old family capitalist could, and of course often did, make large charitable contributions *as an individual.* But he was legally prevented from contributing a penny of his company's money for such purposes unless he owned every share of the company's stock himself; otherwise, if he tried it, he was subject to suit by stockholders for misappropriating company funds. Since the end of the war, states have passed laws permitting corporations to make contributions to charity—and deduct them from federal tax—just like people. As a result, now it is an unenlightened great corporation indeed that does not have its own foundation through which it channels contributions for all kinds of good works, and one of the favorite good works is the enrichment of the local communities in which the company maintains facilities. Such a company, on setting up a new plant in a small town, might first undertake to help out the local hospitals; before long, it might be enlarging the library, bringing speakers and concerts to the local auditorium, setting up a symphony orchestra, establishing a community college, and engaging in a whole collection of other locally beneficial and uplifting activities.

What the community gains from all this is obvious; but it also incurs loss in the form of a certain enslavement, largely psychological rather than economic, to the corporation that is its benefactor. The company town survives in the America of the Sixties, but it is different from the traditional American barony in at least two ways. In the first place, the company, in intent and in effect, is now incomparably more beneficent. In the second place, because of the diffusion of corporate power that I have discussed, the baron himself is now invisible because he simply doesn't exist. He is a committee, or, more likely a collection of committees.

Not the least of the ways in which corporations in recent years have contributed to the life around them has been by making themselves physically a lot less forbidding. The "dark Satanic mill" of the nineteenth century, red-brick, four-square, and threatening with its rows of windows like accusing eyes, still stands slowly crumbling beside the river in many a New England or Midwestern town, but at some time since 1939 it has probably been abandoned as an operating plant. The heavy-industry factory with its rows of smokestacks belching soot still flourishes, of course, but for administrative offices and for factories in the lighter industries that have come into more and more prominence with recent technological change, modern architecture and landscaping have come to be all the rage. The buildings are low and glassy, brightened with cheerful (or, perhaps, garish) patches of color; their large green lawns are often used to display not just the familiar company sign with its trade-mark but sometimes a few pieces of abstract sculpture as well. Unfortunately, these new temples of industry, with their bland, antiseptic quality, sometimes convey a coldness and a sameness of a sort different only in style from that of the old-fashioned brick kind. And the mounting problem of air and water pollution caused by industry attests to the fact that its sense of responsibility to the community still has a long way to go.

4

Obviously, then, since 1939 the great corporation has broadened itself. It has become less a machine designed solely for cranking out a profit and more a complex organism with complex motives. In the course of losing its personal leadership and assuming a personality of its own, it has tended to take over certain human attributes—philanthropic impulses, concern for the humanity of its employees, citizenship—that were formerly the province of its owner as an individual. The reasons for this change are complex, if not downright obscure. Certainly pressure from labor unions, which at the end of the Thirties were beginning to be powerful enough to correct an enormous imbalance in our national life, has been one factor. And certainly pressure from local and federal government—exerted in many ways, from the threat of restrictive rulings and legislation to the awarding of the federal contracts that make up one-tenth of our gross national product—has been another.

It has been said, too, that the progressive separation of ownership and management has often put the affairs of corporations in the hands of men who have comparatively little personal stake in increased profits, and thus are inclined to exercise their power in less restricted and often more public-spirited ways. But, at least in my observation, in practice the thing has worked in reverse; that is, the big companies still more or less family-controlled, where ownership and management are still closely related, are the ones that have shown the most evidence of public-spiritedness, while those where ownership is most widely separated from management are the ones whose bureaucratic managers have been most cautious in undertaking any departure from the business of squeezing out an extra penny or two of profit per share. (The excuse given by the convicted executives of General Electric was that they *had* to fix prices or else lose profits for the stockholders.) Understandably enough, the owner of a dollar feels freer to give it away than does a man who is merely dealing with it as a trustee.

Probably the main reason for the change is the rise of concern, amounting at times almost to obsession, about the thing called the corporate image. (Clearly, one of the best ways to improve your public image, personal or corporate, is by conspicuously doing good works.) Big corporations had their image in prewar days, of course; it was a bad image, and, as we have seen, they were beginning to be worried about it. Their concern, though, was directed mainly to its effect on their relations with labor unions and with the government rather than their relations with the general public. The automobile manufacturer of 1939 did not expect business to be hurt seriously by the image; he expected a prospective buyer to make his choice between Ford, Chevrolet, and Plymouth on the basis not of his opinion of the manufacturers but of his opinion of the cars. Moreover—and perhaps more important—he did not personally have a bad conscience about his company's image. Secure in his faith in the economic ideas of Adam Smith and the social ideas of the nineteenth century, he could still see his company's detractors in terms of old stereotypes like "agitator" or "Socialist."

Now all that has changed; and while the rise of the corporate image has undoubtedly been an integral part of the whole shift of our society in the direction of abundance and publicity, perhaps the chief clue can be found in the word "image" itself, with its suggestion of television. Sitting in his armchair or lying in bed at home, the potential customer can *see* a company as well as its products; he forms an opinion of it on the basis of such things as the people who appear in the commercials and the sort of program being sponsored, and, as many a market survey has shown, he may well decide whether or not to buy on the basis of that opinion as much as on the quality of the product. So there is a cold business reason for developing a good corporate image, as companies were quick to realize. The publisher of *Public Relations News* maintains that there were no more than twenty-five corporate public-relations departments in the whole country as late as 1944, whereas now no major firm of the slightest national pretensions would dream of being without one.

Yet there is more involved than that. As the postwar period has progressed and corporate public-relations departments have become more powerful, the corporate image has tended to separate from the profit motive and live its own life. In many firms a move that promises to endear the firm to the public now justifies itself. The men who propose such moves, and their superiors who approve them, no longer need show concrete and immediate financial results. What will improve the image is "a good thing," and that is that. Perhaps, at bottom, such men often make such moves to satisfy their own inner needs—they want people to think well of their company so that they will be able to think well of themselves.

5

But even in these times of supergiantism and invisible power a giant corporation is still the people who work for it, and especially the people who make the decisions in it. Hacker is not alone in believing that these men are "new breeds . . . whose behavior can no longer be accounted for by conventional rules of conduct." In a brilliant and influential book first published in 1956, *The Organization Man*, William H. Whyte, Jr. argued that the main characteristic of the new businessman operating in a large organization is his abandonment of the "Protestant ethic"—the old belief in hard work and thrift as prime virtues, and of the drawing of moral guidance from interior "character" as shaped by traditional authority—and his adoption of a new "social ethic," whereby one draws authority from one's contemporaries and one's surroundings, assiduously avoids moral confrontations in the belief that they would be evidence of social maladjustment, and concentrates on "getting along" in both senses of that phrase. But Whyte was focusing his attention on the younger executives who in the 1950s were occupying the lower-middle and middle ranks of corporate management. What these men will be like as time passes and they, or a few of them, assume the more powerful top ranks of management and become the moving forces in corporate life is beyond the scope of Whyte's study. As to present top and near-top management, I'm convinced that while the change here over the past generation is fully as great as the one Whyte describes, it is of a more complicated and somewhat different sort.

The business leader of the late 1930s swore by the Protestant ethic, all right. Henry Bamford Parkes has summed up the big businessmen of the great era of expansion following the Civil War by saying that "they could preach laissez-faire as vigorously as Adam Smith . . . and could denounce the growth of government as bitterly as Thomas Jefferson." Three-quarters of a socially eventful century later, the bosses of the Thirties still clung largely to those beliefs; Sewell Avery, the tough, fiercely independent, cash-hoarding, depression-fearing chief of Montgomery Ward, was prototypical of the time. Like most of his peers in the business elite, Avery had grown up in well-to-do circumstances and been given a first-class education that had provided him with a fully satisfactory set of practical and moral underpinnings for his conservative policies. Like most big businessmen of the time, he does not seem to have suffered much doubt about the rightness of his decisions. He *knew* he was right.

Now much of that is changed; the characteristic business manager of the 1960s is more optimistic, more venturesome with capital funds, more group-minded and therefore less venturesome with personal policies, more social-minded, less conservative in politics, less sure of himself in all things. For one thing, he begins as a somewhat different sort of fellow—that is, he is apt to have had a different background. "Recruitment of business leaders from the bottom is taking place now and seems to be increasing," writes the sociologist W. Lloyd Warner. "Mobility to the top is not decreasing; in fact, for at least the last quarter century, it has been increasing." In other words, the famous Horatio Alger legend of rags-to-riches has become more, rather than less, factual than it was in Alger's time. The difference is that, what with ballooning national affluence, the "rags" have become more figurative than literal (and what with the incessant complaining of executives about how taxes prevent them from building up a large estate out of their high salaries, the riches may have become somewhat figurative, too).

The characteristic big-business leader of today is the child of good-citizen, lower-middle-class parents who were ambitious for him and scraped together their pennies to give him a fairly good education; he is seldom the product of real poverty, equally seldom of inherited wealth. Moreover, he has had more formal education than his predecessor in the earlier America. (Almost 60 percent of the big-business leaders of 1952 were college graduates, as against only a little more than 30 percent in 1928; and only a tiny fraction in 1952 had never finished high school, as against more than 25 percent in 1928.) On the other hand, he is less likely than formerly to be a graduate of one of the old Ivy League colleges of the Northeast. These famous institutions have long supplied the backbone cadre in the professions and in finance, and they continue to do so; but their graduates, many of whom still were content with or even enthusiastic about big business as a career as recently as 1939, are now inclined to shy away from the prospect of taking their chances in the "rat race" of a vast organization interested primarily in results and less so in educational or social backgrounds—except, of course, when they enter business by way of specialized graduate training at some leading kingmaking institution like the Harvard Business School, and thus come into the corporation already marked for leadership.

Far more often, the big-business boss of today is a graduate of some smaller and less celebrated college. And he is far less likely than formerly to be an Anglo-Saxon Protestant whose forebears have been in this country for many generations. The melting pot has done its work, as far as business leadership is concerned. One of the striking and little-noticed phenomena of contemporary life is the gulf—in social life, ways of thinking, communication, and personal contact of any sort aside from occasional meetings in some board of directors room—between the leaders of big business on the one hand and the people sometimes called the Establishment, who come from old families, went to Ivy League colleges, and wield much of the power in finance, philanthropy, and government, on the other. The notion that there is a single, homogeneous power elite in the United States is as wrong as it could be.

Conspicuously, the new business leader is embarrassed rather than smug or exultant about the extent of his power, as evidenced by his unwillingness to admit, perhaps even to himself, that it really exists. "As is well known," W. H. Ferry has written, "this country did not seek its role as world leader, but stumbled into it. By similar chance and circumstance, the corporation stumbled into the leadership of American society." One might well carry the argument a step further and say that the big businessmen stumbled—or would have you believe he stumbled—into his position as the leader of the leader. John Kenneth Galbraith has put the matter with his characteristic acid wit. For one thing, he says, the big businessman finds it convenient to deny his exercise of economic power so that he can logically justify his unwillingness to accept federal regulation. Furthermore, says Galbraith, he finds a deeper reason for avoiding the appearance of power in the American cultural grain:

> The privilege of controlling the actions or of affecting the income and property of others is something that no one of us can profess to seek or admit to possessing. No American ever runs for office because of an avowed desire to govern. He seeks to serve. . . . The same scrupulous avoidance of the terminology of power characterizes American business.

Was a Commodore Vanderbilt, a Henry Clay Frick, or even a Sewell Avery reluctant to affirm that he exercised power? Emphatically not. He had no trouble believing that he was competent to exercise it, that his exercise of it was wiser than would be that of somebody else—even, in certain cases, that he was born to exercise it. Contrast, then, the attitude of Roger M. Blough, whose stand on pricing in the steel industry in 1962 set off the greatest confrontation between government and business in recent history, and who as chairman of U.S. Steel is probably among the half-dozen most powerful businessmen in the country. At a conference in Corning, New York, in 1961, Charles Wyzanski, a Boston judge who happened to be sitting across the table from Mr. Blough, was emphasizing how the diffusion of power in modern corporations waters down the power of individuals. Not without a mischievous intent to provoke, Judge Wyzanski remarked that "Mr. Blough has far less power than his predecessors in the United States Steel Corporation. He can't do half the things. He is a constitutional monarch with the diffused power of the Queen [of England]." As Mr. Blough well knew, the Queen has virtually no substantive power at all, while Mr. Blough, in spite of all diffusion, has a great deal and does not hesitate to exercise it on occasion. Everyone turned to Mr. Blough, expecting him to enter at least a mild demurrer to this downgrading of his function. Not at all; instead, Mr. Blough objected to the word "monarch" as making him sound too omnipotent!

Undoubtedly the biggest single change in the big businessman has taken place within his mind. In 1939 his creed was clear enough: competition and the free-price system—Adam Smith's "invisible hand"—insure that business' pursuit of self-interest will serve the public interest. By and large, he still believes that creed, at least in theory, but in practice he does not always live by it. And for good reason; with the influence of government what it is today and with government being far and away business' biggest customer, business can ill afford to give government the back of its hand as Adam Smith would have wished. As *Business Week* put it in 1964: "Cut defense spending, the businessman says, but not my contract and not in my region. Increase international trade, but don't touch my tariff. Down with government subsidies—but not mine." *Business Week* went so far as to suggest a parallel between the two faces of modern business and the two characters of Dr. Jekyll and Mr. Hyde—tactfully omitting to say which face of business it considered to be Jekyll and which Hyde.

And beyond the matter of his own and his company's interest, the big businessman no longer finds enough justification in the unvarnished Adam Smith philosophy to satisfy him personally. He may allow, and even encourage, his spokesmen like the National Association of Manufacturers and the U.S. Chamber of Commerce to parrot it over and over again, but he fails to practice it. Under the Smith system a business that did something not in the interest of profit was not merely eccentric; it was actually subversive of a beneficent system. Now, as we have seen, businesses do things not in the interest of profit all the time. The writer George Lichtheim has suggested that the way to sell capitalism to the people in backward countries is by calling it socialism; perhaps it is not too much to say that United States business now, upon occasion, sells socialism to the American people by calling it capitalism.

6

Thus big business, as so exacting a social critic as Daniel Bell allows, has "become decent." Well, is the new-style business leader more fundamentally decent than was the old-style one? I rather doubt it. In the first place, by his own standard, the Adam Smith code, the old-style boss was being decent, even socially commendable, when he stuck to his profit-making and eschewed all other activities. Besides, when a new-style boss perpetrates some conspicuously "decent" deed, there is often reason to question the purity of his motive; it often appears that he is influenced as much by public pressure or by the opportunity for public-relations coup as by his own inner morality. Henry Ford II, generally considered to be the very model of an enlightened modern business leader, gained great esteem for a speech entitled "Business Ethics in 1961" that he made in Minneapolis two months after the sentencing of the electrical companies and their executives in the price-conspiracy case. "There is really only one thing for top executives to do at such a time as this," Ford said. "That is to forget the alibis and the explanations and have the fortitude—the plain guts—to stand up and say: 'This is our failure. We are chagrined and sorry. It will not happen again.' " Bold and candid words; yet a few weeks earlier, at the annual stockholders' meeting of General Electric in Syracuse, New York, Ford had sat on the platform as a director of General Electric and had resolutely refused to stand up and say that or anything else; in fact, he had refused to answer all questions directed to him by stockholders about his attitude on the matter. What was decency in Minneapolis had not, apparently, been decency in Syracuse.

It can scarcely be questioned, though, that leading businessmen now are far more concerned about their ethics, in the sense of the social consequences of their acts, than they used to be. Back in the Thirties the Harvard Business School segregated the subject into a single course, which could soothe the conscience like a Sunday morning church service and be forgotten the rest of the week; now the matter of ethics permeates practically all the school's courses, and its catalogue promises that a student there "develops a concept of ethical values and social responsibility . . . to the American society as a whole." Harvard's Divinity School does not claim as much! In practice, the application of the concept of responsibility still has its limits. To take only one of the most publicized cases, when U.S. Steel was accused a few years ago of not doing enough to combat racial injustice in Birmingham, Alabama, a city that it dominates economically, Chairman Blough said, in effect, that improving race relations in cities where it operates was not within his company's scope of operations. On the other hand, following the assassination of President Kennedy in Dallas in November, 1963, a leading Dallas businessman, J. M. Shea, made public his highly unpopular view that the Dallas business community as a whole bore its share of responsibility for the tragedy, and lost his job as a result of the recriminations that followed. Such a courageous and soul-searching attitude as Shea's would have been quite unlikely in a 1939 business leader. And so would the sequel have been unlikely. Far from becoming a martyr, Shea, on the wave of favorable national publicity that his act brought him, landed a fine new job in a San Francisco advertising agency. For him, ethics had paid off.

And the changes in the corporation itself and in our society as a whole have brought with them other changes in the character of the business boss. Drawn now largely from the vast middle class rather than from a self-assured, traditional elite, he is inclined to be rather rootless and insecure. Just where, he is apt to ask himself, is his justification—in profits honorably earned, in service to the community, or perhaps in something else? In his confusion, or questing, he often turns toward aesthetic interests, sponsoring concerts, collecting rare books or art, even having a go at painting himself. Everyone knows that the classic American tycoon was an art collector, but he was inclined to keep his collection in his home or in his private office, away from the public eye. The present-day successor shares his treasure with others—or, if you please, flaunts his aestheticism. David Rockefeller fills the hallways and offices of the Chase Manhattan Bank building with iconoclastic modern paintings, and lesser financiers by the thousands follow his example by embarking on a frantic quest for cultural cachet. At parties in the late 1950s in East Hampton, Long Island, a summer community shared by successful artists and leading businessmen and financiers, I used to play the game of guessing which were which. As often as not, I found that the group discussing the stock market was made up of artists, while the group discussing art consisted of businessmen. The only remaining reliable hallmark was a beard; to my knowledge, no leading corporation president yet goes *that* far forward—or back.

7

Underlying all these shifts in the character of the corporation and of the people who lead it is a profound transformation of basic economic ideas.

We have seen how the laissez-faire philosophy of Adam Smith still ruled the roost in business circles at the end of the Thirties, while the great challenge to it was centered, certainly in Russia and in influential circles in the United States as well, in the diametrically opposed ideas of Karl Marx. But even then, and increasingly in the years that were to follow, the Smith view was in the process of coming to seem outdated and quite inadequate to an entirely new situation. It was not only that Smith's advocacy of minimum government interference in business affairs seemed to be less and less in the interest of business itself. Beyond that, it was becoming clearer and clearer that the free market no longer always led to the production of the most and the best goods for the lowest prices; the Invisible Hand could be a cruel one. And beyond that, some of Smith's ideas now appeared simply egregiously wrong for the American situation. Smith had insisted, for example, that the corporation as an institution would never come to much because in it men are working for others rather than for themselves, and under such circumstances, Smith believed, they work ineffectively. Could it be that the semiofficial American economic philosopher was an opponent of the *corporation*? That would hardly do.

Meanwhile in Russia, the home of the opposed philosophy of Marxism, *it* was losing ground, and would continue doing so. More than two decades after the Revolution, the state was showing no signs of "withering away," as Marx had predicted that it would; instead, the Russian state was more powerful and more ruthlessly tyrannical than ever. And in the years since 1939 Russia has made the strange discovery that it can increase the production of goods by introducing, little by little, Adam Smith's beloved profit motive! Smith and Marx both, then, have tended to become lost faiths, mere altars where the empty forms of worship continue to be observed for purposes of self-encouragement. Into the void, in the American situation, has come a new faith, and its prophet is the British economist John Maynard Keynes.

Keynes, a brilliant, aesthetically inclined Cambridge don, who collected modern art, ran a theater, and showed his practical side by making a fortune playing the markets in his spare time (mostly, it is said, while lying in bed mornings with a telephone at his side), believed passionately in capitalism, and believed, above all, that its apparently built-in cycle of inflation and depression, of boom and bust, must be interrupted by the leveling hand of government action. Specifically, he thought that the economy of a free country had to be government-managed through correctly timed deficit spending and control of demand through tax-rate changes. It may not be too mischievous to suggest, at this stage in history, that Keynes represents pretty well the working of the Hegelian system of change—thesis-antithesis-synthesis—so dear to the heart of Karl Marx. Smith was all for capital and no government interference; Marx was for government control of everything and no free capital; Keynes was for capitalism *managed* by government. Smith was thesis, Marx antithesis, Keynes synthesis. Above all, Smith and Marx were economists for times of scarcity; Keynes had the genius to see that an entirely new approach was needed to bring into being the new time that was coming in the West, a time of abundance.

In 1939 Keynes' key work, *The General Theory of Employment, Interest, and Money,* was only three years old, and even though he was already living in semiretirement and was to die in 1946, his ideas were not widely disseminated in the United States. Where they were known, they were far from universally accepted; in fact, in many quarters they were regarded as dangerously subversive. After all, some of the most important of them flew squarely in the face of America's oldest and most cherished notions—for example, the idea that saving (more often called "thrift") is an absolute virtue, an idea tracing its American lineage back to that prototypical philosopher of economic scarcity and our first national sage, Benjamin Franklin himself. Savings, Keynes said, both personal and governmental, can have the effect, by taking money out of circulation, of reducing production, depressing prices, and causing unemployment; indeed, at the wrong time they can be the proximate cause of depression and an unequivocal economic vice. What would the author of *Poor Richard* have had to say to that? One hesitates to think, but, at any rate, many of his countrymen of a later day, and particularly those engaged in business or finance, were duly appalled.

Nor were Keynesian ideas by any means wholeheartedly accepted in government circles. True, the basic economic program of the New Deal—deficit spending by government as a cure for depression—was Keynesian. But anyone who thinks of Roosevelt as a confirmed Keynesian need only read a letter Keynes wrote to Roosevelt in 1938, urging the American President to adopt a less hostile attitude toward business in the interest of making it more amenable to government persuasion. The wooing of business by government is a basic Keynesian tenet. "You could do anything you liked with [businessmen]," Keynes wrote, "if you would treat them (even the big ones) not as wolves and tigers, but as domestic animals by nature, even though they have been badly brought up and not trained as you would wish." President Roosevelt ignored this piece of fatherly advice; indeed, he appears not to have answered the letter.

Roosevelt's successor as President, Truman, was an in-and-out, or schizophrenic, Keynesian. He believed in stimulating the economy and producing jobs with government spending on the New Deal model, but he was fanatically devoted to the idea of balancing the national budget on general principles—which is to say, on the Ben Franklin principle that solvency is a precondition of virtue—and when Congress insisted on a tax cut in the face of a threatened deficit, he was horrified. Eisenhower, with his continual insistence on the crucial importance of government economy, was, of course, no Keynesian at all, at least in what he said. But like so many businessmen in the time of his Presidency, he was a partial convert in spite of himself, because the armaments and missile race gave him no choice but to raise the budget and run a federal deficit.

Seymour E. Harris has described how John F. Kennedy was highly chary of Keynesianism at the beginning of his term as President, and then gradually became a wholehearted convert, largely through the influence of his chief economic adviser, Walter Heller. His early disposition to taunt big business, symbolized by his 1962 confrontation with the steel industry, gave way to assiduous wooing that would have made Keynes smile in approval; and it was he, after all, who was the architect and advocate of the huge tax cut that took place in 1964, a few months after his death—the largest tax cut in our history, and the only one ever made in a time of *planned* budget deficit. This arch-Keynesian act—accomplished in the Presidency of Lyndon B. Johnson, who appears to be our most thoroughly Keynesian President so far—clinched the matter. Keynes had replaced Smith as our national economic philosopher, and the change was apparently ratified by Johnson's landslide at the polls that fall. If further ratification was needed, it was to be found in the fact that the Harvard Class of 1939, in a questionnaire for its twenty-fifth anniversary yearbook, answered the question, "Are you in favor of or opposed to the ideas of John Maynard Keynes?" with more than four ayes for every three nos. How would the Harvard men's fathers have responded to the same question back in their sons' graduation year of 1939? One hesitates even to think.

One of the most striking and significant changes accompanying the rise of Keynes has been a shifting of the battle lines between those long-standing antagonists, the liberal economists in government or the universities on the one hand and practical businessmen on the other. Many liberal economists at the end of the Thirties believed that the economy was approaching a state of stagnation—population growth was declining, the physical frontier was long gone, the growth of monopoly hindered economic expansion by putting a wrench in the machinery of the free market—and the villain was the monopoly-seeking capitalist. The practical businessmen agreed that something like stagnation existed, but they saw a wholly different cause of it; in their view, the trouble arose chiefly out of government tampering with the economic system as embodied in the New Deal programs. So the lines were clearly enough drawn. A partial truce in this ideological war was declared after Pearl Harbor, when all other considerations had to be subordinated to the production of weapons as efficiently and rapidly as possible. But the two sides emerged into the postwar era with their conflicting faiths essentially unshaken.

It was then that new events at last began to put old ideas out of business. The expected postwar depression never developed; population grew by leaps and bounds; as business expanded, wages went up along with profits, and without serious inflation; and everybody seemed to be winning. For both economic armies, the key question was: How could this be? The liberal academics saw monopoly, at least in the sense of corporate bigness on a scale previously unimagined, constantly gaining ground, and yet it did not seem to be having the evil consequences that they had so confidently foreseen. The practical businessmen saw government "meddling" going on, even after Eisenhower brought in a businessman's government, and yet they could not deny that their profits were fatter than ever before.

Obviously, ideas had to be changed. The change, though subtle, was remarkably rapid. When Charles E. Wilson, the former head of General Motors who became Eisenhower's Secretary of Defense, let drop, with his characteristic bluntness, the remark that what was good for General Motors was good for the country, there were howls of anguish from the academy and elsewhere, and even those who agreed with Wilson, sensing instantly that he had disturbed the even tenor of things by firing an unnecessarily provocative salvo in the old battle, took to calling him Foot-in-Mouth Charlie. Yet only about five years later A. A. Berle, the former arch-New Dealer, was concluding that Wilson had been about right: in the new situation, by golly, it *did* seem that what helped General Motors turned out to be in the public interest. Another arch-New Dealer—the former chairman of the "Socialistic" Tennessee Valley Authority, David E. Lilienthal, who was now in private business himself and finding, to his considerable surprise, that it was fascinating, stimulating, and challenging—was saying as early as 1952 that monopoly could serve the public interest, that bigness in business was generally salutary, and that the antitrust laws themselves, as administered, were largely obsolete. "Big business," Lilienthal wrote, "represents a proud and fruitful achievement of the American people . . . in big business we have more than an efficient way to produce and distribute basic commodities, and to strengthen the nation's society; we have a social institution that promotes human freedom and individualism." He was called a renegade by a few of his harder-shelled colleagues from New Deal days, but their voices were almost drowned out by the flood of new facts on his side.

More and more as the 1950s proceeded and the 1960s began, the big businessman came to be accepted back into the firmament by the liberal economists, and his response was, of all things, to accept the firmament as his own. Deficit or no deficit, the 1964 tax cut encountered very little opposition from business, and a great deal of enthusiastic support. Here was the watershed point; in supporting such a move, business was, beyond cavil, Keynesian. And for good reason. Many businessmen, Richard Rovere wrote early in 1965,

> have reached a point where they look upon such enterprises as the War on Poverty and the Civil Rights Act somewhat as their European counterparts in the last century looked upon the conquest of colonies. . . . If some forty million people, about half of whom are Negroes, can be hauled up into our great middle and lower-middle classes, there will be as much new buying power as there is today in, say, all of Latin America. The Great Society should be very good business indeed.

To a great extent, the economic warriors of 1939 have met at their Elbe and embraced each other; the result is what President Johnson likes to call a consensus.

8

The basic economic change in America—from scarcity to abundance, from the allocation of insufficient resources to the allocation of surplus—was both cause and effect of the emergence of the supergiant corporation. Growing abundance meant more buying power to fatten the corporation; the fatter corporation meant fatter payrolls, further increasing buying power; so the interaction went on, spurred by the Cold War and guided by an increasingly Keynesian government. The change was not without its dramatic moments and, perhaps, its tragic figures. To Sewell Avery, a rich man's son who in the haunted Thirties had built up Montgomery Ward (a mail-order house, that most nineteenth century of American businesses) by pursuing a rigorous policy of thrift, the economy of scarcity was like an article of faith. Eric Larrabee has suggested that he may have been our last real scarcity businessman. Almost everyone remembers the photograph of him that appeared in newspapers and magazines in 1944, when he refused to leave the Ward premises after the federal government had seized the firm because of its failure to settle a labor dispute. Two military policemen were carrying him bodily out of his office—and there he sat, coolly and commandingly at ease, his gaze as level and his body as relaxed as if he were still in his executive chair. It was a grand gesture, and the beginning of the end of an era.

The last act remained to be played out. In the postwar years Avery, restored to his executive chair, grimly went on ignoring economic trends, shunning expansion or modernization, hoarding his firm's resources against the depression he was sure would come. At the 1952 annual meeting he assured stockholders that the national economy would probably "topple very soon." At the 1954 meeting he said, "From the looks of things, the country is in a distressful condition." The national boom went on, but not for Montgomery Ward. As a result of Avery's policies, it lost more and more ground in relation to its leading competitor, and in 1955, when the stock was selling almost twenty dollars below book value, an insurgent slate of more modern-minded directors led by Louis E. Wolfson challenged his control in a proxy fight.

I happened to be present at the annual meeting that spring in Chicago, at which that proxy fight was settled, and I will never forget it. Avery, now eighty-one years old, a frail old man with snow-white hair and a blue suit, looking vulnerable rather than commanding, took the podium to report on company affairs. He mumbled about "when the economic rain arrives"; he was silent for long, agonizing pauses, and sometimes he appeared about to topple over bodily; he snapped back querulous answers to taunts from the floor; and only once, when he spoke of the $700 million, debt-free, that Montgomery Ward had put away in its treasury, did his voice rise to a semblance of strength. When the scene became almost too much to bear, a subordinate gently escorted the old man to a seat and took over the meeting himself. Avery, who had powerful Wall Street backing, won the proxy fight by a narrow margin, but three weeks later he retired, to be replaced by a man who adopted most of Wolfson's policies. Thus the era of scarcity finally ended, with a dying victory that was all romance and no substance.

III. MONEYMEN, SALESMEN, AND PHILANTHROPISTS

1

Other changes in our economic life, accompanying and more or less related to the transformation of the corporations, provide convenient windows through which to look at the larger change in the nation as a whole.

The rise of philanthropic foundations is such a window. These institutions, which exist for the sole purpose of giving away other people's money, were quite scarce before the war. The *Britannica Book of the Year* for 1939 declared that they numbered "above three hundred," and that the capital assets of the 121 largest totaled $945 million. They now number about fifteen *thousand,* and were recently reported to be proliferating at a rate of one hundred per month; their combined assets were recently calculated at $14.5 *billion,* and have been increasing at a rate of three-quarters of a billion a year; the assets of the largest one, the Ford Foundation, amounted in 1965 to $3 billion, or more than three times as much as the 121 largest had in 1939; and their charitable grants, for projects ranging from the training of magistrates and local court officers in Zambia to the preservation of the prairie chicken in Wisconsin, were recently running at an annual rate of $780 million, or four dollars and change per year for every man, woman, and child in the United States.

Does all this reflect a tremendous welling up of philanthropic impulses in well-to-do Americans? It would be lovely to think so; but the signs are all too unmistakable that it reflects to a far greater degree the federal tax structure, which, of course, grants exemption for donations to certified charitable organizations. Inheritance taxes were for the first time reaching astronomical levels in the 1940s; accordingly, when the founder of the Ford Motor Company and his son made their wills, they left 90 percent of their Ford stock to their private foundation rather than paying nearly all of it to the government in taxes, thereby making that foundation the richest charitable organization in the history of the world—and, incidentally, preserving family control of the motor company, and even relieving the heirs to the other 10 percent of the stock of the necessity of paying any inheritance taxes! The hard-shelled old Henry Ford, who had lived beyond his time, must have gone to his grave in 1947 chortling over how he had beat the government out of his money and made philanthropy pay.

As to personal income taxes levied on the living, even though they had been rising steeply through the 1930s to what many even then considered outrageously high levels, and even though in 1939 the rich were carrying a far greater share of our national tax burden than they do now, nevertheless high-bracket taxes were still some 25 to 30 percent below what they were to be in the postwar era—which meant, quite literally, that charity cost a rich man more of his own money then than it was to cost him later. The rising curve of foundations all too crassly parallels the rising curve of influence of high taxes on economic behavior; indeed, even the little bumps and pips in the curve are synchronous, inasmuch as the short period of 1950-53, when corporation taxes were temporarily higher than immediately before or after, is the very period when about half of all corporation-sponsored foundations were organized. No, the welling-up-of-impulse explanation simply won't do; we must look at the foundations as an economic and social rather than a moral phenomenon. As such, they are highly interesting.

Logically, for instance, they should be the exact opposite of the corporations, since the corporations are in the business of making money and the foundations of giving it away. And in some ways they have been treated as if they were the opposite; witness the unsuccessful Congressional attempts in the early Fifties to establish that the big foundations were Communistic—a charge seldom leveled against a big corporation. Yet, to a striking and paradoxical degree, the foundations actually *resemble* the corporations.

Both corporations and foundations are, for example, great masses of capital with a built-in tendency, in prosperous times, to grow bigger; just as the corporation has its profits, so the foundation has its tax-free dividends and capital gains on its investments, not to mention new donations to its coffers. Like the corporations, the foundations have been accused of being bad in proportion to their bigness; it has repeatedly been charged that they represent dangerous concentrations of economic and social power, and the most persistent foundation critic of all, Representative Wright Patman of Texas, declared a few years ago that the wealthier family foundations, or clusters of foundations, "today bear a frightening resemblance to the bank holding companies . . . of the early 1900s." Again like the corporations, the foundations have succeeded to a great extent in beating this rap. Early in 1965 the Treasury Department itself, in the course of cracking down on the small minority of foundations that appeared to be abusing their tax exemptions, went out of its way to dismiss the charge that the power of foundations in general was dangerous or was being used irresponsibly.

Indeed, it would be possible, although perhaps a bit graceless, to contend that considering their vast power the great foundations—Ford, Rockefeller, Duke, Hartford, Carnegie, and the half-dozen others that together control between a third and a half of all foundation assets—have up to now done the country remarkably little of either harm or good. The loss of federal revenue brought about by their tax exemptions has, it could be said, been balanced but not overbalanced by the good that has come of their benefactions. It is true, as *Newsweek* said in 1962, they have financed "colleges and universities by the score, museums and libraries by the thousands, medical aid and comfort for uncounted millions." (According to recent figures, the 176 biggest foundations, which control more than three-quarters of all foundation assets, devote 46 percent of their grant money to education, 17 percent to international activities, 14 percent to the sciences, 10 percent to health, and the remaining 13 percent to welfare, religion, and the humanities.) It is equally true that large foundations, even more than large corporations, have a cautious, bureaucratic tendency to produce "studies" rather than concrete results, to the utter frustration of their would-be almsmen. A classic foundation story has it that a literary magazine, losing money so fast that it was threatened with extinction, applied to a mighty foundation for a grant to tide it over the crisis, and got the only faintly encouraging response that the foundation would be delighted to tackle the problem—by undertaking a depth study of why little magazines lose money.

Like corporations (and utterly unlike earlier American philanthropies, which seldom cared what anyone thought of them), the great foundations have become intensely public-relations conscious, fretting about their images almost as much as Ford or General Electric. It is hard to see why this should be so; logically, an institution devoted to philanthropy should be the last to have to worry about what people think of it. Perhaps the concern stems from a certain insecurity in the men who work for the foundations. Because they, like the giant corporations, seem to have produced a new breed of men—a breed that Frederick P. Keppel, who was one himself, dubbed a "philanthropoid." As Dwight Macdonald has described the typical philanthropoid, he is "youngish, earnest, sincere . . . unpretentious, and above all, friendly"; he dresses halfway between academic dowdiness and Madison Avenue chicness; his conversation impartially mixes the argots of advertising and sociology; and his job makes him not so much smug as uneasy. Beardsley Ruml, an important foundation man in his time, said that being in the business of giving away others' money "gives you a feeling of complete insecurity," and Paul G. Hoffman, returning to private business after a stint as head of the Ford Foundation, said that it was a huge relief to get back to the earthy reality of a balance sheet. Insecure or not, though, the big-foundation man is near the very heart of that esoteric Eastern seaboard axis—internationalist in foreign affairs, moderately liberal in domestic affairs, and supposedly vastly influential in matters of state —that has come to be called the Establishment. It may be that the foundation way of thinking exerts its greatest influence outside of foundations, through men like Dean Rusk, who was head of the Rockefeller Foundation before he became Secretary of State.

What the many similarities between corporations and foundations would seem to be telling us is that in the present era, when so many old blacks and whites seem to be blending into grays, huge concentrations of money tend to act somewhat alike whether they exist to get or to give. And in a broader sense, if the big foundations have not greatly changed present-day America—which, like them, is something new under the sun—they certainly seem to have come to reflect it. For example, they are exemplars of the tendency to self-analysis that has led Eric Larrabee to call ours the self-conscious society. The foundations, with their endless studies of American transportation problems, American mores, American corporate problems, and American everything else, are vintage navel-contemplators; indeed, they sometimes go beyond studying their country and study themselves (the figures on foundations that I have quoted come from a study published by the Russell Sage Foundation). Anxious to help but worried about their public relations and frequently stumbling over their own bureaucracy, fearful of demonstrating or using their power, beneficent but not from the most pure motives, the big foundations are like the king in Gilbert and Sullivan's *Utopia, Limited,* who was subject to instant execution by a board of Wise Men if he made a tyrannical move, and who in consequence was given to minding his P's and Q's and keeping himself respectable. A little less respectability might make the foundations more socially useful, but it would hardly make them more characteristic of their time or their country.

2

Wall Street—the Kremlin's cherished whipping boy, the respectable man's race track, the well-to-do retired man's daytime serial—

Wall Street is many things to many people, but as the capital market in the world's first society of mass capitalism, it is in a peculiarly favorable position to reflect the new kind of change, social as well as economic. And it has done so.

Wall Street as it was in 1939 differed from many other parts of the American scene in that it was already visibly on the brink of far-reaching change. As Rudolph L. Weissman wrote in a book published that year, "The old Wall Street is dead. The new one is emerging." The old Wall Street, of course, was the free-wheeling, and sometimes freebooting, one that had flourished in the Twenties, with its pool operators pushing the prices of stocks up or down at will, its bank presidents manipulating the shares of their own institutions for their private profit, its underwriting groups handing out desirable new shares under the counter to their special friends, and so on. One is tempted to think that all that had ended abruptly with the notorious 1929 crash, or at least with the coming of the New Deal in 1933, but it was not so. The first reaction of Wall Street to the New Deal had by and large been one of blatant, almost contemptuous defiance; it is interesting to note that some of the most outrageous pool manipulations took place *after* Roosevelt's inauguration. The Wall Street majority violently and irascibly opposed each of the important reform measures that were passed in the early New Deal years: the Securities Act of 1933, which put the burden on issuers of new stock to disclose the essential facts about the issuing company and its finances; the Banking Act of 1933, which brought the power of banks into scale by separating investment and commercial banking functions; and the Securities Act of 1934, which outlawed all forms of stock manipulation and, by creating the Securities and Exchange Commission, supplied the Street with the police force it so badly needed. It was only after initially accepting these and other reform measures with the worst grace possible that Wall Street, faced with a series of *faits accomplis*, began gradually to soften.

By the end of the decade, the Street was finally on the verge of letting bygones be bygones and looking to the future. It was a little like a grumpy old hypochondriac who finds himself feeling better and resents the fact. After all, the 1930s had been a decade in which the trend of the market, after 1933, had been moderately upward. (But it had also been a decade when the prevailing political climate of the country had been leftist, and more than once during it Morgan partners had had to have police protection because of bomb threats.) Under considerable outside pressure, the New York Stock Exchange put itself through a major reorganization in 1938 to eliminate abuses and partially erase the picture of it as a "private club." Meanwhile, Wall Streeters were thawing out only gradually toward government regulation; the Investment Company Act of 1940 was to be the first piece of New Deal financial legislation on which Wall Street offered substantial, if a bit grudging, cooperation.

Curiously, though, there were certain significant survivals of the past era of wild speculation. Even in 1939 loans by brokers to people who had bought stock on margin amounted to the very high figure of $2.6 billion. Evidently, despite the bitter lesson of 1929, it was still popular to take a flier in the market on credit if you had the chance. The percentage of cash required by the Federal Reserve on stock purchases was below 50 percent, as against 70 percent or more through most of the postwar era; even government still looked favorably on a high degree of public risk. A seat on the Stock Exchange cost about $80,000, which, in dollars adjusted for subsequent inflation, is not so very much less than one cost in 1965. Perhaps more to the point, Wall Street in 1939 was yielding ground reluctantly, under pressure—certainly not with anything approaching enthusiasm. The very name of Roosevelt was still anathema—somewhat comically, his victory over Wendell L. Willkie in the 1940 Presidential election was not mentioned until page 6 of the next day's *Wall Street Journal*. There was still scarcely a Democrat above the secretarial or office-boy level to be found from Trinity Church at one end of Wall Street to the East River at the other, and if one *were* found, his colleagues were anything but tolerant of his deviant views. The New Deal was still considered to be galloping socialism, and most of its regulatory measures were still thought of as impudent meddling in private affairs. Dignity and mystery were still Wall Street's watchwords. Conditions had changed; attitudes, for the most part, hadn't.

It was clear in 1939, then, that the seeds of great change had been sown; what could not be seen was either the nature or the extent of the change that was to come, and the reason was that no one could foresee the coming explosion in the economy as a whole. A few figures will draw the picture in broad strokes. Between 1940 and 1964 the market value of stocks listed on the New York Stock Exchange went from $46 billion to $411 billion. Between 1940 and 1958 the daily circulation of the *Wall Street Journal* went from 32,000 to 540,000. An accurate national stockholder census had not yet been taken in the late 1930s, but according to reliable estimates there were between three and four million stockholders all told; the vast majority of these had only minuscule or token holdings, and some three-fifths of all corporate dividends were paid to 150,000 recipients. In 1952 the Stock Exchange counted six and a half million stockholders; in 1962 it counted seventeen million; in 1965 twenty million. True enough, the shares were not very evenly distributed among these numerous capitalists—Robert J. Lampman of Wisconsin calculated that in 1953 the richest 1 percent of all adults owned three-quarters of all stock, and a University of Michigan survey found that only one-sixth of the nation's families owned any stock as late as 1960—but even so the Stock Exchange now had considerable justification for claiming that "people's capitalism" had arrived.

The story of what has happened to Wall Street over the past quarter-century is essentially the story of its activities becoming a great many people's business rather than a few people's. From the public's point of view, the period, which has seen a wholly unprecedented boom in stock prices, offered stockholders an opportunity to enrich themselves many times by doing nothing more than have the self-restraint to leave their stocks alone in their bank boxes. The Dow-Jones industrial average hovered around 150 in 1939; early in 1965 it passed 900. Of course, as brokers are fond of reminding their customers, you can't buy the averages. But no matter; you *can* buy individual stocks, many of which went up as much as or more than the average. Everyone has heard tales of $500 or $1000 investments in obscure chemical or electronic companies whose stock has multiplied in value by a factor of hundreds and made the lucky investor rich, although it must be admitted that the good fortune usually happened to someone other than the teller. But hear the joyful tale of the staid and safe blue chips. Just in the decade between 1945 and 1955, the value of the common stock of General Motors, General Electric, and Standard Oil of New Jersey approximately quadrupled; that of U.S. Steel, Charles Pfizer, and Radio Corporation of America quintupled; that of du Pont, Corning Glass, and International Business Machines sextupled; that of Container Corporation multiplied in value by a factor of nine, and that of International Paper and Minnesota Mining and Manufacturing by a factor of ten. It remains to be added, on the one hand, that it was possible to lose money on stocks during this period (Air Reduction declined from 55 in 1945 to 35 in 1955, and Acme Aluminum Alloy from 22 in 1945 to 6 in 1955), and on the other, that virtually all of the stocks I have listed are traded today at prices far, far above their 1955 levels.

One thing the postwar stock-market boom has meant is that most families that were rich before the war or even by the end of it are richer now, no matter how prodigal the sons or inept the investment advisers. The John P. Marquand–Tennessee Williams theme of gentility impoverished has, in the last couple of decades, become strikingly inapplicable to American life. We have among us few *nouveaux pauvres,* and those that we have are mostly the widows of improvident and underinsured executives or entrepreneurs rather than the custodians of the remnants of vanished fortunes. Going beyond that, by putting together the sensational rise in stock prices during the postwar era and the fact that there are now twenty million stockholders, one might conclude that the market had provided not only the long-rich but also a large segment of our population with a free ride to greater affluence. The catch, of course, is that the twenty million didn't own their stocks in 1945. As we have seen, the stockholder population was still then comparatively small and the holdings highly concentrated, while as late as 1956, when stock prices were already up to all-time record levels, the stockholder total was less than half what it is now. The rise in stockholder population has not so much accompanied the rise in stock prices as followed it; often enough, the little fellow has been the sucker who came in at the top, while the lion's share of the profits have gone to the few who were lucky enough to hold large blocks of stock in 1945 and to avoid being taxed out of them in the years following, or to the covey of talented and energetic professional stock-traders and corporate wheeler-dealers who sprang up in the postwar years. Even so, the general public *has* benefited from the postwar market rise, however modestly; and Wall Street, realizing that the general public is on the way to becoming its leading customer, has transformed its methods, its mores, and, to a certain extent, its morals.

One of the interesting things that has been happening is a decline in the power of the investment bankers, parallel to, and in large measure resulting from, the rise in the power of the corporations. Traditionally, it was the Morgans, the Kuhn Loebs, the First Boston Corporations and their ilk, with their power to grant or withhold funds for expansion, who were in charge; it was they who put together the nineteenth-century railroads and the mighty Steel Corporation; it was old J. P. Morgan himself who singlehanded averted a national financial panic in 1907; in general, it was the bankers who had called the tune for American industry up to and even for a time after the passage of the Banking Act. Government regulation alone could not humble the power and prestige of the banks; it took the counterweight of the vast new corporate power to do the job.

In the postwar years the top corporations became so rich that they were usually able to finance expansion from their own profits rather than by borrowing, and even when they did go to the money market for new cash, they were so well equipped with fiscal acumen that they could perfectly well have conducted their own bond or stock sales, although few of them did. By the middle 1950s the investment bankers were willing—indeed, all too anxious!—to admit what had happened. The Morgan Stanley man who conducted the $325 million General Motors stock issue in 1955, the largest industrial financing ever undertaken up to that time, was glad to admit he knew perfectly well that General Motors could sell its stock by itself if it wanted to; it was using the services of Morgan Stanley chiefly for reasons of tradition and to achieve the widest possible distribution of shares. The investment bankers, it seemed, had come to exist, or at least to flourish, by the leave of the great corporations.

And Wall Street, seeing the handwriting, began to woo its newly important customer, the general public. In this it was only following belatedly in the footsteps of every manufacturer of soap or home remedies, but in the case of Wall Street, with its tradition of dignity and mystery, the process was particularly anomalous, and frequently entertaining. Dignity was replaced by press-agented antics, mystery by almost indecent self-exposure. Wall Street wiped off its old grim scowl and assumed a rather fatuous smile. Savings banks held do-it-yourself shows in their basements, just like suburbanites, and passed out ballpoint pens or clock radios to anyone who would open an account. The Chase Manhattan Bank became almost manic on the subject of how friendly it was. Your corner broker urged you to drop in and have a chat, no obligation. The firm of Merrill Lynch, by being particularly quick and energetic in going after the small investor, put a large amount of daylight between itself and its nearest rivals in the brokerage trade. Even the formerly most forbidding of investment men began to approach the subject of publicity in newspapers and magazines. First they approached it gingerly, as if it were a hot stove they couldn't help touching; then they came to accept it with frank delight; and finally they were grasping at it like an alcoholic at a tot of whiskey.

Among the most striking responses of the investment community to the new situation was the proliferation of mutual funds, those open-ended investment companies designed chiefly to enable persons with small sums available for investment to get diversified stock holdings under expert management—in exchange for a sizable commission and fee. Mutual funds existed in the 1930s, but just barely; for the year 1936 their sales reached a then record high of $123 million. Sales for the last three months of 1964 alone amounted to slightly under one billion dollars, and the total assets of the mutual funds at that time were above $28 billion. The sales methods used for mutual funds in the late 1950s and early 1960s were comparable to those applicable twenty-five years ago to shampoos or Fuller brushes; many fund salesmen were part-time workers picking up pin money, and the door-to-door approach was commonplace.

The final irony occurred with the appearance, in the early

1960s, of mutual funds specializing in tax-exempt state and municipal bonds. Tax-exempt bonds, of course, appeal particularly to persons in the high income-tax brackets; yet mutual funds, as I have said, are intended for the general public. Wall Street seemed to have concluded that "the general public" was now in the high-tax brackets.

An unhealthy spirit of easy money, of "everybody wins," came to suffuse Wall Street and its wildly growing national clientele. With the blue chip stocks already at such high levels that there was hardly any room for them to go higher, public interest tended to turn to the "cats and dogs," the low-priced speculative issues—and especially to newly formed companies exploiting publicity about the new technological developments in electronics. Overnight fortunes were being made by promoters who did little more than line up two or three likely-looking young men with scientific Ph.D. degrees, think up some futuristic company name like Atomic Dynamics Corporation or Global Orbitronics, Inc., arrange for suitable publicity, and then get a high-powered, and occasionally slightly shady, underwriter to peddle stock. One such promoter went so far as to call attention to how valuable his Ph.D.s were by having them conspicuously accompanied by Pinkerton policemen wherever they went. Eventually, of course, the company often found itself bankrupt—but not before the promoters had unloaded their own stock, leaving the public holding the bag. The SEC tried valiantly to keep on top of this sort of operation, but it simply hadn't enough personnel to do the job.

The comeuppance for all of this nonsense came with the two-day market collapse of May, 1962, the worst crash since the classic one of 1929. The fact that this one never got entirely out of hand, and that an orderly recovery followed it in due time, provided evidence that the national economy remained in good shape, and, perhaps even more, that the regulatory legislation of the 1930s had done its work well. Wall Street emerged soberer and wiser—but not sober enough, or perhaps too wise, to abandon its new friendliness and affability.

Meanwhile, as its approach to the public was undergoing such a dramatic about-face, what was happening to Wall Street's attitudes toward government regulation and toward its own responsibilities? Two examples of its recent conduct will point to the answer.

In 1962 the SEC published a huge study of the stock market in the course of which it recommended various reforms in the technical operation of stock exchanges, especially with reference to the activities of the specialist, a kind of broker-dealer on the floor of an exchange whose personal trades are intended to increase liquidity and prevent sudden violent movements in stock prices. Late in 1963 the SEC followed up its study by issuing a new rule governing specialists; among other things, the rule flatly required specialists under certain circumstances to buy or sell stocks, *risking their own money,* in the interest of stabilizing the market, whether the specialists felt personally inclined to take such risks or not. True, for years the SEC had been *recommending* that specialists do just that, but now it was *ordering* them, on pain of possible suspension from their posts. And what was the reaction of Wall Street to this rule, which an unbiased observer might safely call socialistic, at least in theory? Well, the presidents of the nation's two leading stock exchanges, the New York and the American, promptly commented that the rule "came out of our talking" with representatives of the SEC, and represented "agreement on basic principles." Far from screaming to high heaven about an encroachment on private-property rights, Wall Street now appeared to be bent on claiming part of the credit.

The other incident came about late in 1963 when the sudden failure of a large Stock Exchange firm, Ira Haupt & Company, threatened some twenty thousand persons who had stock-and-bond accounts with Haupt with the loss of part or all of their money. After a dramatic two days of soul-searching—it was the weekend of President Kennedy's assassination—the Wall Street leadership, consisting of the Stock Exchange, its member firms, and several leading banks that happened to be Haupt creditors, got together on a deal whereby, at their own expense to the extent of tens of millions of dollars, they guaranteed the unfortunate Haupt customers their money back. The rule of *caveat emptor* had vanished from Wall Street, perhaps once and for all.

One striking parallel between the Wall Street of the 1930s and the present one stands out—but it is a parallel with an ironic twist. In 1937 SEC Chairman (later Supreme Court Justice) William O. Douglas spoke of the leading stock exchanges as "private clubs."

During 1963 a successor to Douglas in the SEC job, William L. Cary, used the very same language in speaking of the New York Stock Exchange. Yet a few months later, in the Haupt affair, that institution was to show that if it was indeed a club, the membership now seemed to include all those millions of stockholders from coast to coast, making it perhaps the least exclusive club in the world. Truly, what seemed to have happened was something like a reversal of roles. Wall Street had changed more than Washington had noticed; it was the government reformers who were behind the times now.

3

There is a widely held impression that advertising has become more pervasive in American life over the past quarter-century. How well does the impression stand up under examination?

Undeniably, the absolute amount of advertising has vastly increased; total national expenditures for it amounted to just under two billion dollars in 1939, and to over thirteen billion in 1963. This also meant a huge increase in the amount of advertising per capita, since the population had increased by less than half since 1939, and —perhaps more to the point—it meant an even huger increase in the amount of advertising per square mile, since apart from the addition of Alaska and Hawaii as states the nation's area had not increased at all. But advertising, after all, is an economic activity, and perhaps it deserves to be judged primarily in an economic context. As it works out, advertising expenditures amounted to exactly the same percentage of gross national product—2.2 percent—in 1963 as they did in 1939. That is, the advertising industry has grown at no greater and no lesser rate than the economy as a whole. It is interesting to note further that advertising, like so many other businesses, was in a relatively depressed condition in 1939; its gross billings then were nearly a billion and a half below the peak they had reached in 1929, and as early as 1920 advertising expenditures had run to $2.9 billion, or more than 3 percent of the gross national product for that year. Perhaps it should be added that the motorist enraged by ugly and distracting billboards or the television watcher nauseated by deodorant commercials is rather unlikely to gain much comfort from considering their insignificance in relation to the gross national product.

There are various other ways in which the national advertising situation resembles the one that existed just before the war. Consumer spokesmen and intellectuals denounced advertising as frequently and energetically then as they do now. (In fact, they had been doing so for a generation; as early as 1919 S. N. Behrman had written, " 'Publicity' is the reigning philosophy, the magic conjuring word. . . . The advertising man is the *enfant terrible* of the time, unabashed before the eternities.") "By a variety of modern refinements upon the methods of the circus barker," Thurman Arnold said in 1938, "advertising is used to build up public preference for the products of one producer or manufacturer solely because he has the most advertising money and can make the most noise." "The air is full of buncombe and bilge," J. Donald Adams, that gallant die-hard for the gentlemanly ideal, wrote in 1965.

The federal government was then, as it is now, engaged in a seemingly permanent tug of war with business and its advertising agents as to the extent to which advertising should be supervised to ensure truth. In 1939 the Federal Trade Commission was enthusiastically wielding the new, increased powers it had just been given under the Wheeler-Lea Act and the Federal Food, Drug, and Cosmetic Act, and advertisers were duly complaining about the resulting hardships. The most entertaining, if perhaps not the most significant, recent manifestation of this continuing battle was the sandpaper controversy: If a razor-blade manufacturer in a television ad shows his product efficiently shaving a piece of sandpaper, should it be required that the blade *really* be capable of shaving sandpaper—that is, that the test be on the level—or should it be assumed that the consumer knows the test is metaphorical and lighthearted, thus rendering a little trickery harmless? This intricate ethical question went before the Supreme Court late in 1964. (It decided that you can't shave fake sandpaper in a TV ad—only real sandpaper.)

Finally, even the leading advertising medium remained the same over the period in question; in 1939 newspapers got forty cents of the national advertising dollar, and although they were down to twenty-nine cents in 1963, they were still more than thirteen cents ahead of the nearest competing medium.

But, of course, there *have* been important changes in advertising, and the mention of advertising media leads us straight to them.

As one looks back now at the advertising of the late 1930s, the keynote seems to be simple-mindedness. "The advertisers whose ascendancy began in the depression were the manufacturers of patent foods and medicines, vitamin pills and nerve tonics," E. S. Turner writes. Nerve tonics, indeed! Does it not seem probable that a modern copywriter who used such an expression in an advertisement would be hooted off Madison Avenue? In style, prewar advertising was just coming out of the old "They Laughed When I Sat Down at the Piano" school; Pond's was still assuming that all young girls yearned to look like debutantes if not to be debutantes, Listerine's manufacturer was still warning that failure to use his product might result in one's being "Always a Bridesmaid, Never a Bride" and the hottest thing in radio advertising was the new jingle "Pepsi-Cola hits the spot," which in 1941 was played 296,426 times over 469 stations. (It was even on jukeboxes, and people paid the nickel they might have spent on Pepsi just to hear it.) The first of all program-rating services, Hooper, was in its infancy, having been founded in the mid-thirties. The testing of ads was attempted in what now look like primitive ways; one method considered avant-garde consisted of strapping a presumably typical subject into a lie detector or similar machine and seeing what happened when he was exposed to the advertisement under test.

In sum, the ads of 1939 may sometimes have been lies—and far more often than those of today, they most certainly were lies—but at least they were straightforward ones; they were nothing more nor less than they seemed to be. As surely as they were less truthful than current ads, they were also less subtle. The qualitative change in advertising in the postwar period is related to the popularization of depth psychology and the development of commercial television. Radio advertising in the early, pretelevision, postwar years was marked, as I remember it, by a kind of sophisticated revolt. Frederic

Wakeman's very popular novel, *The Hucksters,* had awakened the public to the existence of the advertising business—"Madison Avenue"—and had alerted it to the cynicism of some advertising methods. The result was a Henry Morgan. Mild kidding of commercials by popular entertainers on radio had been going on occasionally for years, but Morgan lighted into the commercials *he* was paid to deliver with the venom of a dedicated hater. "Push-pull, click-click," was the slogan of a razor-blade dispenser that he was assigned to advertise. "Push-pull, click-click, tinkle-tinkle—that's the razor blade falling on the floor; the thing doesn't work," said Morgan. A shock of uneasy laughter at such blasphemy ran around the country. The predictable end came swiftly: industry saw it had a cuckoo in the nest, and Morgan ceased to deliver commercials; but advertising had had its grandest remonstrance up to then—or, probably, since. The fact that Morgan has turned into a tame quiz-show panelist is worth noting, with sadness.

Then, of course, came television. As an advertising medium it was like nothing ad men had previously more than dreamed of. Not only did it combine the virtues of newspapers or magazines with those of radio; it went beyond both by allowing for motion as well as sight and sound. Not only did it allow the pitchman, in effect, to come right into millions of living rooms; it allowed him (or her) to bring there the most intricate and persuasive of props—refrigerators, X-rayed stomachs, breath tests, automobiles. If charm had been proved effective in selling some products, television could be charming; if deliberate irritation had been proved effective in selling others, it could be infinitely more irritating than anything else in creation. Advertisers were not slow in catching on. Expenditures for television advertising went from a pittance in 1947 to $57.8 million in 1949, $170.8 million in 1950, $332.3 million in 1951, and $809.2 million in 1954; in 1955 they passed the billion-dollar mark, and in 1963 the two-billion-dollar mark. As to the new medium's effectiveness, there is no reason not to believe that television advertising deserves its full share of credit for the boom in consumer expenditures that accompanied its rise.

Coincidentally, a Republican administration took over the national government just as television was getting a good foothold, and in the fat years of economic expansion and business-oriented government that followed, criticism of advertising was muted. The government was generally disinclined to interfere, and the public was too busy enjoying the fruits of rising pay and upward social mobility. Riding the crest of this wave, advertising went daring, not to say wild. Motivational research became the Madison Avenue fashion; copywriters earnestly sought to have a favorable effect on their audiences' egos and libidos, and researchers on the trail of helpful clues counted the eye-blink rates of women in supermarkets. In 1957 and 1958 there was a brief flurry of excitement over a frightening-sounding technique called subliminal advertising, which consisted of showing brief slogans on a screen so fast that they were not consciously perceived but presumably lodged themselves in the subconscious; the flurry passed, partly because the government threatened to ban subliminal advertising and partly because tests seemed to indicate that it didn't work. But motivational research went on, undeterred even by the disaster of the Edsel, the car that was promoted according to plans based on its supposed sexual symbolism, and that it turned out to be the greatest commercial flop in history.

While so many television commercials took ample advantage of the medium's possibilities to etch their message in the viewer's mind by making him wince, shudder, or gag, a few were not only benign but entertaining. One remembers particularly the Piel brothers, the cartooned, imaginary manufacturers of Piel's beer, and their imaginatively conceived dialogues about their business problems, which did not rib the product or even the industry after the Henry Morgan pattern but which did something perhaps better—that is, succeeded in being diverting through wit and character. But after a time, Madison Avenue in its inscrutable wisdom decreed that the Piel brothers should vanish.

It should be noted that along with the expansion of advertising went even more rapid growth of the related business of public relations, which has been defined—loosely, and over the violent protests of the public-relations men—as getting free advertising. The American public-relations man at his lowest level goes back to the circus advance man and the barroom song plugger, while at his highest level he goes back to Ivy Lee, who whitened the name of old John D. Rockefeller; the powerful and ultimately pathetic public-relations man J. Ward Morehouse was one of the major figures of *U.S.A.*, John Dos Passos' famous novel about the time of the First World War and its aftermath. Yet despite all this, statistics show clearly enough that by subsequent standards public relations was still in its infancy in the late 1930s. Only a handful of corporations had their own public-relations departments then, while now every self-respecting corporation has a large and elaborate one. The publisher of *Public Relations News* says that there were about one hundred independent public-relations firms in the country in 1944, as against fifteen hundred in 1964. The most characteristic public-relations gesture, the "press junket" by plane, boat, helicopter, or bobsled to some pleasant place in rather disreputable exchange for newspaper or magazine space for the client's product, became a commonplace of the late 1950s. When the business adventurer Robert R. Young set out to seize control of the New York Central Railroad in 1954, the man he chose as his "chief of staff" was a public-relations man. Nowadays hardly anybody in public life, from a President of the United States to a young model trying to break into television, dreams of operating without a public-relations man or a battery of them.

The Sixties and the New Frontier brought with them something of a return to a critical national view of advertising and its adjuncts. In the course of Senator Philip A. Hart's truth-in-packaging hearings, which began in 1961 and continued for several years thereafter, witnesses cited deceptive packaging practices in baby foods, cereals, cooking oils, canned goods, detergents, frozen foods, bread, toothpaste, and many other products. But the trouble was that the American consumer didn't seem to care very much. He or she—except for the poor, who didn't buy much fancy packaged goods anyhow—had such a good income, or was so bemused by advertising of the products in question, or both, that being cheated a few cents on each household purchase could not seem important enough to make a fuss about. At the same time, the economy as a whole was growing, making it possible for advertising and packaging spokesmen to argue that any criticism amounted to a destructive rocking of the national boat; as the editor of *Printer's Ink* put the argument in 1964, "tampering . . . with the high economic momentum" might result in bringing it to "a grinding halt." So "tampering" stayed at a minimum, and the advertising business went on expanding—particularly in Europe, where the newly affluent Common Market countries were beginning to see the benefits of American advertising methods, with the result that by 1965 some leading Madison Avenue agencies had as much as half their total billings overseas.

It is significant of the national mood that in the field of drug prices—a field where high prices *do* matter vitally to consumers, especially to aged ones with small retirement incomes—Senator Estes Kefauver's long campaign for government-control legislation was stymied by a number of factors, public apathy among them, until an entirely irrelevant event, the scandal over the effects of the drug thalidomide, finally jolted Congress into action.

And meanwhile how were the men of Madison Avenue themselves thinking about their responsibilities to society?

In the innocent prewar days the principal moral issue within the advertising business was the simple one of truth. To be sure, in those days many men made their initial leap into the advertising business feeling that they were doing nothing less than trading in their souls and their talents for material comfort; the story of the young newspapermen or artist who "sells out" to advertising or to the movies had been a staple of American folklore for a generation, assuming finally the status of a sort of debased version of the Faust legend. Once he had taken the unholy orders of Madison Avenue, though, the latter-day Faust's professional moral life was vastly simplified. Already inducted into depravity, he need not ask himself whether an advertisement was tasteful or of literary and artistic excellence—only whether it was true enough to suit the Federal Trade Commission.

In the postwar world the light on the moral landscape has changed, and even the terrain itself has shifted. On the one hand, the area of perdition, as descried by novelists and academics, widened vastly; it now included not only advertising and motion pictures but also the vast and vastly expanding fields of television, public relations, and the big-circulation magazines—that is to say, the whole complex of activities that came to be called "mass communications." Nor did young men entering this complex now do so reluctantly, under the terms of a forced bargain with the Devil; on the contrary, as Louis Kronenberger has written, they did so as "exultant volunteers." On the other hand, now that Hell, like the big corporations, was so commodious, it, like them, began to develop a complicated moral system of its own. One could, it seemed, be a good or bad fallen angel.

In advertising, the new polarity was between advocates of the Hard Sell and those of the Soft Sell. The Hard Sell man defined advertising as "salesmanship"; the Soft Sell man defined it as "communication." The Hard Sell man believed in repetition, irritation, calculated bad taste, skirting the brink of deception itself—all in the name of more effective selling; the Soft Sell man believed in restraint, good taste, literary competence, and emphasis on the good name of the manufacturer rather than the real or imaginary "unique" qualities of the product. The Hard Sell man was truculent about what he called the "profession" of advertising, resenting all attempts of outsiders to tell him how to run his affairs as impudence. The Soft Sell man adopted almost a *mea culpa* attitude to his calling (or, at least, to members of it other than himself); a leading Soft Sell man wrote in the early 1960s that advertising had "no tradition of excellence" and "no standard of conduct," and that, as a result, it was "at its lowest ebb of respect." All this he proposed to change by such methods as urging copywriters to tone up their prose by reading Yeats, Houseman, and Emily Dickinson in their spare time. If he found an anomaly in the suggestion that writing to the order of a commercial client can be compared to writing in response to an inner urge, he did not say so.

Even with its wistful pretentions and its tendency to a certain mealy-mouthed quality, the Soft Sell, from a public point of view, is certainly preferable to the Hard Sell; if we are to have advertising at all—and we most certainly are—we must be grateful for people who try to produce advertising with taste and restraint. Which philosophy was winning in the mid-Sixties? Alas, despite a surge of Soft Sell blandness around the turn of the decade, there was evidence that Hard Sell intransigence was still in control.

Take the case of the leading industry that devotes the highest percentage of its receipts to advertising, the tobacco industry. After certain medical reports issued in 1953 and 1954 had raised the strong probability that excessive cigarette smoking was a contributing factor in the causation of lung cancer and heart disease, tobacco advertisers engaged for a number of years in a noisy, unseemly, and frequently irresponsible competition to try to prove that their respective brands contained the least tar and therefore were least likely to induce disease—until the whole thing was called off in 1960 as the result of closed-door negotiations between tobacco men and the FTC. And it was not until after the Surgeon General's Committee report of January, 1964, had shown the smoking-cancer link even more persuasively that the tobacco industry and its advertising agents finally adopted a comparatively mild code of ethics establishing standards as to appeals to the very young, and restricting representations with respect to health.

That fall, when Emerson Foote, chairman of one of the largest advertising agencies and a man who had devoted most of his life to selling cigarettes, abruptly resigned in what appeared to be a crisis of conscience, did other advertising men rally to his standard? They did not. Instead, the leading voices of Madison Avenue either questioned Foote's sincerity or assigned ulterior motives to him; agencies without cigarette accounts, like the Pharisee, comfortably thanked God that they were not as other men, while agencies with cigarette accounts went on advertising cigarettes—and energetically fighting further regulation.

Or, to take another example, consider the attitude of an official advertising spokesman to Mrs. Esther Peterson, President Johnson's Special Assistant for Consumer Affairs, when in 1964 she toured the country holding a series of meetings at which consumers were invited to air their complaints. The mere implication that consumers *had* any complaints seemed to be cause for astonishment and outrage. "The very fact that she is holding these meetings is a definite and damaging inference that something is seriously wrong with the way the consumer is being treated by American business and advertising," cried Mark F. Cooper, president of the Advertising Federation of America. Did the consumer need the protection of Mrs. Peterson, or anybody else? "This may have been necessary fifty years ago, but not today," Cooper assured the country. A leading advertising man, Frederic Papert, said later that he disagreed with Cooper on the subject —"although I guess I'm the only one in my business that does."

On balance, Madison Avenue does seem to be moving toward public responsibility, but slowly. It is now, perhaps, at the stage of last-ditch truculence, and of imminent and drastic change, where Wall Street was in 1939. And perhaps it needs few apologies for being relatively laggard. For one thing, it is younger—after all, it got its start in life half a century later than Wall Street; and for another, advertising is so close to the heart of our culture, seems at times to come so perilously close to *being* our culture, that asking advertising men to feel out of step or behind the times is asking quite a lot.

IV. THE LAND'S CHANGING FACE

1

Twice in my life I have devoted the summer months to an automobile trip around the country, and the years, as it happened, were 1940 and 1964. From the earlier trip I retain a small parcel of memories: the glow of blast furnaces in the sky over Pittsburgh; the wind rippling the lake at the feet of Chicago; perfectly straight two-lane roads leading through farmlands to the horizon and beyond, with an occasional grain elevator standing against the sky; Denver against the mountains; the endless intermountain desert, in which one could travel for hours without seeing another human being; and at last the thrilling hills, fogs, and cold air of San Francisco. The cities, as I look back on them, seem a little old and shabby and tired—certainly new buildings were scarce in them; and in general, to an Easterner making his first comprehensive tour, the people of the country seemed comparatively few and humble in relation to the overpowering natural wonders around them. I recall a constant awareness of time passing, with infinite slowness, in hotel rooms. Perhaps the two words that best contain my remembered impressions are beauty and loneliness.

After years of reading in the newspapers about urban sprawl and overcrowding and despoliation, I set out in 1964, a quarter-century later, expecting to find everything changed, mostly for the worse. I did find many things changed for the worse; but I also found many things changed for what seemed to be neither better nor worse, and I found surprisingly many things a good deal the same.

From dull gray, the cities had changed to black and white; now one continually saw sparkling new glassy buildings standing almost directly beside the most appalling slums, and what would formerly have been considered routine old apartment houses suddenly looking architecturally distinguished by comparison with the new rectilinear rent-collecting machines. The much-advertised sprawl around the cities was there in force, usually trailing off into uninteresting suburban developments and clusters of the oversized trailers called mobile homes. (In 1963, I read later, the more than 150,000 mobile homes sold amounted to about 10 percent of new housing starts of all kinds; in 1964 there were 16,000 mobile-home parks in the nation and more than a thousand new ones were being built each year.) And from the point of view of one seeking sights of beauty or interest, the road facilities seemed to be arranged exactly wrong. East of the Mississippi, open or sparsely settled country is now most conveniently traversed at sixty or seventy miles per hour on mammoth six-lane highways from which the driver sees hardly more scenery than he would from an airplane, and far more billboards (our national expenditure on outdoor advertising has increased 3.5 times since 1940). Formerly a motorist traveling across the eastern half of the nation *had* to look at scenery; now he may do so only by taking a deliberately perverse and circuitous route. Contrariwise, it is in the ugly and blighted urban areas that the turnpikes fade out or narrow into bottlenecks; one limps and struggles through traffic jams, and is thus afforded more than ample opportunity to look at the sorry sights of urban blight and decay.

Other changes seemed merely entertaining; it was diverting to discover, for example, that a bowling alley is now apt to house the main restaurant in small towns in Colorado and Idaho, and that what was once the most celebrated bordello in Cripple Creek, and had not been out of business so very long in 1940, is now a tourist sight with admission charged and a guide provided.

But other things, and important ones, had changed far less than I had anticipated. The billboards and the urban sprawl are as ugly as they are said to be, but Crater Lake and the Garden of the Gods are as beautiful and just about as pristine as they ever were. The commercialization of tourism is as deadly as it has been described—even the trinkets in the shops at many famous places don't bother to be indigenous to the particular region; they are just bland, generalized "souvenirs" equally applicable to the Great Smokies or Death Valley. Yet the Santo Domingo pueblo Indians of New Mexico have so far resisted commercial lures so heroically that, far from charging admission to their rain dances, they simply ignore the presence of tourists or accept them with an amused tolerance. (In my case, their amusement was increased by the fact that my car got temporarily stuck in the mud caused by the rain they had all too successfully called down from the heavens.)

Above all, I think it is too often forgotten by those who stay at home in and near the cities, or who do their traveling abroad, that there are still plenty of open spaces. True, one may have to wait in a line of cars just to get through the entrance to Yellowstone National Park, and will probably encounter a serious traffic jam around Old Faithful; but one may also find less celebrated but not less beautiful, and hardly less accessible, corners of the same park where hardly a soul is to be seen for hours on end. True, the urban areas are overcrowded; but one can be as alone as one wishes in the Maine woods, or the Arizona desert, or almost any of the wilderness areas of the national forests. It's a big country, and we haven't overrun it—not yet.

Perhaps the greatest contrast of all between my two trips was in the number and style of my fellow travelers. For one thing, they seemed to be vastly more numerous the second time around, and no wonder; Department of the Interior figures show that the National Park system had well over 100 million visitors in 1964, as against some sixteen million in 1940. The much-discussed leisure-time explosion had taken place in the interim, and no traveler could fail to be aware of the fact. It is an interesting sidelight that a number of the tourists I encountered in 1964 were Europeans; I don't remember seeing a single identifiable European in 1940. But most of all they were Americans traveling *en famille,* frequently in three-generation depth, piled into a station wagon with a trailer behind or a car-top camper fitted onto a pickup truck. These huge and necessarily slow-moving, family-camping contraptions are a menace to the driver of an ordinary passenger car, as anyone knows who has been repeatedly caught behind them in mountainous country; but they are also the hallmark of a new way of life. In 1940 living in a trailer usually meant poverty and desperation; now it means a kind of liberation—except, of course, from family responsibilities and tensions, which come along even on vacations.

For those who roam the country sleeping indoors, as I did both times, the way of life has changed, too. I remember in 1940 a seemingly endless succession of so-so hotels—I was traveling then with a college professor whose taste ran to the shabby-genteel. We would reach the hotels by threading our way through the streets of an unfamiliar city; we would get our baggage to our rooms by a clumsy process involving a mandatory tip to a bellboy; there would often be a problem about where to put the car; and, finally, we were often kept awake at night by street traffic.

Most of that has been changed, long since, by the invention of that marvelous device, the motel, which in the course of its rise has practically killed the hotel. In 1940 the nation had about fourteen thousand year-round hotels with twenty-five or more guest rooms, while by the end of the 1950s, despite a huge rise in the population, the number was down to just above ten thousand. As to motels and tourist courts, there were about 13,500 of them in 1939 and more than 41,000 in 1958; moreover, over the same period the typical motel had been transformed from a shabby row of unheated little boxes, sometimes with peeling paint and often without indoor plumbing, charging $2 or $3 a night, to the luxurious—and expensive—place it is today. (Motel receipts nationally were $36.7 million in 1939 and $850 million in 1958.) In many parts of the country air-conditioning, television in every room, and a swimming pool are practically standard motel equipment, and it is not infrequently that one encounters such friils as a sunlamp in the bathroom or a special machine that, on command, makes your bed jiggle to relax your muscles. Gone (or nearly gone) is the problem of putting away the car; gone are the inconvenience, expense, and perhaps embarrassment of dealing with a bellboy about the luggage; gone is the traffic noise, drowned by the soothing whir of the air-conditioner; and, of course, gone is the charm of the town hotel or country inn. With its functional comforts, its admirable adaptation to its purpose, and its almost belligerent lack of grace, the motel, I think, has to be counted one of our most characteristic new institutions.

2

What have we done to our land? Basically, I think, to the extent that we have despoiled it we have done so by trusting too much to laissez-faire economics, which had their beginnings in Europe and were never intended to be applied without restraint to a mass society spread across a vast continent. Not that we have not been conscious of the problem of conservation since Theodore Roosevelt's time, and not that we were unconscious of it at the end of the 1930s. Indeed, the New Deal with its Civilian Conservation Corps and its many reclamation projects was in one sense a high point in the annals of conservation. Boulder Dam was finished in 1936, Shasta begun in 1938; in 1939 four major dams were completed and twelve others, including Grand Coulee, were under construction. Other determined government efforts were being directed toward the conservation of mineral resources, petroleum, and natural gas; so great was the interest in conservation that in 1938 there had been an unsuccessful legislative attempt to change the Department of the Interior into a Department of Conservation.

But there is an important distinction to be made here: conservation in the 1930s was very largely an economic rather than an aesthetic matter. It was directed toward dams that would bring people electric power, agricultural programs that would prevent the impoverishment of farmers through dust storms, mineral- and timber-saving programs that would keep us from depleting our national resources—

but seldom toward keeping the landscape beautiful or providing better facilities for recreation. (It is interesting to note that the building of dams and power plants in naturally unspoiled places is thought of now as the exact opposite of conservation. A plan of the Army Corps of Engineers to build two power-producing dams on the Upper Missouri River was denounced by the *New York Times* in March, 1965, as "an act of vandalism" and "a desecration"; the following month, a speaker at a Wilderness Conference in San Francisco happily predicted the eventual *tearing down* of all our hydroelectric dams except perhaps for Hoover, which would be preserved as an historic monument. In a quarter-century the meaning of conservation to most people has been precisely reversed.) National parks were then being looked on quizzically. In California the view was growing that the creation of more parks there would conflict with the state's economic welfare. A resolution was actually introduced in Congress in June, 1939, proposing the abolition of Grand Teton National Park. At the end of the longest and by far the most disastrous depression in our history, we clearly did not feel that we could afford the luxury of worrying about beauty.

And, in any case, at the end of the Thirties the great forces that work toward the destruction of beauty—industrialization and urbanization—were temporarily pretty much at bay. Our farm population had remained nearly constant for many years, and, indeed, it was slightly higher at the end of the 1930s than it had been at the end of the 1920s (although nothing like so much higher as the urban population was). As industrial jobs became more and more scarce during the depression and labor-management strife more and more destructive, a back-to-the-land movement of significant proportions—surely the last such movement in the nation's history—developed. "The estimate in 1935 that there were almost two million Americans in the countryside who had not been there five years earlier may have exaggerated the extent to which that represented an actual return to rural living," Oscar Handlin has written, "but the trend was nevertheless significant. Largely these were fugitives from the depression, people who had sought their fortunes in the cities and failed, and who now returned to family homesteads; for although these were already 'fished-out ponds,' the security they offered, poor as it was, was preferable to the unlimited risks of life in the towns." A practical guide to how to conduct a small farm, *Five Acres and Independence*, originally published in 1935, had run through five editions by 1940, and by the end of the war it had sold half a million copies. Malcolm Cowley in *Exile's Return* tells about how hundreds of writers in the Thirties left the cities and settled in old farmhouses without central heat or plumbing—not out of any desire to be close to the land, but simply out of a desire to avoid the necessity of doing hack work in order to pay city bills.

Others, though, were returning to the land primarily for spiritual and ideological rather than practical reasons; disillusioned with the contemporary scene, they were making nostalgic excursions into the simpler, sweeter American past. Such a one was Charles Allen Smart, Harvard '26, who left a city job to take over a small farm that he had inherited in southern Ohio, and who described his experiences in a popular and charming book entitled *R.F.D.*, published in 1938. Smart and his wife brought quite a good many of their city attitudes and artifacts to the farm with them—they put reproductions of Toulouse-Lautrec, Laurencin, and Chirico in their WPA-built privy—but he was genuinely and quite movingly rhapsodic about the farm life:

> The harvesting of wheat . . . is like sowing seed, or the births of the animals, or the making of wine. Flesh and blood, bread and wine, seeds and death . . . no thank you, gentlemen, you can keep your offices and trains, your files and accounts, your wing collars and umbrellas. . . . Farming is immeasurably more sympathetic to thought than is business, for example, and it is more stimulating and vitalizing to it than is teaching in a school.

How little the Americans of 1939 saw the shape of the urban problems ahead is dramatically shown by the World's Fair Futurama. Here was a frank attempt to envision perfection in the human use of land and its resources. Among the chief elements that made up the vision were bigger and more efficient highways designed to convey more automobiles into cities faster (with little said about parking facilities); disruption of existing urban areas by the intrusion of these highways; and the rigid compartmentalization of cities into residential, commercial, and industrial areas. Even allowing for the fact that the Futurama was presented on behalf of an automobile manufacturer, it appears now as a remarkable essay in reversed values. As I have noted before, many of its prophecies of Heaven have become facts; the only trouble is that now that they are here they look more like the lineaments of Hell.

3

What the nation considered its "conservation" problem in 1939—the problem of making the most of natural resources, and thus raising standards of living—has been triumphantly solved; now it is exclusively the problem of those remote places that we call underdeveloped (or, more delicately, "less developed") countries. It is significant to note that David Lilienthal, who became famous in the Thirties as one of the heads of the pioneer resource-development project, the TVA, now heads a firm that specializes in similar projects for foreign countries. And one effect of the solution was to help cause a shift in the center of gravity of national life from the farm to the city and its suburbs, with an accompanying change, almost amounting to a reversal, in the national style of living.

Many things contributed to the shift. On the one hand, the growth of industry, accompanied as it was by the rising power of labor unions, made for millions of appetizing high-pay jobs in urban areas, where industry was concentrated. On the other hand, the products of industry—new machines, fertilizers, and pesticides that have become the marvels of the agricultural world—tended to reduce the amount of human labor necessary to farming and thus do the farm hand out of his job, and also to convert successful farming from a small, individualistic enterprise into a vast, impersonal business. What could the small farmer do? Despite government subsidies, he had to sell out to a big combine, go to the city, and take an industrial job.

Specifically: we now produce 60 percent more food than we did in 1940 from about the same number of acres of farmland. In 1940 we had a little more than six million farms of which 2.2 million consisted of less than fifty acres, and 100,000 of a thousand acres or more; in 1959 the national total of farms was down to 3.7 million, of which just over one million consisted of less than fifty acres and 136,000 of more than a thousand acres; and the Department of Agriculture says that a corn farmer now *must* have at least a thousand acres or his costs will make it impossible for him to meet competitive prices. Meanwhile—and here is the key figure from a social standpoint—the number of man-hours of labor required to do the country's farm work decreased from more than twenty million in 1940 to under nine million in 1963.

The annual decline in the farm population has been almost, but not quite, in a straight line. In 1939 we had about 31 million farmers, or not quite a quarter of the whole population; in 1963 we had 13.7 million, or 7.1 percent. After falling off sharply during the war, the total turned upward slightly in the first postwar years, 1946 and 1947, proving that a few ex-GIs could be returned to the farm at least temporarily. There has been a net loss in every year since then except for 1955, and in some years during the 1950s the net loss amounted to almost a million farmers. Between 1950 and 1962, one out of every five farmers became a former farmer.

It is true enough that the process of urbanization in American life had been going on for decades, even generations—hadn't William Jennings Bryan himself, in his famous "Cross of Gold" speech, warned the country, "Destroy our farms, and the grass will grow in the streets of every city in the country"?—but only in the years after the Second World War has the flight from the farm become a rout. And something, unquestionably, has been lost in the process—something very old and very American, not just peasant shrewdness but a straightforwardness, steadfastness, and simplicity of heart that usually more than counterbalanced the lack of intellect or formal education that went with it—something that was never better expressed than by Ridgely Torrence in his poem "The Son":

I heard an old farm-wife,
Selling some barley,
Mingle her life with life
And the name "Charley."

Saying: "The crop's all in,
We're about through now;
Long nights will soon begin,
We're just us two now.

"Twelve bushel at sixty cents,
It's all I carried—
He sickened making fence;
He was to be married—

"It feels like frost was near—
His hair was curly.
The spring was late that year,
But the harvest early."

The seventeen million farmers who have left the land in the past quarter-century are urbanites now, and must be considered in an urban context; but for those who have stayed, life has changed, too. The nature of the change is nicely documented in two books on a more or less typical farming community in the Ozark foothills of Missouri—*Plainville, U.S.A.*, by James West, describing the community as it was in 1939, and *Plainville Fifteen Years Later,* by Art Gallaher, Jr., describing it in 1954.

West in 1939 found Plainville a small, relatively isolated community where farming methods were technologically backward, and where farming was not just a living but a way of life. Although there was a rising discontent, based apparently on exposure to national mass communications media, with the traditional local social structure, nevertheless that structure remained firmly in place. Essentially, it consisted of a two-class system based not so much on wealth as on such other matters as whether one lived in the hills (that was lower-class) or on the prairie (upper-class). And nonmonetary values extended, West found, into the conduct of work; harvesting, threshing, butchering, and sawing wood were often group or even community activities, and a farmer would "lend a boy" to his neighbor for a day or two when the neighbor needed extra help, expecting nothing in return other than similar consideration when *he* had a problem. Plainville had some of the aspects of a kind of primitive socialism—never, needless to say, called by that name. "The roots of her tradition," West wrote, "are still in the frontier."

Three crucial things had happened to Plainville by the time Gallaher studied it in 1954. A highway going through it had been completed in 1940; television had come to it, as it had to almost every other place in the nation, soon after 1950; and the technical revolution in farming methods had been progressively affecting it over the whole period. As a result of these things, Gallaher wrote, "Plainvillers are increasingly drawn into the mainstream of modern urban America"; in particular, they had become less cooperative, more individualistic, more technology-minded, and, above all, far more devoted to the almighty dollar: "The major desire of Plainvillers is [now] more money." The population of the town had dropped 12 percent between the census of 1940 and that of 1950. The number of farms in the county had dropped 37 percent in the years between the end of the war and 1954, and the size of the average farm had increased from 151 acres to 217 acres. Meanwhile, Plainvillers had become far richer—the average gross annual sales of the local merchants went from $5,300 in 1939 to $27,600 in 1949—and this, combined with their increasing exposure to national ideas as to styles and standards of living, had changed their aspirations; living conditions that had been thought satisfactory in 1939 were now thought substandard as the new ranch house with its jalousie windows and its antenna replaced the old homestead with its backyard outhouse. Largely gone was the two-class system based on traditional ideas, replaced by a new hierarchy based frankly on affluence; gone was the habit of offering and expecting mutual help on work.

And along with all this went a basic reversal in attitude: the old nostalgia for the past and indifference to technology had been replaced by a sense of superiority to the past and an almost religious devotion to technological change as the potential solution to all problems. Plainville, Gallaher found, now looked instinctively for authority not to its own past but to the rest of the country—above all, to the rich cities with their skyscrapers and washing machines and shiny new automobiles. Not only had the method of the farm been industrialized; in the process, it seemed, the mind of the farmer had been industrialized and urbanized too, and in that sense even those who stayed on the farms did not remain farmers at heart.

4

And what of those exploding cities? To begin with, changing facts and necessities were shaping new attitudes to them, all but destroying the deep-rooted and long-cherished American belief that they are inherently wicked, or at least vastly inferior to the countryside as places of human habitation. Like so much of our traditional thought, this belief has roots in the Old Testament; it was nourished in the nineteenth century by the agrarian idealism of Jefferson, and, needless to say, exploited by many politicians before Bryan. What tended to break it down now, as both farm jobs and the farm way of life disappeared, was the sheer need to make a virtue of necessity, combined with the fact that the former farmer found, sometimes to his surprise, that urban life with its gadgets and two-car garages and late rising hours was downright easier than farm life.

City-bred sociologists and professors might go on idealizing the rural life; the farm boy was apt to be the last to do so. A famous anthropologist, talking at a conference a few years ago with Barry Leithead, a former farm boy who had grown up to become the president of a great clothing manufacturing company in New York City, pointed out in behalf of the rural life that the blood pressure of a certain group of South Africans had gone up significantly after they had moved from the bush to a big city. "I can only tell you that mine went down," retorted Mr. Leithead. "I didn't like milking cows at 4 A.M."

But dissatisfaction with city life remained—indeed, as the cities grew, it increased. A recent survey of a group of Harvard graduates showed satisfaction with their living environment to be in inverse proportion to the size of their communities; those in large cities pronounced themselves least content, and those in places with populations under 3,500 most content—a result that may have some significance in spite of the probability that few Harvard men even in the smallest communities milk cows at 4 A.M. In plain truth, there were plenty of reasons for urbanites to be discontented.

One of the troubles seemed to stem from the fact that the cities, being unable to expand much further vertically, tended to expand horizontally into acres and acres of sprawling suburbs. The amount of such expansion, familiar as it must be to everyone from both reading and personal observation, is almost beyond belief when shown statistically. Of the thirteen million dwelling units erected in nonfarm areas during the period of 1946 through 1958, about eleven million, or 85 percent, were outside central cities—which, to all intents and purposes, means in suburbs. Between 1952 and 1962 a million and a half people left New York City alone for the suburbs. From the farms and the cities, people were converging on communities that scarcely existed yet—that, in fact, were springing into existence day by day and almost hour by hour, appearing in the nick of time to catch the new arrivals, like the beams that, in old movie cartoons, used to swing into the path of a man walking on girders just as he seemed about to step out into space.

And if the quality of life in the new communities comprised of those eleven million new dwellings—whose inhabitants, conservatively allowing a family of four to each, make up almost a quarter of our whole population—is often as alarming as its quantity, the blame, in the opinion of most students of the subject, is mainly assignable to lack of planning, or the leaving of "planning" to the Invisible Hand of the free market. Suburbs made up of row upon row of identical or nearly identical houses, each on its minuscule plot of what was formerly farmland or countryside, are, of course, the most profitable kind of suburbs for the real-estate developer. And, no doubt of it, the postwar era has been a golden age for such a man. The whole economic machinery of the country, and often local and national laws as well, have worked in his favor. "Because of government mortgage insurance, bankers and investors run practically no risk [on suburban development]," writes the architectural critic Wolf von Eckardt.

> The builders and promoters themselves invest little more than their judgment on where and what to put up. The "where" is easy—on the cheapest possible land near the most crowded metropolitan concentrations. . . . The county governments are happy to welcome them and present them with the essential sewers and local roads. Most county councils are dominated by people whose main cash crop is land. . . . The "what" is answered with clever packaging and public relations. Wrap a shoddily built house in a fashionable façade, stuff it with gadgets, put a gaslight or something in front for that extra bit of nostalgia, give it a romantic name and you'll have the suckers beating a path to the sales office.

As an index to the financially gratifying result, between 1950 and 1960, while the consumer price index on all goods and services was rising about 10 percent, suburban land values went up by anywhere from 100 to 3,760 percent.

This is no place for a detailed rehash of the subject of the characteristic style of life in the new suburbs—which has certainly become in recent years, whether we like it or not, the characteristic style of life in America. That has been amply and excellently chronicled many times. But it is the place for a brief summary of those chronicles. Consisting essentially of similarly priced houses appealing to families situated similarly in life, the description goes, the new suburbs tend to be homogeneous to the point of extreme provinciality. Children may grow up in them believing that everybody—everybody "real," that is, as opposed to the shadow-people seen on television—is more or less alike; and even television often does its damnedest to give back suburbia an image of itself. Hastily erected schools force local taxes sky-high, and are nevertheless so overcrowded that children have to attend them in two-a-day shifts; thus elementary education, which ought to be a leisurely and thoughtful awakening process, becomes a kind of crisis program, with certain similarities to the production of bombers in wartime.

As for the parents, their dominating emotions are too often frustration and, above all, disappointment. They have moved to Prettyville with stars in their eyes, idealizing the notion of neighborly relations in a small community as surcease from the drudgery of farm life or the competitive tension of city life. Too often they find drudgery and competitive tension have followed them, and that small-town neighborliness, as practiced here, means chiefly a galling lack of privacy. The father being a commuter—perhaps, in effect, a mere nightly and weekend visitor—the mother must play the role of both parents most of the time, spending her days visiting the supermarket or ferrying the children to and from school, the playground, the homes of friends, the doctor. Imprisoned in the second car, she wonders when she will find the time to enjoy community life or, for that matter, to recover from the boredom of having too much of the wrong kind of thing to do. The father, meanwhile, may find even his evenings and weekends pre-empted by work on the perpetually unfinished house, which requires him to serve as an unwilling, inexperienced, and ill-equipped carpenter, painter, gardener, and plumber. As Walter C. McKain, Jr., an expert on suburbia, sums it up, the wife has become a chauffeur; her husband, a handyman.

Certainly this picture, for all its grim verisimilitude, is exaggerated; resourceful people can make the most of almost any environment, and one quality Americans have in abundance now as in the past is resourcefulness. I have no doubt that full lives are being lived in the most architecturally monotonous suburbs, and that suburbia will produce not only good citizens but major scientific and artistic talents in the second half of this century, just as farms and towns have produced them in the past. But this is not to blink at the fact of the enormous and pervasive change that the emergence of the new suburbs has had on our national life at almost all levels. To return to the context of this book, let us quickly compare the suburb now with that of 1939.

They are hardly comparable at all! Basically, the earlier one was an upper-middle-class affair. Its typical property was no longer the pretentious and rather mysterious estate of a Jay Gatsby—that sort of thing had gone with the crash—but rather the ample, oak-beamed, individually designed home, on a large plot with large trees, of a man who had arrived in the world of affairs. The 1939 suburb was the world of J. P. Marquand's novels: expensive, smug, snobbish, exclusive, a little pretentious but not too much so, often outrageously discriminatory as to race and religion, and redeemed, if at all, by a rueful sense of its own limitations. Its spiritual center was its country club, not its shopping center, playground, or school. It was a goal, an end, rather than a makeshift place to sleep and eat; to live in Greenwich or Shaker Heights or Winnetka in 1939 was in itself something of a mark of success. In short, it was in every respect more attractive to the eye and less pleasing under the surface than its successor. To give the new suburb its due, the old one was probably just as potentially boring to live in, just as provincial—while its typical inhabitant, stuffed shirt that he was all too likely to be, was quite probably *more* boring to meet than are those harried chauffeurs and handymen of Prettyville.

5

It came to be said in the 1950s that no one remained resident in the big cities except the very rich and the very poor, and while this was far from strictly true—of the middle class, there conspicuously remained the army of unmarried and aspiring young, mostly recent college graduates, who have always brightened and invigorated our cities, and also a sizable cadre of older people both married and single whose tastes enabled them to take the city on any terms and the suburbs on none—nevertheless there was too much truth in it for the cities' good. What drove away the bulk of the middle class were the commonplace urban drawbacks: high rents, bad schools, traffic jams, dirt, noise, sometimes dangerous streets. But, in addition, the cities were losing much of their charm. In 1939, as we have seen, scarcely anything had been built for years, and, as a result, many cities had a sort of faded grandeur and grace almost reminiscent of a classic ruin. The postwar business boom brought with it a huge boom in new urban construction, some of it apartment houses, but the great bulk of it office buildings. Expenditures for private commercial construction, which had been only $292 million in 1939 and much less than that during the early depression years, amounted to over $1.1 billion in 1946, $3.2 billion in 1954, and $5.2 billion in 1963. The figure is still headed upward.

The sad truth is that most of these new buildings that have almost overrun our cities are ugly and graceless. They are so because no one has restrained their builders' entirely understandable—and, according to classical economics, proper—desire to have them produce maximum rent for minimum construction costs, rather than serve some such irrelevant aim as the adornment of their environment. The one feature of the best modern design that was widely adopted by the postwar commercial builders was simplicity, which they seized upon apparently because it combined a touch of artistic respectability with the admirable advantage of saving them money. The result was not cleanness of line or freedom of form, but sheer, rectilinear, dispiriting monotony. In the 1930s the downtown districts of most cities had still been dominated by gargoyled and filigreed temples and palaces of commerce, no doubt blatantly pretentious, no doubt illustrative of Veblen's theory of conspicuous consumption, but distinctive, able to capture the imagination and assert their existence by being different from each other. If one were suddenly unblindfolded downtown in an American city in those days, one could still get a good idea what city it was with a fast look around.

In the postwar years the fancy old office buildings went down under the ball and hammer of the wrecker one after another, to be replaced by bloodless masonry or glass boxes like barracks in the one case, greenhouses in the other. In the early stages, the better-designed new buildings stood out by contrast with the old ones around them, but soon the contrast was gone. Lever House, the first modern glass office building on Park Avenue in New York, at first presented a striking and actually exciting contrast to its staid old neighbors like the Victorian Renaissance Racquet Club, but soon so many of the neighbors had disappeared and been replaced by near-replicas of Lever House that it had all but been swallowed. Now one's eye traveled not to it but to—the old Racquet Club! The final outrage to Park Avenue was the great, monolithic, shapeless, utterly uninteresting Pan Am Building, which, viewed from the north, actually succeeds in completely blotting out the sky at the end of that famous canyon—not just maiming a thrilling vista, but simply obliterating it.

Far from opposing these tendencies, local and federal laws have generally encouraged them. Often city zoning ordinances rather than architects have appeared to be the designers of new buildings; for example, under the ordinance in effect in New York City during the 1940s and 1950s the typical office building was a truncated pyramid with a series of right-angle setbacks, while shortly after the enactment of a new ordinance now in effect, the characteristic form changed to a plain block with sheer walls and a prescribed amount of clear ground space.

Peter Blake, in his eloquently titled book *God's Own Junkyard,* explains the forces behind mediocre city architecture in recent years. In the first place, the huge amounts of capital needed for new buildings come not from architects or devotees of the city but from investors and mortgage bankers, who professionally care little about architectural quality and everything about getting a good return on their money; therefore they insist that the builder avoid radical departures of any kind in favor of a design that has reliably yielded profits before. In the second place, if the builder is determined enough to defy his backers and insist on an unconventional design, he has let himself in for months or years of bickering with building-code officials, planning boards, contractors, and eventually rental agents. In the third place, the federal government, under tax regulations that have been in effect since the early 1950s, allows a building syndicate to "write off" most of its construction costs as depreciation during the first seven or eight years after completion—thereby encouraging the syndicate to sell out after that period, eliminating the pride in ownership that would come with putting up a building one intended to keep indefinitely, and actually putting a premium on buildings designed to last only a decade or so. Finally, some cities—most notoriously, New York—frankly put an extra tax on architectural quality. The excellent Seagram Building there found itself being taxed at a rate about 50 percent higher than its junky but otherwise comparable neighbors; when its owners inquired why, the city explained that they had to pay more on it because of the added prestige that they were deriving from its superiority. Everyone, from investor to city assessor, seemed to have his face set against quality in city building.

6

Then, of course, the cities had their slums, as they had had them in 1939, and, indeed, since before the turn of the century. The New Deal had mounted a resolute attack on the problem, and at the close of the 1930s it was getting results; by the end of 1939 the first twelve decentralized public housing projects sponsored by the United States Housing Authority—in Florida, Michigan, New York, Ohio, South Carolina, and Texas—had been completed, and had provided decent, low-cost quarters for some thirty thousand former slum-dwellers. That was only a drop in the bucket in a time when there were nine and a half million unemployed, but at least it was a start. As a leading housing expert wrote at the time, "The year 1939 may well be considered one of the most significant in the contemporary social history of the United States. For in that year the slums of the nation began to decrease as the principles of public housing were transformed into the reality of projects."

But such optimism was not to prove to have been justified. New civilian housing of all kinds, whether or not assisted by federal or local government, was to drop off sharply during the war years, and by the time the old programs of the hopeful New Deal planners had been resumed or replaced by new postwar ones, the cities were in the process of developing a whole new and quite different set of problems to add to their old ones. The shiny new office buildings springing up everywhere under private auspices were leaving abandoned shacks, tenements, and rat-infested lofts standing almost at their feet. Nearly every slick and gleaming downtown area was soon surrounded by its ring of decay.

At the same time, the suburbs were draining downtown of its nighttime population, except for night watchmen and derelicts; it was becoming a part-time city, tidally swamped with bustling humanity every weekday morning when the cars and commuter trains arrived, and abandoned again at nightfall when the wave sucked back—left pretty much to the thieves, policemen, and rats. A visitor from a distant planet, landing downtown in an American city after dark, might have thought the region plague-swept. He would have been lucky to find a place to sleep: in the whole postwar era there has not been a single even third-class hotel in New York City less than two bleak miles from the Wall Street area, the financial center of the world and long ago the center of some of the most brilliant social life of the continent. (The population of New York south of City Hall in 1960 was about two thousand by night, perhaps a million and a half at noon.) Worst of all, downtown was abysmally equipped to cure its own ills; having scarcely any real citizens at all, it could hardly expect to have devoted and responsible ones able and willing to give it good government.

Not far from downtown, the slums remained. The new economic boom was passing them by—it simply did not trickle down that far—and, by the stark contrast it created, making them a worse scandal than they had been before. As the children of Jews and other early-in-the-century immigrants from Europe rose in the world and moved to the better city neighborhoods or the suburbs, Puerto Ricans and Negro migrants moved in to take their places. Even the products of the highmindedness of the 1930s, the pioneer low-cost housing developments, often tended to assume the proportions of slums themselves; their rooms became overcrowded, their facilities deteriorated, their elevators and lovingly planned grassy plots became the arenas for violent crimes.

The initiative in tackling these problems might well have come from the businessmen, the creators and likewise the chief beneficiaries of the boom, whose home at least from nine to five was downtown. And in some notable cases they did—but too seldom. "The evidence is overwhelming that they don't care," the Boston planner Edward J. Logue said in 1965 of New York businessmen. "They live in apartments on the East Side and look at the river and go somewhere else on weekends." The initiative, such as it was, came from the federal government, and was embodied in the urban-renewal program, which was begun during the Truman Administration by enactment of the Housing Act of 1949. Characteristically for the postwar era, this law provided not for outright government action like the housing measures of the 1930s, but rather for federal subsidies primarily to promote private action—holding a carrot in front of business to persuade *it* to do the good works. Specifically, the 1949 Housing Act and subsequent acts authorized an arm of the federal government to make grants to localities equal to from two-thirds to three-fourths of the net cost of condemning slum property, clearing it of structures, and selling it to private developers at less than the price the localities had paid for it. The developer got his discount, and the community eventually got new buildings—of one sort or another.

Urban renewal was off to a comparatively slow start during the Eisenhower years; as late as 1959, a decade after the enabling legislation, only a little more than a billion dollars in federal funds had been spent on it. But by the end of 1963 thirteen hundred projects in seven hundred different cities and in forty-two states were completed, under way, or authorized; 250,000 slum housing units had been demolished, 157,000 families relocated, and 33,000 businesses displaced; built or abuilding were some six billion dollars' worth of new housing, commercial and industrial buildings, and public buildings of various sorts; and the cumulative federal commitment was up to three times what it had been in 1959. Furthermore, this unprecedented government-engineered building boom, it appeared, was only in its early stages; Urban Renewal Commissioner William R. Slayton said confidently in 1963, "Most of the results we expect from urban renewal lie ahead."

One might think from these figures that the slums were swiftly and surely being wiped out, to everyone's benefit. But was this really so? Idealistic as it may have been in conception, urban renewal from the first ran into trouble from those banes of our mixed economy, private greed and public bureaucracy. For one thing, the federal and local governments lacked the authority (and also, quite possibly, the capacity) to tell the private developers exactly what sort of buildings they should put up, and too often the result was buildings that architectural authorities had no hesitation about declaring to be inferior both structurally and aesthetically to the slums they had replaced. The "superblock" of high-rise apartment houses, its unadorned walls as forbidding as prison walls and its lawns with their "Keep Off" signs not much more enticing, has become an unhappy hallmark of our cities, partly as a result of urban renewal. As for the cost of the new housing, it is usually far beyond the reach of the people displaced by the demolition; according to the calculations of an avowed enemy of the urban-renewal program, Dr. Martin Anderson of Columbia, the median monthly rental for private residential apartments built under urban renewal in 1962 was $195—a rental inappropriate for a family with an annual income of much less than $10,000.

Which leads us to the most urgent difficulty of all, that of relocating the slum-dwellers displaced by the federally sponsored bulldozer, who in the early 1960s totaled about 25,000 families a year. (Many of them were Negro, a fact that added another dimension to the problem. "Urban renewal means Negro removal," said an official of the NAACP—"with some justification," in the opinion of Federal Housing Administrator Robert C. Weaver. During the Kennedy Administration about half of the displaced persons were nonwhite, while nonwhites ended up in fewer than 15 percent of the new housing units built under the program.) Where were these people, many of whom were getting on in years and had never for a moment thought of themselves as living in slums, to go now that their homes were being sacrificed—at the choosing of others—to the cause of civic betterment? Local housing authorities worked valiantly at the problem and in the majority of cases found reasonably satisfactory solutions, in public housing or in private housing that was officially "standard"—this is to say, nonslum by official criteria. Still, one can't help being disturbed by the moral aspects of the matter, especially since the involuntary self-sacrifice is all on the part of the slum tenant and none on the part of either the owner of the slum or the builder of what replaces it. To the latter, especially, as *Business Week* pointed out, urban renewal is a pure bonanza.

Is the medicine worse than the disease then? Some people think so. Almost everyone agrees that urban renewal has had its successes —more in commercial and cultural developments, like New York's Lincoln Center for the Performing Arts and shopping centers in various cities, than in residential building—but the fact is that in the early Sixties the outcry against its weaknesses was growing increasingly loud and influential. Even the federal government's own General Accounting Office, after investigating a Cleveland urban-renewal plan in 1963, reported that the only reason the existing buildings were being condemned was because they failed to pass the urban-renewal authorities' arbitrary tests for what is and isn't a slum—tests involving jargon like "incompatible uses," "blighting influences," "obsolescence," and the like. As a matter of fact, said the GAO, many of the old buildings at the Cleveland site were in perfectly sound shape, and some of them had recently gone through extensive renovation.

A couple of years earlier, arguing on similar grounds, a group of residents of a section of Greenwich Village in New York, led by the redoubtable architectural writer Jane Jacobs, had succeeded in quashing an urban-renewal project that would have wiped out their homes and that was backed by the whole panoply of municipal and federal authority. These people, fortunately for themselves more articulate and knowledgeable about publicity and political pressure than the average prospective candidate for relocation, simply would not be convinced that their carefully tended old nineteenth-century brick houses, intermingled with loft buildings, garages, corner groceries, and other modest establishments, were in fact slum dwellings, "incompatible uses" and "blighting influences" to the contrary notwithstanding. And, for a wonder, they won.

Back in 1939, it may be interesting to note here, neither these buildings nor many of the other structures so far demolished under urban renewal would have been considered slums. A slum in those hard days meant a place that was too cold, unsanitary, overcrowded, or unsafe—more or less literally unfit for human habitation. And there are still too many like that, in our cities and outside of them. But the rise of general affluence has brought changed standards, exalting the new at the expense of the old, even when newness means cheapness and flimsiness and oldness means sound construction and mellow grace. The point has been reached where the speculator's or the bureaucrat's eye, falling on an old street that to its residents is a satisfactory place to live and to an architectural historian may be a place that ought to be preserved by law, sees quite simply and clearly a slum to be removed. Slums, it now has come to appear, are often in the eye of the beholder.

7

Meanwhile we were abusing our countryside, one that was originally as lovely as any in the world, and remains so in many places; briefly put, we were simply littering it, the air above it, and the water around it with the debris of affluence. We were polluting the air with smoke and industrial gases (to say nothing of, for a short but ominous period before the test-ban treaty with Russia, nuclear fallout) to such an extent that the East Coast, continually exposed to the rest of the country's used air borne on prevailing westerly winds, was sometimes described as standing at the end of a kind of sewer. We were polluting our rivers and bays with industrial wastes and poisonous insecticides to the point where the balance of nature was being seriously disturbed—shad and salmon no longer came up many rivers to spawn, huge schools of killed fish floated to the top of lakes or were cast up on beaches, and certain species of wild fowl virtually disappeared. In 1965 only one American river running near a major metropolitan area—the St. Croix between Wisconsin and Minnesota—remained unpolluted.

Those clusters of hideous "mobile homes" defaced the view from the highways along which they arranged themselves in untidy strips. Nor could mobile homes always be excused as the resort of the poor and struggling who could afford nothing else, because for some unfathomable reason a few of the rich affected to live in them, too; in Palm Springs, California, millionaires took to buying them for $15,000 or so and then investing four or five times that much in converting them into Egyptian tombs, Georgian mansions, or Oriental pagodas. As for billboards, they have been under constant public attack for many, many years, but lobbies in Washington and in state capitals just as fiercely defend them, and how triumphantly they survive! After a long and gallant fight by the late Senator Richard Neuberger of Oregon, Congress in 1958 approved a plan granting a bonus of .5 percent on highway funds to any state that meets federal standards of billboard regulation; five years later only one state, Kentucky, had claimed and collected its bonus. As President Eisenhower said ruefully—and rather characteristically—at the height of the ruckus, "I am against those billboards that mar our scenery, [but] I don't know what I can do about it."

The single thing most often chosen as symbolic of national aesthetic disgrace is the automobile graveyard. Let us try to get some idea of how this phenomenon, the very hallmark of affluence in other rich nations as well as this one, has grown. There are no exact statistics on how many motor vehicles were junked in 1939, but, based on sales in the preceding years and the known tendency of owners to keep cars for a long time in those days, the total may well have been below one million. In 1950, according to the Automobile Manufacturers Association, we junked 3.25 million, and in 1955 4.4 million, while in 1961 we finally topped the five-million mark, not quite four and a half million of that year's crop of derelicts being passenger cars. Considering that junked cars often stay where they are thrown much more than a year, how many of them are decorating the American landscape at this moment? Twenty million? Thirty million? Nobody knows. (The Department of Commerce knew in 1965 that there were about 17,500 automobile graveyards, junkyards and scrap-metal heaps along our highways—one every 14.6 miles of main highway in New York, every 10.1 miles in Texas, every 4.5 miles in North Carolina.)

What is to be done with the junked cars, inasmuch as the jaws of metal-pressing machines obviously lack the appetite to consume them all? Dump them into the sea? Impractical, and an insult to the sea in any case. Produce fewer cars, and ones that are designed to last longer? Here, of course, is the crux of the matter. Say what you will against it, the annual-model-change and quick-obsolescence system of manufacturing and merchandising automobiles has been one of the chief main stays of the whole postwar boom, and one of the chief reasons the national standard of living, coldly measured in terms of money rather than those of such intangibles as the charm and compatibility of one's surroundings, has gone up to levels unprecedented in the history of the world. Take the present system away and we would reliably have a recession or far worse. The slogan "You auto buy now" that was bandied about so much during the 1957–58 recession may have been an atrocious abuse of language, but it was pretty sound economics.

The automobile along with its appurtenances like the highways has repeatedly been singled out as the nemesis of national beauty. Such city planners as Victor Gruen have accused the automobile of the virtual rape of our cities, and have done their best to banish it from them by creating pedestrian malls downtown. Conservationists, moreover, have pointed out that its voracious demands for paved ground have not only destroyed natural beauty but have also seriously disturbed natural ecology, with effects that may be felt only years from now; it has been estimated that an area of American land the size of Louisiana now lies entombed under concrete and asphalt. Nevertheless, we have continued to encourage the automobile and its use through federal action. The pivotal point came in 1956. At that time, with the country clearly facing a transportation crisis as population and commerce rose steeply, we might have turned any of three ways: toward modernizing and expanding public transport, toward concentrating on the private automobile, or toward creating a balanced system. The die was cast for the private automobile when Eisenhower proposed and Congress authorized a nationwide interstate highway system to provide nonstop, limited-access, high-speed car travel on 41,000 miles of new roads—enough to cross the country coast to coast more than a dozen times—at a cost of $41 billion.

This made sense for a variety of business interests and probably, in the short run at any rate, for the economy as a whole, but not, oddly enough, for motorists even in the short run. As Ruth and Edward Brecher have pointed out, there is an "apparently inexorable rule that new roads soon attract enough new traffic to jam them." As federal and state highways proliferated, so did traffic jams, and no wonder; our total vehicle miles traveled amounted to 458.2 billion in 1950 and some 75 percent more—just short of 800 billion—in 1963. Despite the popularity of airlines, 90 percent of all our intercity travel was still by private car. When Robert Moses refused to permit express buses on New York City parkways in order to leave them clear for "pleasure driving," Gruen remarked sardonically that "If a law permitting only pleasure driving on parkways were to be enforced, there would not be a single car left on Mr. Moses' parkways."

Finally, in Boston on December 30, 1963, It—the ultimate traffic jam that would be permanent and would provide such a rich mine of material, what with each fossilized car and driver frozen in place, for the archaeologists of the far future—almost happened. It began in midafternoon. Bruce Talford, helicopter-borne traffic reporter for radio station WHDH, noticed it developing. As he wrote later,

> It was quite obvious when we took off from the heliport at 3:45 P.M. that we were in for an unusual afternoon. The northbound side of the Central Artery was already showing congested traffic at that early hour. We decided to track the congestion to its source and found traffic backed up through Leverett Circle underpass. . . . Then we swung over the Boston Public Garden and Boston Common. . . . Traffic was literally bumper to bumper and completely stalled. . . . At each of the intersections traffic looked like something you'd expect to see in a cartoon. . . . By 4:45 P.M. the entire downtown area . . . was completely snarled. We began to refer to [it] as an emergency area.

Strangely enough, all this had no special cause such as a construction bottleneck or a multitude of stalled cars in key places; its cause was simply too many cars. At 7:40, Talford said, downtown traffic was "still at a near standstill." At 8:10, "the downtown area looked like a typical 5 P.M. rush-hour period." "When would it end?" Talford must have been asking himself—or perhaps even "*Will* it end?" And then, almost mysteriously, it did end. Shortly after nine o'clock, more than five hours after the jam had begun, conditions returned to near normal. It had not quite happened, but that was no guarantee that It wouldn't, next time.

8

In the early 1960s the consensus at home and abroad seemed to be that we had made a general mess of our environment. "The archvillain in the despoliation of our landscape, it sometimes seems, is American capitalism," Edmund K. Faltermayer mused in the March, 1965, issue of *Fortune*, which does not ordinarily go in for depicting American capitalism as an archvillain. "To one returning here after a long sojourn abroad, the impression gathered is one of pathologically profit-minded enterprises striving to outdo each other in the creation of eyesores." That same season there appeared a book by an Englishman, Ian Nairn, who had recently made a ten-thousand-mile tour of the United States and who declared flatly, "America has made the biggest hash of its environment in the history of the world." Not even Mrs. Trollope, the grand dame of British America-scolders, had gone quite so far as that.

But a change of attitude was in process. The quality of our life, as reflected in our environment, was coming to be a matter of public concern. There had been turns in this direction before—when the first great national parks had been created with extraordinary foresight in 1872 and 1890, when Theodore Roosevelt had dramatically brought the problem of natural-resource conservation to public attention—but my impression is that the current turn is the most decisive of all. Certainly, after free enterprise's landscape-littering orgy of the 1950s, it is the most sorely needed. In part, the turn stems from changes in our leadership. President Kennedy eloquently looked forward to an America that would no longer be afraid of grace and beauty, while President Johnson, in his 1965 inaugural, called for a combining of the old conservation aimed at the protection of wildlife and woodlands with a new conservation designed to "salvage the beauty and charm of our cities."

But just as much, I think, the cause was a spontaneous feeling of revulsion and remorse on the part of millions of us on realizing the harm we had been doing with our carelessness. "Is public ugliness the price America must pay for its incredibly high level of public consumption?" Faltermayer asked. His answer was no. But even many of those more pessimistic, who suspected the answer might be a qualified yes—not a majority of these, surely, but a highly influential minority—were and are unprepared to pay the price any longer, and are increasingly willing to sacrifice a measure of affluence in the interest of grace and beauty. The new mood is not yet a general one, and sometimes it seems hardly more than the equivalent of a political splinter party. But there was reason in the mid-Sixties to think it would grow, especially after Congress passed a first, cautious road-beautification measure late in 1965.

As to suburban life, the new mood was represented by a small tendency to build in a new way, replacing the familiar, mindlessly ranged rows of identical houses with planned communities containing dwellings in tight clusters or attached rows; large plots of open ground for use by everyone; provision for commercial, industrial, and civic activities as well as eating and sleeping and schooling; and provision for a planned diversity of residents, including insofar as possible all races, incomes, family sizes, and social levels. The aim was to remove all the worst aspects of the typical postwar suburb or convert them into assets to convenient and graceful living. The nearness of school, market, and friends' homes would largely free the lady of the house from chauffeurhood; the elimination of the endless multiplication of lawns and flimsily built ranch houses would tend to raise the man of the house out of the status of handyman; while the town-style living and the common recreation grounds would foster a sense of community. These developments were called New Towns after similar planned communities in Britain and Scandinavia. (The nearest thing to a precedent for them in this country was to be found in the few Greenbelt towns built at government expense during the late 1930s.)

"The country is on the verge of a New Town boom," Ada Louise Huxtable wrote in the *New York Times* in February, 1964. That was putting it pretty strongly, since there were only a handful of New Towns planned, and most of those were still on the drawing board. But the promise was there, and fulfillment of it seemed to be on the way. The most heralded New Town was Reston, Virginia, eighteen miles west of Washington, where a Harvard-educated developer named Robert E. Simon, using an imaginative plan developed by a New York architectural firm, had started work on what, on paper at least, looked like a dream community—seven neighborhoods of clustered "town houses," situated on plazas reached by walkways inaccessible to automobiles, grouped around an artificial lake, opening on acres of wooded and terraced land reserved for the use of all, with shops within easy walking distance of every dwelling. In an access of enthusiasm, Wolf von Eckardt wrote in *The New Republic* that Reston was "an architectural ensemble resembling a modern Portofino." It opened officially in December, 1965.

The strangest and most heartening aspect of New Towns was that they were being built for profit, with no government assistance except that granted to other forms of development. However "planned" they might be, nobody could anathematize them as one more example of socialistic government meddling in private affairs. Their proliferation, therefore, depended on the financial success of the first ones, and such success was far from assured; some experts believed that most Americans simply don't *want* to give up their chauffeuring and chore-doing or live within walking distance of shops and friends' houses, even though they could accomplish this and still have a view of woods and lake. Certainly the pioneer developers found many obstacles in their way; conservative capital often shied away from them because they were commercially untried, and the Reston plan, superior as it was in so many respects, ran into an entirely characteristic roadblock: it turned out to be clearly illegal under local zoning requirements. But the point is, after much tribulation the zoning laws were changed and enough capital raised to make possible the beginning of construction. Indeed, by 1965 the very phrase "New Town" had caught on to the extent that it was beginning to be used, quite cynically and improperly, as a promotion gimmick by developers who were actually planning huge suburban subdivisions of the most routine sort. And maybe that was a good sign for the future of New Towns; in America what is exploited turns out to be what has succeeded.

As to the city proper, there were various portents of the new mood. There began to be much talk and some action in favor of an alternative to the slum-clearance kind of urban renewal—that is, rehabilitation of structurally sound existing buildings, either by professional builders or by the residents themselves, with various forms of public encouragement, some of it from the Urban Renewal Administration, the personification of the "federal bulldozer" itself. Pleasant nineteenth-century urban areas like the section west of Rittenhouse Square in Philadelphia, which had become woefully rundown and were sometimes fast on the way to becoming slums, were fixed up into places whose restored charm was no less genuine for being largely based on nostalgia.

There is much to be said for rehabilitation—certainly the cliché that "They don't build the way they used to" is true enough—but, unfortunately, up to now it has worked well chiefly in providing housing for people with plenty of both money and taste, who are self-evidently the ones best equipped to solve their housing problems under any system; rehabilitation for the underprivileged has yet to prove itself. Meanwhile, there came to be a few signs of a rising revolt against mediocre commercial building in our cities. A New Yorker said to me recently, "The Pan Am building is a turning point. It has finally shown us all the possibilities of badness—after it, new office buildings will *have* to be better." (I must say I was more impressed by his spirit than his logic.)

A growing revolt against the urban incursions of the automobile was indicated by such things as a moderate proliferation of downtown shopping malls, and the loud and prolonged public outcry against a plan for a downtown expressway across Manhattan Island that, besides encouraging still more automobile travel to the city, would displace dozens of small businesses and the homes of several thousand persons. Attacking the same problem from the opposite end, a few cities were putting on heroic drives to keep out automobiles by planning improved public transit. Atlanta, Boston, Los Angeles, and Washington were among them, but perhaps the prize example was the San Francisco Bay area, whose new rapid-transit system, scheduled for completion in 1969, was expected to provide nothing less than seats for every rider—wide, foam-padded seats, at that—and to have an average speed of fifty miles per hour, allowing for stops. The public-transit improvement trend seemed likely to be speeded on its way by the Urban Mass Transportation Act of 1964, which, provided it was followed by adequate appropriations of funds, would take much of the staggering cost of well-planned new transit off the shoulders of the cities.

And in the mid-1960s it seemed that at last—almost too late—we were becoming interested in preserving national landmarks from destruction by speculators, or simply from the natural process of decay. Natchez, Mississippi, passed a preservation ordinance as early as 1951 and Annapolis, Maryland, in 1952; Philadelphia came along in 1956 and New York in 1965—in the last case, far too late to save anything of the seventeenth- and eighteenth-century city, which had long since been wiped out by fire or demolition. Other old cities like Boston, St. Louis, and Atlanta had no legislation but could boast of energetic and effective private groups, most of them recently formed, fighting the battle of preservation. Fashion, often a stronger force than law, was turning toward landmark preservation. Suddenly it was "in."

The tremendous threat to the appearance of our landscape and the quality of our life posed by the previously unimaginable increase in our population, the amount of our leisure time, and the demand for outdoor recreation created by both factors, was coming to be fully recognized at the federal level; in 1962 the National Park Service had plans to not quite double its 26 million acres of park lands. Needless to say, it would not achieve these goals without overcoming great difficulties. Local political opposition to each new park, rooted in real or imagined threats to local economic interests, is predictable—and predictably fierce; popular opposition to federal "land-grabbing" runs deep in the American psyche; and besides, the cost of our land rises so fast that every month lost in political maneuvering brings closer the day when our government simply will not be able to afford to buy the land needed for our common recreational use.

And billboards? Well, hear the small case that Peter Blake jubilantly cites as evidence that American rough justice in the frontier tradition may eventually rise to smite them down. "On a Sunday morning in June, 1958," he writes,

> one or several "persons unknown" sawed down seven billboards along a rather handsome highway leading from Santa Fe to Los Alamos, in New Mexico. This act of terrorism raised a serious problem: since the billboards had been located on Indian Pueblo Land, it was difficult to determine just exactly what law enforcement agency—local, state or

federal—should investigate the outrage. While officials conferred for several days to decide the issue, citizens of surrounding areas telephoned newspapers and radio and TV stations expressing support for the terrorist or terrorists unknown. Only two telephone calls expressed disapproval: one complained that the lawbreaker had not cut down enough billboards; the other complained that the terrorist (or terrorists) had frustrated plans of a large group of New Mexico citizens who had scheduled a mass burning of billboards for later in the month.

Now Los Alamos, a government-sponsored community full of high-domed atomic scientists, is not exactly the typical American small town, nor is art-conscious Santa Fe the typical American city; the tale is heartening all the same.

But I must not be too optimistic. True, our national attitude toward our environment seems unmistakably headed in a healthy direction. In the Thirties we were so naïve that we often thought of natural beauty and economic development as going hand in hand, but we were too poor to suffer very much from the consequences of that notion. In the Forties we were too busy in first fighting a war and then recovering from the war to think much about the whole question of beauty. In the Fifties we thought about it, but, except for a small minority, we thought about it negatively—beauty was something one sacrificed with the deepest regret to a higher value, profit. In the Sixties, it seems, we are finally getting things into perspective.

Yet the whole idea of conservation fights upstream in America, now as in the past. It fights upstream against our cherished though so often dishonored economic philosophy of laissez-faire and the social value of private profit. It fights upstream against the embodiment of that philosophy in tax laws that encourage quick-buck real-estate speculation, localities that oppose new parks, federal programs that promote automobile travel, and state legislatures that decline to lift a finger against billboards. Rehabilitation of streets to look as they did in 1810 or 1820, like the preservation of landmarks, goes against our deepest emotional commitments to change. In almost all its manifestations, conservation fights upstream—and will probably always have to do so. When one stops to consider the matter, the word itself is an antonym of change.

8

And—to compound the paradox—in many of the nascent changes for the better that I have mentioned there is more than a touch of coming full circle. A revolt against the cult of the automobile can't help having overtones of horse-and-buggy days. The rising New Towns bear certain striking resemblances to the old towns—Boston and Gloucester and Marblehead and Trenton—that sprang up on the virgin soil of the New World before the republic was formed.

In miniature, and in speeded-up time, the sense of coming full circle is beautifully exemplified in the development of the motel during the past twenty-five years. I have said that in the course of becoming the favorite American form of lodging and of practically finishing off the old-fashioned hotel, the motel has progressively fancified itself almost to the point of absurdity. But it has done something else. What were the distinguishing characteristics of the motel, as it was originally conceived? That it was situated on the open road, not in the heart of the city; that it had only one story, or two at most; that it usually had no restaurant of its own; that one carried one's own bags; and, most basic of all, that one could park the car at one's door.

In recent years, motels have tended more and more to invade downtown; whole chains make it their main selling point that they are right in the middle of things, and even New York City now has its Motel Row a few blocks from Times Square. They have tended to become multistory structures—who wants to spend a bundle on a piece of downtown real estate and then put up a one-story building? They have tended to incorporate restaurants—in the case of the more expensive ones, first-class restaurants complete with dim lights and French chefs; in many small towns the dining room of the fanciest motel is where local people go to dine on the town. They have come to include service—nominally "optional," to be sure, but just try to duck the braid-bedecked bellhop at some of them! Finally, and crushingly, they have begun to run out of parking space. Obviously the high-rise ones can't supply a place to park beside everyone's door, but not even the parking lot—the remaining gesture toward motelhood—is always adequate to its job. Coming back to my room at a downtown motel in Minneapolis late one evening in August of 1964, I found the lot full. There was nothing to do but hunt down a place to park on a public street nearby.

Has the motel, then, become a hotel by another name? Not quite. In the course of circling it has moved. It has fewer flunkies and a more impersonal air than the old hotel had. Its coldly modern lobby and corridors have a deserted air even when every room is occupied. To find life one goes to its tiny, crowded swimming pool—which is obligatory even in the sootiest cities. The people who drink free coffee in its lobby of a morning do not speak to or even look at one another. The informative cards and announcements that one finds on one's dresser have the air of not having been written by human hand. One feels efficiently provided for—and faintly depressed—and turns on the TV. That, quite evidently, is the way we want the motel to be; and the curious, spiraling manner of its evolution may be a lesson in the manner of change in the United States.

V.
WHEN EVERYONE IS SOMEBODY

1

That extraordinary institution, the income tax, is both a leading actor in and a painstaking recorder of the drama of social change. By extracting revenue from citizens at progressive rates that are, always in theory and some of the time in practice, scaled according to ability to pay, it has a cumulative leveling effect between the rich and the poor. Meanwhile, by requiring everyone who gets more than a pittance of annual income to report his precise income under what amounts to his oath, it provides the government with a mine of information, far more accurate than can be derived from census or polls, about how much money how many Americans take in. This information is collated and published in due time by the Internal Revenue authorities. Let us press the income tax into service in its recording role.

In 1939 somewhat over four million Americans, out of 130 million, declared income in any amount above $2,000 for the year. In 1960 more than 25 million, out of 180 million, declared more than—not $2,000, but $5,000.

In 1939 200,000 persons declared more than $10,000, and 42,500—a fair-sized football crowd—more than $25,000. In 1960 five and a third million declared over $10,000, more than half a million over $25,000.

In 1939 only 3 percent of the population had sufficient income to require them to pay any income tax at all. In 1960 48 million—more than a quarter of the national population, and well over half the adult population—had to ante up in some amount.

In 1939 the nation's two-thirds of a million of the richest taxpayers accounted for 90 percent of all income-tax money collected. In 1960 it took the top 32 million to provide that percentage. To put it another way, while the population was rising by 38 percent, the number of persons who had to chip in to supply the bulk of federal receipts had increased by nothing less than 4,600 percent.

These figures, I am convinced, attest to one of the most dramatic redistributions of income that any nation ever went through in so short a time. The very rich we still have with us, but they are increasingly insignificant as to relative numbers and relative economic importance (though the political importance of the long-established rich, oddly enough, may be rising); the moderately rich have increased in number moderately; the distinctly well-to-do have become commonplace; and the comfortably off have become our great central mass. Furthermore, the less-than-comfortably-off have in recent years been declining sharply not only relative to the population but in absolute numbers as well; from 1952 to 1961 returns declaring less than $5,000 decreased from 43 million to 33 million, while the national population was rising from under 160 million to over 180 million. Like the farm, the low-income brackets seem to be in the process of being depopulated.

"They's change a'comin'," says one of the Okies in *The Grapes of Wrath.* "I don't know what. Maybe we won't live to see her. But she's a-comin'. They's a res'less feelin'." On such evidence, will anyone gainsay the general statement that since 1939 the change has come, and that in terms of personal income it has been a change from something like frank oligarchy to something approaching democracy?

2

The answer is that some will. Various commentators have contended that the national economic leveling has been far less marked and less socially significant than is generally believed; a few have been so rash as to talk about the "myth" of income redistribution, and one, the late C. Wright Mills, stubbornly insisted that a small "power elite," consisting chiefly of business, political, and military men, but including, curiously, café-society celebrities, still rules the nation. I must say as a layman in these matters that such analyses seem to me to rest for the most part on prejudgments, personal theories, and the torturing of fragmentary statistics.

There is no denying, though, that the redistribution has been laggard, scandalously so, in reaching to the two extremes of the economic spectrum. The very rich and the very poor clearly survive as important elements in our national life. To take the rich first, those who already possessed fortunes before World War II have succeeded pretty well in keeping the fortunes intact despite death and taxes. Tax loopholes like exempt bonds, executive stock options, and the famous or infamous depletion allowances on mineral investment have saved many of the very rich from paying high tax rates they are nominally subject to, and a similar array of escape hatches has lessened the death duties that nominally prevent great fortunes from passing from one generation to the next. The strange case of the dozen or so men with incomes of more than a million dollars per year who annually find perfectly legal ways of paying no income tax at all is only the most spectacular example of how the rich and powerful effectively resist the national tendency toward economic democracy.

Moreover, the rich have increased their numbers in the postwar period. If the estimates of the National Bureau of Economic Research, the Federal Reserve, and other government agencies are right, the country in 1953 held some 27,000 millionaires—persons owning net assets of one million dollars or more—and in 1965 held some ninety thousand. According to the same sources, five thousand newcomers were entering the millionaire class annually. Millionaires were getting to be a dime (or perhaps, allowing for inflation, one should say a buck) a dozen.

The nature of the new, less scarce millionaire is nothing like that of the old one. From post-Civil War days, and to a great extent as late as the 1930s, the millionaire characteristically thought of himself as an empire builder, changing the face of his land with his railroads or skyscrapers or automobiles, shaping the lives of his employees in ways that he fondly assumed to be benevolent, living in baronial splendor and isolation from the eyes of the vulgar throng. The post-war millionaire is quite another matter. He makes his money by manipulations—buying and selling existing companies, engaging in intricate speculations in convertible debentures and the like—that often change little or nothing except his wealth in relation to that of others. Frequently it simply does not matter much which group of investors holds the controlling interest in a company that is effectively run by its professional management, and in the vast financial markets of today even the richest of individual speculators can cause scarcely more than a momentary ripple by comparison with the panic-breeding storms whipped up by a Jay Gould or Jim Fisk. The new millionaire lives in luxury, to be sure, but not in either isolation or splendor; he prides himself on his low hedge and the democratic accessibility of his premises. Above all—with a few spectacular exceptions like the late Robert R. Young, whose drive in life seemed to be a sort of nostalgia for the piratical days of the Fisks, Vanderbilts, and Harrimans—he is not interested in power as such; it is a convenient by-product of money that may make it easier for him to make still more money, but beyond that it is almost irrelevant to him.

At times it seems that he is not much interested even in money. He usually does not know much about how to spend it, and apart from learning to buy the works of thoroughly accepted artists, he does not have much time or inclination to widen his horizons. He sees himself—as he has told me himself time and time again over the past fifteen years—as a player in a game of which the object is to outwit the other players and the tax laws, and he devotes himself to the game for its own sake day in and day out, with a sort of monkish intensity. Occasionally in a fit of boredom or conscientiousness, if he can't pull off the standard rich man's leap into government service, he quits the game in middle life and suddenly takes up something of obvious social utility like professional philanthropy, teaching, or even medicine; but, as often as not, his old addiction soon grips him and he goes back to making more money.

Far from feeling superior to or contemptuous of the rest of society, he yearns for greater acceptance by it—in particular, by intellectual and artistic society. Sometimes he appears almost as a wistful and pathetic character. It is a further cry than we often realize from the Robber Baron to the Wheeler-Dealer, and the former would have a certain justification in scorning the latter as just a ribbon clerk at heart. When it comes to millionaires, in short, they aren't what they used to be; the social leveling has been even more pronounced than the economic.

Poverty, suddenly rediscovered by the Johnson Administration, had, of course, been with us all along, although during the Fifties it had usually been kept brushed under the rug in the interest of preserving the notion that day by day in every way we were all getting richer and richer. We were not. True enough, the number of Americans who lead lives of deprivation because of poverty has been decreasing steadily—and the percentage of our population comprising such persons decreasing more rapidly—over the past twenty-five years; but the rate of decrease has not been nearly fast enough, and the reason is that the industrial system when left to its own devices simply does not provide for the automatic economic uplifting of those who are not situated or equipped to profit from it—the people who have been called the "losers" in industrial society.

To put the problem in the context, we must remember that in the second half of the 1930s poverty was not a problem so much as a condition of the nation, and that definitions of poverty are, as they should be, relative to conditions at the time they are formulated. A young reporter visiting a migrant-labor camp in California in 1939 asked the landowner why he didn't have plumbing installed in the workers' shacks; because, he replied blandly, they were too uneducated to know how to use it. The answer speaks eloquently of both the conditions and the attitudes of the time. Consider that the 1964 officially accepted "poverty line" of a family was an annual income of $3,000, which, adjusted according to Bureau of Labor statistics consumer price figures, amounted in 1935-36 to $1,330. Well, in 1935-36, according to census figures, 11,650,000 American families, or 38 percent of all American families, had annual incomes of less than $1,000—and were thus not just below the latter-day poverty line but far below it. President Roosevelt's "one-third of a nation, ill-housed, ill-clad, ill-nourished" seems to have been, by the standards of the Sixties, much too low a figure. More like four-tenths of us were then living in what we now call extreme poverty.

But as everyone was to be aware by the time the federal anti-poverty program came along in 1964, the big postwar boom had simply by-passed many people, by no means all of them isolated in unlucky "pockets" of poverty. As early as 1957, when the everybody-wins spirit of the Fifties was near its apogee, a careful study made by Robert J. Lampman of the University of Wisconsin resulted in the conclusion that 20 percent of the population was then living below the poverty line defined in current purchasing power. A University of Michigan study made two years later arrived at just about the same figure, and estimated that another 10 percent of the nation's families were living right *on* the line. The psychologist Bruno Bettelheim and the sociologist Morris Janowitz declared in 1964 that "downward social mobility seems to affect as much as 20% of the male population"—meaning, in plainer language, that in a time of unparalleled economic growth one in every five men apparently had lower status in his community than his father had had. And the rate of emergence from the ranks of the poor was declining, according to the calculations of authorities; Lampman concluded that between 1947 and 1957 about 800,000 a year rose out of the poverty zone, and only 500,000 a year between 1957 and 1962. Michael Harrington, in his passionate book *The Other America,* which soon after its publication in 1962 became almost the embodiment of the nation's conscience with respect to its poor, summed up his case thus:

> The poor in America constitute about 25% of the total population. . . . At this point I would beg the reader to forget the numbers game. Whatever the precise calibrations, it is obvious that the statistics repre-

sent an enormous, an unconscionable amount of human suffering in this land.

Nor was poverty confined to a few locations of social groupings. There was much talk about poverty in "Appalachia," the mountainous region made up of parts of ten Mideastern and Southern states and all of West Virginia, which was down on its luck because of bad roads, automation of coal mining, prevalent flood conditions, and a disinclination of industry to settle there—but Appalachia was simply the worst region of poverty, not the only one. The situation was bad among Negroes, since 44 percent of Negro families were said to be below the poverty line in 1964, but not all of the poor were Negro. It was bad among farmers, among whom 43 percent were said to be below the line, but not all of the poor were farmers. It was bad among old people and fatherless families—almost half of each category was poor in 1964—yet at the same time about one-third of all poor families did not seem to fit into any definable disadvantaged group at all.

And in many cases it was clear that booming commerce and industry were not merely failing to uplift the poor but were actually contributing to their plight by involving them in installment-buying contracts that they had little or no hope of fulfilling. The enormous national installment-credit total of about $54 billion in 1965—about ten times the 1940 figure and between three and four times the 1950 figure—was heavily concentrated in the lower-income groups. "There are large numbers of poor people who discover that they have a binding obligation to pay a finance company for furniture never delivered or a TV set that never worked," Nicholas Katzenbach, then Acting Attorney General, said in 1964. "There are large numbers whose cars or washing machines are repossessed after months of payments . . . who have no idea they are entitled to return of their equity." In effect, then, though certainly not always through intention, something quite against the American tradition of this century was going on: in certain cases the business boom that was alleged to be bringing affluence to all was actually fattening itself and its beneficiaries by bilking the poor.

All this resulted, hearteningly if hardly surprisingly, in stirrings of guilt, sympathy, and responsibility in the well-off majority; and in 1965 social legislation aimed at correcting the problem of poverty was flowing out of Congress far faster and more vigorously than it had at any time since New Deal days.

3

But to repeat: despite the survival of the rich and the poor, the middle class was enlarging itself and ever encroaching on the two extremes. How big was the middle class, or, as some commentators were taking to calling it, the middle mass? There was no sure answer, because nobody could precisely define the group. But there were plenty of helpful guideposts. We might begin with one of the most reliable hallmarks of middle-class status, the condition of having children in college. In 1939 about 15 percent of college-age Americans were attending college; in 1957 the figure was 32 percent, while in the early Sixties it was above 40 percent and heading fast for the 50 percent mark. We might take the relative numbers of white-collar and blue-collar workers—in 1956 white-collar workers took the lead for the first time in our history, and in the subsequent years the gap widened rapidly—except that many blue-collar workers are now, by economic criteria, firmly established members of the middle class. Or one might turn to the informed estimates of authorities: Andrew Hacker, for example, estimates that between 60 and 70 percent of the population may now be considered to belong to the vast new middle class, which he describes—justifiably, I feel—as "a corporate creation." The idea that our society is moving inexorably toward a universal middle class has become so commonplace that social commentators habitually drop it into subordinate clauses.

The most striking effect has been the emergence, perhaps for the first time since the early days of the republic before the rise of industry created the split between capital and labor and the opening of the frontier created the split between the Easterner and the Westerner, of a clearly predominant national style of life. So much has been written about that style of life that perhaps I may be forgiven, in putting it into the context of this book, for doing so rather elliptically and discontinuously.

It is a style of life, then, based on relatively high income, but just as much on the expectation of and sometimes the actual need for still higher income. Sometimes it seemed that the higher the income, the more a man ran into debt; high taxes, private-school bills, liquor bills, insurance premiums, major appliance bills, sports-car bills always seemed to stay one step ahead of rising income. In his book *The Exurbanites*, A. C. Spectorsky described feelingly the plight of the commuter who makes $25,000 a year and just can't *quite* live on it; and while many who manage to scrape by on a fraction of that sum must have read about the poor exurbanites with certain feelings of superiority and scorn, the almost incredible problem is nevertheless real. Take a group at the very top of the middle class, the graduates of Harvard. Twenty-three years out of the Yard, in 1962, the Harvard graduates of 1939 had a median annual income of $23,800—and thought that what they needed to fill the wants of themselves and their families was $27,000. More than one in ten of them admitted to spending more than he earned in an average year. Compare the situation of an earlier Harvard man, the gentleman farmer Charles Allen Smart, Class of 1926. "The gruesome fact," he confessed in 1938, "is that I need thirty or thirty-five hundred dollars a year to live in the luxurious style to which I am accustomed." Gruesome, nothing—subversive of the national economy!

Debt means living on credit, and the credit card is an authentic artifact of the new style of life. It came into being in 1950, when the Diners' Club was founded to provide collective credit privileges at a handful of restaurants in the New York City area; fifteen years later, the Diners' Club had 1.3 million holders of its cards, and the nearest competitor, American Express, had 1.2 million. "There are no specific qualifications for membership," reported the Diners' Club, adding cheerfully, "The main requirement is stability. We are looking for people who don't change from job to job. . . . There is no definite earning requirement, but you can readily figure that if a person doesn't earn $7,500 a year, he won't qualify." By 1965 credit cards would get you credit not only at restaurants, motels, travel agencies, airline counters, and the like, but also at tourist attractions, pet shops, and wig-making establishments. Delinquencies in this enormous new industry were strikingly low, amounting to less than a quarter of one percent of the value of merchandise bought on the cuff.

Indeed, an almost compulsive honesty in small matters, whether based on pure affluence, on exaggerated fear of social disapproval, or on high-mindedness, is one of the marked features of the new middle class. In 1964 the public library of one of the richer suburbs of New York City simply stopped doing anything about pursuing unreturned books. There were, it found, so few instances of them that enforcement activities were not worth their cost. (On the other hand, in far-from-suburban Brooklyn the public library announced a few years ago that its annual losses from book thefts amounted to $500,000.)

In 1939 a charge account was still something you had at a department store, and buying a meal in a restaurant on credit was practically unheard of.

It is a style of life marked by big families. The percentage of American families with four or more minor children nearly doubled between 1950 and 1963, and a surprising number of these families were well-to-do and entirely happy with their large broods. The 1939 Harvard graduates—just the right age to be parents of the postwar bumper crop of babies—in 1964 averaged 1.3 daughters and 1.4 sons; practically all those with four children thought that number was "just right," and 88 percent of those with six heroically declared *that* number to be just right. The most common explanation of the phenomenon of big families among the well-off is that given by Lincoln and Alice Day:

> Growth in our society has increased the impersonal quality of many of our social contacts. . . . The employee of a large, bureaucratic-type organization [may find that his job] offers little in the way of meaningful personal relationships. . . . In this mushrooming of size and anonymity, the family stands out as a haven of intimacy. . . . Children are seen as providing security.

But then, as the Days graciously allow, "Americans may also desire more children because they like them." In 1939, at any rate, few middle-class Americans felt they could afford more than two or three.

What with bureaucratic rat races in the office and children races in the living room, it is, notoriously, a high-tension style of life, and that means resort to soothing preparations—what an earlier era might have called "nerve tonics"—and alcohol. The new tranquilizer drugs, the consumption of which (apart from their use in mental hospitals) has been almost exclusively a middle-class affair, came along just at the right moment to meet the organization-man crisis. Sales of tranquilizing drugs zoomed from zero in 1955 to 462,000 pounds worth $2.2 million in 1958 and 1,159,000 pounds worth $4.75 million in 1959 before slacking off somewhat as their effectiveness began to be called into question. At the height of the tranquilizer craze executives used to take the most popular product, Miltown, before every important conference; harried mothers used to gobble the stuff like candy when the kids were getting out of hand; and pretty but shy girls at dinner parties occasionally broke out in ugly red welts because they had imprudently taken tranquilizers to which they happened to be allergic as a preparation for the rigors of meeting people. The story has an ironic footnote: In 1965 the *U.S. Pharmacopoeia,* published for pharmacists by the Food and Drug Administration, dropped Miltown from its listing of drugs; Miltown, the *Pharmacopoeia*'s learned editors had belatedly decided, is not a true tranquilizer after all. In some circles, announcement of the omission was bound to have a shattering effect. Couldn't a man count on anything any more? Next they would be discovering that aspirin doesn't kill pain, nor coffee keep you awake. It was, as W. H. Auden had noted before it had fairly begun, an age of anxiety.

As to drinking, a study resulted in the conclusions that between 1946 and 1964 the percentage of regular drinkers in the adult population rose sharply, and that the amount of rise was directly proportional to income level. As against a nationwide drinking figure of 71 percent in 1964, the findings were that 89 percent of college-educated persons, 87 percent of those with incomes above $10,000, and 100 percent of the study's sample of dentists, lawyers, judges, and physicians were drinkers. And what with the rise in popularity of the lethal Martini, it can hardly be disputed that the national trend was toward stronger wine as well as more. Stories of revelry in the club car of the afternoon commuter train became folklore. In 1963 the folklore achieved its epic. Three men were arrested in Stamford, Connecticut, for extortion on the charge that they had ridden the New York commuter trains regularly, kept systematic count of the Martinis consumed by each rider, and then threatened to report their findings to wives and employers unless they were paid off.

4

It is an outdoor style of life. In the 1939 Sears catalogue, garden furniture was skimped in a couple of pages, "shorts" for men meant underwear or athletic equipment and nothing else, and the only sun preparations mentioned were for the relief of accidental sun*burn* rather than the promoting of sun*tan*. Except for specified occasions, in the middle-class family outdoors was still chiefly for children; the adults remained firmly inside, or ventured out to what was called the "glider" on what was called the "porch." I am exaggerating, of course —the bohemian wing of the middle class already had its beloved pools and patios in 1939—but in a general way the middle-class move outdoors over the past quarter-century, the consequences of which I find myself unable to decide on with any assurance, can hardly be exaggerated. And it is a change that has been reflected in house design and interior decoration. The much-maligned picture window surely indicates not so much a desire to contemplate the other picture window across the street as a desire to get away from the dark, enclosed, small-windowed rooms of an earlier America, built that way to keep out the North American continent's bitter cold in winter.

Parenthetically, ours is a style of life that has brought with it not only record-breaking profits for the manufacturers of plate glass but also new hazards for the middle class. The American Medical Association reported in 1963 that an estimated forty thousand people a year "try to walk through glass doors, glass walls and picture windows," and that almost six thousand of them wind up in the hospital. "The usual injuries are severe lacerations of the arm, hand, or wrist, and disfiguring facial cuts are not uncommon," *Consumer Reports* said. "Less frequently, arteries may be severed, leading sometimes to massive hemorrhaging and death." O pioneers!

It is a style of life without permanent domestic help. The live-in "couple," or even the single full-time maid, was far from a fixture of middle-class life during the depression, but was a common enough feature so that Bell Wiley, in a marriage manual aimed at the middle class of 1938, could write: "Once you have a child the situation alters. You can still get along without a maid, and if you do so I admire you for it. But you would be justified in having one." In short, the problem as Miss Wiley saw it was not economic but moral: must the young mother show her fiber and liberalism by going it alone, or may she forego solidarity with the proletariat in the interest of family comfort? She did not need to agonize for long; wartime and postwar industrial jobs and wages were soon to remove the moral dilemma by putting the price of full-time help beyond the means of all but the rich. The number of women born before 1910 who learned to cook for the first time in their lives after 1939 must be astonishingly large—and I must say that in my observation they have become excellent cooks, perhaps because they attacked cooking in relative maturity as an art or as a lark rather than in adolescence as a chore.

Living-in maids, the Census Bureau tells us, declined from over 200,000 in 1950 to under 160,000 in 1960; meanwhile, living-out female household workers increased from 1.2 million to 1.6 million, reflecting chiefly the rise of the baby-sitter, so integral a part of present-day middle-class life that omission of mention of her (or him) in such a discussion would be thoroughly improper. (Certainly there are millions of teen-age regular or occasional baby-sitters who do not appear in the census figures.) Interfamily feuds arise out of competition for baby-sitters; their unavailability has become the standard dodge of parents for ducking unattractive social engagements; and in the 1950s Lou Little, coach of the Columbia football team, publicly offered his players as baby-sitters on evenings other than those preceding important games. In 1939 the very term "baby-sitter" was not yet in any dictionary.

The rapid disappearance of the full-time maid from middle-class life has, of course, been met by the proliferation of labor-saving household devices, which are so expensive and so prone to break-down, become so quickly obsolete, and are financed at such high interest rates that they may well be relatively as great a burden on the breadwinner as were the low wages of human workers under the old regime. But surely most of us would agree that the decline of domestic service as a lifework for Americans is a healthy national phenomenon. What is beyond question is that the decline has been a big factor in the change to more informal family life. If life *must* be informal, the middle class has decided practically, then let's make a virtue of necessity. In 1939 the coat and tie at home for the head of the middle-class family were still in vogue, even in hot weather, for the good reason that the open-necked, short-sleeved shirt to many people was still a badge of the manual worker. Or consider blue jeans. In 1939 they were worn chiefly by cowboys, laborers, and children at play; in 1965 150 million pairs of them were sold in the United States for wear by men, women, and children, and titles of fifty American songs began with the words "blue jeans," and Bing Crosby had a pair converted into the pants for a Tuxedo. A round young female rear tightly enclosed in a well-patched pair is one of the most familiar and stimulating of contemporary American sights.

The household furniture shown in the 1939 Sears catalogue ran to the oppressively overstuffed; bent wood made only a small, tentative appearance, and wrought-iron no appearance at all. Bell Wiley advised, not without irony, that in the kitchen "you must hide everything that looks like a utensil." The living room with bare hardwood floor, sling chairs, and a high-fi set with all the works showing, and the kitchen with all its brass pots and gadgets in serried ranks assembled, belonged to the future.

Almost everything about interior furniture has gone through an about-face, the lounging chair perhaps most dramatically. Formerly we had masses of comfortable-looking stuffed ones that were intended to be sat on decorously; now we have spare, angular-looking shapes of iron, cloth, and plastic that are intended to be sprawled in. The national posture at home has become deplorable by former standards—what modern parent ventures to deliver the standard admonition of a generation ago, "Sit up straight"?—and the prevalence of the slipped disc may be directly related. One commentator, Sylvia Wright, claims to find cultural importance in the relaxation of our posture standards, and argues that certain bizarre phenomena of the Twenties and Thirties like flagpole-sitting and marathon dancing reflected postural malaise and symbolic revolt against the social pressure to sit straight. Siegfried Giedion declares that "posture reflects the inner nature of a period." Whether the present middle-class tendency to sprawl reflects a revolt against authority or a wish to lie down and accept authority is a question beyond this layman's purview.

It is, notoriously, a child-centered way of life. The 1939 survey that I cited earlier showed that in most middle-class families parents took joint responsibility for the upbringing of their children; now the basic terms of the family compact have changed so radically the very question thus framed sounds quaint, and it seems more apposite to ask whether parents assume joint responsibility for the *acts* of their children. Parents scarcely bring up children now; they finance them. (Of the Harvard '39 fathers reporting in 1964, 6 percent said their main problem in handling their children was moral values, and 78 percent said money.) Children seem to be born believing that they enjoy full equal rights with their parents, and our society encourages —very nearly compels—them to retain that belief. The ostensible reason for the move to the suburbs in the first place is usually "for the sake of the children."

Life with Father, the famous Lindsay-Crouse play that began its long Broadway run in 1939, was the last gasp of the Victorian father who eats lamb chops while the rest of the family settles for stew, and rules his roost like a pasha. True enough, *Life with Father* was a satirical and nostalgic sketch of an era already past, but in 1939 it contained elements of contemporary truth, too. As Phyllis Lee Levin has pointed out, the "television father" of the 1960s stands in stark contrast. The attitude of Mr. Anderson in the sarcastically titled *Fa-*

ther Knows Best toward the eccentric adventures of his offspring was: "Let's keep out of it and see what happens." Uncle Bentley in *Bachelor Father* was eternally flummoxed by his niece and brow-beaten by his houseboy, while the helpless and bewildered nonhero of *Make Room for Daddy* abdicated responsibility to his wife because she "talks the loudest." Yet children, at least in the findings of a University of Illinois study, actually crave paternal authority: they want their fathers to be moral, calm, relaxed, strong, decisive, consistent, predictable, strict, and not to spoil them—or so they say to the pollsters. And perhaps the form of their response—complaint—is more revealing than its content.

Through whosever fault—parents', children's, or society's—the process of "bringing up" children has become more an entertainment for which one pays (dearly) than the responsibility to be discharged that it used to be. In such circumstances, small wonder that there have been organized attempts to make the community itself into a firm parent through teen-age codes of conduct. The writing of such codes has been spreading across the country since about 1960; they are entirely voluntary and unconnected with local law, their enforcement is left up to individual parents, and their effectiveness is in dispute. Their provisions, in their early years, varied quite widely from place to place. A Columbus, Georgia, code discouraged friendship rings and other symbols of sexual possessiveness. One in Maryland condemned party-crashing and decreed that "going steady" was permissible only when practiced through double or group dating, while one in Houston forbade car ownership before the age of eighteen unless transportation to a job was involved. What the codes indicate clearly enough is a move in the direction of the community child-rearing advocated long ago by Plato and practiced with modifications in the kibbutzim of Israel. One wonders whether the harassed parents who abdicate to codes always realize the implications in terms of the individualism they are nominally committed to.

It is accused of being a style of life that encourages sexual infidelity. Is it really? Here statistics are bound to fail us, despite the conscientious (and maybe a bit humorless) efforts of Dr. Kinsey and his associates. Certainly the changing circumstances of middle-class business life—the home farther and farther from the office as the suburbs push out, the commuter railroad harder and harder to face of an evening as its deficit rises and its service declines, the business trips to other cities (with female colleagues going along, in some instances) more and more frequent, the spare pocket money more and more available, the girls in the office more and more seductive as technology cranks out new packaged beauty aids—put temptation continually in the way of the commuting husband. And meanwhile, there is plenty of evidence that his personal morality and cultural environment do less and less to persuade him to resist that temptation.

No foundation study is needed to establish that community authority in general and the management of places of accommodation like hotels (and motels!) in particular are less censorious of extramarital sex than they used to be. In our teeming and boiling society, cops and room clerks have other things to worry about. (What, I wonder, was the last American novel in which a girl, on checking in at a hotel, turned a ring on her finger to make it look like a wedding band, and then, on reaching a room, said to her lover, "I feel dirty"?) On another level, the anthropologist Margaret Mead has said that marital infidelity is rooted in our culture because of our commitment to freedom of choice in other matters such as jobs, places to live, and political parties. Perhaps; but not Cressida nor Don Juan nor Emma Bovary seemed to need either commuting life or a culture committed to freedom of choice as a precondition for infidelity.

5

It is a style of life marked by mobility, often enforced but usually welcomed, too. The "mobile home" may not really be much more mobile than a tree once it has been firmly planted, but its name has symbolic importance. Its occupants, like those of the mass-produced split-level, assuredly *are* mobile, from city to city as the company goes through its ritual procedure of transferring the young executive to broaden his scope, from the suburb to the cottage at the beach for weekends and summers (in 1965 there were some two million "second homes"), to the superhighway for the vacation trip. I am not much impressed by all the talk about "the new leisure," at least as far as the middle class is concerned; it seems to me that one way or another most of us during our working years are busier than our fathers were, and, far from finding time hanging heavy on our hands, have more trouble than ever fitting in the things we want most to do. We spend so much of our time simply going from one place to another, not like rats running on a treadmill but like ants hurrying from place to place because they are ants and have legs.

The old American restlessness has taken naturally to cars, jet planes, and long commutation. A novelist trying to capture the flavor of a segment of American life in the 1950s called his book simply *Go*, and another called his *On the Road*. We swarm over the Champs Élysées and Saint-Germain-des-Pres in July, evoking pitying stares from the natives, damaging our national monetary position, and turning these places temporarily into parts of America. We also swarm over our own once exclusive resorts, littering them with used paper cups and cigar bands and homogenizing out of them their old snobbery and also a good deal of their old flavor. Sun Valley, built in 1936 for the rich and used in its early days as a sort of junior Olympus for the gods and goddesses of Hollywood, has fought social change with a will—and has lost the battle. In 1938 the family trade could peek through the keyhole at this earthly paradise in a movie with Sonja Henie called *Sun Valley Serenade;* in the Fifties and Sixties the family trade went there in person. "We had a good group," an old-time Sun Valley patron reminisced recently for the *New York Times*. "The Ray Millands, the Gary Coopers . . . Evie and Van Johnson. Our pet ski instructors were always welcome, but anyone else got frozen out fast." The gambling house in nearby Ketchum went out in 1948; the casino has become a supermarket. The boiler room at the Sun Valley lodge has been prettified and become The Boiler Room, where mobs dance to a steel band. Nobody gets frozen out.

Language always participates in social change, and certain favorite middle-class words have undergone striking alterations in nuance of meaning since before the war. Russell Lynes has noted how the word "lady" has through most of American history been used indiscriminately as an honorific, or simply a factual, term for any adult female; only in recent years, I think, has the word taken on in the minds of millions an unpleasant overtone of fake elegance, of mincing euphemism. Lynes notes that listings under "Ladies" still outnumber those under "Women" two to one in the Manhattan telephone book, but this seems to represent social lag. He also points out that we have dropped "common" and "vulgar" in the sense of "uncouth." Well we might; to be uncouth is no longer so very common, or vulgar either! The list could be expanded. "Wealthy," now that it describes a condition so much more . . . well, common, has lost its former connotation of elegance, and is eschewed in many middle-class circles for the blunter "rich." Our halting approach to candor in speaking of sexual matters in "polite" (a vanishing word itself) circles is perhaps reflected in the fact that one would now hesitate to speak of having relations in Duluth if one wished to convey that one's aunt and uncle lived there.

Finally, it is a style of life beleaguered by all sorts of moral dilemmas that caused no trouble in 1939. Mention the subject of "natural childbirth" at almost any middle-class dinner party, and what happens? Within five minutes the young mothers present will be at each others' throats on the question of whether giving birth without the help of anesthesia is participation in a great experience or an act of contemptible masochism. Barely hint to well-off urban parents that they are contributing to the decline of the public schools by sending their children to private ones, and the fat will be in the fire. Nor do suburbanites lack for up-to-the-moment worries: a church in Old Greenwich, Connecticut, not long ago conducted a well-attended symposium of its parishioners on the subject of "overcoming guilt about having deserted the urban core." And consider the woes of a couple in Rockland County who decided to build a swimming pool. All through the months that it was under construction, they found themselves being progressively ostracized, even by their best friends. They persevered, until at last the pool was finished, filled, and put into service—and everyone smiled at them again. Now it could be told what had been the matter: word had gone around that the construction was not a swimming pool at all, that they had been committing the utimate gaffe of secretly building a fallout shelter.

Other times, other agonies, big and little.

6

What is to be made of all this largely familiar but all too true material? The temptation is overwhelming to assume that the middle class's approach to universality somehow implies an approach to homogeniety—that the members of the huge new middle class are as like each other as were the members of the quite small old one, and that therefore, by logical extension, most Americans are alike. The fact is that the new middle class is a hotbed of cultural and ideological differences and disputes, and that their number and intensity are increasing in proportion to the group's size.

Politically, the middle class has no party. Its traditional affiliation with the Republicans had been severed well before 1939—to be specific, in 1932, as a result of the crash and the depression. The Democrats, aided by hard times, war, and postwar prosperity, held it fairly well in line for twenty years after that, but then it got too big and too prosperous for them to hang onto any longer; and the subsequent eight-year hegemony of the Republicans was based largely on the personality of a single man, Eisenhower. The middle class was overwhelmingly Republican in 1956 and overwhelmingly Democratic in 1964. Its chief political characteristics now seem to be its independence of parties and its tendency to vote on men rather than on issues. Of course, it can be argued that these characteristics really reflect homogeneity, since the issues between the two main parties are usually not nearly so clear-cut now as they were in the 1930s. But surely this cannot be said of the savage fight in the early 1950s over McCarthyism—a fight that was very largely a middle-class affair.

I do not intend here to give McCarthyism anything like the attention it would deserve in a chronological history of the past quarter-century, because it seems to me to have been a transient eruption of the authoritarian and anti-intellectual tendencies that have always existed just under the surface of American life, rather than a manifestation of social change. The episode showed, however painfully, that we can still lick such tendencies when we have to. What I do want to suggest is that, as Senator McCarthy himself broadly hinted in a few unguarded moments, the fight was not really about the menace of Communism at all, but rather about the deep gulf of suspicion, distrust, and even hatred between various segments of the middle class—on the one hand, a coalition of the intellectual, the civic-minded, and socially assured, and the academic forces, concentrated in but by no means confined to the East and West Coasts and the university centers—and, on the other hand, a coalition of the rural, the less-educated, and the more recently recruited members of the midle class regardless of place of residence.

There was really no economic issue; members of the rich, the near-rich, the well-off, and the struggling were to be found on both sides. In retrospect the quarrel seems to have been about an issue so long established in American life that it was a main theme in Mark Twain's work, and considered so disreputable, not to say childish, in modern society that it had to be kept covert: that is, the question of whether anyone is better than anyone else by virtue of education. And what a quarrel it was—precisely because this issue is a generally unacknowledged sore point, a disreputable social disease, of the new middle class. From the heyday of European immigration through the boom of the Twenties, there was a strong consensus in favor of the idea that education conferred automatic superiority. Then the reform movement of the Thirties, with its idealization of the untutored manual worker, almost reversed the consensus; and the immediate legacy of the vastly increased availability of education in the postwar years was this outbreak of envy on one side and scorn on the other. If everyone was to be somebody, to paraphrase *The Gondoliers,* then who would be anybody? Communism, demogoguery, trial-by-smear were and are real issues—but the McCarthy fight was, I suggest, at bottom less abstract.

Nor has the rise of the middle class ended regional differences. The scope of this book requires that, for the most part, the country be treated as a whole; another series of books could surely be written about the changes since 1939 within specific regions—the South, for example, or the Southwest. My point here is that the old, slyly expressed hostilities between the regions have changed surprisingly little, and where they have changed, it has usually been in the direction of divergence rather than concurrence. The Texan, notoriously, is more Texan now than ever—and especially when he finds a foil in somebody from the "effete East." The Nevadan, with his sense of open space combined with a feeling of being federally hemmed in that stems from the fact that the national government owns the lion's share of his state's land, has a difficult time agreeing on anything with a fellow member of the middle class (or the Republican or Democratic Party) from a crowded industrial state like New Jersey or Pennsylvania. The Chicago businessman is still as anxious as ever to convince you that in no sense but population is his bailiwick "the second city" to New York. The Colorado gas-station attendant still looks pityingly at the misguided owner of a malfunctioning foreign car with a New York license plate (although the Volkswagen is an exception—for some reason, it is socially acceptable to mechanics from coast to coast).

And, of course, a common economic status has done nothing at all to dampen the progressive exacerbation of differences on the race issue between the middle classes of North and South. In college just before World War II, I recall, and in the services during it, white Northerners and Southerners who became close friends as a result of being thrown together often maintained their relationships by simply avoiding the subject of race, or by touching on it only in jest. In the early 1960s it was a good deal more difficult to do that; the nicknames "Yankee" and "Rebel" cannot now be considered so gay and carefree as they were then.

The middle class has not come to *feel* like a class; its growth up to now has not brought to it the slightest sense of identity or solidarity on a national level. And not only regionalism divides it. Social differences based on family and community tradition sometimes appear to become firmer as economic differences disappear. We fight against homogeneity with a tenacity so great that it seems to stem from a national instinct.

For a couple of decades I have spent part of every year living at an East Coast summer resort. Rather, it has become a summer resort; when I moved there it was primarily a light manufacturing town beyond New York City commuting range, dominated by a small but strong business and professional middle class with a rich sense of the local past. At first the "summer people," with their quaint city ways, were accepted without question as amusing eccentrics who were good for local commerce. As the newcomers' numbers increased, two things began to happen: the local middle class began to enlarge, partly because of the influx of city money, and its social relations with the city people began to deteriorate. Jokes about summer people's oddities became local staples. First covertly and then less so, some local stores maintained two price scales, one for locals and one for summer people. New distinctions of almost theological nicety began to appear: if summer people stayed for the winter, far from becoming ordinary residents, they found themselves "year-round summer people." Some of this new-found reserve, certainly, stemmed from direct political competition—a few of the summer people had been trying to move in and run things—but for the most part, I feel sure, it stemmed from the local people's fierce drive, often perhaps unconscious, to save themselves from being absorbed into a faceless and colorless mass. They wanted to have their affluence and keep their pawkiness—and to a great extent they seemed to be succeeding.

Even in suburbia, the heartland of middle-class conformity, a constant rear-guard action goes on. There are always the husbands who deliberately let their lawns go to crab grass, there are always the wives who discourage the invasion of their privacy by unannounced callers; and if these people jeopardize their popularity by their unorthodoxy, they are willing to pay the price. I am convinced that comparatively few suburbanites are any longer able to feel committed to suburbia as a way of life. The national preoccupation with middle-class conformity that began in the mid-Fifties has been to some extent a self-correcting phenomenon. A reader who feels that he just can't face one more treatise on the subject may perhaps take comfort from the thought that every description of American conformity helps make it less true.

7

The greatest split within the middle class is between white-collar and blue-collar. It has become popular to assume the contrary; the U.S. Department of Labor itself asserted in 1959 that "the wage earner's way of life is well-nigh indistinguishable from that of his salaried co-citizens. Their homes, their cars, their baby-sitters, the style of the clothes their wives wear, the food they eat, the bank where they establish credit . . . are alike and are becoming more nearly identical." But this view—an appealing one, surely, with its democratic implications—is coming to be looked upon by many observers as largely a myth.

Dr. Mirra Komarovsky of Barnard College, reporting in 1964 on a study of sixty working-class married couples, said that she had found the entry of skilled and semiskilled workers into the economic middle class to have been rather strikingly unaccompanied by adoption of middle-class manners and tastes. The physical surroundings of her subjects were middle-class enough—pleasant if modest houses duly equipped with modern furniture, washing machines, and television sets—but their values and attitudes Dr. Komarovsky found "reminiscent of the past" and reflecting a life "insulated from contemporary currents of thought." For example, in bringing up their children they relied for guidance certainly not on Freud and generally not on Dr. Benjamin Spock either, but on the methods used by their grandmothers. Their social life was confined to two or three other couples. The wives did not expect the husbands to help with household chores, nor did they expect to be invited along when the husbands went out of an evening. "As the interviews progressed," wrote Dr. Komarovsky, "I felt further and further removed from the world of the Twentieth Century. . . . From all appearances, the working-class style of life—its values, attitudes, institutions—remains in many respects quite distinct from the dominant . . . patterns of contemporary American society."

All sorts of trivial but telling habits of life can be cited as pointing the contrast. Let us imagine for a moment two families, each consisting of a couple in their late twenties and two or three small children, living side by side in one of the longer-established and therefore more heterogeneous suburbs. Mr. White is a white-collar man—an employee of a book publishing firm, say—and the Whites live in a rambling old house from the 1920s that they picked up for practically nothing when it was on the verge of falling to pieces and have diligently "done over," almost entirely with their own hands. Mr. Blue next door is a garage mechanic, and his house is a small, trim rancher less than five years old. Mrs. White buys her clothes in the city, scanning the sales and discount stores for copies of Paris fashions; the local dress shop is good enough for Mrs. Blue. The Blues' lawn looks like a putting green, and Mr. Blue manicures it regularly with a sit-down power mower, even though it covers only a quarter-acre; the Whites' lawn is studded with gray spots and weeds, and when Mr. White gets around to cutting it, he does so with a hand-pushed machine. (He does this job wearing Madras shorts, which Blue wouldn't be caught dead in.) The Blue car is a three-year-old Chevrolet, the White car is a timeless Volkswagen.

Both families consume alcohol moderately but in totally different patterns: the Whites have a cocktail or two daily, with some ceremony, often outdoors in full view of the neighbors, and they discuss their drinking freely, while the Blues abstain through the week except for Mr. Blue's occasional beer for TV-watching, and on Saturday night they sometimes get moderately drunk on boilermakers, behind drawn blinds, with a certain furtiveness. The Blues flaunt their knowingness about TV program characters; as for the Whites, TV-watching is the thing *they* do furtively. The Blues shout to each other, from room to room of their house or from corner to corner of their lot, without self-consciousness; the Whites modulate their voices to the point where they sometimes can't hear each other. When her children were under two years old Mrs. White sometimes let them play naked in the backyard wading pool, a practice that moved the Blues to ill-suppressed titters, though not to outrage.

The Whites, naturally enough, have many books, and, indeed, use books as the main decorative motif of their living room; the Blues haven't a book in the house, and even the occasional ones that Mr. White presses on them as a gift soon disappear mysteriously. Once every two years the Whites pay off their social debts by having a fairly large outdoor cocktail party; the Blues, pretending with elaborate politeness to be otherwise engaged in their own backyard, watch over the hedge with tolerant amusement. Here, in sum, are two families with hardly anything in common except their citizenship, yet their respective family incomes are practically identical, in the neighborhood of $8,000 a year. They share, in fact, inarguable membership in the middle class.

It is true that Mr. White's *expectations* of income are far higher than Mr. Blue's and that those expectations along with his different education and background, color his whole view of his life. The blue-collar man has expectations, too, but they are largely illusory—and, perhaps sadly for him, he halfway knows it. The sociologist Ely Chinoy found the automobile production-line workers of the 1950s to be firm believers in the traditional American idea of "getting ahead." They told themselves that eventually they would get out of "the shop" and go on to something that would pay better; the fact that they seldom did this they attributed not to their stars but to themselves. "I guess I'm just not smart enough," one of them told Mr. Chinoy. "Sometimes I look at myself in the mirror and I say to myself, 'Pat, you dumb so-and-so, you could have been somebody if you'd only set your mind to it.' "

8

The kind of "getting ahead" that most blue-collar workers have settled for in the postwar world has consisted of receiving more money for the same work or less work, as a result of a rapidly rising wage scale, brought about by general prosperity in conjunction with the effective efforts of the unions. And how the unions have changed in the process of becoming so successful!

In 1939, although not yet anywhere nearly so powerful as they were to become, they were, in a sense, in their glory. The great organizing drives of the depression years—made possible in large part by the passage in 1935 of the National Labor Relations Act, which gave unionism official status in our national life—had pushed up union membership from under three million in 1933 to almost nine million in 1939. But as significant as the numbers was the *élan*. Capitalistic company management, the working man could still legitimately assume, was the enemy. Didn't it still often use finks to spy on the union and goons to break the heads of pickets? Hadn't it been only two years ago, in May of 1937, that at the infamous Battle of the Overpass at River Rouge, Harry Bennett's army of Ford Motor Company antiunion hoodlums had set upon unarmed union organizers, breaking one man's back and brutally kicking and mauling the fallen bodies of many others, including some women? Against this enemy, the union was the worker's shield and buckler. "You can't scare me, I'm stickin' to the union," the popular labor song of the time went. The formation of the CIO in 1938 had crystallized the trend of the labor movement toward militant, politically oriented industrial unionism and away from the traditional small-shop trade unionism. Unionism, in short, was a social and moral force. The production-line worker didn't dream of having the right to get spiritual satisfaction from his job; apart from his religion, he expected to get that from the union.

The next two decades were to see the really big growth of the labor movement—and its spiritual decline. First the necessity for war production brought enormous increases in the sheer numbers of blue-collar workers eligible for union membership, and then the postwar consumer-goods boom extended the process. Labor had its problems through this period—the factional disputes of the Thirties expanded into epic struggles within unions against domination by Communists or gangsters, and the Taft-Hartley Act of 1947 weakened labor's hand in several ways—but union membership and its concomitant, union power, went on increasing at breakneck speed. By 1945 union membership nationally was up to 14.8 million, and in 1956 it stood at about 18.5 million. There it leveled off, and a bit later began to turn downward. Between 1960 and 1962, unions suffered a net loss of nearly half a million members; between 1955 and 1962 the proportion of the total labor force that belonged to unions decreased from 24.4 to 22.2 percent. Such an old friend of labor as Murray Kempton began to speak of the twilight of the American labor movement.

And figures do not begin to tell the story of the reversal; in fact, the decline of unionism *as an idea* had been going on long before the number of members had turned downward. Seen in hindsight, the decline had begun as early as during wartime, when unions, for good or ill, had tended to drop their social and political goals, their dream of remolding an America nearer to their hearts' desire, to concentrate exclusively on "market unionism"—getting more pay for less work. In the postwar period they continued this policy, with superb effectiveness. But in the process they became, to the rank-and-file member, merely an enormous bargaining agent with whom he felt not much more identity than he did with the corporation itself.

How did labor come to lose so much of its soul? By its success in bargaining with the Devil, an old-fashioned moralist might say. But there is more to it than that. For one thing, part of the process has been a tendency of the Devil to become less and less devilish: while the corporations grew fat, as we have seen, they tended to become more bland and benevolent; management goons and spies largely vanished from the scene, and many postwar pay raises were granted almost voluntarily, not so much in concession to union power as out of concern about the company's "image" and the desire to create new potential customers.

The labor authority Solomon Barkin insists that union militancy is not dead, and he cites how in 1959 the whole labor movement rallied to the support of the steelworkers in their strike. He attributes the numerical decline of union membership largely to such factors as the shrinkage of employment, brought about by automation, in well-organized industries; the tendency of industry to move its plants from the East and Midwest, where unions have been strong, to the South, where they have not; and the loss of interest in unionism on the part of white-collar workers.

Again, there is, I believe, more to it than that. Part of it has to do with the union member's relationship with his leaders. In the old days those leaders were young, fiery, underpaid, ascetic, radical—

a surprising number of them were Marxists of one sort or another—and intellectual. Nowadays, whether they are the same men twenty-five years later or different men, they are inclined to be old, highly paid, high-living, often self-seeking, public-relations-conscious, politically neuter, unintellectual—taking on, as Daniel Bell has said, "the grossest features of a business society." In 1965 the twenty-nine-man executive council of the nation's great labor-union organization, the AFL-CIO, included fifteen men over sixty-five years old, nine over seventy, and one over eighty. Most of the serious intellectuals had long since deserted the labor movement; Herbert Hill has written, "Ever since World War II, it has been estranging the people who produce, distribute, and conspicuously consume ideas. . . . Many of them no longer regard the labor movement as protector of the underdog."

It is significant that the great issue of the United Steelworkers of America's 1965 presidential election was the alleged "Tuxedo unionism" of the incumbent of many years, David J. McDonald—a man who, his opponent maintained (and won by doing so), had become fonder of associating with big-business executives and government officials at "Twenty-One" or the Stork Club than meeting with rank-and-file members in union halls. If their leader was so much like a company president, how were the hard-hat men to make of him a champion of the oppressed, much less a prophet? Again significantly, McDonald had not always been like that; the son of a poor Welsh steelworker and pioneer of militant unionism, he was a night-school college graduate who had made his own way in the world. The modern union leader, as Hill has written, is "the Siamese twin of the versatile entrepreneur who has built the business from scratch." One might add that he is the ironic embodiment of the old capitalist dream of the self-made man.

And there is perhaps another reason for this drastic loss of spiritual commitment of blue-collar union members to their unions. Television, movies, magazines—the whole world of what is grossly called mass communications, changes in which I mean to consider next—have sold him a bill of goods: he belongs to the middle class now, by the unimpeachable evidence of his weekly pay check, his quasi possessions, his installment-buying contracts, so he should believe in middle-class ideals, which assuredly do not include the ambition to belong to an embattled working class. "If one can pay one's bills and meet the installments on the house, the car, or a new refrigerator and still save a little money, then one is moving forward," Chinoy comments of the automobile workers. "[They] have to a large extent retained the form but lost the substance of the American tradition of opportunity." Indeed, they hew to the form far more now than they did in 1939, when it was still an estate of honor and perhaps of nobility to be a "working stiff," or even—to use a word now gone from American life—a proletarian.

So in officially joining the middle class the blue-collar man has largely kept his cultural style, gained in material comforts, and lost his ideological fire—and with the last, one fears, some of his self-respect.

VI. "PLEASURES OF A KIND"

1

The most striking thing about the arrival of television on the American scene was certainly the almost apocalyptic suddenness with which it became a fully established part of our national life, complete with a huge audience and an established minority opposition, affecting not only all our other communications media and the whole world of our popular arts but also our manners, morals, habits, ways of thinking. By comparison, the much chronicled automobile revolution earlier in the century had been positively Fabian in its gradualness.

To use the product of the first change as a metaphor for the second: like a racing car revved up, thrown into gear, and then held back by brakes until the signal for the start of the race, TV (as it seems to have been called by universal consent from the very first, although the words "radio" and "phonograph," scarcely shorter than "television," have never been thought worth reducing) was primed by circumstances to get away from the mark fast. As we have seen, its technical development was virtually completed in the 1930s; then its commercial exploitation was held back for an extended period, first by the war, later by the postwar economic reconversion and governmental delay in assigning channels and licenses. As late as 1948 there were still fewer than twenty TV stations on the air, and only 172,000 families had receiving sets. Then the explosion began. During 1949 and 1950 sets were installed at a rate sometimes as high as a quarter of a million a month. In June, 1950, there were more than one hundred stations operating in thirty-eight states; coaxial cable, the device by which reception is extended beyond a station's normal range and network broadcasting is made possible, reached along the East Coast from Boston to Richmond, and westward as far as Milwaukee and St. Louis; and the census of that year found five million families with TV sets in the house.

All the figures were, of course, to be vastly increased in the subsequent years. But the extent to which TV had "arrived" in 1950 may be judged from the fact that people were already making surveys of its prevalence and pundits were already deploring its possibly pernicious influence on the young. And some of the figures in the surveys are so high as to seem scarcely credible. One 1950 study, for example, reported that some junior high school pupils were spending twenty-seven hours a week watching TV, while the national *average* for children aged seven to seventeen who lived in homes that had TV was three hours a day. And all to look, much of the time, at rigged wrestling matches, the stand-bys of the little screen in those early days.

What happened next is already history. Set ownership rose at a rate of roughly five million a year during the 1950s. Here, surely, was something totally unprecedented in world history. Neither in this nation nor in any other had anything like five million families per year ever acquired for the first time any wholly new thing of any sort. (Radio at the height of its growth had added about two million American families per year to its audience.) The combination of technology and affluence had achieved a kind of miracle, however equivocal. By 1962 nine-tenths of all households had at least one set, and 13 percent had more than one set in the house. We have already seen how dramatically the TV advertising expenditures of American manufacturers rose in response to this fantastically broadening audience. At no time during this period does there seem to have been a trace of the prewar skepticism about TV's commercial success.

Everyone accepted the idea that it was *the* new medium, while as to its cultural potentialities, it was hailed almost daily by some commentator or other as the most promising and important technological advance since the invention of printing.

One recalls the excitement with which the residents of remote Western communities greeted the arrival of the first coaxial cable that would bring the wonders of New York—and, eventually, of Hollywood—into their living rooms. The contrast points up the reversal in our national attitude toward change, and particularly technological change, that had taken place since the war. In 1939 change was something to be looked upon skeptically, even fearfully, since it could demonstrably bring disaster as well as progress; now it was welcomed without question or reservation, for its own sake.

Nor did television ownership begin at the top of the economic scale and filter downward. There was never even a fleeting moment when TV was the plaything of the rich. Nearly all sets cost $150 or more in the early years and, for obvious reasons, it was some time before used ones at low prices became plentiful; nevertheless, the poor man was as ready to go into hock for this new thing as he was for a car. Max Lerner has said that TV is "the poor man's luxury because it is his psychological necessity," and undoubtedly Lerner is right, difficult as it is to conceive of something previously nonexistent becoming a psychological necessity the moment it arrives on the scene. Television seems to have filled a gaping void by offering solace to American loneliness. The remotely situated farmer could hear bright voices and see bright faces from far away; 3 percent of rural households had TV in 1950, and 80 percent in 1960. But the poor family in the city seemed to need such solace, too; forests of antennas sprang up over the slums as soon as they appeared over the farms and suburbs.

There were moments in the late Fifties, when television had become all-pervasive and yet still retained the sheen of a new toy, when it seemed almost to bring our national life to a halt. The year 1954 saw the "TV dinner" make its appearance; it also saw the city of Toledo make the astonishing discovery that water consumption rose startlingly during certain three-minute periods that turned out to be the time of commercials during popular programs. In a small town that I know, at certain hours no one was to be seen in the streets; the stores and restaurants were almost deserted, and a strange hush fell; and even a telephone call was generally answered curtly and with ill grace. No one could be very much surprised at the results of a national survey made by Westinghouse Electric shortly after the beginning of the 1960s. More man-hours per year in the United States, Westinghouse found, were being spent watching TV than were spent working for pay.

The one laggard group about admitting the new wonder into the house was not economic but social—the academics and urban intellectuals. For a few years many such persons resisted TV entirely without too much difficulty, and one was even able to imagine that it would become permanently a pure "mass" phenomenon, like comic books, ignored or misunderstood by the teachers and opinion-makers because they simply were not exposed to it. But that possibility soon vanished. More and more during the early 1950s, one began to hear teachers or intellectuals saying, a little sheepishly or defensively, "We have one but we never turn it on," or, "We got it to take the kids off our hands at cocktail time." Some were convinced by individual events; the Kefauver crime hearings undoubtedly made hundreds of thousands of converts, the political conventions of 1952 and 1956 and, of course, the celebrated Army-McCarthy hearings many more. Gradually the area of resistance narrowed until it approached the vanishing point; I have heard only one person speak of missing the events following the assassination of President Kennedy because of not owning a set. "Just because they don't have TV doesn't automatically make them intellectual," ran the caption of a 1965 *New Yorker* cartoon—nor could it by any means be said then that possession of a set meant nonmembership in egghead ranks. Let us look a last time at those 1939 Harvard graduates—hardly a solid block of intellectuals, but a good cross-section of the well-educated upper-middle class. In 1964 92.5 percent of them reported that their families had at least one TV set, 13 percent of them said they had three or more sets, and two men admitted to six! Clearly, the opinion-makers have joined the TV audience.

Almost as sudden as the arrival of TV was the emergence of

the critical counterattack. (And it's worth noting here that being critical of TV does not necessarily imply not watching it constantly or even not enjoying watching it. One highbrow wit twitted another in the 1950s by saying that his taste for corny popular culture, though "largely negative," was nonetheless "genuine.") As I have said, pronouncements viewing with alarm TV's possibly deleterious effects were being made as early as 1950, and in 1961, when Federal Communications Commissioner Newton Minow delivered the celebrated speech in which he called TV programs "a vast wasteland," his words were only the first major government endorsement of a view that had been widely held and expressed for a decade.

In particular, the attacks had been, and continue to be, focused on the effects on children, an audience so numerous and so devoted that some TV men say they constitute, collectively, a virtual tyranny dictating the timing and nature of programming. Does the child whose TV-watching is unrestrained parentally, and who sits mesmerized in front of the screen twenty or thirty hours a week, suffer any lasting effects from the experience? Are the eyes damaged? Does the violence of the programs predispose to a life of crime? Does the passivity of the act of watching damage initiative? While none of these charges has been definitely proved, none has been definitely proved false. A report to the American Academy of Pediatrics in the fall of 1964 declared that excessive television watching can lead to a specific physical sickness—the "tired-child syndrome," characterized by fatigue, headache, loss of appetite, and vomiting, and curable only by abstinence from television. Nor is excessive exposure to such hazards an exclusively American phenomenon; a United Nations study published in 1965 showed that childhood TV-watching habits in Japan and England are about the same as they are here.

2

Television is here, and here to stay; like fire, it is better as servant than as master, and sometimes one wishes that the bringers of television, like the bringer of fire in the Greek myth, might be chained to a rock to have their livers pecked at by vultures. I have begun this discussion of our popular culture and communications media with television because its long shadow has fallen so strongly over almost the whole field in the past fifteen years. But before going on to consider the nature of that shadow, let us glance back at the same place before the shadow fell. In retrospect, there is a quaint, almost naïve quality to the news and entertainment world of 1939. A friend of mine, a critic of the popular arts, says he thinks now of that era in association with the Victorian one. There are nonsense songs today that are comparable to "Mairzy-Doats" or "The Hut-Sut Song," but now they are sung exclusively by the young, not by the general population. There are soap operas now on television, but they are a backwater, an anachronism, a time-filler in the network schedules, rather than the common currency among housewives that they were when they flourished on their natural medium, radio. There are wild dance steps indulged in by teen-agers now, but they are often self-conscious, almost scholarly derivations from African dance patterns rather than the spontaneous expression of pleasure in motor activity that the jitterbug was. There is inane and illogical liberal faith now in the automatic natural goodness of any Negro, just as there used to be in the goodness of any working man, but the earlier fallacy was held, I think, in a more heartfelt and less hypocritical way. In the summer of 1939 I was earning extra money for college by working as a door-to-door salesman. I'll never forget the nice young housewife who opened her door one day and, with an expression of innocent delight in new excitement, gave me the news of the Nazi invasion of Poland by asking, "What do you think of this little old war we're having?" I admit with a certain horror that I felt the same innocent excitement myself. It was that kind of a time.

It was a time, of course, when the movies ruled our popular culture, as they were to continue to do until television came. It is hard now to remember, but nonetheless true, that in 1939 the unmodified word "show," in the city or in the country, on the East Coast or on the West, unmistakably meant "movie"; even a few blocks from Broadway itself one had to say "play" or perhaps "legit show" to designate a live drama. As the young novelist and screenwriter Budd Schulberg wrote that year, "Hollywood's voice . . . has become the most powerful in the world. But it's like an overgrown child who is still encouraged to talk baby-talk." The recent cult of the Humphrey Bogart movies of the late 1930s and early 1940s among young people who were not born yet in 1939 shows that the baby-talk had a kind of innocent, escapist charm that was more than ephemeral.

And as for the people who appeared in those movies—the "stars"—they were accorded a degree of adulation that TV stars never attain now. "Hollywood gods and goddesses," Ruth Suckow called them. Leo Rosten, in his study of the movie colony made in the years 1938-40, saw Hollywood as the last embodiment of the old American dream of unbounded personal achievement, replacing the earlier symbol of the poor boy who becomes a mogul in business or finance. People followed their stars' every move with an intensity now accorded chiefly to attractive people in positions of world political leadership, like the Kennedy family. "Never in history," Rosten wrote, "has the public been so avid for information about mortals who earn a living by posturing."

Self-contemplation by Hollywood had become a surefire movie theme; in films like *Boy Meets Girl* (1938) arch jokes about stock Hollywood types like the tyrannical producer, the ex-novelist who for $1,500 a week writes dialogue for a horse, and the dumb blonde star, or about Hollywood folkways like previews at which the stars are mobbed by admirers, were the delight of millions. But the posturing had a kind of naïve sincerity, even when it included the use of newly minted superlatives like "supercolossal." "How's your picture doing?" Rosten quotes one producer as asking another. "Excellent!" says the other. "Only excellent? Too bad," says the first. And the stars, being superhuman, could violate the social norms of society not only with impunity but to their greater glory; if they tended to be epicene in their clothes and language, and if they customarily regarded marriage as a short-term thing, these specific violations of American norms only served to emphasize their apartness from the common run. Hollywood was "glamour" in a very pure form, and because of its insouciance it ruled the national consciousness far more tyrannically than cautious TV, with its constant feeling of the public pulse, rules it now.

3

The tale of what has happened to our movie industry since 1950 is essentially one of decline. In the decade between 1948 and 1958 average weekly movie attendance dropped from ninety million persons to about half that figure, and the amount of national income originating in the motion picture industry dropped about 25 percent. The village or neighborhood movie theater often took to showing pictures only on weekends, and sometimes it closed its doors entirely. Just between 1954 and 1958 the number of operating movie theaters went down from 14,700 to 12,300 (although the loss was mostly recouped by the rise of outdoor drive-in theaters, which catered to our passion for cars while allowing small children to be stashed in the back seat to sleep, and of which more than four thousand were operating by 1958). The former movie theater converted to something else has been a familiar sight since the late 1950s; some became apartment houses, others bowling alleys, still others supermarkets whose owners provided sacrilegious reminders of the noble past by posting news of the latest packaged-food bargains on the very same marquees, and in the very same block letters, that once carried the names of Ginger Rogers, Clark Gable, and Norma Shearer. Even more pointedly, some of the old movie theaters in New York City became television studios.

Coincidentally with the coming of television, a structural change in the motion-picture industry profoundly affected the nature of American-made films. In February, 1950, a federal court in New York decreed the dissolution of corporate combines made up of the producer-distributor and the exhibitor. The effect of this bill of divorcement, reinforcing the effect of TV, was to all but put an end to both the old low-budget B movie—the stinker that made up the other half of the double feature—and also the low-budget effort made for art or just for the hell of it. The new emphasis (after a period of experimentation with gimmickry like 3D) fell heavily on high-priced blockbusters, of which the ill-starred, $42-million *Cleopatra* was to become the awful and wonderful prize specimen. So great was the investment in these blockbusters that everything had to be pretested, every inch of film weighed over and over again to be sure that it was sufficiently stimulating, yet at the same time inoffensive. The film-maker was on the horns of a dilemma: he had to be "daring," either by showing an unusual amount of female anatomy in one well-calculated scene, or else by taking up a supposedly controversial theme like anti-Semitism or Communism—and yet he also had to avoid being so daring that anyone would be repelled into staying away. Gone in the squeeze was the sudden intuition, the directorial hunch, the go-to-hell attitude that had accounted for many of the good things in American movies of the older, simpler days.

"From now on, art is out," announced the producer of *The Treasure of the Sierra Madre,* after his highly praised, and indeed first-rate, film had achieved only an indifferent gross. Coming from any Hollywood producer, such an outburst had its laughable aspect—art, one might say, had never been very far "in" in Hollywood—but certainly the new conditions seemed to place it further out than ever. Meanwhile, wave after wave of generally superior European-made films was rolling over the American movie scene, first flooding the large-city "art-film" houses and eventually seeping into the boon-docks as well. At length, many Americans went to Hollywood films, if they went at all, mainly to satisfy a sort of sociological curiosity rather than to be entertained in the traditional sense. Toward the end of the 1950s Hollywood capitulated to television by making available for showing on the home screen most of its whole library of past works; a bit later, many of the long-abandoned Hollywood movie lots began to be refurbished for TV production, and in 1965 the cycle was complete—Hollywood was a boom town again.

Television has not replaced movies in our national life, and it almost certainly never will. The living room is, according to circum-stance, either not convenient or else all too convenient for the tradi-tional movie-house activity, necking, and—as dozens of commenta-tors before me have noted—the flickering little box cannot hope to compete with the large screen in the dark, peopled theater as a me-dium for conveying large romantic dreams. Television, for another thing, is simply too available; what may be indulged in at any time for any length of time at no cost can hardly be the treat that going out to a movie is. Television's performers, similarly, suffer from being in such ready supply; seeing them so often, the public soon tires of them, and their terms as Olympians are consequently far shorter than those of movie stars. It is surely significant that the big stars of television entertainment are mostly comedians rather than romantic heroes and heroines. Perhaps the flickering little box, with its tendency to miniaturize rather than aggrandize, suits our wry and sophisticated times.

4

The effect of TV on radio is obvious without argument or statistics: radio has been squeezed almost out of the picture as a medium of dramatic entertainment and been forced to rely largely on news (which television can do a great deal better, but not for people who want it frequently and quickly or while riding in their cars) and music (which it can do just as well as television, and in some cases better). The spread of classical music via radio, mostly FM, is a subject I mean to come back to. As a purveyor of current popular music—the stock-in-trade of that most modest of our new culture heroes, the disc jockey—radio has become something it seldom was in 1939, the secret friend and solace of the young. Children clutch their transistors (which didn't exist until after 1950) to their hearts as if the squalling little gadgets were talismans against all the confusion and phoniness of the adult world. The expansion of the popular-music business that this youthful enthusiasm, or addiction, has brought about is shown by the fact that in 1939 there were 1,000 popular-music composers and 137 publishers, while in 1964 there were 18,000 song-writers and 10,000 publishers. "We initiated the present era in disc jockeys and the music they play," proclaims the young writer Renata Adler, who can barely remember the Lone Ranger, the Shadow, and the Green Hornet. "This is no trifling matter." Indeed it is not. The rasping beat of the New Sound—successor to rock 'n' roll—and the code-like language in which the disc jockeys introduce it are surely playing some sort of role in the formation of the next generation of American adults. Inasmuch as the songs are generally goodhearted in a witless way, Miss Adler thinks that, after all, it may not be a bad role.

What has happened to the press is surely not all television's doing, but just as surely it is partly so. The great trends in our daily press—toward fewer daily newspapers and toward consolidation of the ownership of the remaining ones into great regional or national chains—had been going on long before 1950, or even 1939. Many years ago, when we were a nation of comparatively few people, we were also one of many newspapers. In 1909 we had 2,600 dailies for 90 million population; by 1939 we had about 2,000 for 130 million. The decline has continued since then, both relatively and absolutely. According to Census Bureau figures, the number of morning dailies was 473 in 1939 against 357 in 1958—a loss of just about 25 percent—and meanwhile the total of afternoon dailies was going down by 10 percent.

But probably more significant than this over-all decline, from a social point of view, has been the progressive disappearance of newspaper competition in our larger cities. New York City in the 1840s had sixteen dailies for a population of 400,000—a sort of continuous town meeting of press voices, exposing the public to just about every conceivable shade of opinion on local and national events—while as late as the 1920s there were still fourteen; in the early 1960s, with a population of nearly eight million, the city had only six dailies of general circulation, and in 1966 the number was to be reduced further. In virtually no large American city has new newspaper competition appeared since World War II, and in 1960, of the 1,461 cities that had any dailies, 1,400 had only one, while in many of the remaining cases the competition was illusory since the two "competing" papers were under a single management. "American cities with competing newspapers will soon be as rare as those with two telephone systems," A. J. Liebling mourned.

Why had these drastic shrinkages taken place? Certainly rising labor and production costs in the publishing business were a factor; certainly the national trend in all business toward consolidation of many small enterprises into a few large ones was another; and certainly, since about 1925, competition from radio, newsreels, and news magazines as suppliers of national and international news has cut into the market for the local paper. But among the most serious blows to the vitality of the local newspaper has been the latest one, the coming of television.

One reason the effect has been so great has been because TV news coverage, in contrast to TV entertainment, has generally been on a high level. Both in daily handling of routine news and in more thorough coverage of selected events in special programs, the networks have set a high standard of accuracy and, generally speaking, responsibility that has frequently been followed by local stations. So much important news "happens" on TV, particularly in the case of pronouncements by public officials on Sunday interview shows like *Meet the Press,* that often the front pages of the Monday morning papers read like rehashes of the previous day's programs. Abetting the process, many public figures have taken to saving their most newsworthy statements for the TV cameras rather than the press, so as to get the widest possible exposure.

But beyond all this, certain unique advantages for on-the-spot coverage are inherent in the nature of television. By making certain events far more vivid and immediate to the public than newspapers or magazines could hope to make them, it has altered the *effect* of the events. Two examples will suffice. "It is the almost instantaneous television reporting of the [civil-rights] struggle in the streets of Selma, Alabama," James Reston wrote in the *Times* in March, 1965, "that has transformed what would have been mainly a local event a generation ago into a national issue overnight. Even the segregationists who have been attacking the photographers . . . understand the point."

And aside from making news coverage itself a powerful catalyst to social change, TV has the ability to etch events into our minds in a wholly unprecedented way. The sad and sickening drama of the three or four days following the assassination of President Kennedy has been apprehended by a whole huge nation in a way that surely not even the death of Julius Caesar was apprehended by the compact community of ancient Rome. The event and its grotesque sequel have become a permanent part of the consciousness, and doubtless of the unconscious as well, of almost every American who was alive at the time and old enough to understand speech. It will be remembered by tens of millions in the year 2000, by millions probably as late as 2025—and it does not seem too much to predict that for many of these it will still loom then as one of the most intense experiences of their lives. Undoubtedly, television has made millions of new fans for the news; for those not naturally compatible with the printed word it has opened up the painful fascination of the never-ending serial story that is the modern world. But it has not made fans for the newspapers.

Forced to rely more than previously on local news, on news analysis (usually syndicated from New York or Washington), and on entertainment, the newspapers might have turned to sensationalism of the sort that flourished so wildly in earlier American journalism, and it is surely to their credit that for the most part they have not done so. Nor have the trends toward consolidated chains and one-paper towns accentuated the long-standing tendency of the American press to be solidly Republican (in response, of course, to the opinions of its businessmen owners); indeed, the press clearly went Democratic in the 1964 Presidential election, for the first time in generations, and the prospects in the mid-1960s were that publishers, like businessmen in general, would henceforth be increasingly independent in their politics.

Despite these portents, I can't evade the conclusion that our newspapers have gone downhill since 1939. A one-newspaper town necessarily has a one-party press; and in many of our good-sized cities the news is so sketchily and slantedly covered, in the limited amount of space left between the advertisements, that one *must* turn to network radio or television to find out what is going on. Particularly in the small-town weeklies (of which more than six thousand survive) American journalism seems too often to have degenerated into a crass, profit-mad business, blithely flouting the most elementary journalistic ethic by openly trading plugs in the news columns for paid advertisements, and being careful never, never to tread on the toes of influential local businessmen—all under an editorial-page colophon quoting Voltaire or Lincoln on free speech. For generations a favorite dream of the journeyman newspaper reporter (an almost vanished breed) was to start a small weekly with high standards. The dream still exists and is even occasionally carried out, but there is a dearth of William Allen Whites to be the voices and the consciences of our remaining small communities.

5

In the magazine field, rising literacy and the rising advertising outlays of a booming economy acted as counterbalances to the effect of television, and brought about what looks at first glance like a magazine golden age. In 1965 one of the many "surveys" to which publishers and advertising men incline such an attentive ear found that *McCall's* had almost fourteen million adult women readers and the *Ladies' Home Journal* almost twelve million, while *Time*, long the leader among weekly news magazines, was claiming almost fourteen million readers of both sexes. Between 1950 and 1963 advertisers' faith in magazines led them to more than double their expenditures for space, and, in the case of certain products like drugs, insurance, and travel, the percentage increase was far greater.

Yet the truth is that in the mid-Sixties few of the large-circulation magazines were flourishing, or had been for some years. Ruinous competition for circulation, repeated management upheavals, and uneven editorial quality resulting from these factors dogged many of them. In the Fifties it was discovered that temporarily increased circulation could almost literally be bought, though at an enormously high price, through outlays for advertising and promotion combined with drastically reduced subscription rates for new subscribers; moreover, with the indispensable advertisers paying such close attention to circulation figures, in some cases the circulation *had* to be bought if the advertising was to be kept away from the competition. Thus a vicious circle was closed, and thus arose the strange new phenomenon of the magazine that ceases publication when its circulation is rising, killed by the unbearable cost of participating in what came to be called "the numbers game." *Collier's*, a weekly with a long and generally distinguished history, gave up the ghost under these and related pressures in 1956, while the venerable *Saturday Evening Post* became a chronic money-loser in the 1960s. Indeed, almost the only group of magazines that were able to increase their profits substantially after 1950 were the more intellectual ones of limited circulation like *Harper's*, *The Atlantic*, *The Reporter*, and *The New Yorker*, which were properly situated to take advantage of the rising standard of education and to win the affection of advertisers more interested in the buying power of comparatively few readers than in mass circulation. One might note that, in the listing of magazines by circulation for 1963, *The New Yorker* ranked nearest, not to such celebrated names as the *Post* or *Look*, but to a couple of publications called *Hairdo* and *Secrets*.

And what were the magazines saying? *Life* and *Look* were introducing more long and serious text studies roughly on the model of TV news documentaries, but were still basing their appeal primarily on pictures. *Time*, the *enfant terrible* of the 1920s and 1930s, when it had been noted for its undergraduate-style brashness, freshness, ability to raise hackles, and often originality, became staider, more reliable, more responsible—and usually duller. Among the magazines of a million-plus circulation, only *McCall's* in the postwar period seemed to hit a new and responsive chord. While its chief competitor in the women's field, the *Ladies' Home Journal*, was doggedly pursuing the conception of the American woman as a creature apart (although, it ought to be added, considerably widening the conception by introducing more and more discussion of women's psychological and sexual problems), *McCall's* was sensing a newer current and relentlessly considering women as a part, and probably the dominant part, of their families: hence "togetherness," the most ridiculed and by the same token most successful magazine slogan of recent years. Like Winston cigarettes, which are advertised like a cigarette shouldn't be, *McCall's* succeeded largely by adding a repellent expression to the language.

Mass magazines have shown, at least, that television does not supersede them, although it has certainly been a factor in their difficulties; what largely remains for them to show is that either electronic or intramural competition can stimulate them to improve themselves.

6

It is a temptation to see the hand of television behind every recent change in communications and the popular arts and entertainment—and one that I mean to resist. For example, in sports, live coverage of which has become a TV staple, the new medium seems to have magnified old tendencies rather than created new ones. With our high regard for action, strength, and physical competence of all kinds, we have been a sports-mad nation for generations, and never more so, perhaps, than in the years after the First World War, when a Black Sox scandal, involving the fixing of a World Series, could shake the morale of most of the country's youth and that of not a few adults, and when a ballplayer could become probably the single American most widely known around the world. ("To hell with Babe Ruth!" Japanese soldiers are supposed to have cried as they charged out of the South Pacific jungles in 1943 and 1944.)

No such intensity pervades our attitudes to sports now, yet a far greater proportion of the population watches or participates in sports, or does both, than in the 1920s or 1930s. With sports, as indeed with sex, we seem to be more familiar and at the same time more casual. Undoubtedly TV contributes to the familiarity. It has helped make millions of converts to participation in bowling; it has put on the map of mass-audience spectator sports one in which no more than a few thousand persons had ever seen a top-flight tournament before 1950—golf; it has elevated professional football from comparative obscurity to a popularity far surpassing that of baseball itself; and as to boxing, perhaps the sport it is most perfectly equipped to cover, it has often had the effect of emptying the arena of in-person spectators, making the fighters and their backers dependent on TV receipts for a living, and, in effect, converting the ring itself into a kind of studio. The ultimate accolade to the power of TV in sports consists of their pointed exclusion from it—as in the case of recent championship fights, which were shown only by closed-circuit TV in theaters where admission was charged.

A further and interesting effect of this change in boxing—a minor but long-established part of our popular culture—has apparently been to make it become less of a sport and more of a stage-managed and artificial drama. In the 1930s and 1940s, the heyday of Joe Louis and Primo Carnera, the fighters usually beat each other to within an inch of their lives for the public delectation, while their noncombatant backers and handlers ended up living high on the earnings—a scandal that Budd Schulberg angrily recorded in his documentary novel *The Harder They Fall.* In the 1960s, on the contrary, the fighters seemed to be shrewd entrepreneurs rather than victimized gladiators; a whole series of heavyweight championship "fights" ended in early "knockouts," which the victims, tens of thousands of dollars richer and usually looking fresh as a daisy, were entirely willing (and able) to explain in detail to the press five minutes later. The ringsiders, bilked by these sham epics, were the ones who were getting "murdered" now, and who could deny that there was a certain poetic justice about it? Despite the occasional sickening report of a death in the ring in some minor fight, television seemed to be taming championship boxing from a dangerous blood sport into a big-money con game, harmless to everyone but the gulled customers.

Television has pretty well killed popular interest in the minor leagues in baseball by enabling persons who live in minor-league towns to watch major-league games; by the same token, it (together with the easily portable transistor radio and the car radio) has focused national interest on the major leagues to an extraordinary degree. At the key moments of a close World Series, no one in any American city can help being abreast of the action almost play by play, and work virtually stops until the last out. But the change, I think, is a technological rather than a social one. Had the communicating tools been so readily at hand in the days of Ruth and Lou Gehrig, they would have been used just as passionately then.

Nor has television been more than one of the factors, and very likely not the most important one, in the proliferation of the signs and materials of serious culture throughout the country since the end of the war.

7

Here is a highly charged subject; the "culture explosion," if such it be, has been under heavy attack since even before the Kennedy family, in the act of promoting it, called it to public attention. Certainly the squabble over it is a uniquely American phenomenon, demonstrating if anything ever did our celebrated penchant for self-criticism, and perhaps the survival of the streak of anti-intellectualism that has run through our life since the frontier was opened up and we began to declare spiritual as well as physical independence from Europe. Can anyone readily imagine an outcry of influential voices in, say, France, against an increase of interest in cultural matters in the villages and farms? Such a patently "good" development would surely be greeted with quiet satisfaction if not with smugness. Perhaps, indeed, in the American case the squabble itself holds as much interest as the event.

Reliable and generally irrefutable statistics, here gathered from various sources, attest to the existence of a quantitative cultural boom. The number of local art museums has increased fourfold and that of opera-producing groups sevenfold since the 1930s, while symphony orchestras have something like doubled their number even since 1950, and no American city with a population of fifty thousand or more is now without one. Meanwhile, public support has been keeping pace; attendance at the Detroit Symphony, for example, rose from 300,000 to 700,000 a year in the decade before 1965. Sales of phonograph records nearly tripled over the same decade, and—the Beatles and rock 'n' roll notwithstanding—the share of classical records in this expanding market was meanwhile rising from 8 to 18 percent. FM radio stations daily scheduling excellent classical music sprang up in many parts of the country. By 1965 cultural centers were recently completed or under construction in dozens of communities, and more than a hundred had arts councils at work, as against a mere handful a decade earlier. In books, the greatest single development of recent years, leaving aside the greatly increased sales of books in all categories, has been the rise of quality paperbacks. The paperback book industry, inaugurated in 1939, has become part of our way of life over the past quarter-century, and accounts now for a fairly steady 300 million books a year, of which an astonishing number are classics ranging from the Greek myths through Shakespeare to the most respected works of contemporary art and scholarship. And so on.

Significantly, too, all this growth has been pretty general throughout the country; scarcely a state or region can be said not to have participated. I have no figures on Alaska, where the struggle against nature—that old American preoccupation—may up to now have left hardly more time and energy for pursuing culture than it did along the Oregon Trail in the last century; but I do know (by way of Eric Larrabee's book *The Self-Conscious Society*) that in the South, which H. L. Mencken had no hesitation about denouncing as a cultural desert in *The Sahara of the Bozart*, in 1959 had sixty-five symphony orchestras and museums by the score, of which at least one maintained a huge van for carrying exhibits to the backwoods. And what of Sinclair Lewis' citadels of Babbittry, the small towns of the Midwest? In March of 1965 Tyrone Guthrie, artistic director of the celebrated repertory theater in Minneapolis, on paying a random visit to one of them—Cherokee, Iowa—pronounced himself full of both admiration and amazement at finding a symphony orchestra, a local theater group, and a high-quality museum in a town of eight thousand persons.

And yet—some disturbing facts remain. The vast majority of our towns, and even some fair-sized cities, contain not a single bookstore, and the number of bookstores in proportion to population is actually decreasing. The well and widely reviewed novel of unquestioned quality that does not "catch on" and achieve the magic circle of best-sellerhood characteristically has a pathetically small sale—in many cases smaller than it would have had ten, fifteen, or twenty-five years ago. The lion's share of those fast-selling paperbound editions of Shakespeare, Dostoievsky, and *Moby Dick* is sold not to adults making a free choice to sample the classics, but rather to the fast-growing army of high school and college students who are virtually compelled to make the purchases, since the books are assigned reading; indeed, some paperback publishers affirm that they are entirely uninterested in issuing books that do not have possibilities for the academic market. There is evidence that many of those growing flocks of concert- and museum-goers are more interested in seeking status than culture.

Furthermore, almost everyone knows a small town or village that is not at all like Cherokee: where the mysteries in the paperback rack in the drugstore are almost the only books to be seen; where playing classical music on one's phonograph brands one as pretentious or eccentric; where the smallest reference to literature, music, or art in conversation is the signal for an ironic response, really a boast, in the old and truly disreputable tradition of the frontier, about how the interlocutor doesn't have much truck with such things. That is to say, a community, in President Kennedy's words, afraid of grace and beauty. "The count of symphony orchestras is . . . inflated," the Russian emigré composer Igor Stravinsky said in 1965. "Of those deserving the name we have more likely grown [not from 800 to 1,350 since 1950, but] from eight to thirteen . . . and I am certain there are not thirteen capable of preparing first-rate performances of the new works of our outstanding younger composers." Stravinsky, who went on to issue a warning against "statistical fictions" in what he called "culture publicity," is not known for being a moderate man; nevertheless, his opinions can scarcely be dismissed.

8

In short, a flank attack on the "culture explosion" is based on the thesis that it doesn't exist, or exists only in a shallow way; however, the central offensive, led by New York intellectuals associated with *Partisan Review* and other magazines of that ilk, admits its existence but considers it a bad thing on the ground that the more culture spreads, the more it tends to become corrupted and commercialized—transformed from the real thing into what Dwight Macdonald scathingly calls "midcult." "The danger to high culture is not so much from [mass popular culture] as from a peculiar hybrid bred from the latter's unnatural intercourse with the former," Macdonald wrote in 1961. "A whole middle culture has come into existence and it threatens to absorb both its parents. . . . It pretends to respect the standards of high culture while in fact it waters them down and vulgarizes them. . . . A tepid ooze of midcult is spreading everywhere." At a cultural conference held that same year, the critic Alfred Kazin attacked from a slightly different angle: the trouble with American culture, he said, is that in the very act of expanding in response to the spread of industry and affluence it destroys itself by aping the patterns of industry—packaging, huckstering, and selling itself as if it were so much soap. As Louis Kronenberger wittily put the case, the businessman interested in the arts, in applying his tried-and-true business methods to them, was just as much a businessman as ever—"Babbitt had been split up two for one."

So went the counterattack; meanwhile, the defense, carried out in large part by the charitable foundations that devote much of their money and energy to promoting the spread of culture, was based broadly on the proposition that such a spread is inherently so good for the country in the long run that any temporary ill effects are overbalanced. I do not feel that this is the place to take sides in the controversy, except, perhaps, to remark that one side's tendency to identify increasing quantity with increasing quality seems extremely vulnerable, while the critics like Macdonald who imply that culture and democracy are irreconcilable seem at times to betray a chagrin rather like that felt by landed aristocrats overtaken socially by a new industrial class. What I can try to do is put the debate in the context of social change.

In 1939, then, high culture in America *was* in the hands of an elite, as the statistics amply show. But more important than the fact was the national attitude: the fact represented a situation that few people aspired to change. There were, as we have seen, few charitable foundations making the grants and beating the drums for a greater dispersion of culture; the pioneer paperback book firms started that year were originally intended not to spread the classics but to get a larger audience for unashamedly commercial books; and the community theaters that were a particularly charming flower of the time existed much more for the amusement and distraction of their staffs and their small audiences than for any such elevated purpose as furthering culture, while surely the plays in their repertories were usually unpretentious enough. Even the occasional grand and highly publicized "cultural event" in a big city—the first showing of Picasso's "Guernica" in New York in 1939, for example—almost always had a political or social purpose, like raising money for the Spanish Loyalists or for relief of Nazi refugees, rather than existing for its own sake as it probably would now.

There seem to have been two reasons for this national lack of cultural ambition. One of them, certainly, was the presence on all sides of pressing economic problems. Those comparatively few who were interested in cultural matters and lived in or near large cities could pursue their interests at moderate cost, but the notion of making mass converts to culture among sharecroppers or production-line workers scarcely crossed anyone's mind—and indeed, even in retrospect, such a notion appears as preposterous sentimentality. The enrichment of people's lives could hardly be considered until their subsistence had been provided.

But there was another reason, perhaps deeper. There was in those days a sort of treason against culture being committed by those who created it. A pervasive suspicion of the urban aesthete or intellectual, stemming back to nineteenth-century populism, and greatly reinforced by the New Deal worship of the simple working man, ran deep in our thought, and in our literature itself. It was open season on highbrows in the novels and plays of the time. The aesthetically inclined Robert Cohn had been the "goat" of Ernest Hemingway's vastly successful *The Sun Also Rises* a decade earlier, and Hemingway's famous staccato, monosyllabic style—the very epitome of American expression in those years—was designed, among other things, to suggest (with immense but carefully concealed craft) that the simple, untutored man expresses the essence of life better than the graduate of academies and universities. Or consider the attitude toward "culture" and "love of beauty" embodied in Thornton Wilder's *Our Town*, the Pulitzer Prize play of 1938. "Is there any culture or love of beauty in Grover's Corners?" a lady asks Mr. Webb, the newspaper editor who serves as the author's spokesman. "Well, Ma'am, there ain't much," Mr. Webb replies,

> not in the sense you mean. . . . But maybe this is the place to tell you that we've got a lot of pleasures of a kind here: we like the sun comin' up over the mountain in the morning, and we all notice a good deal about the birds. . . . But those other things, you're right, ma'am, there ain't much. "Robinson Crusoe" and the Bible; and Handel's *Largo*, we all know that; and Whistler's *Mother*—those are just about as far as we go.

The strong implication that the ability to enjoy "pleasures of a kind" such as watching birds or the rising sun makes appreciation of art unnecessary to a full life tells us a lot about the quality of American life at the end of the 1930s. True enough, *Our Town* is set not in 1938 but in 1901, but the author himself has disclaimed any intention to document a specific time or place, and his play obviously struck a responsive chord in its own time. That the deepest pleasures come from the simplest things, that the most meaningful speech is that of the untutored man innocent of good grammar and punctuation, that ignorance of almost all art is no occasion for resolve or even regret: whether such propositions are right or wrong, a country that holds them would not appear to be on the verge of a culture explosion.

9

But the United States was, and the reasons for the rather abrupt change of direction are so familiar that they need not be labored. New affluence has brought millions the leisure and the cash to explore the possibilities of culture; an enormous broadening of higher education (of which more in a later chapter) has put millions of youngsters in the way of culture whether by their own choice or not, and some of them, perhaps, have later served as cultural emissaries to their less-educated parents; and the mass media have served culture—at their best as its self-effacing purveyor, and at their worst as its huckster.

These media in the latter role provide the opponents of proliferating culture with their most effective weapon, and the country at large with a most disheartening phenomenon. Cultural events have, for example, had a checkered career on television, and for reasons not hard to find: the industry's economic stakes have grown far faster than national interest in culture, which has therefore tended to be priced out of the market, particularly at convenient viewing hours. Without consulting the networks' own figures on time devoted to what they consider cultural events, I have gained the impression that in the mid-Sixties such events of real interest turn up on TV far less often than they did a decade ago. One is allowed to see a great, publicized event like the opening of New York's Lincoln Center, with celebrities like Governor Nelson Rockefeller and Mrs. Jacqueline Kennedy on hand—cultural huckstering of a high order, with a high-minded corporation as sponsor—but one is no longer, for example, allowed to see even an occasional performance of the Metropolitan Opera, as one was in TV's salad days.

The plastic arts, whose end products are objects as tangible and salable as manufactured goods, are the arts most readily susceptible to commercialization, and it is in painting and sculpture that the recent broadening of public interest has been accompanied by the most disconcerting evidence of equivocal motives. Rapidly rising art prices in the 1950s, combined with the charitable-deduction and capital-gains provisions of the federal tax code, made art collecting in that period a hobby for the well-to-do that was not only pleasant, ego-enhancing, and prestige-bringing, but frequently profitable, too. Obviously, such a situation made the sincerity of the collector's interest in art suspect. It was not necessary for a business or professional man to have the slightest interest in art to make him want to become a collector; he needed only to be interested in making money! The old "I know what I like" saw was subjected to a switch: the credo of many of the new collectors, whose enthusiasm for Abstract Expressionist painting was being so widely acclaimed as a national cultural gain, might well have been: "I don't know anything about art *and* I don't know what I like, but I know what's going up in price!"

Paintings were welcomed by businessmen as a new, morally elevating, amusing, and fashionable form of growth stock in which to trade. What could be more soul-satisfying than to combine a neat profit with a mention in the newspapers as "the prominent art patron"? Conversely, the sincere or naïve new art enthusiast, on realizing that his collecting was little more than another form of the buying and selling for profit that he had hoped to rise above, might be and sometimes was dismayed into a revulsion against art.

In New York, where the ranks of the professional merchants of art, the dealers, had swelled from a few dozen in 1939 to several hundred in the mid-1950s, the art world's all too sedulous aping of the business world reached a kind of apogee in April, 1960, when the Parke-Bernet Galleries conducted a mammoth auction of important modern paintings, drawings, and sculpture donated to the sale for the benefit of the Museum of Modern Art. So that collectors around the country could bid without sending their representatives to New York, the auction room there was linked by closed-circuit television to similar rooms in Chicago, Dallas, and Los Angeles, from which bids could be relayed to the auctioneer as fast as they were made. (In 1965 the same firm was to conduct its first international auction via Telstar, the communications satellite.) The event was a huge success: as the coaxial cables under America pulsed with the copulation of art and commerce, a Utrillo oil was knocked down to a Dallas bidder for $20,000; a Juan Gris went to a Los Angeles man for $23,000; a magnificent Cézanne stayed in New York for $200,000; and so on. On almost every item there was spirited intercity bidding, enthusiastically encouraged by the auctioneer ("Come on, Chicago, you're not going to let Dallas steal it, are you?"). Only once was the smooth tenor of the occasion disturbed, when a gallery attendant inadvertently placed a Hans Hartung abstraction on the auction easel upside down, and the bidding from several cities was approaching the $10,000 mark before anyone noticed.

Here, then, was a true copy of the Stock Exchange in action, on a nationwide basis just like the bidding for U.S. Steel or General

Motors, with the useful additional element of open competition based on local and regional pride, long familiar to American businessmen, thrown in. What can one say about why such an event would have been impossible in 1939? The fact that technology had not then advanced far enough to provide the closed-circuit television is only the beginning; in truth, if that auction had been described in 1939, it would have sounded like doings on some other planet.

Are we going through an artistic renaissance or a period when culture is engulfed and drowned by money? Very likely neither; culture is destined to survive, but Athens in America seems a long way off, too. It does seem a bit pathetic to boast of American interest in high art in the second half of the rich and enlightened twentieth century when one recalls how the Italians of the nineteenth, the vast majority of them poor and illiterate, made Verdi their national hero. Certainly the institutional way culture is being promoted nowadays is enough to give any amateur of the arts a feeling of queasiness. The very concept of a generalized thing called "culture" is repellent to those who are deeply moved, whose lives are deeply affected, whose existence on earth is made bearable, by works of art. No one loves culture; one loves *Otello* or the "Ode to a Nightingale." But perhaps it isn't fatuous to believe that increasing exposure to works of art under the new conditions may accidentally create one such devotee of a single work for every hundred—or thousand—profiteers and culture-climbers, and that therefore the unseemly brouhaha is in a good cause.

10

If one of the major effects of the transformation of communications techniques (and surely this has been one transformation for which the word "revolution" is not too strong) has been a filtering down of ideas and attitudes formerly held by the small educated middle and upper-middle class to the new middle mass, the prize example must be not culture but psychoanalysis. Apart from its role as actual therapy—which, because of the enormous amounts of time and money required, has up to now been marginal in American life—psychoanalysis at the end of the 1930s was a way of life, a devotion, a kind of religion to an elite that could probably be numbered in the tens of thousands, and just a word, not even a joke word, to everybody else. The death in 1939 of Sigmund Freud, the founder of psychoanalysis, was the occasion for much debate about the validity of his methods and their effectiveness as treatment. Orthodox medicine was far more skeptical than it has since become; as a prominent Johns Hopkins doctor wrote in 1940, "Medicine should be grateful for the extension of methods and of ideas in psychiatry, but should also be cautious in evaluating claims, especially of therapeutic results."

But this skepticism was not shared by the more intellectually chic echelons of the middle class, who had taken psychoanalytic ideas, or at least an approximation of them, to their bosoms in the 1920s and continued to clutch them there. Psychoanalytic jargon terms were bandied about freely in conversation in such circles, while the chief application of the ideas came in the care and rearing of children. Mothers worried about toilet training and sent their children to progressive schools, where, in accordance with psychoanalytical theory, permissiveness reigned and competition was discouraged in the interest of releasing creativeness and avoiding the formation of neuroses. Psychoanalytic ideas were certainly the key factor in the rising vogue among parents, in these limited circles, for closely observing and studying child behavior almost minute to minute. The famous books on child behavior by Arnold Gesell and Frances L. Ilg, *Infant and Child in the Culture of Today* and *The Child from Five to Ten*, appeared, respectively, in 1943 and 1946; with them in the house, a baby born in 1939 or 1940 could be and often was kept under constant scrutiny for the slightest deviation from the behavioral norms for his age.

This, considered as a group phenomenon stemming from psychoanalysis' emphasis on the crucial importance of infanthood and early childhood on character formation, was a new and key trend in American life. But, as I have said, in 1939 it was a statistically small trend; if nothing else, the ever-pressing economic concerns of most American parents in those days would have been enough to limit their intensity of interest in the fact that "the eighteen-month-old child is relatively self-contained," while the three-year-old expresses independence, and so on. Since then, the psychoanalytic concern of the well-educated and relatively well-heeled group—what may be called the traditional middle class—has declined, while that of the huge new middle class has risen. A graph of such interest in the two groups would show crossing curves.

The members of the traditional middle class who were themselves brought up on psychoanalytic ideas in the 1930s and who are now the parents of teen-agers have tended to shy away from those ideas; many of them feel varying degrees of dissatisfaction with their own progressive-oriented educations, many sense in their own children the actual appeal for greater parental strictness of which I have spoken earlier, and, of course, many have discovered what Samuel Butler (arguing for the opposite conclusion) pointed out so vividly in *The Way of All Flesh*: that the surest way for a parent to have a tranquil life is to be a severe parent.

But, meanwhile, the emerging new middle class was going in the opposite direction. Television, not only in its rash of "psycho" melodramas but more subtly in its family-situation comedies and even in its "adult" westerns, was insinuating an often watered-down version of psychoanalytic ideas into the minds of its viewers, and the serious Broadway theater was being swamped by them, while huge-circulation magazines like *Life* were treating the subject in an explicit and not necessarily cheapened or "popularized" way. The notion that the themes of violence and perversion, so prevalent in our postwar popular literature from Mickey Spillane to Norman Mailer, represented a devious outlet for a national libido frustrated by our traditional sexual Puritanism gained more and more currency in the postwar years. Harvey Swados makes the interesting point that while the favorite courtroom drama in our popular literature of the 1930s was the Sacco-Vanzetti case—a political drama turning on justice to radicals—the comparable favorite of the 1950s was the Loeb-Leopold case—a psychiatric drama involving juvenile delinquency, resolved by a "compromise between revenge and therapy dictated by psychiatric testimony." "Psychoanalysis today is an aspect of American popular culture," Harold Rosenberg wrote in 1965; indeed, to a great extent America had become the *home* of psychoanalysis, a situation not without its irony in view of the fact that Freud himself had made no bones about being a classical European anti-American.

But alas! there is evidence that what the popular media have succeeded in planting in the American mind is nothing Freud would have recognized or approved—certainly not a system of thought with its own demands and disciplines, but rather a stray idea here and there, often snatched at apparently because it provides a rationale for antisocial behavior. Thus for the parent with a tendency toward irresponsibility, those half-grasped ideas give license to be neglectful of the children ("Don't repress them, you know?") and, conversely, for the parent with a tendency toward doting, they give license to run a child-centered household ("Babies need love or they'll grow up basically insecure"). The psychiatric tests that have become so popular with employers and educators often seem to be a combination of unjustifiable invasion of privacy and plain nastiness; Vance Packard in *The Naked Society* cited one in which, on the basis of their reaction to a group of cartoons, testers presume to determine schoolchildren's "oral eroticism" and "Oedipal intensity"—matters which are surely none of the testers' business in the case of normal children, whether or not the tests can truly determine them.

Perhaps worst of all, psychiatric concepts half understood, perhaps willfully half understood, have become a new and particularly damaging weapon in personal relations—a sort of social dumdum bullet replacing the old standard cartridge. The marital quarrel that in 1939 was generally conducted with the familiar old epithets and perhaps with a few pieces of crockery, could end and leave no aftermath; the up-to-date one, involving a questioning of the other's unconscious motives, leaves doubts in the minds of the parties to it. And so in the most casual of hostilities. "What are you, sick or something?" is a good deal more unforgivable, not to say uglier, a crusher than "Get lost" or "Dry up and blow away" or the familiar old stand-by, canonized in the play *Born Yesterday*—"Drop dead."

11

A little learning, then, is still a dangerous thing; and occasionally the danger is to the half-learned himself, as was apparently the case with the American automobile manufacturers of the middle 1950s, many of whom became convinced that people bought the kind of cars they did more to gratify conscious status drives and unconscious sexual ones than to achieve the most efficient transportation at the lowest cost—and who eventually got their comeuppance for their presumption. The wide, low-slung, tail-finned, chrome-hung, gadget-bedecked, souped-up kind of automobile that was very likely the most preposterous product of our postwar popular culture suddenly stopped selling in 1957 and 1958. (The hulking beetles of 1939 would have made hardly better status symbols, and possibly worse sex symbols, than the Volkswagen does.) The mid-1950s cars cannot, of course, be attributed to psychoanalysis, but it is explicit in the annals of the manufacturers that some of their features can be blamed on the popularization of psychoanalysis. The specific and decisive turn of the public against them may have marked, in a roundabout way, the beginning of a more discriminating national attitude to the subject.

The emphasis that psychoanalysis puts on the bad effects of the repression of unacceptable thoughts—the mind's self-censorship—is closely related to the remarkable national reaction over the past twenty-five years against censorship of print and other media.

It was in 1943 that the American writer Henry Miller—already well known in Europe for his candid, sometimes hilarious, and often outrageously exhibitionist novels like *Tropic of Cancer,* and enjoying a certain underground fame for them in his own country, even though they could not be sold there or imported legally—explained in an open letter how he felt about the matter.

> It seems so ironical that I, who "by common consent of the critics" should be considered "one of the most interesting figures on the American literary scene," am obliged to call attention to myself as a water colorist. . . . Such a condition is a sad one. . . . And yet, if tomorrow by

(United Press International Photo)

STREET SCENE, 1939: Detroit WPA workers protesting cutbacks.

(United Press International Photo)

TWO CAMPUS MOODS: Goldfish-eating at Boston College, 1939, and a protest rally, University of California at Berkeley, 1964.

SENATORIAL STYLES: Tom Connally (D., Texas) in 1940, Robert F. Kennedy (D., New York) in 1965.

(Wide World Photos)

(*Dorothea Lange Collection, Oakland Museum*)

WARTIME MOODS:
War plant workers, Richmond, California, 1942.

(*Wide World Photos*)

President Roosevelt in Hawaii, 1944.

V-J Day, Times Square.

TOP: Columbia vs. Princeton, May 17, 1939—the first televised sports event.

BOTTOM: Republican National Convention, 1964—politics in the TV fishbowl.

(Wide World Photos)

(Cornell Capa-Magnum)

PAINTING:

TOP: "Georgia Jungle" by Alexander Brook (1939).

BOTTOM: Jackson Pollock at work (1950).

(Collection of Museum of Art, Carnegie Institute, Pittsburgh)

(Hans Namuth)

(Wide World Photos)

WAYS OF LIVING:
Levittown, Pa., in 1952 and Reston, Va., in 1965.

(The New York Times)

PROPHESY AND FULFILLMENT: Part of the General Motors Futurama at the New York World's Fair, 1939-40, and the intersection of Santa Monica and Harbor Freeways, Los Angeles, 1966.

(General Motors)

(Wide World Photos)

NBC

(Thomas D. McAvoy, LIFE Magazine © Time, Inc.)

(Wide World Photos)

Governor Wallace and Deputy Attorney General Katzenbach at the University of Alabama, 1963.

(Wide World Photos)

The Spirit of '76 en route from Selma to Montgomery, March, 1965.

Marian Anderson at the Lincoln Memorial, Easter Day, 1939.

Three Presidents who bridged two eras.

The United Nations in the October, 1962, missile crisis; Adlai Stevenson representing the U. S.

(Wide World Photos)

Sewell Avery of Montgomery Ward, among the last of a breed, 1944.

(United Nations)

President Johnson signs the Medicare Bill, July 30, 1965.

(United Press International Photo)

Automobile assembly lines, 1940 and 1963: landscapes with and without figures.

(Wide World Photos)

(NASA)

(Ford Motor Company)

(Arthur Schatz, LIFE Magazine © Time, Inc.)

THE WORLD OF 1965:
A Connecticut child gets a boost on her math homework from a computer.
Astronaut Edward H. White II takes a walk in space.

(Lynn Pelham, Rapho-Guillumette, LIFE *Magazine © Time, Inc.)*

American beach scene, 1965.

a decision of the Supreme Court [a] half-dozen terrifying words were restored to currency, if I, like the great English writers of the past, were permitted to use them, I should undoubtedly be sitting in clover . . . but unless I am vastly mistaken, not all the King's horses nor all the King's men can bring about such a miracle . . . we are deathly afraid of a few good old Anglo-Saxon words—*in print*. Alors, *tant pis pour moi*!

Hardly anyone needs to be told now that Miller was "vastly mistaken." *Tropic of Cancer* was published in the United States by Grove Press in 1961, and although it ran into censorship troubles in many localities, more than two and a half million copies were sold and the Supreme Court duly affirmed the legality of such sales. Miller achieved a seat of clover—*tant mieux pour lui* (thanks largely to the fair-mindedness of his publisher, who, for technical reasons, need not have paid him any royalties)—and the good old Anglo-Saxon words he had spoken of, far from continuing to be interdicted, have become more or less obligatory in the works of young novelists, female ones included.

Censorship of printed matter to eliminate candor about sex goes far back into the American past; the first federal antiobscenity law was passed in 1842, more were passed in the 1850s, and in the 1870s, the heyday of the famous censorship crusader Anthony Comstock, state after state passed such laws of its own. Ever since then, as Morris Ernst has written, "courageous defendants and their lawyers had to chip away at the great stone monument to Comstockery piece by piece." A few important chips had been taken before 1939—for example, the famous New York District Court decision allowing James Joyce's *Ulysses* in 1933—but the really broad-based assault on book censorship had to wait until the postwar era, when a general relaxation of the Puritan ethic had made the temper of the country ripe for change. The key case was that of *Lady Chatterley's Lover*, the touching, if perhaps rather quaint by present-day standards, D. H. Lawrence classic of the 1920s about the affair between a titled lady and her gamekeeper, which had been published here only in expurgated form until it was issued in full (again by Grove Press) in 1958. The Post Office Department brought suit to stop its distribution, the book was cleared by a federal judge in New York, the decision was sustained on appeal—and our public communications moved into a new era. The floodgates were open; even spicy books like the eighteenth-century *Fanny Hill*, for which only modest literary merit was ordinarily claimed, and which had circulated for generations among undergraduates in bootleg editions, made its formal appearance in due time. In 1965 it was hard to imagine the federal government attempting censorship along Comstock lines of any book of the slightest literary merit.

Movie censorship has been slower to give ground. The film industry has censored itself ever since 1930 by requiring adherence to its celebrated code, and in 1965 that code was going through its first major overhaul ever. While a revolution in American moral standards had been taking place over more than a generation, official Hollywood had sat behind drawn blinds. What had changed substantially over the years was the code's interpretation. Its detailed provisions like the general prohibitions of nudity and discussion of brothels were honored in spirit as well as letter before the war, an era when, in retrospect, movies appear to have been as innocent as a newborn baby (one recalls with astonishment what a shock it came as when Clark Gable in *Gone with the Wind* uttered the epoch-making line, "Frankly, my dear, I don't give a damn"). But in the changed temper of the postwar years, movie-makers took to circumventing the spirit while adhering with grim or tongue-in-cheek technical exactitude to the letter; nobody, for example, could have mistaken the brothels in *East of Eden* or *A Walk on the Wild Side* for anything else—and, of course, nobody was intended to. At times, in such productions as *Some Like It Hot*, the making of films seemed to have become an intricate game, comparable to that played by politically dissenting writers in totalitarian countries, in which the movie-makers and the audience were in cahoots to communicate in a secret language that made a mockery of the code without violating the most picayune of its provisions. Which would seem to indicate that, if only in the interest of preventing the perpetuation and indeed dissemination of a spirit of hypocrisy, liberalization of the code was overdue.

But meanwhile, for enemies of censorship there were certain less heartening trends. For one thing, as sexual censorship lost ground in the late Forties and early Fifties, political and ideological censorship gained; particularly in the movies and in television, the McCarthy-era witch hunt for Communists and fellow travelers, epitomized in the plight of the blacklisted Hollywood Ten and the television writers smeared in the broadcasting blacklist *Red Channels,* represented an abridgment of the First Amendment perhaps unprecedented in American life in peacetime.

Further, the relaxation of official censorship often seems to be having the effect not of releasing art and expression from confining shackles but rather of creating new shackles; what is called "hard-core pornography" has been given an inadvertent but nonetheless substantial boost, while, as I have suggested, even serious and high-minded young writers now feel a kind of obligation to include in their works the words that would previously have been censorable. It seems obvious that such a feeling, where it exists, represents the opposite of a release of the writer's creative powers, while for loyal readers the results tend to become so tedious that even the heartiest advocates of free expression among them feel a certain dampening of their enthusiasm for the anticensorship cause. Doubtless, too, resentment caused by licentious use of the new freedom is partly responsible for a recent backlash of censorship, in the old Comstock tradition, at the municipal level. Even in the 1960s, a film was banned in Chicago because it contained the words "rape" and "contraceptive," and another was banned in Memphis because its treatment of poverty among tenant farmers was thought to "reflect on the South"; a high school library in Phoenix, Arizona, put Aldous Huxley's *Brave New World* and Thomas Mann's *The Magic Mountain* on its restricted list; while in Pontiac, Michigan, a parent group effectively prevented the assignment to high school students of what is surely among the purest as well as among the greatest of American novels, *The Scarlet Letter*. Comstockery is a weed that continues to flourish in the untended hedgerows of our national life, in spite of the liberalized attitude toward censorship that has come with the general broadening of our collective mind.

12

For it *has* become broader: television, books, magazines, cultural events, even half-grasped psychoanalytic concepts have tended to widen our field of vision, and the great question is whether in the course of being broadened our view has become less penetrating. What it has not become, I am convinced, is more standardized. The case that the mass media have forced nearly all of us into a single mold is a weak one; if television were effectively such a mold, surely one of the first things to become standardized would have been our speech, and yet regional accents in many cases seem to grow more pronounced as time goes on. The American of the 1960s has been exposed to many ideas and experiences that were simply beyond the ken of the American of 1939; often he has resisted the experience or been baffled and confused by it; and often he has tried to close his mind and soul to it. In vain; willy-nilly, he has added new facets to himself, and he will be adding more.

VII. MIRRORS UP TO NATURE

1

In 1939 the American novel, almost always a sensitive recorder and sometimes a creator of our preoccupations and aspirations, was at the climax of a phase of nationalism, regionalism, and social realism. The disruption of life and the intense suffering brought about by the depression had turned novelists' eyes and thoughts away from Europe and the rest of the world and toward their own country, past and present. So strong was this tendency that not even the rising menace of Hitler had yet been able to affect it much, except perhaps in a certain militant glorification of America that was beginning to appear just under the surface of novels ostensibly meant as critiques of our economic and social system. Popular historical novels like Elizabeth Page's *Tree of Liberty,* Vardis Fisher's *Children of God,* and Bruce Lancaster's *Guns of Burgoyne,* among many others, were set in the American past rather than in some exotic place. Particular regions, with their characteristic flavors and problems, were taken up in such books as Robert Penn Warren's *Night Rider,* about race tensions in the Kentucky tobacco country, and John P. Marquand's *Wickford Point,* a witty and wistful tale based on the conflict between a snug and quaint New England community and one of its members who has left it, in body if not wholly in spirit, to be part of a larger world.

Above all, the subject for novelists was the depression, almost always approached in a reformist spirit. To seek the novel of the late Thirties with a contemporary American setting that ignored the depression would be like looking for a needle in a haystack, and to search for the one that took the side of management or ownership in the social struggles of that time would be equally futile. The pervasiveness of this orthodoxy is shown by the fact that it affected even writers not normally concerned with social reform. In 1939 the most recent novels of Ernest Hemingway, whose vision of life was ordinarily not political or social but highly personal, and of James Gould Cozzens, who was later to declare himself both in his writings and in public statements as a decided conservative, were both characteristic depression-time celebrations of the simple and humble man as against the corrupt rich. In Hemingway's *To Have and Have Not,* the reader's nose is rubbed in the circumstance that the good characters are poor and the bad or corrupt ones rich, while in Cozzens' *The Last Adam* the whole point is the nobility of an unlettered country doctor who puts work and service above the values of the marketplace. Even F. Scott Fitzgerald, the celebrated lyricist of the leisured, and a writer accused with some justice of being unduly fascinated by the rich, was at work in 1939 on a novel about Hollywood—*The Last Tycoon,* fated to be left unfinished at his death—in which Communists and labor violence were to play a large part.

The overt depression novels of the late Thirties fell into several groups. There were tracts more or less openly preaching revolution, some of them written by open Communists. There were strike novels, taking advantage of the obvious dramatic and emotional possibilities of the violent clash of management and labor. There were novels on the concomitants of widespread poverty, such as the wave of banditry, more or less in the Jesse James tradition, that was affecting much of the country. And there were the novels about particular groups among the poor, of which much the most celebrated and probably the best was John Steinbeck's *The Grapes of Wrath,* an account of the migration from Oklahoma to California of a family of dispossessed sharecroppers, which first appeared in March, 1939, to great acclaim, and became the best-selling book of the year.

The Grapes of Wrath is at once a moving story and a catalogue of the accepted social attitudes of its time. Rereading it now, in a time when few Americans who read books have ever known the sensation of wondering where their next meal will come from, one is struck by how distant its story and its setting seem; it now appears as almost as much a historical novel as the tales of the time of Jefferson or of the early days of Mormonism that were published in the same year. The Joad family piled in their malfunctioning old truck, talking their quaint rural Fundamentalist talk, literally counting pennies because they must to live, or being amused and delighted by their first exposure to modern plumbing in a government-run migrant camp, seem like characters out of a remote past—and yet they live because of the author's marvelous ability to identify with them. *The Grapes of Wrath* overflows with love of humanity, the feel of poverty, and overblown Biblical prose. Some of its best passages have to do with machinery in relation to Americans; when Al Joad repairs the truck, the parts involved are described in loving accuracy and detail, and Al's fulfillment of himself through correctly handling and fitting them is splendidly projected.

It is also a book untroubled by moral complexity. Bankers and the rich are inhuman, poverty-stricken sharecroppers are human (although not always entirely good). When a poor man who runs a company store overcharges the Joads, we wonder whether an ambiguous element is being introduced—but no; the storekeeper, basically good, is merely a helpless agent of his employers. The problem of Communism among organizers of the migrant fruit-pickers is quickly handled. A picker is told by an orchard owner, "A red is any son-of-a-bitch that wants thirty cents an hour when we're payin' twenty-five," and the picker logically concludes, "I ain't a son-of-a-bitch, but if that's what a red is . . . we're all reds." The reader feels that while the author knows his Joads intimately, he does not know or understand his villains, the bankers who dispossessed them; the bankers never appear. More than a moving historical document, *The Grapes of Wrath* is a morality play in the old tradition that has since been destroyed by the moral ambiguity of recent years; and in both ways it suited its readers when it appeared.

It is also significant that *The Grapes of Wrath,* like most of the novels of its period, is not written in a technically experimental way; in the Twenties Fitzgerald and Hemingway had been preoccupied with style, and in the early Thirties Dos Passos had introduced a number of new techniques to American fiction (and meanwhile across the Atlantic, James Joyce, Virginia Woolf, and others had been formally revolutionizing the novel); but toward the end of the depression, matter triumphed over manner in American writing, and the tale came again to be of more interest than the teller. This tendency, for obvious reasons, carried over into the early postwar years, when the matter of the American novel became the great experience of the war.

There was little or no formal experimentation in the big batch of "war novels" that appeared between about 1946 and 1952. The war had washed away the depression and replaced it with a whole new experience, and the recounting of this experience as exactly and truly as possible became the novelists' preoccupation, overwhelming any urge to produce self-conscious art. That is to say, the war novels, like the depression novels, remained in the storytelling tradition out of which the novel itself had originally arisen, setting particular people against a certain factual social background and following them through a series of vicissitudes. These novels fell generally into two categories—those concentrating on bringing the news of what combat had actually been like, on reporting "how it was," and those emphasizing the reaction of provincial Americans to the unfamiliar cultures they encountered in the course of their life in the military service.

Far and away the most celebrated novel in the first category was Norman Mailer's *The Naked and the Dead,* describing the adventures of one combat platoon, made up of men with widely varying social and geographical backgrounds, in the Pacific war. Strongly derivative in technique and style from various writers, most conspicuously from Dos Passos and Hemingway, strongly critical of American business society from the point of view of a rather naïve political leftism that seemed to be a hangover from depression attitudes, *The Naked and the Dead* excelled in its memorable depictions of some types among

American civilian soldiers—the sensitive, educated young lieutenant, the brutal sergeant who takes to Army life like a duck to water—and in its remarkably vivid projection of the precise feelings of soldiers in combat. Books like Mailer's said to the parents of soldiers all the things that their less articulate and gifted sons had been unable to say.

In the other category, the novels of self-discovery in the war, the classic was John Horne Burns' *The Gallery*. Made up of a series of sketches of men and women brought by the circumstance of the war to the Galleria in Naples, and tied together by the comments and reactions of a first-person narrator who stands for the author, *The Gallery* is not so much a formal novel as a hymn to the Italian temperament; the tale it has to tell is of how a young American falls in love with Italian warmth, generosity, spontaneity, and humanity—even with Italian cruelty and squalor—casts off his earlier values based on Puritanism, money, and social position, and goes through a kind of rebirth. Perhaps the book's most poignant figure is Momma, a fat Italian lady who presides with vast love and without even a shadow of disapproval over a Neapolitan bar frequented by homosexuals; the implication that such tolerance, and more than tolerance, would be next to impossible in an American city is clear.

The generally materialistic course of postwar society in this country would seem to indicate that the kind of wartime rebirth abroad described by Burns was not a sufficiently general experience with our servicemen to have a significant effect on our national life. "Greece, though conquered, made Rome her captive"; Italy, however, hardly seems to have made the United States her captive, nor does Japan, although the appearance of Zen Buddhism and other elements of Japanese culture in a sort of American subculture of the 1950s testifies to the fact that many members of our postwar army of occupation in the Orient went through an experience not unlike Burns' in Italy. The popularity of *The Gallery* seems to have expressed a dissatisfaction with American values and temperament and a rueful wish for something different, rather than a change or a resolve to change.

So the war novel bridged the country's transition from war to peace, giving readers vicarious participation in what was recently past rather than clues to what was just ahead. As affluence became more general and the postwar society took shape, one might have expected the novel to turn its attention to the quality of that society, denouncing its hypocrisies and satirizing its fatuities; but, in general, this did not happen. Instead, society directly treated—the manners and mores of a certain time and place, which had always been the core subject of the novel—tended to fade out of it entirely. And the reason is not far to seek. What with such new elements as the supergiant corporations and the need to conform to their ways, the Cold War and McCarthyism, supermarkets and stock-market booms and the threat of nuclear extinction, the reassuring moral blacks and whites of 1939 tended to fade into the common gray of 1955, and social comment in fiction could no longer have the fixed moral background that traditional storytelling requires. The social tragicomedies of Marquand, set generally against the relatively fixed society of New England, began to seem more parochial; Southern writers for a few years after the war found the kind of stability they needed in life below the Mason-Dixon line, but then violent social change in that region destroyed it as a backdrop for human idiosyncrasy or a subject for gentle ribbing. The American novel of manners lost ground in the 1950s and early 1960s. Sociology—science of a sort, and thus entitled to be amoral, as art is not—tended to take over from the novel the function of giving an account of society.

2

Indeed, the novel began to turn away not only from society and toward the isolated individual experience, but even away from the elements that had always been its *sine qua non,* story and character. Form and style became more important than content, and the characteristic form became a sort of personal essay that in 1939 would scarcely have been called fiction at all. Malcolm Cowley, assuming that a nation's fictional stereotypes are part of its emotional climate at any given time, has written that the stereotype of the late 1930s was the martyred striker, that of the 1940s the civilian soldier, and that of the 1950s the young man ruined by his mother. The situation of the last-named, whatever its relevance to American Momism, is hardly the jumping-off point for an investigation of the country at large that the earlier two were. Essentially, it is a personal dilemma.

And along with the turning away from society as a subject went a resort, often frantic, to symbols in an effort to make order out of moral chaos. Too often the effort on the novelist's part appeared to be to *seem* to mean something rather than to mean it. After all, who, in the midst of postwar complexity and ambiguity, could know exactly what to mean? Who could have the beautiful certainty about the proper interpretation of current events that the author of *The Grapes of Wrath* had had? The most successful of the few brave novelists who still attempted to grapple with the broad sweep of American society found it necessary to adopt highly eccentric and oblique approaches. Ralph Ellison in *Invisible Man* (1952), in order to show what life in America is like for a highly sophisticated and sensitive Negro, used methods closely analogous to those of the Surrealist painters. John Updike in *Rabbit, Run* (1960) tells his story from the point of view of an antihero, a sex-obsessed young man of decent impulses and haunted by religious ideas but with so little moral spine that in effect he is a kind of monster—so utter a slob that the reader who still hopes for his country is almost forced to reject the resulting vision of American life, however great its verisimilitude.

It is odd to find that probably the most satisfying fictional picture of the physical, and to some extent the moral, aspects of postwar America is contained in a book written by a man for whom English is the second language and the United States the last of several homelands. The book is *Lolita* (1955), by the Russian emigré writer Vladimir Nabokov; its "hero" is a seedy and depraved refugee scholar who earns our sympathy more than Updike's Rabbit chiefly because he is certifiably insane; its "heroine" is a rudderless and wickedly sexy American preadolescent; and its description of an automobile tour of the United States taken by this pair—complete with hotel bedrooms, a hospital, an historical reconstruction, highways, roadside joints, and countless motels—is funny, sad, and oddly unforgettable. Sick and confused people, then, to show the reflection of a sick and confused civilization; what we have seen of ourselves in the fictional mirror has not been reassuring.

Meanwhile in 1961 the war novel came in for what may have been its curtain-call appearance, in *Catch-22* by Joseph Heller. In the decade since the war novel had come to the end of its first phase, there had been quite a change. Gone now was the earnest effort to impose order and meaning on the war experience by rendering it in precise detail, or by making of it a symbol for universal suffering; gone, indeed, were all earnestness and all hope for meaning. The wind of Existentialism and "absurdity" had swept over literary America in the interim, and now the dominant note was unrelieved cynicism and hysterical laughter at the meaninglessness of war—and, perhaps, of everything else. The high-level bungling and destructive futility of many of the military operations described in *The Naked and the Dead* had shocked many readers, but these things appeared pale by comparison with the goings-on in *Catch-22*. Here we have a bomber group in which most of the members are attempting to avoid combat by proving themselves insane—only to discover the catch, that the authorities consider the desire to avoid combat as *prima facie* evidence of sanity; here we have an American officer in the entrepreneur tradition who makes a deal with the Germans to bomb his own base for cost plus 6 percent; here we find a single character who is cool and courageous in combat—only to discover that in human relations he is a savage and a criminal. *Catch-22*, a tedious book in some parts and a very funny one in others, cannot be written off as sophomoric iconoclasm; it is a telling hoot of derision, not so much at war as at what came after. It is the only World War II novel whose real subject is postwar America.

3

As an index of change, let's compare an important 1939 novel and an important 1964 one that have certain marked similarities. Both *The Web and the Rock* by Thomas Wolfe and *Herzog* by Saul

Bellow are essentially romantic autobiographical projections in which the central theme is a neurotic love relationship. Yet how differently is this time-honored subject treated in the two books, and how different they are in almost every other way!

Certainly, the two heroes present a contrast. Wolfe's Monk Webber is an Anglo-Saxon Protestant from a small town in the South; Bellow's Moses Elkanah Herzog is a Jew from Montreal and Chicago. Webber is presented as masterful, dominating, in the heroic mold, energetic, physically strong, attractive to women; Herzog, although his good looks and passivity fascinate aggressive women, is a middle-aged drifter with a partially failed career who has been cuckolded over a long period by his best friend. Webber is creative, a budding novelist; Herzog is a philosopher-historian, a shrewd critic whose self-expression takes the hobbled form of writing letters, usually unsent, to public figures. Webber is proud and self-congratulatory, never wry or rueful; Herzog is self-deprecatory. "If I am out of my mind, it's all right with me," he says in the book's first line. Webber is naïve and humorless in the tradition of romantic heroes; Herzog is sophisticated, witty, ironic. And each of them expresses the popular view of the quintessential American in the time when he was created.

In form both books are, strictly speaking, plotless and episodic. But Wolfe, striving to be in the tradition of epic narrative, labors valiantly to seem to be telling a story, using a number of literary devices to that end, while Bellow simply sets down Herzog's thoughts, writings, conversations, and movements during a few not particularly crucial days in his life, in the course of which he goes from New York to Martha's Vineyard to visit friends, returns, has dinner with a woman, visits magistrate's court, goes to Chicago to see his stepmother, his daughter, and an old colleague, becomes involved in the book's only action—a minor automobile accident—and returns to his house in the Berkshire hills. The notion that the novel should be a story has given way to the notion that it should be pure expression.

It is in certain key attitudes, explicit in the main characters and implicit in the point of view of the authors, that the contrasts between *The Web and the Rock* and *Herzog* are most enlightening about social change. Webber, for example, seems never to read the newspapers, and is apparently unaware of the world outside the borders of his own country until it touches him personally; the existence of Nazism as a rising world menace strikes him all of a heap when he is beaten up at a festival in Munich. Herzog, on the other hand, knows about everything, and broods about the state of the world constantly; Khrushchev, Eisenhower, Adlai Stevenson, and many public figures in nonpolitical fields are among those addressed or discussed in his admonitory letters. Webber is a patriotic American provincial who has no emotional connection with the rest of the world apart from a sentimental affection for his imaginary version of German culture. Herzog is a cosmopolite, feeling little identification with the United States, and the author seems to expect such cosmopolitanism in the reader, since the book is dotted with untranslated passages in Yiddish, Italian, and even French as garbled by a Japanese. Webber, as a country boy, idealizes the big city, while Herzog, a city boy, idealizes the countryside; he thinks of his old house in the Berkshires as a solid foothold in Anglo-Saxon America, and there he bumbles around ineffectually trying to "do for" himself, a parody of a pioneer. Webber is scathingly patronizing toward immigrant groups in America, and his strongly ambivalent attitude toward Jews, explicit in his relations with his sophisticated Jewish mistress, would be called anti-Semitism now. Herzog is openly patronizing toward Anglo-Saxon Protestants ("Because the government gave much of the continent away to the railroads," he remarks, "the Wasps . . . stopped boiling their own soap circa 1880, took European tours, and began to complain of the Micks and the Spicks and the Sheenies"); a Jew himself, he does not so much hate the non-Jews as simply stay out of their way, the only non-Jewish characters in *Herzog* being a working-class New England couple and an inept, unperspicacious psychiatrist.

Or consider the two men's attitude toward love and sex. Webber openly believes in the old double standard—he announces to his mistress that he is entitled to have other concurrent affairs and that she is not; while Herzog comes close to reversing it—he assumes his wife has a perfect right, without provocation, to leave him for another man and take the children with her. The key activity of Webber's woman is cooking delicious dinners for him; that of Herzog's wife is studying Russian literature in order to compete with him more effectively, and refusing to sleep with him because it interrupts her studies. Webber's Esther keeps a spotless house, while Herzog's Madeleine keeps such a messy one that he has to straighten it up himself to make it livable. And, of course, there are sexual details and taboo words in *Herzog*, none in *The Web and the Rock*.

Finally, consider how the two authors leave their heroes. We last see Webber, having broken with his mistress in order to pursue his career and his self-development through writing, sentimentalizing his affair in rolling rhetoric: "What glory was ever greater than our own! . . . Who has ever loved as we did? Who ever knew the glory and the grief and all the lovely times that we have known together?" And Herzog? He fades out about to fall into the clutches of another woman, and, in the momentarily tranquil anticipation of this event, finding that he is cured of the compulsion to write letters; he has achieved a sort of peace not by releasing his creative powers but rather by exorcising them. Both of these novels enjoyed great popular success; that they appear now as black and white, odd and even, heads and tails, is no accident.

4

Meanwhile the serious Broadway theater, beset by crippling and almost insurmountable financial troubles as production costs went sky-high, tended to immerse itself progressively in psychopathology that provided intellectual puzzles for the highbrows and sex and violence for the lowbrows, while "serious" music tended to plunge so incautiously into technical experimentation—the use of electronic equipment and other devices to produce outlandish new sounds, the increasing abandonment of traditional tonality and rhythmic structure—that to the music-loving layman it no longer seemed to do what in his view music must do, that is, stir emotion. An indigenous form of American music, jazz, has been described by Whitney Balliett as "a largely subterranean but still major strain of American artistic expression." But Balliett, a lover of jazz, may be too modest in his claim for it; a case could be made that since 1939 jazz has been closer to the surface of our national life, both artistic and social, than any other kind of American music.

At any rate, the interaction between jazz and society has been specific and obvious; the evolving course of jazz over the past quarter-century is a miniature social history in itself. At the end of the Thirties jazz was dominated by the kind of music called swing, characteristically played for dancing by large bands. The most popular of these bands were made up of and led by white men, although some of the best were those of Negroes—always the innovators of jazz, and, of course, the founders of it—like Count Basie and the incomparable Duke Ellington. Of the trumpeter Louis Armstrong, the father of swing music, Martin Williams has written: "There is not necessarily any 'new' rhythmic device in Armstrong's musical vocabulary. . . . He employed inflections, accents, metrics and phrasing in such a way as to give the music a new kind of momentum." But, as the decade turned, the momentum was running out. This fact, combined with the specific disruptions of the war—the military draft, gasoline rationing, a stiff wartime entertainment tax—spelled the end of the big bands. In about 1944 there emerged a whole new style; called either bebop or modern jazz, it was played by small ensembles mainly for listening rather than dancing, it was looser rhythmically and more advanced harmonically than any jazz that had preceded it, and its chief prophets were the alto saxophonist Charlie Parker and the trumpeter Dizzy Gillespie.

Almost contemporaneously with bebop there arrived a separate though related movement that soon came to be called cool jazz; like so much of the jazz before it, it was invented by a Negro (Lester Young) but largely popularized and exploited by white musicians (notably Stan Getz and Gerry Mulligan). Its mood of withdrawal and restraint was an utter reversal of the famous spirit of uninhibited freedom that had hitherto dominated jazz from its infancy in the Deep South. And this new mood seemed to respond to and to embody a subtle disappointment in the quality of life in postwar America. The wartime dream of what the peace would be like was somehow not working out, all this was not quite what had been expected, and the response was a kind of music that expressed a certain disillusionment, a certain withdrawal, a certain creeping into the shell analogous to that of the veterans who settled down after the war, buying a house and beginning to raise a family, and seeming to lose any real interest in anything else. At the other extreme, cool jazz was to become the inspiration for the bohemianism of the 1950s, the so-called Beat movement, which was another sort of revolt through withdrawal.

While all this was going on, jazz was acquiring not new adherents—indeed, it had lost many thousands of followers with the collapse of the big dance bands—but new status: it was coming to be taken seriously by the intellectuals, and regular columns criticizing it seriously and intelligently were beginning to appear in popular publications. Jazz musicians themselves developed self-consciousness as artists. Benny Goodman in the 1930s had felt compelled to establish his musicianship by showing that he could play Bach with the violinist Szigeti; the Charlie Parkers and Dizzy Gillespies now were content to show their artistry in jazz itself.

Parker died in 1955, and, more than coincidentally, the year marks a watershed in the development of jazz. Beginning then, another new breed of musicians gradually emerged. Most of them were Negroes, but they had little in common with their grandfathers who had played New Orleans jazz on dusty tailgates in the South. These men were urban, intellectual, highly sophisticated musically; many of them were graduates of the leading music schools like Juilliard in New York or the New England Conservatory of Music. Like Ellington, but few others among their elders, they could make their own music from start to finish; the new jazzman was composer, arranger, and instrumentalist. Not surprisingly, what they produced was a kind of jazz far closer than what had gone before to developments both in "serious" music and in the other arts. They composed in classical forms like the rondo and fugue, or they experimented with entirely new forms; they flirted with atonality, after the manner of Schoenberg; they abandoned completely the traditional set-length chorus. Then just before 1960 there appeared a new star in the alto saxophonist Ornette Coleman, who was immediately hailed as a genius —as few jazzmen had been before him—by some of the leading names in the established music world. That Coleman himself feels like an artist rather than a journeyman music-maker is dramatically shown by the fact that, after being a great success for a couple of years, he withdrew entirely from public performances and worked in seclusion for almost three more years in order to perfect and advance his music.

"O strange new world!" this strange new music, hard to listen to and almost impossible to dance to, but haunting and evocative, seems to be saying. Like recent novels and recent works in painting and sculpture, it is stretching or even abandoning traditional formal limits in reaching to express the puzzled and puzzling mood of its time. And the jazz world seems to be abreast of its time in a more explicit sense; a new social element began intruding in the form of tension between the races. For decades, white and black jazzmen had got along strikingly well together, despite the tendency of the whites, by intent or not, to cash in on the discoveries of the blacks; but after about 1960, as the civil-rights struggle nationally was moving into a more activist phase, Negro jazzmen began to introduce into their music a certain element of violence, often overtly antiwhite. Curiously, the music of the Negro equality movement is not jazz, the Negro's own music, but "folk songs" written by white men. But, as Balliett reports, in New York City there emerged a few years ago a curious organization called the Jazz Composers Guild. At its meetings, white and Negro members held "discussions" of the race issue that tended to become uninhibitedly acrimonious; then when tempers were thoroughly worked up, the antagonists would play together, putting their hostility into their music. Perhaps it is not too much to hope that this surprising use of ugly but deep-seated feelings to serve creative ends may prove to be prophetic for the future of race relations in a wider context.

5

Like so many other things, American painting in 1939 can be seen now to have been at a point of end and beginning. The reigning style, as in the novel, was straightforward realism; the reigning subject, again as in the novel, was the American scene, often treated with strong overtones of patriotism. So it had been all through the depression. The American painters who had lived in Paris in the 1920s, absorbing European culture into their lives and often European painting styles into their work, had come home in the years after the 1929 crash, and their return had proved to be spiritual as well as physical. Beginning in 1935, when the federal government through its WPA artists' project had become by far the country's largest art patron, artists had had practical reason to become patriotic in their work, but at the same time there can be no doubt that the sentiment was genuine. In all the arts Americans of the time were finding strength in their own roots.

Regionalism was riding high, and the most favored region was the one so often thought of as most characteristically American, the Middle West. The big four of American-scene painting of 1939 were Thomas Hart Benton of Missouri, John Steuart Curry of Kansas, Grant Wood of Iowa, and Charles Burchfield of Ohio. By way of further parallel with the trend in the novel, there was also a group of painters of political and social protest including such men as William Gropper and Jack Levine, but even some of these, during the later New Deal years, often tended to emphasize the romantic and creative things in national life—the building of dams, the winning of the West—over the darker themes of poverty and deprivation. Again, the quest for what was quintessentially American combined with the depression-time idealization of the poor and untutored led to a large-scale rediscovery of American folk art. Art dealers and collectors culled the farms and villages of the country in search of Sunday painters whose works might be diamonds in the rough; it was in 1939 that the pawky canvases of the upstate New York painter then called Mother Moses, and later promoted to Grandma Moses, were first put on display in New York City.

Folk art's simplicity, gawkiness of proportion, and lack of perspective even had their effect on highly sophisticated artists; Grant Wood's "Parson Weems' Fable," painted in 1939, and showing a tiny but fully uniformed and adult-faced George Washington being chided for chopping down a cherry tree as round as a globe, managed to combine folk-art tendencies, American-scene painting, and national folklore into what one critic scathingly called a "daintily patriotic whimsy." It was a painting of a much less currently fashionable sort that won the year's most important art accolade, first prize in the Carnegie International Exhibition in Pittsburgh, that year. The winner, Alexander Brook's "Georgia Jungle," showed a Negro family standing beside a meandering stream in desperately poor farmland, with tumbledown shacks in the background and a dull sky overhead. Yet the values in the work were not anger or social protest, certainly not patriotism, not the neatening up of messy things that is characteristic of primitive painting; rather, they were lyricism, sympathy for humanity, and artistic craftsmanship. Even so, "Georgia Jungle" was American scene-painting, all right.

Despite occasional triumphs, there was a tiredness, a played-out quality about much American painting in 1939, and this was felt by critics both at home and abroad. The critic and museum director James Johnson Sweeney spoke of "a fundamental dissatisfaction with the results" of both regionalism and social satire, while *The Nation*, referring to the reception accorded United States exhibitions sent to Paris and London that summer, reported that "a good many sly remarks were made by French and English critics . . . their main view seems to have been that American art is imitative . . . of French art, or else only weak and sprawling." French and English critics had been saying such things about American painting for more than a century, so it was nothing new. Yet, oddly enough, it was precisely in imitation of French art that the wellspring of a powerful and indigenous postwar American art movement, which would eventually rise to confound the Old World, was to be found.

6

New art movements are always born when old ones are still in the ascendancy, and in the late Thirties there were underwater currents running in American art. In 1936 the Museum of Modern Art had put on a show of European fantastic art, Dada and Surrealism, and while the main thing the American public derived from it seemed to be a set of jokes based on the Swiss surrealist Oppenheim's "Fur-Lined Teacup," this sensational exhibition may have served to condition some Americans to the idea of the outrageous in art. A small group of American abstract painters meanwhile had formed themselves into an association and, beginning in 1937, held annual exhibitions in New York, to very little fanfare. This is not to say that either extreme distortion of reality or outright abstraction were new in American painting; there had been a first wave of abstraction before the First World War and a second in the Twenties, but they had been swept away by the realism of the depression years. Now, though, a third wave was about to begin in earnest, and part of the wind behind it was the sudden influx to New York of European painters as war refugees. Max Ernst, André Masson, Yves Tanguy, Marc Chagall, and Piet Mondrian were only a few of those who had arrived by 1941, and their effect on the American art scene was immediate and explosive, reinvigorating it and compelling it first to imitation, then to new directions of its own. By an accident of history, the traditional direction of artists across the Atlantic had been reversed, with benefits to the new hosts that the old ones had apparently never derived.

Out of this wartime ferment came the movement that has dominated not only American art but world art in the postwar period, the movement called Abstract Expressionism. One by one, in the years just before and after 1945, the pioneers of the movement—most of whom had previously been painting more or less in the accepted manner of depression days—went through periods of being under the influence of the Europeans, then moved on to evolve the unprecedented styles that were to make them famous. Characteristically, the result presented a striking challenge to the imaginaton of the viewer in that it looked like nothing he had ever before been asked to think of as a picture, much less as a work of art. Great gobs of paint were splashed, slapped, or dripped on huge canvases, apparently without plan; little rivulets that had run down erratically from the big strokes of color were allowed to stay; and the absence of any recognizable object, or even the bare suggestion of such an object, became an article of faith.

Franz Kline's paintings consisted of wide black strokes at seemingly random angles on a white background; to some, they suggested concentration-camp barbed wire, but to others the reference was not so specific, and what Kline seemed to these to be conveying was a generalized sense of modern tension. Mark Rothko, a Latvian-born Jew, painted great pools of solid color ringed by fuzzy clouds of another color, somehow suggesting a kind of desperately achieved tranquillity. The great, gaudy slashes of paint characteristic of the naturalized Dutchman Willem de Kooning unmistakably embodied violence; later, in his most celebrated work, de Kooning was to violate the school's no-object tenet by painting a series of women—but what women! Violently distorted, horribly grinning, menacing, with an almost nightmarish sexiness but at the same time a quality of endearing helplessness, they seemed to stand for a society that had lost its bearings.

Jackson Pollock, the generally acknowledged leader of the school, went through an evolution typical of it: a young man from Wyoming, he first did American-scene paintings under the tutelage of the old master Benton himself; then for several years he experimented with strange faces and animals distorted in the Surrealist manner; then in about 1948 he abandoned his brush and easel, laid canvas on the floor, and took to dripping paint on it. As Rudi Blesh describes the process, Pollock "raced around it with pails, hurling gushes of violent hues to splash and flow, to gut and to congeal. . . . Hours went by before the pails were empty and the fury over. Pollock squatted on his heels in a corner, trembling and spent." Strangely, the result was not always chaos, nor the decorated linoleum that Pollock's work has been compared to; in the happiest cases it was a blend of unleashed violence and hidden order that has the power to bring tears to the eyes.

What was it all about? Partly, no doubt, it expressed the desire to shock and the need for something new; in no other form of art is novelty at such a premium as in the plastic arts. But there was something else. Harold Rosenberg, in an essay that became an Abstract Expressionist manifesto, explained it this way:

> At a certain moment the canvas began to appear to one American painter after another as an arena in which to act—rather than as a space in which to reproduce, re-design, analyze or "express" an object, actual or imagined. What was to go on the canvas was not a picture but an event. . . . What matters always is the revelation contained in the act. . . . With traditional aesthetic references discarded as irrelevant, what gives the canvas its meaning is not psychological data but . . . the way the artist organizes his emotional and intellectual energy as if he were in a living situation.

A fantastic theory? To be sure—Mary McCarthy objected that you can't hang an action on a wall—and certainly one destructive to art itself, in the long run. But for the moment—a certain moment around 1950, in the national twilight zone between peace and war, scarcity and abundance, the past and the future—Abstract Expressionism managed to express contemporary America more completely than any previous American art had ever expressed the country in its time. Here were all the confusion, the latent violence, the love of ostentation, the doubt, the belief in action as a resolver of doubt.

Perhaps, indeed, it expressed something more, something endemic all around the world; because the movement was soon recognized and honored in almost every country where painting is practiced or followed. Suddenly American exhibitions were in demand everywhere. The American style became the International style as artists in other countries imitated it. In London, Paris, and Rome, the European capitals that had so long condescended to American art, museums and collectors vied for the latest works of the Americans, and young painters studied them as Americans of earlier generations had studied the Europeans. The tables were turned: the world capital of contemporary art had at last, and temporarily, crossed the Atlantic.

7

We come now to the years of Abstract Expressionism's popular glory, which were also the years of its artistic decline. In this chapter, in trying to show how works of art have both revealed and enriched the changing civilization from which they sprang, I have tried to treat the works apart from public reaction to them, but here that procedure becomes impossible, because in the 1950s the American public reaction to Abstract Expressionism was part of, and had an enormous effect upon, the course of the work itself.

What happened was that Abstract Expressionist painting became a craze, a big-money fad. I don't mean, of course, that the mass of Americans, the production workers and secretaries and farmers, were suddenly converted from calendar art to Pollock and de Kooning, because of course they were not. But among the few thousand museum and gallery people, critics, and collectors who make up the art world, the conversion took on overtones of a stampede—particularly after Pollock's death in an automobile crash on Long Island in August, 1956, had elevated him in the knowledgeable but vulgar mind to a position of pseudomartyrdom not unlike that occupied by the late young actor James Dean in the minds of movie-mad teenagers. First the more esoteric media of public information publicized the movement as they had never publicized any American art before, and eventually the mass popular media joined in. The *Saturday Evening Post*, after hooting at Abstract Expressionism by comparing it to the paintings of a chimpanzee in 1957, emphatically joined the ranks of its admirers in 1959. But the key factor in the popularization was the collectors, who bid the prices of individual paintings up from hundreds of dollars to thousands, then tens of thousands, and eventually, in a few cases, more than a hundred thousand. The new movement seemed to fit perfectly the status and culture aspirations of the newly affluent members of a fantastically expanding economy.

Paradoxically, these open-handed collectors did not always become art-world powers, latter-day Medici; more often, indeed, they were closer to the role of victim. Were these smearings and drippings art? Were they culture? Were they worth money? How could a simple businessman know, except by what he was told by the "experts"? If he admitted that a painting had no meaning for him, he might be showing his obtuseness; on the other hand, if he raved about it and bought it, he might, for all he knew, be serving as the "mark" in a confidence game. The art public was caught between the Scylla of being a philistine and the Charybdis of being a sucker; for the first time in our history the artist and his dealer seemed to have the collector over a barrel.

But the effect of such money and acceptance on the artists was to make them better businessmen and poorer artists. Deprived of the role of outcast that had long been traditional to the artist in America, they tended to embrace the most conventional of middle-class attitudes and prejudices. A whole second generation of Abstract Expressionist artists appeared who, generally speaking, were as minutely conscious of status, as eager for advancement by fair means or foul, and yet as cautious about giving offense in the wrong place, as any gray-flannel man in corporation management. Frank Getlein, the witty art critic of *The New Republic*, saw these painters as artistic equivalents of cautious, middle-of-the-road Eisenhower Republicans, and he took to describing their style as "Ikeonography."

And, indeed, the number and closeness of the parallels between Abstract Expressionism in its later phase and the prevailing national ethic of the late 1950s are striking. In a time when bad design, sloppy handiwork, and "built-in obsolescence" in product-manufacturing were becoming notorious, Abstract Expressionism made a kind of principle of careless craftsmanship and unsound use of materials. In a time when the popularization of psychoanalysis was exalting insight over reason and gesture over thought, Abstract Expressionism was looking upon the slightest hint of appeal to the rational mind as heresy. At a time when the role of advertising in our national life seemed to loom unprecedentedly large, the Abstract Expressionist artists took to advertising themselves with "manifestos" that shared the incantatory quality and the doubtful grammar of plugs for cigarettes or lipstick. ("To be right is the most terrific personal state that nobody is interested in," said Franz Kline, and the art world earnestly brooded about the sentence for several years.) At a time when the country was getting rich and wanted everything, like money, to come easy, Abstract Expressionism offered a kind of art that rejects the past and in which, therefore, anyone can become an instant authority with scarcely any effort. In a time when mass production was the key to industrial success, Abstract Expressionists, including some of the old masters of the movement, took to painting virtually the same picture over and over again—presumably because they, like an automobile manufacturer, knew there was a ready market for that picture but might not be for some other one. Finally, in a time when many were forgetting the rights of minorities and adopting the attitude of a bully toward them, some of the high priests of Abstract Expressionism were turning so savagely and vindictively on the artistic underdogs of the time, the traditional representational painters, as to recall the methods of Senator McCarthy himself.

Small wonder that the movement, having run out of creative steam and become a kind of unintentional parody of bourgeois life, eventually spent itself and was succeeded in the early Sixties by new fads—the stale jokes and meaningless shocks of "pop art" and the childish trickery, based on long-known techniques to achieve optical illusion, of "op art." The disastrous decline of Abstract Expressionism—a kind of art that in its first rapture deservedly brought the United States high esteem in the eyes of the rest of the art world—was one more example, and will perhaps stand as the classic one, of how success in the arts defeats itself in a materialistic society like ours. The superficialities and banalities of pop and op do not reflect the deep-running currents of national life, as scene-painting did in the 1930s or Abstract Expressionism did in its early years at the end of the 1940s; instead, they reflect merely a few superficial aspects, such as a desperate love of chic and a vague sense of disorientation. But we can take heart from the probability that the doldrums will not last. Something better in art, better both under eternity and under the current American sky, is probably having its beginning as this is written.

VIII. FROM PARADISE TO BERKELEY

1

If we compare, even cursorily, the pertinent figures on U.S. education in the prewar years with those for the mid-Sixties, we will not fail to find a picture that must by now be familiar to readers of these chapters, that is, a picture of increase so great as to make the term "growth" seem inadequate. Just to begin with, proportionately far more Americans are young now than used to be; in 1965 about 40 percent of us were aged seventeen or younger, as against less than 30 percent in 1940, and the percentage is almost sure to increase still further over the next few years as the famously numerous "war babies" go through their peak child-bearing years. Enrollment in schools of all kinds and at all levels has not merely kept pace with this increase; it has greatly exceeded it. The nation's elementary and high schools, public and private, had about 28 million scholars in 1940; they had over 50 million in 1965. As noted previously, the average adult American of 1940 was an elementary school graduate; of 1965, a high school graduate. Enrollment at colleges and universities in 1940 amounted to 1.5 million, or 15 percent of persons aged eighteen through twenty-one; such enrollment in 1965 amounted to over 5 million, or more than 40 percent of persons in that age group, and, moreover, the increase for 1965 over the previous year alone exceeded the current *total* enrollment in all British universities. In 1940 fewer than 200,000 bachelor's degrees were conferred on young Americans; in 1965, almost half a million. Finally, money: in 1940 our total national outlay from all sources for formal education amounted to $3.4 billion, while in 1965 it considerably exceeded ten times that sum.

What had happened? There was more to know—some science-oriented educators in the 1950s took to talking roundly, if not precisely, of a doubling of the total store of human knowledge every ten years since 1945; there was more urgent reason for as many as possible to know as much as possible; and there was money available to hire the job done. But if only the process were as simple as that! In fact, the quantitative increase in U.S. education over the quarter-century was accompanied by the rise of new methods and the decline of old ones, the appearance of new and intractable problems, and a series of dramatic ebbs and flows in the collective character of the people being educated, the nation's raisers of hopes and bringers of despair, its incessantly scrutinized youth.

2

Let us recall a little of what American education was like twenty-five years ago.

Ideologically, it was in those days strongly influenced (although not actually dominated) by the movement called progressivism, putting emphasis on permissiveness and on education as a social process, and by an idea compatible with both progressivism and the national spirit of the time, the idea that the schools should concentrate on producing good citizens rather than merely well-stuffed minds. An important education conference held at Columbia in August, 1939, took as its theme the responsibility of education "for the defense and advance of democracy." The ivory tower was not in fashion. The Progressive Education Association, with almost ten thousand teachers and educators in its membership and generally considered to be the spearhead of educational advance, beat the drums for sparing the rod and creating "the child-centered school." (The "child-centered home" would, as we know now, come next.) Although its theories were put into practice most explicitly in private schools and colleges, progressivism's influence was felt in public education as well, and some public schools, like the elementary ones of Los Angeles County, were wholeheartedly and enthusiastically progressive.

But for all the advanced thought, American education was in many ways backward, hardly out of the frontier era. For one thing, the old-style one-teacher school was still very much in evidence; coast to coast, 130,000 such public schools were entrusted with the elementary or high school education of several million children. A New York survey made in 1939 showed that some of the school districts in that state still had the same boundaries that had been given them in the year 1812; more than a century and a quarter of population increases and shifts had gone unremarked by the authorities. Nationally, although three out of every four students at all levels were in elementary schools, enrollment at such schools was actually decreasing, partly in response to the depression-time decline in the birth rate and partly because depression-time dislocations made it impossible for many parents to send their children to school at all.

Why this picture of practical stagnation at a time of high theoretical hopes and ideals? The chief answer is that the schools, like so many of their students, were desperately poor. Expenditures on public education had been decreasing, sometimes sharply, during the 1930s. The burden of school financing still fell almost exclusively on real-estate taxes in local communities, and as assessments went down or properties lapsed from the tax rolls through default, the money needed for school maintenance, to say nothing of improvements, was often simply not forthcoming. The situation was dramatically shown in the autumn of 1939 when the public schools of Toledo had to be closed for two months because of a lack of funds to keep them running.

Despite straits like these, the idea of federal aid to education had not been accepted by the country. In 1939 the federal government did manage to spend the hardly trivial sum of $2.7 million on aid to education through various programs, but even this was almost an over-the-transom kind of thing. People simply did not like the idea. Under the Constitution was not education a residual power of the state? Even when in desperate need, should the states sell out their precious independence to federal control? Again, there was the question of aid to parochial schools. Was not the separation of church and state a fundamental American principle? Even President Roosevelt himself, asking in 1938 for federal education grants amounting over a six-year period to the then huge sum of $855 million, was circumspect on the subject. "No one," he said, "wants the federal government to subsidize education any more than is absolutely necessary. It has been, and, I take it, will continue to be, the traditional policy of the United States to leave the actual management of the schools and their curriculum to state and local control." The consensus still felt, better the overcrowded one-room schoolhouse, with its single undertrained teacher and its leaky roof, than the surrender of even part of the authority to educate one's children to the sinister octopus of Washington.

Finally—to touch fleetingly on a topic that will be treated more fully elsewhere—in 1939 the races were, broadly speaking, educated apart, to the clear disadvantage of Negroes. There were no mixed schools of any kind in the South, where the "separate but equal facilities" doctrine had the backing of law; there were few indeed in the North, where economic disparities and the geographical isolation of Negroes in ghettos made it all too possible for liberals to hold integrationist views and still send their children to lily-white schools. The Negro college graduate was a rarity, and the Negro graduate of a white college was almost a freak. Integration? The very term in its present meaning was not in common usage. "The year 1938 has experienced a definite trend toward the integration of school subjects," an educational authority wrote in 1939; he was talking about relating subject matter in various fields, like history and literature, to one another.

The first force for postwar change in our educational system was, of course, the baby boom. The tidal wave of new young Americans meant constant pressure on physical facilities and the supply of teachers at the elementary level. Meanwhile, growing national wealth led naturally to increased demand for berths in colleges, so the pressure was on there, too. But these things were only the beginning. As if American educators did not have enough problems in providing for a vast increase in the number of pupils, they were simultaneously faced with—indeed, they were doing much to create—a rising demand for a complete overhaul of educational methods. In the face of the new scientific and technological advances, the old methods that in many cases had seemed good enough for a century or more suddenly came to appear as dangerous anachronisms. Education, it began to be said, was technologically an underdeveloped country; it was due for its belated industrial revolution.

During the 1950s various researchers in various places were working, largely unnoticed by the general public, to help bring such a revolution into being. Radical reforms in teacher-training methods were proposed by such bodies as the Fund for the Advancement of Education, an arm of the Ford Foundation. New researches into children's learning capacities culminated in the trail-breaking, much-quoted, and, of course, highly controversial conclusion of the Harvard psychologist, Jerome S. Bruner: "Any subject can be taught effectively in some intellectually honest form to any child at any stage of development." Here was a complete reversal of orthodox doctrine. We had been believing young minds must be carefully protected from overstrain; now we were abruptly told that they must be protected from atrophy arising from disuse. An enterprising MIT physicist, Jerrold Zacharias, concluded that in view of new developments the teaching of physics in American high schools was obsolete and had to be overhauled completely to take account of questions of quantum and the atom that were now indispensible knowledge to anyone wanting to understand modern science. Another Harvard psychologist, B. F. Skinner, was pioneering in the development of the technology that came to be known as "programmed instruction"—the usurpation of part of the teacher's function by mechanical devices of one sort or another. "Any teacher who can be replaced by a machine should be," as Skinner put it.

3

But all this was going on largely in the laboratory. In practice, the American educational system, bursting at the seams as it was, continued to struggle along largely on traditional methods, because that was what most people wanted it to do. Teach five-or seven-year-olds quantum mechanics or economic principles? The idea seemed preposterous. Replace, or completely retrain, the high school science teacher who had been good enough for a generation of students, and who, on the side, was perhaps coach of the county championship basketball team? Indeed not. And on a more serious level, the upholders of the humanistic, liberal-arts tradition that had always been so powerful a force in our concept of education found themselves recoiling instinctively from the very notion of mechanized instruction that would reduce or perhaps eliminate personal contact between student and teacher. Schools, they said firmly, are not factories, and should not become factories.

The country at large thought its schools, with all their problems, were doing their job adequately; there did not seem to be much concrete evidence that they were failing, and in the absence of such evidence the old ways were good enough. People do not much like to think about educational problems if they can avoid it. The education of one's own child is a topic that bores almost no one; on the other hand, the education of everybody else's child is a topic that bores almost everyone. A jolt to complacency was needed to bring the educational industrial revolution into being, and, of course, in due time the jolt came.

On October 4, 1957, Soviet Russia successfully launched Sputnik I, the first man-made earth satellite, an 184-pound sphere that circled the earth every hour and a half in an elliptical orbit. A month later, she launched Sputnik II, this one weighing more than a thousand pounds and carrying a live dog. The effect of the Soviet feats on American public opinion can hardly be overestimated. A long succession of scientific and technological world "firsts," of which the fission and fusion bombs had been only the most spectacular, had given us an illusion of permanent scientific pre-eminence. Everyone knew in 1957 that space exploration was the next item on the scientific and technological agenda, and almost everyone assumed that the United States would lead the way as usual. Now came the rude awakening. It wasn't so much that we were militarily threatened by the new developments—apparently, for the present, we weren't—as simply as that we had been beaten. Nor did the new sense of chagrin and unease disappear when we managed to orbit our own first satellite early in 1958. Our scientific leaders told us emphatically that we were now decisively behind in the space race; our education authorities added with equal emphasis that we were behind in the education race.

These humbling discoveries had far-reaching effects in many areas of American life, but probably in none so decisively as in education. In the first place, education began to become recognized for the first time as a national concern of such overwhelming importance as to override the familiar objections to federal aid. Federal funds in large sums for student loans, for school construction, for new teaching materials, began to be available with the passage in 1958 of the National Defense Education Act, which was later greatly extended by amendments, and in the seven years after the first Sputniks our national outlay from all sources for public education doubled. (Meanwhile, colleges and universities were benefiting from vastly increased individual contributions from their loyal alumni, amounting in the 1960s to around $100 million a year—a surprising amount of it going to public state universities as well as the private ones that have always relied on alumni support.)

Then in 1965 came passage of a historic aid-to-education law—*Teachers College Record* was not alone in calling it "one of the most historic pieces of legislation ever enacted"—pledging more than a billion dollars in federal aid, mostly to school districts containing many needy children. This act even went so far as to achieve a compromise on the old sore point of federal aid to parochial schools that had paralyzed so much proposed legislation in the past. At last the country had decided that it was in a period of education crisis that called for broad relaxation of long-held principles and narrow interpretations of Constitutional rights.

And along with sudden affluence came a turning of education to new goals—or, more precisely, a turning away from goals entirely and toward techniques. Progressivism, the beacon of idealism in the 1930s, fell into disfavor. It had been in decline long before the Sputniks. The practical realities of wartime had flown in the face of its pacifist bias, and in the early postwar years its high-minded emphases on free expression, unstructured curriculum, and avoidance of academic discipline had come to appear to more and more people as interesting but somewhat quaint relics of a past time. It was suddenly discovered that substantial numbers of young Americans had never learned to read properly, and the blame was promptly put on progressive methods of instruction. Now, with the country evidently faced with the necessity of rapidly turning out masses of scientists and technicians who could beat the Russian ones, progressivism's delicate concern for young psyches came to appear as a form of self-indulgence.

So education's industrial revolution took place. The new techniques that had been under development for a decade or so, and had hitherto remained under wraps, were put into use on a large scale. As they had done so long ago in American life in general, mechanization and mass-production methods took command of American education. Television, both closed-circuit and broadcast, was the prime "hardware." In 1963 closed-circuit TV was already being used in over three hundred educational institutions apart from armed-forces training centers, and broadcast TV was a staple of the curriculum in thousands more; in a few spectacular cases an especially equipped airplane, a "flying classroom," was used to spread educational programs over a much wider area than would otherwise have been possible.

Even the very symbol of the new age, the computer, came to have its uses in education in the management of data about students, the grading of papers, the sorting of equipment; and one education authority said, "There is good evidence that automation will gradually extend into the classroom itself." The mania for technical innovation even extended to the very walls, roof, and ceiling of the classroom: movable walls came to be considered important school equipment, and one authority solemnly reported, as a modest research "breakthrough," his finding that "since most classroom noise emanates from the shuffling of feet and the movement of chairs, *the floor and not the ceiling should be the surface that is acoustically treated.*" Finally, and crucially, mechanized teaching, in many manifestations from simple language tapes to computerized systems of instruction capable of conducting an entire class without human aid, came into general use. The horrified outcry of *Brave New World* and *1984* was not stilled, but under the stress of crisis conditions it became muted. "It is possible to use machines in education without turning schools and colleges into factories," Ronald Gross and Judith Murphy insisted a bit grimly, pretty well expressing the general view of the reigning educators. "Indeed, at a time when students come in tidal waves, technology's labor-saving teaching devices can free the time of the best teachers for more personal and specialized teaching. It may be the only way to *avoid* regimentation."

4

But was it not inevitable that in all this dehumanization, all this emphasis on technique, numbers, facts, and immediate results, something priceless should be lost and a new kind of "education crisis" arise? Did not the rise of science and math, and the disposition to teach them and everything else by production-line methods, mean a crushing blow to the study of literature, history, philosophy, music, and art—the subjects concerned with man's greatness and vileness and oddness, that is to say, his humanity? Indeed it did; at all levels of instruction these subjects tended to be relegated to a back seat, and many bright college students shied away from specializing in them because of the ever-larger disparity between the starting job salaries offered graduates in the sciences and those in the liberal arts. There were predictions by leading educators that the liberal-arts college was doomed to extinction.

But a strong counterattack appeared almost at once, showing, perhaps, that the tradition of humanistic learning in America runs deeper than many people suspect. More money earmarked for the humanities became available from the foundations; a new law passed in 1965 established a national foundation to channel federal funds into the arts and the humanities; leading men of science, up to and including President Kennedy's science adviser, Jerome B. Wiesner, made the point that scientists themselves were coming to be hampered in their work by the one-sidedness of their training; and, all in all, in the mid-Sixties the cause of the humanities in America appeared far from lost—although it had had a close call.

But there was another, deeper-running ill effect of the new developments, related not specifically to the curricula of colleges but to the mood and atmosphere of the institutions themselves. One of the forces that had compelled the depersonalization and mechanization of education, the huge numbers of college students, was both directly and indirectly the cause of a new kind of student discontent. College students had become so numerous that they were metaphorically a mob, and sometimes they became one literally as well.

The sheer expansion of college facilities, the very fact that college and university walls encompassed two and a half million students in 1955 and five million in 1965, must be accounted a kind of miracle. Localities did a heroic job of setting up so-called community colleges, generally offering two-year programs not leading to degrees, while established degree-granting institutions, using both private and public funds, stretched their capacities in response to the demand. It is safe to say that up to the time this is written every young American endowed with the intellectual capacities to enable him to benefit from college and the often quite modest financial resources to enable him to pay the bills has been able to find space in some college somewhere.

How well his expectations concerning his college experience have been realized is another matter. Under the new setup, the typical huge and famous American university, with tens of thousands of students, is much more than a citadel of learning. It is a service center for a vast and complex society, closely related to that society's established institutions—business, local, state and national government, labor, national defense. It engages in subsidized research; it attunes its teaching programs to specific needs; its faculty is an available pool of specialized talent as much as an instrument of education; its administration is a huge bureaucracy like that of government. By the mid-Sixties Harvard, Cornell, and the Massachusetts Institute of Technology had become famous for their pioneer work in underdeveloped countries; the University of Wisconsin was so deeply committed to involvement in Wisconsin urban service and renewal that its president said, "The boundaries of the campus are the boundaries of the State"; and even Yale, traditionally dedicated to academic purism, had lately begun to play a large role in school reform, urban renewal, and antipoverty programs in its local community. In the traditional sense the great American university of the Sixties is hardly a "university" at all, and a more appropriate term, "multiversity," has been invented to describe it.

To the idealistic student admitted, after hard work against fierce competition, to a leading "multiversity," what he found often fell far short of what he had dreamed of. The famous professors he had looked forward to studying under, nationally and internationally known for their writings or their Nobel Prizes, were there, all right, but he seldom so much as saw them. Their research, their writing, their private lives in their inaccessible homes preoccupied them, while face-to-face teaching was generally turned over to assistants. The student came to feel that far from being the reason for the institution's existence, he and his thousands of fellows were the least important and least considered element in a vast, mechanized maze. He seemed to be the odd man out. To the faculty and the administration, it seemed to him, he was not a person at all but merely an IBM punch card without human existence, and without even meaning except as interpreted by the mindless lights and dials of an electronic machine. Disillusioned, he was apt to become cynical and adopt the terms of this unpleasant and unexpected game—that is, devote himself to learning the craft of "beating the system," getting, with as little effort as possible, the proper codings on his IBM card so that after receiving his degree he would slide easily into the gears of the next mechanical maze on the production line, the huge corporation. Gone in the process, needless to say, were both the ideal and the reality of achieving the kind of true education that would draw forth his best talents and abilities.

Students' unrest about their role (or lack of role) in the giant knowledge factories was largely underground, and largely unnoticed by the lay public, until a revolt of frightening scope and dimensions took place at the University of California at Berkeley late in 1964. That it took place where it did was symbolic and by no means accidental. Here was the most sought-after state university—by some accounts the most sought-after university of any kind—in the country, with a renowned faculty, a gorgeous campus in a near-perfect climate, a magnificent library, scientific facilities famous around the world. Berkeley was the multiversity typified, and indeed, its president, Clark Kerr, was the man who had coined the term in a speech at Harvard in 1963; considered the leading spokesman for the new style in American higher education, Kerr had said, "The university is being called upon . . . to respond to the expanding claims of national service; to merge its activity with industry as never before."

Whether because of the claims of national service and industry or for some other reason, at the start of the 1964 fall term the Berkeley authorities decided to begin enforcing an old but long-neglected rule that abridged the right of students to engage in political activities on campus. When eight students were suspended for disobeying or too vigorously protesting the rule, about a thousand others responded by staging a three-day sit-in strike in and around the administration building. Classroom activity was all but paralyzed; large-scale violence was narrowly averted; the liberal-minded Kerr hesitated and temporized; and before the sad and ominous episode was over, state police had been ordered onto the campus by the Governor of California to make mass arrests, many of which led to jail terms. Perhaps worst of all, in the interest of maintaining law and order President Kerr and the other university authorities had been forced to support the police action; the hallowed old idea of "benefit of clergy," of exemption of the university from civil law in the interest of academic freedom, could apparently no longer apply in the multiversity.

Ostensibly, the Berkeley revolt was about student political freedom, but many people came to feel that the political issue was largely an excuse, and that the real target of the strikers, hidden just below the surface, was the bureaucratization and mechanization of higher education. But could anything be done about this? With so many students and so many pressing demands on education by society, was not the multiversity with all its drawbacks a historical necessity? And if so, could higher education in the traditional sense survive? These, in the middle Sixties, were agonizing questions for American educators, and for the rest of us, too.

5

The situation of the country's youth in 1939—its problems, its attitudes, above all its economic status—appears to us now as a weird combination of the familiar and the unimaginable. Of the roughly twenty million persons then between the ages of sixteen and twenty-four, more than half were not in school (though the term "dropout" was not yet in general use); of that ten million plus, some seven million had part-time or full-time jobs, and the other three million were, as John Chamberlain put it, "just hanging around." In the light of such figures, the few hundred thousand jobs of a sort that could be provided by the federal programs of the Civilian Conservation Corps and the National Youth Administration were hardly more than a drop in the bucket.

The mood of youth seemed to be one of deepening apathy. Earlier in the decade youthful high spirits had manifested themselves in various ways; on the one hand, there had been the involvement of hundreds of thousands of youngsters in the antiwar movement centering on the Oxford motion, and, on the other, there had been so many teen-agers of both sexes leaving school and taking penniless to the road that youth hoboism had come, briefly, to be thought of as a national problem. Now there seemed to be neither the will nor the energy for mass political protest or grasping for self-sufficiency by leaving home to become a tramp.

The economic problem had become an incubus pressing down

the spirit of youth. The signs are to be found in the results of a poll of 13,500 youths made in Maryland in 1936, in which 60 percent of the respondents said they considered "economic security" synonymous with the phrase "youth problem in general." The inability to earn a living often led to a loss of self-confidence and a brooding sense of inadequacy: "I feel stupid about not being able to get a job," a Middletown youth told the Lynds, "and I've got to pretend I don't care." Gone, or almost gone, was faith in either the old creed of rugged individualism or the newer economic solutions of the political Left; only one in ten in the Maryland poll believed that their earning power could be raised through "individual effort," while even fewer put their trust in any "new economic system." "What is youth thinking?" Chamberlain asked, and replied, "When I see an eighteen-year-old listening hour after hour as the radio 'entertainment' drools on . . . I doubt that youth is thinking at all." But in retrospect it appears that youth had one thought, all right: it thought it had a right to feel sorry for itself—as perhaps it had.

The privileged minority was another matter. The young people in college, and especially those in the old Eastern colleges, were still few enough to consider themselves an elite corps. It is odd now to recall that by 1939 the privilege of college attendance was thought to have been immensely democratized in a generation, and a good many aging Tories were grumbling that *anybody* could go to college now; after all, when the fathers of the class of 1939 had been in college back in 1910 or 1915 they had represented only 5 percent of their age group rather than 15 percent. At the other extreme, it is equally odd to recall that many college graduates drafted into the democratic catch-all of the Army in 1941 or 1942 found that in order to be "one of the boys" they had to sedulously suppress their backgrounds, their relatively cultivated tastes, even their tolerably grammatical speech. An Ivy Leaguer in particular was a princeling, assumed (often quite wrongly) to be rich; nowadays, if he has anything to live down as a GI, it is the charge of intellectual rather than social superiority.

Like his unprivileged confreres of his own age, the prewar college man was apathetic, but in a very different way. He tended to disdain rather than despair. He might hold liberal political views, but he hesitated to press them loudly or publicly. (It would have seemed ludicrous, Walker Gibson, Yale '40 and now an English professor, wrote in 1965, for any member of his college class to risk much for the cause of civil rights—"only meatballs did that sort of thing.") In attitudes, and even to a certain extent in dress, he was something of a dandy; college men still held the position of men's fashion leadership from which they have long since quite spectacularly abdicated. His academic goal was all too apt to be the "gentleman's C," and he tended to look on academic excellence with suspicion, if not with hostility, as the province of the fellow too clever for comfort or the "greasy grind." The kind of excellence he honored was generally in athletics—or even in the ability to absorb vast quantities of beer without showing the effects. "Joe College," the stereotype of an earlier era, had survived the rigors of the depression to a surprising extent.

In sum—and allowing for the fact that I have exaggerated—he was by sole virtue of his attendance at college and the values he acquired there a member of an "officer class," a fact explicitly certified by the military services themselves, which through the war years, with notable exceptions such as the case of battlefield promotions, tended to treat a college degree as a kind of union card for membership in the officer corps. And their status as officers made the college graduates of circa 1940 all the more conscious of themselves as a privileged group with shared attitudes and shared experiences; on battleships in the Pacific, on islands in Polynesia, at airfields in Britain, during the tedious stretches of wartime service, conversation among young officers would drift wistfully to events not so long past at Charlottesville or Ann Arbor or New Haven, places that appeared in retrospect as nothing less than lost Paradise. And the reminiscers may have constituted the country's last well-defined caste.

6

College life in the early postwar years was, of course, dominated by ex-servicemen, some of them returnees whose college careers had been interrupted, but hundreds of thousands of them newcomers on the GI Bill of Rights. As might have been expected, the veteran was an entirely new and different kind of college student. Uninterested in the social frills of college life and even, to a certain extent, in athletic events, he was grimly determined to absorb as much knowledge as possible in as short a period as possible so as to make up for lost time. Often married and the father of infants or young children, he focused his emotional life on his family rather than on the traditions and "spirit" of the institution he was attending. The blow he dealt to Joe College would probably prove to be the final, fatal blow.

Moreover, the influence of the veteran on college life was to extend to the first postwar generation of nonveteran college students, the youths who had been too young to be in the war and who reached college age between 1945 and 1950. Understandably taking the older, more experienced, collectively heroic ex-GIs as their models, these young people became studious, earnest, rather humorless, bent on getting an education not for its own sake but because it clearly would, under the emerging national system, lead surely and inevitably to a good job and the solution to *the* youth problem of not so long before—economic security.

Above all, these early postwar students were disinclined to rock the boat. Involvement in national political issues, or in campus issues, or, indeed, voluble or individualistic self-expression of any sort whatever could, they felt, only land them in trouble and jeopardize their chances to benefit from the new affluence spreading across the country. "The silent generation," they came to be called, and for good reason. They were in college at a time of many crucial and controversial happenings—the early bomb tests, the reconstruction of Europe, the expansion of corporations, the rise of television, the Korean War, the erosion of civil liberties by the Communist witch hunts—yet in retrospect it almost seems that from 1945 through the McCarthy era American youth had lost its voice.

And American youth, like everybody else but more spectacularly, was getting rich. A combination of burgeoning national wealth and the settled national habit of indulging the young was putting unprecedented cash sums into their hands, and a short digression on this phenomenon is in order here. Whether he came from a background of poverty or of wealth, the student of 1939 usually considered himself lucky if he had two bills to rub together in his wallet. Generally speaking, the financial treatment of youth by its elders was based on the same principles that had prevailed in the nineteenth century, when putting money in the pocket of a college student had been looked upon as a sure way to destroy initiative and create a wastrel. Testators and trustees still designated twenty-one, or twenty-five, or even thirty as the age at which a fortunate heir might, with luck, be mature enough to deserve to get his hands on an inheritance; and free spending was still considered the telltale sign of pretentious, newly rich parents.

Exactly why, in the postwar era, Americans abruptly reversed a tradition as old as the nation and began fairly showering their offspring with cash in practically unlimited sums is a puzzling question not, I feel, to be satisfactorily answered with glib talk about child-centeredness and parental guilt. That such a reversal occurred is beyond question; in the mid-Sixties it was being claimed that Americans between thirteen and twenty-two were spending $25 billion a year, or half as much as the cost of our entire military and defense establishment, and that their purchases were responsible for 43 percent of the take in the phonograph-record industry, 44 percent in the camera industry, 39 percent in the radio industry, 53 percent in the movie industry, and even 9 percent in the national economic balance wheel, the new-automobile industry. Moreover, some experts went further and estimated that these figures fell short of telling the whole story—that teen-age influence on adult buying decisions made the true economic impact of youth several times greater.

That the change constituted an economic revolution was soon recognized by industry itself. No longer did the storekeeper, big or little, shoo the kids away from his door with an exasperated injunction not to bother him; on the contrary, the Ford Motor Company set up a lavish road show to tour the colleges wooing business, the AM radio business in many localities was virtually turned over to programs beamed to youngsters, and even, of all things, the issuers of credit cards—those philosopher's stones of the age of affluence—found an increasingly numerous and welcome market in teen-agers. "The youngsters often pay up quicker than their parents," said a spokesman for the National Retail Merchants Association, adding, with delicious if apparently unconscious irony, "They don't have a lot of other fixed obligations."

That the change has been a social revolution is less clear. When poppa gets the bill—and there is no evading the fact that eventually in one way or another he gets it—does he complain? Perhaps, but if so, his stifled cries are inaudible, and on the record his protest does not reach the point of rebellion. More to the point, are the recipients of his largess corrupted, as all previous generations of Americans have unquestioningly assumed they would be, by such treatment? Some say they have been, or will be soon; the *Times*' education editor, Fred M. Hechinger, feels that a "passion for possession" produced by affluence in youth may be putting a spiritual blight on a generation.

The evidence, up to now, is spotty. Youthful drinking and its sometimes tragic consequences in the well-to-do suburbs have been much publicized, and the nasty, increasingly ill-tempered riots of youngsters rich enough to have their own cars that take place in Florida almost every spring, and at resorts all across the country almost every Fourth of July and Labor Day, certainly suggest that indulgence has had the bad effect our forebears expected it to have. (The five hundred youths who threw chunks of cement, rocks, beer bottles, and other missiles at police in Arnolds Park, Iowa, on July 4, 1965, were apparently incited to riot when one of their number shouted to the chief of police, "Hey, punk, we're going to take over the place." Whether or not that boy's father punished him by, say, taking away his credit cards for a month, is not recorded.) But to one brought up the Puritan way, as I was, what is most surprising is that such episodes have been as few as they have. Indeed, given money but not a sense of responsibility, youth has even shown some tendency to invent the sense of responsibility for itself. Hechinger, a close observer of youth, reported in 1965 that "many young people are fed up with the hucksters" who sell them goods.

7

What with its full wallet, its open-handed but unguiding parents, its head stuffed full of conventional ideas of progress, its materially secure but spiritually dreary future assured as never before, we may understand that an important segment of American youth in the mid-1950s should have got its belly full of the whole thing—that is, that it should have adapted a stance of revolt, not against too little but against too much of the wrong things. The classic shape that the revolt took was the form of bohemianism that came to be called the Beat movement.

Originally it was a literary movement—its writer-founders invented what they called the "beat generation" in a conscious attempt to make themselves the successors to the famous "lost generation" of writers that had come along after the First World War—but it was never to produce any important literature, and as time went on it tended to become less and less literary and more and more a social movement of youth. (One of its chief tenets, passivity as a response to a hostile society, militated directly against writing or any other form of creative activity.) The truth is, Beatnikism hit a national nerve, filled a deeply felt need. It reacted against the dishonesty and hypocrisy that are built into a market society. Suppose one had plenty of money, the chance to go to college, and the prospect of a successful future in a corporation; of what value could all that be if the whole system that made it possible were based on the mutual deceit of people selling each other, through the systematic use of lies, articles they knew in their hearts to be mediocre or downright shoddy? The idealism of youth was outraged, as had been the idealism of the youth of the 1930s—and here we may draw a specific comparison.

"I feel stupid about not being able to get a job," the Middletown youth had told the Lynds. "I feel stupid about being able so easily to get a berth in a society for which I feel only contempt," the Beatnik said. The Middletown boy had felt he was entering an unjust adult world; the Beatnik felt he was entering a phony one. The most familiar complaint of conventional society against the Beatnik, that he was afraid of honest work, gave him just the opening he needed to state his case. "Our affluent, mass-production, automated, advertising-oriented society makes the line between honest work and sheer opportunism hard to draw," he could reply (and in one case did). "Perhaps I could go to work selling soap or hair dye and in fifteen years work myself up to a $60,000 mortgage, and carry my wife's pocketbook for her through Europe. No thanks, I'd rather stick to my own mud puddle."

The attitudes and outward aspects of Beatnikism became familiar to everybody during the latter 1950s. Like all the bohemianisms of the past, it adopted eccentric habits of dress and grooming—beards, pony tails, dirty sneakers, peasant blouses, and so on. Its chief centers became the Greenwich Village area of New York and the North Beach area of San Francisco, from which vantage points it sneered at the self-deluded organization men and women "uptown." Sometimes it took to petty crime, more as a protest than as a revenue source. Its devotees ritually experimented with drugs, usually the less dangerous and nonaddictive ones like marijuana, and they came to look upon these experiments as religious experiences, freeing them from the constricting cruelties and absurdities of society.

Indeed, as the Beat movement developed it took on more and more of a religious cast. "The holy barbarians" a sympathetic commentator went so far as to call the Beatniks, and their own high priests made the belated discovery that the word "beat," as applied to them, did not refer to the condition of being battered or ill-used, after all, but was really a contraction of "beatific." Needless to say, the form of religion adopted was seldom the Protestantism, Catholicism, or Hebraism of one's parents; far and away the most popular Beat religion was a version, perhaps not always a very well-understood version, of Oriental Zen Buddhism, which had the advantages of being exotic, of putting its emphasis on the achievement of grace through life style, and of rigorously avoiding anything suggesting a conventional code of laws or precepts governing everyday conduct.

But, unfortunately, revolts have a tendency to come full circle—the son who hates his father grows up to be the father's carbon copy, the successful overthrower of a tyrant becomes a tyrant himself—and the Beat movement, which had within it the seeds of a helpful corrective to the failings of postwar American society, failed to accomplish much in the way of reform or even in the liberation of the souls of its members, because it so quickly turned into a ghastly parody of everything it set out to oppose. Conformity in reverse has, of course, in one degree or another been the fate of all bohemian movements, but the Beat movement was an extreme case. Its mode of dress became as stylized and invariable as the sober dark suit of the young corporation executive. Its special language, featuring words like "pad," "kick," and "dig" mostly borrowed from the world of jazz, became as threadbare and flat as Madison Avenue jargon. Its conscientiously attended marijuana sessions sometimes came to have more than a little in common with the conventional suburbanites' bored but regular attendance at Sunday morning church.

If conventional society was the photographic positive, Beat society, it seemed, was merely the opposite yet identical negative; in fact, conventional society seemed to be more sensitive in reacting to correct its own tendencies to conformity—the gray flannel suit, in the literal sense, almost disappeared following the vogue of Sloan Wilson's famous novel, and Madison Avenue men virtually abandoned their jargon after it had been through a certain amount of lampooning. Further, the Beat movement was corrupted within by the conventional economic aspirations of some of its leaders; the cat is out of the bag when, for example, we find that one of the central episodes in Jack Kerouac's novel *The Subterraneans,* a key Beat text, involves the writer-hero's chagrin that one of his rivals has been paid a larger advance by a publisher than he has. What kind of contempt for market standards, one may well ask, is that?

So Beatnikism, a protest with a valid point and sometimes a touching honesty but not enough positive content of its own, gradually faded out by being assimilated into the mainstream of American life, and thus losing its point. It reached the end of the road when Beatniks came to be tourist attractions, goggled at by vacationers as if they were a national resource like the Grand Canyon; thus the assimilation was completed.

8

A casual, at times almost bored, attitude toward sex was part of the Beat philosophy, but meanwhile there was much talk of a revolution in sexual mores sweeping through American youth on a far broader front.

Whether or not such a revolution has actually taken place is a question that must remain in some doubt because of insufficient data. For one thing, sex, as Kinsey and his associates were not the first to discover, is a subject on which it is hard to get truthful answers from persons of any age, and, for another, the view of older people toward the sex customs of younger ones is clouded by contrary tendencies to undue alarm and unrealistic complacency. Nevertheless, both the data and the attitudes, past and present, are worth our attention.

In 1939 Bruce Bliven, while allowing that "with the authority of the home destroyed . . . responsibility rests with the young for their own behavior," expressed his opinion that the vast majority of the rising generation was "good" in the strict sexual interpretation of the word. In 1965 *Time* magazine, while allowing that national attitudes on sex were now far more easygoing than formerly, nevertheless declared roundly that "mostly, sex among teenagers is a joking game." It seems more than possible that both Bliven and *Time,* a quarter-century apart, were indulging in a certain amount of wishful thinking. As to the earlier period, it is worth remembering that for many penniless young people of the depression years sex was almost the only pleasure that was free; the Lynds, reporting on an informal poll of Middletown persons of both sexes in their twenties, stated that seven out of ten said they had had premarital relations.

As to the better-heeled middle-class youth of the time, Dorothy Dunbar Bromley and Florence Haxton Britten, on the basis of a study of more than a thousand college girls, reported in 1938 that a small promiscuous minority had given popular college girls in general a "reputation for loose living." To the extent that Mary McCarthy's novel *The Group* may be considered as social research, it is interesting to note that its account of the sexual adventures of young woman college graduates in the 1930s shocked many readers after the book was published in 1963. Was all that, they asked themselves, going on way back *then*? The illusion that sex has been invented within the past generation seems to be a perennial one.

But it would be astonishing if the social winds of recent years—the spread of psychoanalytic ideas, of uncensored books, of youthful affluence, of youthful freedom from parental restraint—had not brought with them an increase in sexual freedom, and apparently they have. The firmest statistical indicator, although a far from definitive one, is the incidence of illegitimate births to young girls; according to figures of the Department of Health, Education, and Welfare, between 1940 and 1960 the annual number of such births to girls between fifteen and nineteen considerably more than doubled, while the total number of girls in that age group was increasing less than 10 percent. Despite various confusing factors—and a less censorious national attitude toward illegitimacy is surely one—these figures argue convincingly in favor of rather dramatic change.

So much for quantitative analysis of sex among youth. No doubt a more helpful topic for dissertation is changes in the quality of youthful sexuality. The old American problem of the creation of a false, overly glamorized, and "romantic" picture of adult sex relations by mass public entertainment media has, if anything, grown less acute since 1939. Television, with its natural tendency to miniaturize life, can hardly bring about such misleadingly extravagant expectations of love as the movies used to, and it shows little inclination to try. And according to Gael Greene, a young writer with an astonishing ability to elicit candor from college girls and who interviewed some six hundred of them on more than one hundred campuses during the early 1960s, there had been other important changes, most of them very recent and initiated by the girls rather than the boys.

Just since the middle 1950s, says Miss Greene, college girls in significant numbers had abandoned the traditional arbitrary distinction between "nice girls who don't" and "bad girls who do." "The truth is," she quoted a nonpromiscuous college student, "nice girls do"—and the chief condition under which they do is the existence of a relationship involving affection, seriousness, and monogamy so stringent that it almost approximates common-law marriage. Gone, in the view of Miss Greene—and that of many other observers—was the traditional idea of "playing the field" while in college in order to set up a basis for selection: "The monogamy of most collegiate lovers is positively tame," and except in the South, where social tradition is most tenacious, "stag lines have just about disappeared. . . . Couples become each other's property, sticking together through bliss and boredom in an imitation of married life that often leads to married life." (In 1961 12 percent of women college students were already married.) And along with all this, says Miss Greene, goes a rise in the power and influence of young girls relative to young men, reflecting a similar power shift in adult society: the college girls of today, more sophisticated and far more sexually aggressive than their mothers, or for that matter than the college men of their own time, are far from being "wild" or even "immoral"; instead, Miss Greene found them in the process of forging a new code of sexual morality.

If this is right, a dramatic change is indeed in progress, and what has been lost in terms of traditional morality has perhaps already been gained in honesty and surcease from long-established hypocrisy. But we should be chary; the next generation might confound us by evolving still another code with positively Victorian overtones, and we may do well to leave this subject with the thought that if there is any field in which the *"plus ça change"* theory of social change is overwhelmingly convincing, it is that of the sexual mores of youth, in which, for reasons that modern psychology makes plain enough, *every* generation must stage a real or token revolt against its parents.

9

After the Sputniks, when, as we have seen, the forms and the methods of education on all levels changed so rapidly and drastically, the character of the students inevitably changed, too. Two trends stand out: the rediscovery by college youth of the ability to assert itself, and particularly of its voice in politics and world affairs; and a rising tide of lawlessness and misbehavior, some of it based on principle and some not, some of it among the underprivileged and some not, some of it rigorously nonviolent and some not, but all of it deadly serious rather than carefree or prankish as of yore.

The return to political involvement was undoubtedly related to the change in national political leadership in 1961. The Eisenhower Administration had usually appeared to college youth as the perfect expression of the alien and vaguely hated world of parents, the world of business. By contrast, the Kennedy Administration, with its youthful, energetic leader, seemed almost youth's own. Kennedy's words, many of his ideas, and above all his exuberant style roused the young from their long lethargy, made them think of politics as something that could interest them, and even made them feel again part of the national scene. No doubt the reawakening was overdue and would have come in time anyhow; certainly the inspiring presence of the doomed young hero at the head of government hastened it.

Berkeley was only the visible part of the iceberg. The trend ran broad and deep. "Yesterday's ivory tower has become today's foxhole," said the president of Hunter College in 1965. Student pacifists picketed and paraded against our Vietnam policies, and in 1965 staged demonstrations on many campuses—even at normally conservative institutions like Columbia and Cornell—in protest against Reserve Officer Training Corps graduation ceremonies. Students were always in the forefront of the great campaign for Negro civil rights, and as time went on their participation increased. The three martyrs of the Mississippi Negro voter-registration drive in the summer of 1964 were students, as were nearly all their fellow workers who survived, while the historic Selma-to-Montgomery march of early 1965 was organized by a nominally student organization, and its white participants were largely students and clergymen.

Meanwhile, at the farther reaches of political protest, an organized, generally non-Communist student Left—so conspicuous by its absence throughout the 1940s and 1950s—made its appearance; it was small in numbers, having in 1965 a hard core of some five hundred members, but it had considerable influence on dozens of campuses. Its target was broader than Vietnam policy or racial segregation; it chose as its villain the whole spectrum of evils of the middle-class society of which its members were a part. "This generation has witnessed hypocrisy as has no other generation," a typical student radical said. "The churches aren't doing what they should be doing. There is lie after lie on television. The whole society is run and compounded on lies." So had the Beatniks said, in their passive and oblique way, but now a segment of youth was saying it loud and clear; the Silent Generation was emphatically over. It was almost as if the United States, for the first time in her history, were about to have, like Latin-American and Oriental countries, a youth with the political muscle to influence the actions and decisions of its elders on a national scale.

Many thoughtful adults view this prospect with alarm, and reasonably so; youth, after all, is impetuous and inexperienced, and matters of state are grave. But then age is rigid and timid; that youth has refound its political voice, however raucous a voice, is occasion for rejoicing.

To say that the rising incidence of youthful antisocial behavior and outright crime in the 1960s is merely an unfortunate by-product of this new mood of self-assertion would, of course, be to oversimplify. Factors are plainly involved that are only indirectly related to political awareness; and the chief one is probably plain boredom, usually brought about by deprivation that may or may not be related to racial matters. At any rate, between 1940 and 1960 the annual number of arrests of persons under eighteen doubled while the population of that age was increasing by only about one-third; entire new problems, such as that of teen-age drug addition on a significant scale and teen-age vandalism as a commonplace in many communities, made their appearance during that interval of years; and in 1963, according to the FBI, persons of eighteen or under accounted for not quite half of all arrests for the crimes of homicide, forcible rape, robbery, aggravated assault, burglary, larceny, and auto theft. (For the suburbs the figure was just *over* half.) The problem of dropouts—one of three high school students in the mid-1960s fail to stay until graduation—does not look so bad by comparison with the frightful prewar situation, but it is bad enough, attesting as it does so eloquently to boredom, impatience, and disillusion, and it is all too clearly related not only to crime but to unhappy and wasted lives.

"What are we to do with such information?" asks the psychiatrist and writer Robert Coles.

> Scream that all those children are spoiled, that they have failed us? Or look more closely at ourselves and what has happened in too many homes between us and our children? Amid the din of parents telling themselves and one another how very much they give . . . their children, how pivotal the concern they have for their children's welfare, the ungracious response of those children seems like an incredible betrayal indeed—until, that is, one begins to listen to some of these parents. . . . Many of them are quite helpless before their children, quite afraid to say no to them on any count.

It does seem as if a whole generation of American parents has been inclined to "give" too much that was tangible and too little that was intangible—perhaps because the tangible things were all they had to give; Coles may be right in saying, "Once and for all we must realize that the life of the child's mind lives intimately with the life of our society."

But before we begin wringing our hands, we may do well to remember that now as in the past many people triumphantly survive, or even turn to account, the worst of upbringings. A generation of parents can't ruin a generation of children if it tries, and some of the most moaned-about aberrations of the current young have their creative side: for example, educators agree that dropouts who later return to school or college learn more than they would have learned otherwise because of their increased maturity. Taking the overprivileged with the underprivileged, the clever with the dull, and the good with the bad, it seems clear that the youth of today is more rebellious yet more independent-minded, less law-abiding yet more potentially creative, and, perhaps above all, far, far better educated than was youth twenty-five years ago.

10

To a certain extent, the Ivy League undergraduate of today occupies a position analogous to that of the undergraduate at any good college or university in the prewar years—that is, he is a member of an elect. But the manner of his election is quite different, and so, by the same token, is he.

For the most part, he is elected on the basis of brains and demonstrable leadership potential. Flooded with applications from every corner of the country—and the number would be far, far greater were it not that many aspirants with only fairly good high school records simply don't apply because they feel they have no chance—the Ivy League admissions directors these days inevitably load their freshmen class rolls with straight-A students, school class presidents, and school debating-society stars. There are, of course, pressures in another direction. The alumni, on whom the Ivy League colleges rely so heavily for financial support, generally want two groups of boys admitted: football players and their own sons. But as often as not, the alumni don't get their way; the almost invariable policy of the admissions directors is to turn down a boy no matter what his athletic ability or genealogical qualifications unless it appears reasonably certain that he has the intellectual capacity to survive four years and graduate—and that capacity, in the 1960s, is not inconsiderable. As to the alumnus whose son is turned down, he complains a bit about how things have gone to hell, sometimes writes a grumbling letter to the admissions office or the alumni magazine—and, to his credit, generally goes on making his annual contribution to the support of his alma mater.

The resulting atmosphere of increased intellectual seriousness and decreased social snobbery at the Ivy League colleges is unmistakable. Largely gone is the old stigma borne by the too-clever or too-diligent student, and the social approval of academic mediocrity; in these days the "gentleman's C" just won't do. Gone, too, are most of the attitudes that went with that one, and arrived is a new sort of sophistication. Where the Ivy Leaguer of 1939 was content and even sometimes proud to think of himself as a "typical Yale man" or "typical Dartmouth man," the Ivy Leaguer of today would be amused by such a designation. And just as he sets himself apart from the generation of his father, so he sets himself apart from the rank and file of his own; if one talks Beatnik language to the present-day Ivy Leaguer of bohemian inclinations, one risks insulting him mortally.

Conventional manners are not his concern—not because he feels superior to them but because he is uninterested in them. The late William C. De Vane, who served as Yale's dean of the college from 1938 until 1963, said in 1965 of the present-day Yale student, "I wouldn't say he has bad manners; I'd say he has no manners." But with all that, De Vane maintained, he is less "wild" than his prewar predecessor, less prone to sophomoric pranks, which he regards as unstylishly childish.

His indifference to careful dress and personal appearance in general is becoming proverbial, but it seems, at least in some cases, to be balanced by a certain fastidious concern about surroundings. A Princeton undergraduate writing in the *Princeton Alumni Weekly* in 1964 patiently explained to the old grads that the styles of student dormitory-room decor at Princeton these days fall into several categories, among them the Suburban (Danish or genuine leather furniture, framed reproductions of Gainsborough or Manet, brass lamps, a refrigerator, a stereo set); the Bohemian (Mexican woven objects, brick-and-board bookshelves, empty paint tubes, no rug); and the Manorial (bearskin rug, sea lion tusks, pistols and daggers, perhaps a tapestry or two). Speaking as one who in 1939 occupied a college room furnished strictly for utility, and which it never occurred to me to think of as anything but four walls between which to sleep, study, and engage in bull sessions, I find myself startled by the very notion of a college room as environment in the sense that a house is in adult life. Any decorative touches to the room in those days were what one's mother applied and one later removed. We decorated ourselves with care and pride and our rooms not at all; now the reverse is nearer the truth.

Perhaps the change is significant; it may mean that the privileged student, and even youth in a somewhat wider context, has shifted attention from self to the world around. "They're not interested in being descendants; they're interested in being ancestors," De Vane said of the present-day Yale students. "They have a large-spiritedness, a public concern that is new." From young people with such qualities a nation's elders are entitled to hope for great things—and hoping and caring are apparently most of what they can do for their children now anyway.

IX. THE RISE OF THE SORCERERS

1

"Some recent work by E. Fermi and L. Szilard which has been communicated to me in manuscript," the letter from a Long Island summer resort began,

> leads me to expect that the element uranium may be turned into a new and important source of energy in the immediate future. Certain aspects of the situation which has arisen seem to call for watchfulness and, if necessary, quick action on the part of the Administration. . . . In the course of the last four months it has been made almost certain . . . that it may become possible to set up a nuclear chain reaction in a large mass of uranium, by which vast amounts of power and large quantities of new radium-like elements would be generated. . . . This new phenomenon would lead also to the construction of bombs.

The time was August, 1939; the signer of the letter was Albert Einstein, its addressee was Franklin D. Roosevelt; it set in motion the sequence of events that led to the making of the first atomic bomb; and it has been called the beginning of the dialogue between American science and American society.

American science, at any rate, was not at the time involved in any significant dialogue with society. Just to begin with, the nation did not yet occupy anything like a key position in the world of science; during the twentieth century up to then Germany, Britain, and France had each produced more Nobel Prize-winning scientists than we had, and Germany had produced three times as many. American scientists of whatever qualifications were, by later standards, markedly few in number. According to *Historical Statistics of the United States*, there were then about 150,000 persons in the United States earning their living as scientists outside universities—and that included foresters, sociologists, and dieticians.

But, of course, the core of U.S. science then was not outside the academy. Nobody but the universities wanted scientists. Private industry, which with few exceptions had yet to discover that pure science pays off, was so uninterested in university scientists that to land jobs in it they often had to conceal their academic attainments. The federal government's outlay for scientific research and development was a paltry fifty million dollars or so, most of it devoted to agriculture. Nor did the universities want scientists badly enough to pay them much more than a pittance; $1,500 to $1,800 a year, offered with embarrassment but nonetheless with a firm "take it or leave it," was the average starting compensation for research scientists with Ph.D. degrees, and the physicist-writer Ralph Lapp tells of a top-flight young nuclear physicist who, on getting his doctorate from a leading institution in 1937, found there were only four research jobs available in the entire country.

Besides being underpaid, the university scientist was underequipped; by necessity he became a master of the art of do-it-yourself. A Johns Hopkins professor recalls how the typical biology researcher used to work: "He made all his own media, did his own sterilizing in a Sears, Roebuck cooker, kept his own stocks without assistance, and was grateful for some help in washing up the glassware." Yet, for all his troubles, the scientist of the late 1930s, particularly if his field was nuclear physics, was excited—and probably happy. He was so because he knew that he or his colleagues in his obscure little fraternity were on the verge of huge and epochal discoveries. "You can be sure that anytime you see two physicists together these days they're not far from [the subject of atomic fission]," one physicist says to another in Dexter Masters' novel *The*

Accident. "It's the glamor theme of 1939, all right." As we all know now, it had reason to be.

But we did not all know that then. In retrospect, the public attitude to science and scientists in those days seems barely credible. Few newspapers or magazines had full-time science reporters on their staffs. "The scientist was pictured as a queer sort of chap who lived a hermit-like existence, dedicated to goals not much different from those of the alchemist of medieval times," writes Lapp, who recalls that many people he met then were so unfamiliar with the word "physicist" that they had trouble pronouncing it. The public stereotype of the scientist, enshrined in the movies and in popular fiction, held him to be "mad," impractical, visionary, eccentric—and harmless. With his test tubes and his wild look, he seemed to have an almost comic irrelevance to a country struggling not to drown in poverty.

The embodiment of the stereotype was, of course, Einstein, the one scientist of whom almost everyone had heard. Had the letter to the White House borne any other signature, its impact might have been smaller—and our era have been totally different. But Einstein was, of one sort or another, a national figure. The European background that he shared with so many of our leading scientists branded him as an "alien" and an "immigrant." His habit of wearing his hair long helped add an expression to the American language. The legend of his inability to assist a little schoolgirl in Princeton with her elementary mathematics homework reassured everyone of his harmlessness and impracticality. Long ago, one had heard, he had devised a simple formula—$E=mc^2$—and although one had little idea what it meant, one was persuaded by its very simplicity that it could not be very important, that it could not have practical application, that it could not really work.

2

When all of a sudden—

In 1940 the wheels of a federal atomic-bomb project began turning; in June, 1942, the Manhattan Engineer District was formed;

in December, 1942, the first self-sustaining chain-reacting atomic pile was operated at Chicago; on July 16, 1945, the first atomic bomb was tested in the desert near Alamogordo, New Mexico; and on August 6, 1945, the second one pulverized the city of Hiroshima.

Because the public knew nothing of any of these events except the last one, its reaction was so much the more stunned. The esoteric scribblings of the amiable eccentrics were shown to have contained the secret relationship of matter and energy; the professors were shown to be the most practical men alive; the harmless madmen were revealed as sorcerers holding such destructive power as no man had ever held before. The dialogue between science and American society was to become the principal dialogue of the age.

Ever since then, American society's part in the dialogue has consisted chiefly in doing what it perhaps knows best how to do, that is, in spending money. The main fact of our present financial commitment to science is fairly well known: the annual federal outlay for scientific research and development runs around fifteen billion dollars, with industry and private agencies throwing in some six billion more. Congress' instinctive reaction to a request for funds for science is to raise rather than lower it, and the magic word "research" has become the master key that unlocks the Treasury to him who utters it. What is not so often recognized is that as a society we have learned the lesson of the 1930s, or what we take to be the lesson: that what looks impractical in science may not be. The practical value, military or other, of being the first nation to put a man on the moon, a project to which we currently devote over five billion dollars a year, is highly problematical, and even high-energy physics, the special study that led to the building of the bomb, is not expected by its practitioners to pay off further in any practical way in the foreseeable future. As Lapp says, "No scientist whom I know has ever maintained that high-energy physics is going to build a bigger bomb or otherwise enhance the nation's security," yet five billion dollars or more of our taxes are expected to go into high-energy physics during the 1970s. Doubtless there is more to our willingness to spend for science than a logical conclusion based on past experience; perhaps there is an element of primitive superstition, of propitiation of a new and fearful god, of

and effort. In one of the most spectacular cases in the 1950s, United States scientists spent several years and large sums of money struggling with a technical problem in military communications, only to discover, after they had arrived at the solution, that the Russians had published the same solution in an unclassified paper in 1950. Laboratory chiefs took to saying that they sometimes found it cheaper and more convenient to conduct an experiment from scratch rather than hunt for the report of its previous undertaking. A whole new branch of technology, called Information Search and Retrieval, concerned with trying to make computers do infinitely more rapidly what human librarians have been doing for centuries, has risen up to meet the problem. But the computers, at least up to the mid-Sixties, do not seem to be very efficient librarians—their main trouble seems to be their limited ability to deal with language, especially when translation is involved—and the confusion goes on. A vast comedy seems to be in the process of being played out: huge sums are being devoted to the new technology that will, it is hoped, enable us to keep track of the fruits of other scientific and technological work on which, of course, even huger sums are being spent simultaneously. Even the papers on Search and Retrieval are already so numerous that they sometimes get lost! Where will it end? Will science, like a schoolboy overcrammed for an exam, get to know so much that for practical purposes it knows nothing? Will the world end in a suffocating cloud, not of atomic debris but of scientific literature? Doubtless not; but if not, present trends will have to be modified.

3

Meshing and interacting with population growth, with increasing material well-being, with the rise of the supergiant corporation, with the approach to an all-urban civilization, and with the tensions of the Cold War, the progress of science and technology has obviously been a mainspring in the transformation of American life that is this book's subject. But what effects has it had on us, the laymen of science, as human beings?

The sense of living under the threat of the extinction of the civilized world, and perhaps of the human race, through a miscalculation by political or military leaders, has often been called something new in the experience of man, but it has also been described as being not essentially different from, for example, the sense of doom felt by Romans in the later years of the Empire. The sudden upsurge in man's self-destructive capacity comes after a long and enormous broadening in his horizons over the centuries. Doubtless we are the first generation since Noah's to contemplate the possibility of the literal extinction of our race; but then, to the Romans, who knew nothing of the limits of the earth or even its physical form, the Empire, emotionally speaking, *was* their race and the barbarian hordes to the north were beings hardly more kin to them than to us are the Martians whose supposed invasion of the earth, projected in a misunderstood radio broadcast, caused hysteria in the Eastern United States in 1938 (and in whose existence, ironically enough, space exploration is just now teaching the layman to disbelieve). A sigh of relief ran around the world when Russia and the United States signed a limited nuclear test-ban treaty in 1963, after years of competing tests, rising fallout levels, rising protests from every corner of the globe, and political fumbling; but the relief may not have been greater than that felt in the past, by the smaller number of persons involved, when any important treaty averted or postponed a potentially destructive war.

Few Americans, certainly scarcely any who were living in major cities, will ever forget their sensations during the Cuban missile crisis in October, 1962, when for several days the world hovered on the brink of nuclear war—and knew it. I happened to be living in New York at the time, and my main concern was about the effect of the crisis on my small children. There was no shielding them from it—the news blared from radios, TV sets, and headlines everywhere, and it was discussed thoroughly (and, I think, properly) in their schoolrooms. "Will we all die?" one of them asked me one evening. So must have asked the children of Troy. But what strikes me in retrospect is that my children were not visibly frightened—indeed, they seemed to be far more matter-of-fact about the situation than I felt. A good part of humanity, after all, seemed to be in the same boat, and it may be that threats to our lives have less power to disturb us in proportion to their magnitude and therefore their incomprehensibility.

Suicide, we are told, may have any number of causes, but, on the record, fear of nuclear war would not seem to be significant among them. In 1940 there were 14,466 recorded male suicides in the country, and 4,441 female, while the figures for the year of the missile crisis were, respectively, 15,062 and 5,145; this meant that in twenty-two years the rate per 100,000 population, male and female combined, had dropped from 14.4 to 10.9. (For 1945, the year the atomic age began, the rate had been 11.2, and it has varied only in small fractions since then.) Over the same period, it is true, the incidence of mental-hospital admissions increased from 1.4 to 2.6 per 1,000 population. No one can measure the extent to which the atomic jitters contributed to this rise, but certainly a factor that cannot be ignored is the enormous improvement since the end of the war in mental-hospital conditions, which has made victims of mental disturbances far more willing to accept hospital treatment and relatives of the victims to commit them to it. On the evidence up to now, it would seem that we can endure the new conditions better than might have been expected. Indeed, if the constant and rapid rise over the postwar years in the amount of life insurance in force is any indication, among the chief effects of uncertainty is to induce us to sacrifice to the future more than ever. That and an increasing tendency to get a slight headache; sales of aspirin and other nonprescription pain-killers went up some 240 percent between 1949 and 1964.

The national space program is probably the most remarkable manifestation of our new emotional reaction to science and technology. The National Aeronautics (curiously old-fashioned word!) and Space Administration set up shop on October 1, 1958; appropriations for its activities amounted to about $340 million in 1959, $520 million in 1960, $1 billion in 1961, $1.8 billion in 1962, and $5.3 billion in 1965. Here we were, then, spending a significant portion of our national income, and more than 5 percent of all government outlays, on a program that did not seem to have any clear purpose beyond that of putting a man on the moon by 1970—and ahead of the Russians.

Why are we doing it? Not, as in the case of the atomic-bomb

project, primarily at the urging of scientists; at the time of the Congressional hearings leading to the establishment of NASA, the scientific community seemed to be relatively unconcerned about the whole affair, and especially about competing with the Russians. Not primarily for military reasons, although despite all protests to the contrary they are certainly a consideration (and will become a more important one with the establishment of the planned Manned Orbiting Laboratory). It is possible to argue that we are doing it chiefly because of the influence of one man, President Kennedy, who proposed the man-on-the-moon program in May, 1961, and who may have been helped in getting it through Congress by a temporary national mood of chagrin following the Cuban Bay of Pigs disaster. But the protests against the soaring expenses, Congressional and public, have been few and feeble enough to make it evident that Kennedy spoke for the nation. Then there is the fact that the annual five billion, under present economic conditions, causes no one to feel any specific pinch; what it does, in fact, is to stimulate our economy at the cost of a certain weakening of our currency, and up to 1965 that weakening had been relatively mild.

Perhaps we would do well to turn for an explanation to American sports madness and human curiosity. With tens of thousands of men and billion of dollars' worth of equipment disposed around the world for every American manned orbital flight, and with television and radio covering it minute by minute, the moon race with Russia is such an Olympics as was never seen (indeed, I can't help feeling it has put the traditional Olympics somewhat in the shade). As for human curiosity, there is no evidence that Americans ever have been, or are now, exceptionally exploration-minded; but we are unique, along with Russia, in having the huge amounts of money and technical skill necessary to the exploration of space. Wouldn't almost any other nation, if similarly blessed, undertake to do the same thing?

Stimulating as space exploration is, though, the very strangeness of it, the enormous complexity of the apparatus it requires, and the fact that it is accomplished by teams and committees rather than by individuals alone tend to take some of the kick out of it, perhaps especially for the young. To return to my own children, I have the impression that they were less thrilled and moved by the flights of Glenn, Carpenter, Schirra, Cooper, and company than I had been at a similar age by that of Lindbergh in 1927. The man alone in the little monoplane being buffeted by sleet over the North Atlantic was something my imagination could encompass; but to my children, a capsule whirling around the earth at speeds beyond reason, apparently controlled by electronic computers on the ground, is just one more item in the vast storehouse of things beyond their understanding, and after the first couple of experiences of it, they became more blasé than I would have dreamed of being about Lindbergh. One of the prices we are paying for the advance of science, and its bureaucratization, is a contraction of a precious human trait, the capacity for wonder.

4

It is a stimulating fact to those with a taste for irony that over the very period in which the human race's hold on life has come to be threatened by atomic and nuclear bombs that hold has been significantly strengthened by advances in medicine.

Inarguably, the pace of medical advance over the past quarter-century has been spectacular. Marguerite Clark, long the medicine editor of *Newsweek*, testifies that in the years before 1940 medicine reporters considered themselves lucky when they found one major medical discovery to write about every six months; while in the 1960s they are more likely to find one every twenty-four hours. By present-day standards, medical practice in 1939 in such key areas as the treatment of bacterial infections was still in its infancy. The clinical use of penicillin had not yet been discovered; the very first sulfa drugs had just been developed and were not yet in general use. Tuberculosis, the leading cause of death among persons aged fifteen to forty-five, annually killed twice as many Americans as automobile accidents; influenza and pneumonia combined killed three times as many. Measles, whooping cough, diphtheria, and typhoid each still caused thousands of deaths every year, many of their victims being children; and, of course, the danger of juvenile polio brought terror to millions of parents every summer. The Surgeon General had recently estimated that one American in twenty-two was infected with syphilis, and that disease or its complications resulted in almost twenty thousand deaths a year.

The roll call of important advances against bacteria and virus disease since then is a familiar one. The bactericidal effect of penicillin was found in 1941, just in time to meet the venereal-disease and wound-infection crises of wartime; then streptomycin was developed in 1945, aureomycin in 1948, terromycin in 1950, izoniazid for tuberculosis in 1952, the Salk and Sabin vaccines against polio in 1953 and 1955. (All of these postwar developments were American.) Although the development of insulin therapy for diabetes in Canada in 1922 remained, in the view of some leading authorities, the all-time most elegant and spectacular achievement of medical science, the infection-fighting drugs produced in the decade and a half after 1940, considered collectively, certainly made a greater change in the conditions of human life than anything medicine had previously accomplished, except perhaps the discovery of aseptic surgery.

The evidence is in the statistics. Syphilis and tuberculosis in the early 1960s caused one-tenth as many deaths per population as in 1939, while measles, whooping cough, diphtheria, and typhoid had become statistically insignificant causes of death, and polio had been all but wiped out, bringing about a release from anxiety all out of proportion to statistics. Infection had not been conquered—the death rate from drug-resistant cases of pneumonia and influenza began creeping ominously upward after a low had been reached in 1954, and an element of infection by viruses began to be suspected in cancer. But it had certainly been hobbled.

From a social point of view, the key fact is that these discoveries were of benefit chiefly to those persons who all through history had most frequently been struck down by infections, that is, children and young adults. It is the swift killers of the young that have been brought low. The life expectancy of Americans born in 1940 was 62.9 years, and of those born in 1962 70 years, but this gain of over 10 percent is largely accounted for by the reduction in early deaths, and comes nowhere near being matched for persons in middle life. Between 1940 and 1956 the death rate for persons between 15 and 34 was just about cut in half; for persons between 55 and 64 the rate was reduced only 20 percent. The life expectancy of the American over 45 is hardly greater today than it was in 1939.

What has most strikingly happened, then, is that the conditions of childhood and young adulthood have changed. The poignant story of sudden death in youth, that staple of nineteenth-century sentimental fiction from Dickens on down the line, has become a rarity. Undoubtedly one of the reasons for the very high American birth rate in the nineteenth century (in general, about twice the rate of recent years) was the expectation that some of the children would die of infection—as some usually did. Grief at the death of a son or daughter may be a maturing experience or a permanently disabling one (think of Mark Twain, old before his time because of grieving over his Susy); at any rate, it used to be a common American one, even as recently as the 1930s, and it is now a far less common one. As for the young themselves, has this firmer grip on the life line changed their behavior and attitudes, or is it in the process of doing so? It is too early to tell, yet the signs are there. As we have amply seen, youth today has a truculence, a self-confidence, an impiety, and at the same time a sense of freedom and possibility that appear to be highly compatible with the knowledge of a firmer grip on life. It used to be taught in pious American families that one should live always ready to die; to live ready to die, but not just yet and not without warning, is something else again.

Of course, by no means all of medicine's recent triumphs have been in the treatment of bacterial and viral diseases. Cortisone, synthesized in 1946, and ACTH, in 1949, although they effect no cures, have proved to be an enormous boon to sufferers from a great variety of inflammatory ailments. Heart surgery, all but nonexistent before the war—even the celebrated "blue baby" operation was developed as recently as 1945—has saved some quarter of a million lives. The discovery of oral antidiabetic drugs has freed hundreds of thousands from bondage to the hypodermic needle. The development, and universal use in mental hospitals beginning in the early 1950s, of a whole cabinet of powerful tranquilizing agents far more mettlesome than the popularly used Miltown has met the rising incidence of mental illness by making most cases much more manageable even though still no more curable than before. The average hospital stay of a mental patient has been cut in half since 1940, and as a result mental hospitals have actually become less populous while the national case total has gone up. The total of patient-days spent in mental hospitals in 1962, relative to national population, was 12 percent lower than in 1940, and in 1960 the famous St. Elizabeths in Washington, D.C., reported the smallest patient population in years—not relatively but absolutely. Madness, although still not understood, has lost some of its age-old terror. And some doctors feel that huge and too-seldom-recognized advances have been made in the treatment of accident cases. Spurred on by new techniques in accident surgery and new methods of treating shock and other complications, the emergency room has changed its whole attitude; as an authority said recently, "It never gives up on a patient, any more."

Not only, then, have a group of previously intractable and often fatal diseases become preventable or curable; in addition, the "long disease" that the sickly Alexander Pope called human life itself has become a dramatically more bearable disease. But what is ahead? Is the recent spurt of medical science over, or is it just getting started on the way to the medical millennium, the conquest of disease?

Here the doctors disagree in classic style. No such millennium is in prospect, say the pessimists—or can ever be in prospect, since disease in their view is an immutable condition of life. The case was perhaps put most eloquently by René Dubos, a champion of the *plus ça change* theory of social change, in his book *Mirage of Health,* first published in 1959. Man, Dr. Dubos says, has always looked forward to freedom from disease, and imagined it in a mythical past: Hesiod in his *Works and Days* wrote of a golden age when men "feasted gaily, undarkened by sufferings" and "died as if falling asleep"; the oldest known medical treatise in the Chinese language, written in the fourth century B.C., refers to a past time when men lived a hundred years without becoming decrepit; while Condorcet and Benjamin Franklin, to name two, predicted an era when men would live for an indefinite span free from disease. Yet in reality, says Dubos, as we conquer one disease we create another—the victories over bacterial disease, for example, were concurrent with the rise of potentially deadly air pollution and the indiscriminate use of poisonous insecticides—and in the end "complete freedom from disease and from struggle is almost incompatible with the process of living. . . . Disease will remain an inescapable manifestation of [man's] struggles." So medical research becomes a gigantic irony, at best a temporary palliative for transient conditions, and medical progress largely an illusion.

But others equally eminent take a contrary view. As they see it, those who believe that medicine has been through a revolution over the past quarter-century haven't seen anything yet; the real revolution, they contend, has been taking place, unnoticed by the layman, in the biochemical lab, and its effects will be felt in medical therapy in the years just ahead.

They point to the isolation in recent years of DNA, the nucleic acid in human genes that appears to be the carrier of hereditary information, and the understanding of which may lead to the ability to direct heredity, or even, when combined with other discoveries, to a way of controlling cancer. They point to the recent research on LSD—the discovery of its properties was a wartime Swiss accomplishment—and the other so-called "psychoto-mimetic" drugs, which, because they are capable of inducing temporary conditions of severe insanity, give promise of showing doctors how to understand such conditions. And they point to many other developments in biological research that at present are still at so abstruse and theoretical a stage that a layman can't make head or tail of them.

The trend of all these advances, according to the optimists, is toward turning medical science away from empirical therapy and toward understanding of causes, with swift practical results almost beyond imagining. Dr. Lewis Thomas, chairman of the Department of Medicine of the New York University School of Medicine, believes that in the foreseeable future—perhaps in the 1980s—medicine will have a basic understanding of all the major diseases, meaning that, although some of them may not always be curable, they will be preventable. Like the old sages, he foresees a time when a vigorous life span of a century may be normal (and he believes, again optimistically, that a sharply falling world birth rate will forestall the catastrophic overpopulation that such medical advances might bring). Are he and those who share his view as deluded by the eternal spring of hope as were Condorcet and Franklin, or is the millennium of medicine really in sight this time around? Since their predictions are comparatively short-term, many of us will live to learn the answer. The course of medical science will be one of the many things that should make the daily news in the years just ahead the most gripping serial story in human experience.

5

But even now the country has found that it must speak of, and deal with, the disturbing consequences of medical progress. The conquest of the killers of youth means more old people, economically unproductive and socially isolated; and decline in the general death rate, unaccompanied by a matching decline in the birth rate, means more people, perhaps too many more, of all ages.

The "problem" of the old (who are often spoken of in uneasy euphemisms like "senior citizens," which in themselves reveal one dimension of the problem) has been discovered in the postwar era, for a number of reasons. For one thing, there are of course many more old people than there used to be; we had 8.75 million persons over sixty-five in 1939, about 16.5 million in 1960, some 19 million in 1965; and it is expected that we will have over 25 million by 1985. (Let the ancient sages note that we had over ten thousand centenarians in the 1960 census, too.) For another thing, the change in family structure that has almost eliminated the three- and four-generation household has often left old people high and dry physically and emotionally. The well-known and none too heartening results are things virtually unheard of in 1939: retirement communities consisting entirely of old people, the emergence of a medical specialty called "geriatrics." Rejected materially by both corporations and children that summarily advise them to go away, and spiritually by a whole society that reverses the ancient tradition of respect for age, the old in America have understandably become snappish and suspicious of their youngers, and taken refuge in huddling together, nursing hurts that all too easily turn to bitterness.

Materially, the country has treated its old people fairly well through rising Social Security benefits, with the glaring exception of the scandalous delay until 1965 in the passage of any Social Security legislation to provide for their medical care, the cost of which had long been the chief cause of real need among the retired. (In 1963 the median net assets of American couples over sixty-five, including real estate, were $11,180, which isn't so bad, once medical contingencies are provided for.) But in equally important intangible ways, we have treated them abominably, and we do not seem to be about to change. Both business and their families seem to want them less and less, progressively to withdraw consideration for and understanding of them. In 1939 we did not exactly look to our old people for mature wisdom as the Greeks in Homer looked to Nestor; nor do we now hold them in such patronizing contempt as Hamlet's court held Polonius. (We still keep, for example, the Congressional seniority system that tends to confer power on the very old; Sewell Avery was not the only octogenarian business leader of the 1950s; and as I have pointed out, now more than ever before the labor unions are run by old men.) But the parallels are there, all the same; the way things are going, the old as a group seem doomed to greater and greater isolation from the mainstream of our life. The best solution—as many younger people looking ahead are coming to realize—may lie in the development earlier in life of resources and interests that can be exploited in the leisure after retirement. But old age, never the best of times in America, is not the best of times there now.

Few Americans talked or thought much about population control in 1939, though they did something about it by rigidly limiting the size of their own families, for economic reasons. It was, as I have shown, a time when the accepted idea among demographers was that our national population curve would level off and eventually turn downward—and when the prospect was viewed with considerable alarm. Emma Lazarus' Golden Door of immigration, which in the peak years between 1905 and 1914 had admitted an average of about one million new future Americans per year from abroad, had been summarily slammed in the early 1920s with the introduction of the quota system and other restrictive legislation. (In 1965 the door was, very tentatively, being reopened a crack.) On the eve of the Second World War, as Oscar Handlin has pointed out, "the volume permitted by the quota system was low and economic disaster had deprived the promised land of its attractiveness. In many cases, the quotas were not filled." In some years during the 1930s we had a net loss in international migration, our emigrants actually exceeding our immigrants. The excess of immigrants in 1939, including war refugees, amounted to a modest 54,000. And meanwhile our birth rate was near the lowest point in our history.

The war changed all that. It brought in its wake a small wave of immigrants, many of them Jewish refugees from Europe especially admitted after the passage (unbecomingly late, I can't help thinking) of the Displaced Persons Act in 1948; altogether, over the decade 1940–50 immigration added almost a million to our population. Far more significant in terms of numbers, Americans began reproducing themselves much faster: there were fewer than 2.5 million live births in 1939 as against 3.4 million in 1946 and 3.8 million in 1947, and meanwhile the rate per 1,000 population was going from 18.8 to above 25. The now-familiar term "population explosion" began to be heard—and even applied to the United States.

But it would be a great mistake to suppose that in the postwar era our birth rate has gone up in a straight line and our death rate down in a straight line. The truth is that both have undergone interesting and significant shifts in direction. The death rate, after remaining almost constant during the war years, began a strong decline that continued until a bottom was reached in 1954; since then it has been in a small, inconsistent uptrend attributable to the increase in the percentage of old people. As for the birth rate, after its early postwar surge it fell back somewhat; then mounted to another peak in the lush 1950s; then, beginning in 1958, went into a really significant decline amounting to some 16 percent over the next six years. By 1965 the total annual number of live births in the nation was running some 300,000 lower than it had been in the peak year of 1957, while the rate in proportion to population for some months in 1965 was actually lower than it had been for the year 1939, and as low as it had been at the blackest point of the depression.

Medical progress, by coming up with more convenient and efficient methods of contraception, has surely played a role in this recent and rather dramatic reversal in the trend of our birth rate; but another, less determinate factor, a turnabout in our official attitude toward birth control, should be considered, too. Traditionally, of course, American office-holders have assiduously shunned the very mention of birth control because of the attitude of the Catholic Church, which, while long an advocate of family planning by the well-known "rhythm method," opposes contraception by mechanical means on moral grounds.

In 1939, since hardly anybody in the United States was seriously worried about overpopulation, politicians felt not the slightest urge to incur the anger of the Catholics by advocating birth-control programs, nor state and municipal governments to do so by setting them up. With the changed conditions of the postwar years—rapidly rising birth rate, marriage rate, and population—some of them may have begun to feel such an urge, but if so, they certainly succeeded in suppressing it well. For a decade and a half after 1945, birth control remained a politically taboo subject. President Eisenhower was probably speaking for the country when he curtly dismissed the subject in 1959 with the comment that birth control was not a proper governmental function (an opinion, by the way, that he was later to reverse emphatically).

Yet strangely enough, almost in a matter of months after Eisenhower's famous dictum, all levels of American government, federal state, and local, were to be deeply involved in birth-control aid. True enough, there was almost never any explicit administrative or statutory authorization for such action, and politicians at all levels continued to circle the subject warily. The official pussyfooting went on, but the programs went forward. In 1962 it came to light, despite some efforts to suppress the information, that the federal government through a number of its departments and offices was financing more than half of all national research dealing directly or indirectly with birth control—and this extraordinary news brought no great outcry. In 1963 there were tax-supported birth-control programs in about a dozen states, most of them in the South, where Catholic influence is generally weak and where for political and social reasons, as distinct from demographic ones, whites were anxious to slow down the rise in the Negro population. In 1965 there were or were soon to be such programs in thirty-three states, North, South, East, and West. All told, in 1963 there were 450 public birth-control clinics; in 1965, 700. And then the pussyfooting abruptly stopped. "I will seek new ways," said President Johnson loud and clear in his 1965 State of the Union message, "to use our knowledge to deal with the explosion in world population." It was the first time any President had flatly referred to the matter of population control in an important policy address, and Johnson's words were widely interpreted as marking an official and irrevocable commitment of our government to an unprecedented course.

What had happened? Had Catholic political influence in the United States declined so much and so abruptly? Hardly. According to the National Council of Churches, some 21 million Americans, or about one in six, were Catholic Church members in 1940, while almost 44 million, or a fraction less than one in four, were Catholic Church members in 1962; and, of course, our first Catholic President assumed office in 1961, at the very moment of the reversal. Or had the availability of a relatively safe and highly effective contraceptive in pill form, Enovid, caused old ideology to yield to new medical technology? On the evidence of the timing of the birth-rate decline, apparently not; the decline began in 1958 and was already in full cry by the time "the pill" came into wide use in 1961 and 1962. Other less visible factors seem more likely to have been behind the change in national attitude: a growing awareness of the existence of a population problem—especially in the world's poor countries, but perhaps potentially here as well; the rediscovery in the 1960s of American poverty, along with the realization that unchecked population growth would almost surely make it worse; and subtle changes in the attitude of the Catholic Church itself. Finally, no doubt the rather frightening implications of medical progress, which now seemed on the verge of being able to hold death at bay, were seeping little by little into our national consciousness.

In population control as in so many aspects of our national life, the 1960s seem to be a time of reason and caution and planning, as contrasted with the all-out, pedal-on-the-floor spirit of the 1950s. Then we were unhesitatingly for more money, more automobiles, more TV sets, more mass-produced suburbs, more babies; now we are picking up the debris left by that binge, and resolving not to go on another one. As regards population, there is cause to believe that reason is coming to prevail: the opponents of birth-control measures have given up much of their intransigence, while the proponents show an inclination to avoid high-pressure tactics and to respect religious principle. Again, as in clinical medicine, the next few years will tell a thrilling story; the American birth rate, with the biggest crop of nubile young women in history on hand to push it up and "the pill" to hold it down, will be a statistic as fascinating to watch as the quotations of one's favorite stock—and with considerably more implications for the country's future.

6

The dialogue between science and society up to now has been at its most bewildering and perhaps least enlightening in the matter of automation and computerization.

The world's first automatic general-purpose digital computer, called Mark I, was completed at Harvard in 1944. Although it contained 760,000 parts and 500 miles of wire, it required about four seconds to perform a task of simple multiplication, eleven seconds to perform one of division. Its first offspring—ENIAC, the first electronic computer—was finished in 1946, and rendered Mark I completely obsolete. Nevertheless, it was not until 1954 that the first practical applications of computers for business purposes were made on anything more than an experimental scale. Since then, measured in terms of numbers of installations and sums invested, the rate of computerization in American industry has been truly startling. About twenty computers were shipped to customers in 1954; the number passed 1,000 for 1957, 2,000 for 1960, 3,000 for 1961, and reached 4,500 for 1964. The cost to the customers was $190 million in 1954, $240 million in 1957, $2.2 billion in 1960, $4.4 billion in 1964. In 1965 there were in use in the United States some 25,000 of these strange—and to most of us, including most of the amiable young women who generally operate them, totally incomprehensible—devices. Also by 1965 the primitive computers of the 1950s were completely obsolete. In 1964 the Census Bureau's original Univac machine was shipped to that repository of the quaintly ancient, the Smithsonian Institution.

The spread of computers, along with the simultaneous spread of the use of automatic machinery in industry, has been accompanied by an acrid controversy on the question, Does automation, by mechanizing tasks formerly performed by human hands or minds, create unemployment, and, if so, to what extent? A whole school of Jeremiahs has sprung up, predicting that automation will take over human labor and consign man to the junk heap; but a contrary-minded school has sprung up to insist that instead it at last will free mankind from drudgery and enable him to realize his potentialities. The sociologist Donald N. Michael said in 1964 that automation "means an end to full employment"; Charles E. Silberman in *Fortune* magazine rejoined crisply a few months later, "There is, in fact, no technological barrier to full employment." A group of influential citizens, mainly social scientists, calling itself the Ad Hoc Committee on the Triple Revolution, sent President Johnson a manifesto in 1964 in which it insisted that automation was eliminating jobs (and especially Negro jobs) so fast that unless drastic steps were taken quickly the nation was threatened with "unprecedented economic and social disorder." Ten months later the respected economist Peter F. Drucker wrote: "Automation and other technological changes, according to all the evidence, have had no unusual, let alone destructive, impact on the total number of jobs available, on workers' wages, or even on job security. . . . Automation is just today's fashionable scapegoat for persistent unemployment."

Figures frequently quoted by responsible persons have it that automation wipes out forty thousand jobs a week, or over two million a year (President Kennedy went so far in 1962 as to give the figure 1.8 million a year); while Chairman Blough of U.S. Steel, who ought to be in a position to know, insists that on balance it *creates* many *new* jobs. "Mechanization and technological improvement in general," he wrote in 1961, "while changing job content and eliminating some jobs, has proved to be a job-creating mechanism of great proportions." In 1965, another famous industrialist—and pioneer manufacturer of computers—confounded the confusion. Automation, said Chairman Thomas J. Watson, Jr. of International Business Machines, may have contributed to unemployment "to some extent—no one knows how much."

And so it goes. Faced with such a welter of flatly conflicting views, a layman can hardly hope to arrive at an intelligent opinion, any more than he can without intensive study more than scratch the surface of the whole subject of automation and its effects. Nor can he safely fall back on employment statistics. Between 1961 and 1964 employment of manufacturing production workers actually increased by one million, while during 1964 roughly 50 percent more factory workers were hired than were laid off, and layoffs ran at the lowest rate since before all the hullabaloo about automation had begun. But who was to say that these employment gains had not been made in spite of the effects of automation rather than because of them?

A layman can, though, make certain observations. He can recall that fears of the job-destroying capabilities of machinery, or hopes for its liberating possibilities, are not new. The Luddites of nineteenth-century England made opposition to mechanization a principle, and Samuel Eliot Morison quotes a publication called the *United States Review* as having declared in 1853 that within half a century "machinery will perform all work—automata will direct them. The only tasks of the human race will be to make love, study and be happy." Those were scarcely the only tasks of Americans in 1903, which happened to be the year the era of mass production and mass employment was inaugurated with the organization of the Ford Motor Company.

Further, a layman who has heard of numerous companies (Melville Shoe is one) which in their initial enthusiasm ordered computer systems and laid off employees, only to discover later that the computers failed to do the job and the employees had to be rehired, cannot help but suspect that the reason so many of the early computers are now considered obsolete is that their capabilities turned out to be far less miraculous in practice than in theory—and he is particularly susceptible to this line of thinking when he knows such random facts as that a single tiny error in a computer's set of instructions resulted in the explosion of an Atlas-Agena rocket as it was being launched at Cape Kennedy, or that the "programming" of computers in the United States prior to 1960 is estimated to have cost two billion dollars. On the other hand, he knows perfectly well that in particular industries—printing, coal mining, and oil refining are classic examples—automation *has* eliminated many jobs. I well remember the eerie feeling I got when, in the autumn of 1963, I visited the Bayway oil refinery in Linden, New Jersey, (the one to be seen and smelled from the New Jersey Turnpike just south of Newark Airport) on assignment for *The New Yorker*. In ten years automation and related factors had reduced Bayway's working population from 4,800 to 1,800. Whole rows of offices in the administration center stood vacant; only an occasional man in goggles and helmet walked like a midnight pedestrian along the streets between the pipe stills; and as I stood beside the catalytic-cracker unit, the Times Square of the whole hissing and clanking complex, not a soul was in sight anywhere.

Most authorities apparently agree on one thing—that if a disastrous "automation problem" for workers in general exists, it exists for the future rather than in the present. Meanwhile, the existence of such a tremendous ruckus on the subject so early in the age of computers provides insight into the temper of the times, and into how it has changed. The idea of robots and mechanical brains with human abilities has fascinated and frightened men since long before Mary Shelley created Frankenstein's monster; even so, the way so many of us have seized upon the electronic computer, even before it has had time to prove itself, as the monster come true, tells a lot about our new view of science and technology as sorcery, our increasing concern about the increasingly uncertain and unpredictable future—and perhaps our increasing love of problems, of intellectual puzzles, as more and more of our working hours (under the influence of science and technology) come to be devoted to brainwork rather than physical labor. It is interesting to speculate what would have happened if science and technology had presented us with, say, the electronic computer, in 1939. Would not the hard-line, backward-looking industrialists of that time have contemptuously thrust aside such a newfangled gadget, confident—and perhaps rightly so—that human workers at those times' low wages could do the same work more cheaply? Would not militant unionists have struck any plant that ventured to replace specific workers with a specific machine, instead of accepting automation as inevitable and often merely using it as a bargaining issue, the way most unions do now? Automation, it would seem, is as much an effect of current conditions and attitudes as a cause of them; so science and society interact in their new dialogue.

7

The rise of air transportation is just one of the more important among the many recent technological advances that have had vast effects on our lives. The number of intercity miles traveled in the United States by airline was only a little over one-fourth of the combined total for railroad and bus as late as 1953; it was about 60 percent of the railroad-bus figure for 1958, about 90 percent for 1962; and in 1963 airline travel took a lead over the other two that it is unlikely to lose ever again. That this rise took place during a period when public ground transportation was tending to become inefficient and uncomfortable, and private ground transportation by automobile progressively slower and more exasperating because of traffic jams, was not so much ironical as characteristic. Time-distance anomalies have come to abound: it is quicker and far more convenient to commute to some parts of New York City over the 250 miles from Boston or Washington than over the fifty-odd miles from Redding, Connecticut, or Ocean Beach, Long Island; on many intercity air trips in the United States one spends more time in buses to and from airports than in transit aloft; and a weekend visit from New York to another climate and another culture in San Juan, Puerto Rico, is as convenient and as usual as was such a visit in 1939 to that New Jersey shore resort whose very name seems to call up a past time: Atlantic City. For better or for worse, the Atlantic Cities of America have been demoted by jet travel to centers for business conventions.

By cutting in half or less the propeller-plane transit time from place to place, the jet transports, introduced by one airliner after another around 1960, have done more than that. They have revolutionized the relations between governments, international businessmen, scientists, and scholars. Heads of state or their deputies turn up in foreign capitals on a few hours' notice in times of crisis; the international scientific or scholarly meeting has become a standard institution, and one of the main activities of the American Council of Learned Societies has come to be the granting of jet-travel expenses for scholars to such meetings. If one assumes that face-to-face encounter promotes understanding, one must, of course, account these changes as tremendous gains. Yet it seems that they bring with them new problems. Recent medical research has confirmed what many jet travelers have suspected since their first experience of it: that long-distance east-west or west-east travel at jet speeds, with its disruption of time schedules, meal and sleep times, and the length of day and night, upsets a human being's "metabolic clock" in a way that may leave him mussed up both physically and mentally for a day or two. Who knows what meetings of foreign ministers, businessmen, scientists, or scholars may have resulted in blank failures of understanding because someone's metabolic clock was out of whack—or may in the future?

Much as Americans love scientific and technological change, we cannot quite keep pace with it; the spirit and the flesh are willing, but not always able. I am tempted, in trying to round out this brief account of such recent change, to resort to the old dodge of following a hypothetical man through a hypothetical day, seeing how many of the objects and events in his routine life are new since 1939.

We begin with him having slept in an apartment house protected against burglars by a closed television circuit, being awakened by his clock radio as he lies under his thermostat-controlled electric blanket, arising to clean his teeth with his electric toothbrush, putting on his drip-dry shirt and his suit with no-iron pants, crossing the vinyl floor of the kitchen to get the frozen orange juice out of the deep freeze and switch on the automatic coffee-maker; and then, a few minutes later, lighting up the day's first charcoal-filter cigarette. . . .

And there we hit a snag so troublesome that I abandon the hypothetical day. Because here the evidence of progress is apparently reversed: our hypothetical man knows perfectly well, and has learned from science within the past quarter-century, that cigarettes whether filter-tipped or not are bad for him, perhaps disastrously so. He began learning this in 1953 and 1954 when the first authoritative reports appeared linking heavy cigarette smoking to cancer and heart disease, and in January, 1964, of course, he found the full weight of his government's Surgeon General put behind the new and crushing evidence against cigarettes. And yet over this period the cigarette's status as a stage prop, as a businessman's piece of incidental business, as a housewife's five-minute relaxer, as a catalyst to courtship among the young—in sum, as a settled part of our national life—has actually become more secure. The mid-Sixties found the sales and net profits of the big cigarette companies at or near record levels. Well and good—the population and the economy had greatly expanded. But wait. Use of cigarettes had also been increasing, and increasing dramatically, *on a per capita basis.* According to Department of Agriculture computations, in 1940 each person in the country aged eighteen or over smoked, on the average, 1,976 cigarettes (5.4 per day). In 1945, when wartime restrictions were lifted, it was 3,449 cigarettes (9.4 per day), and in 1950, just before the first medical reports, it was 3,522 (still under 10). The figure rose every year in the decade from the start of the health scare to the issuance of the Surgeon General's Committee report; for 1963 it was 4,345—a fraction under 12 cigarettes per adult American per day; it dropped somewhat right after the report, then started up again. Meanwhile, use of cigars and pipes, which the doctors generally found to be far less dangerous than cigarettes, was either holding steady or sharply dropping: the average number of cigars smoked per adult of either sex was 61 for 1940 and 60 for 1963, while average pipe-tobacco consumption was 2.81 pounds in 1940 and .92 pound in 1963.

In other areas of American life we have again and again found people in the aggregate reacting with dramatic speed and decisiveness to new situations. Why, then, this astonishing reversal of form in the case of cigarette smoking? There is, of course, no sure answer; even if it were possible to ask every cigarette smoker why he goes on smoking, or takes it up, or increases it, millions of the respondents probably would not know. But a number of possibilities present themselves. Perhaps people don't believe the medical reports. Perhaps they want to break their addiction to cigarettes but can't. Perhaps increasing tension makes them smoke more. Perhaps they are victimized against their better judgment by advertising. Perhaps they feel that their lives are made hugely more pleasant and richer by cigarette smoking, and, weighing the alternatives, decide consciously and rationally to put style of life and small satisfactions along the way ahead of longevity for its own sake.

And there is another possibility, which may not be as farfetched as it sounds. Perhaps, in a time when society's dialogue with science and technology is tending to become a monologue, more than a few Americans, consciously or not, determine to smoke in order to defy regimentation by scientific and technological authority, even at the risk of their own lives.

X. SOME MORE EQUAL THAN OTHERS

1

On Easter day, 1939, the Negro contralto Marian Anderson stood on the steps of the Lincoln Memorial in Washington, giving a recital to some 75,000 persons on the Mall in front of her, and to millions more coast to coast who were listening on radio. Behind her sat members of the President's Cabinet, Senators, Congressmen, and distinguished citizens white and black from the worlds of the arts and public affairs, not to mention the grave stone figure of the Emancipator himself. The event was an act of atonement on behalf of the American people and members of their government for a particular insult to American Negroes that had been delivered several weeks earlier—the refusal of the Daughters of the American Revolution to allow Miss Anderson to sing in Constitution Hall, in Washington, because of her race. In symbolic importance, the Easter concert was an event to rank in American Negro history with the 1963 March on Washington, and was, indeed, perhaps the best thing that had happened to the Negro on the official national level since Reconstruction days. When Miss Anderson, whose voice and musicianship were more at home in grand opera, finished her recital with the singularly appropriate spiritual "Nobody Knows the Trouble I've Seen," a rare thrill of oneness must have run around the country. Or as Walter White, secretary of the National Association for the Advancement of Colored People, put it, "A new affirmation of democracy was felt by all those present."

But the affirmation was hollow.

In 1939 in the capital city of America where Miss Anderson sang, one-third of all the people were Negroes, yet no Negro could go to any theater of any sort except a neighborhood Jim-Crow movie house; no Negro could eat in any public restaurant used by whites except for a few cafeterias in government buildings; no Negro could sit next to a white man on a public bus or ride in a taxicab driven by a white man; and no Negro could register in any hotel. All these taboos were enforced entirely by tradition, yet they were enforced as firmly as if they had the backing of law. The situation regarding the opportunities for a Negro in his country's armed forces or its government was more or less comparable. In the Civil War the hard-pressed Union Army had welcomed Negroes as soldiers, although for a year or so it had indulged in the breath-taking hypocrisy of paying them on a lower scale than the white soldiers; in 1939 precisely two Army infantry regiments and one cavalry regiment were open to Negroes, the Navy accepted Negro applicants only for the job of mess attendant, and all other branches were closed to them entirely. The number of Negroes in civilian government service had been increasing steadily all through the New Deal period, although the practice of segregation in federal offices that dated back to the days of Woodrow Wilson was still generally observed, and the U.S. Housing Authority and the Department of the Interior were alone among government agencies in including in their contracts a clause forbidding discrimination on account of race, creed, or color.

Also on the Easter weekend when the new affirmation of democracy was being felt at Lincoln Memorial, a Negro magazine writer was in Mississippi, where she had traveled by bus from New York, sitting always, during passage through Southern states, in the all-black rear section, and eating food dispensed through special side windows of Southern roadside joints. In a Mississippi town she saw a sign on a store door: "Easter Egg Hunt. White children 9:30 A.M.—

colored children 3:30 P.M." Even in the days of slavery, she remembered having been told, white and Negro children had played together freely and naturally up to the age of puberty; but not now.

A pall of apathy and despair had settled over the American Negro community following the end of Reconstruction in the 1870s and the coming of Jim Crow in the 1890s; and in 1939, when three-quarters of all our Negroes still lived in the South, it had not lifted. A measure of this mood is to be found in the modesty of the Negro-rights movement's aspirations. In 1939 that movement was exulting over what looks now like a dubious triumph. Back in 1896 the Supreme Court decision in the case of *Plessy* vs. *Ferguson* had legalized segregation by establishing the doctrine that states were allowed to provide Negroes with "separate but equal" facilities as to transportation, public accommodations, and education. Over the succeeding forty-three years, the decision had stood; but in practice the facilities, in particular the educational facilities, had tended to grow progressively more separate and less equal, until in the 1930s, in many Southern communities, the "separate but equal" facilities consisted on the one hand of a reasonably new brick building and on the other of a crumbling, unpainted frame one. Nor was there equality, or anything like it, in teacher salaries; it was estimated in 1939 that the teacher-pay differential between white and Negro schools in the nineteen states that practiced official segregation amounted to between $20 and $25 million a year. In 1938 the Supreme Court had ordered the State of Missouri to admit a qualified Negro, Lloyd Gaines, to its law school, or else provide separate facilities that were truly equal. Far from overthrowing *Plessy* vs. *Ferguson* and its segregation doctrine, the decision affirmed them in greater detail; yet it was hailed by Negro leaders as a great victory because it seemed destined to improve the wretched condition of their public education. They were, in short, grateful for a small material gain at the expense of a huge doctrinal loss.

The idea that inequality is inherent in segregated education seems scarcely to have occurred to most Negro leaders and their white sympathizers in 1939. Segregation in itself was scarcely even an issue; integration was scarcely yet a Negro goal. Segregation was a fact—and not just in the South. (A poll taken by the National Opinion Research Corporation three years later, in 1942, would show only one in four white *Northerners* favoring integrated schools.) Of the forty-eight states, only twelve had laws in 1939 forbidding school segregation by race; in fourteen others the law was silent; in the rest segregation was either mandatory or explicitly allowed. And, laws or no laws, integration in colleges existed as a rare and exotic phenomenon. For the academic year 1937–38, the pioneer leaders were New York University, which had 556 Negroes enrolled, Ohio State, which had 309, and the University of Kansas, which had 193; coast to coast there were 2,043 Negroes enrolled in white colleges, and the total of such colleges with even a single Negro enrolled was seventeen.

On the question of voting rights for Negroes in the South, Walter White of the NAACP maintained at the time that 1939 was a year of progress, inasmuch as the number of Negro registrants and voters materially increased in Richmond, Birmingham, Atlanta, and various cities in Texas, Louisiana, North Carolina, and Kentucky; meanwhile in the Northern and Border states, White exulted, "the growing independence and intelligence of the Negro vote . . . caused politicians of all parties to realize that this was a phenomenon which had to be reckoned with." Yet in some parts of the South the "progress" was of a negative sort; the poll tax and various forms of intimidation were combining to continue the long process of reducing Negro registration that had been going on for more than a generation. As the Justice Department was to point out in the mid-Sixties, at the turn of the century 9 percent of potential Negro voters in Mississippi were actually registered, as against 5 percent in 1964—and 1939 was a point along the way in this long, sickening decline from nowhere to nowhere. As to the political influence of the Negro in the North, it is perhaps enough to say that up to 1948 no Presidential candidate of either party ever saw fit—or thought it necessary—to stump Harlem.

When he did vote, the Negro was apt to vote Democratic, especially in the Northern cities, although there were many Negro Republicans, as, of course, there had been since Republicanism had given his race its brief taste of political power during Reconstruction. The Communists had tried hard to make capital of his disadvantaged position in American life; they had collected something like a million dollars for the defense of the Scottsboro Boys, nine Negroes who were sentenced to death in April, 1931, for the alleged rape of two white women on a freight train passing through Alabama. And some Negroes had turned to Communism; a few were high in the councils of the Party, and the National Negro Congress, formed in 1937 as a Popular Front organization with the respected non-Communist A. Philip Randolph as its first president, became outright Communist and after the Nazi-Soviet pact in 1939 took to proclaiming that no American Negro would fight against Soviet Russia. But the National Negro Congress, a Communist leader like Benjamin Davis, and such a celebrated Negro Communist as Paul Robeson were exceptions; in that time of widespread leftist tendencies in America, Communism never captured the collective imagination of the American Negro and never was able to enlist his membership in force. One is tempted to speculate why. Perhaps he was too apathetic, too enervated by long oppression; perhaps he was too shrewd, able to see through the pie-in-the-sky promises that Communism made him to a new form of potential exploitation; perhaps, for all the mistreatment he had suffered so long, he was too stubbornly loyal to traditional American dogma. Or perhaps Murray Kempton is right in saying that "the typical Negro, through the Thirties and today, has been bored by the Communist."

Economically the Negroes had reason enough for disaffection; their plight was desperate. Always employed marginally, they made up what was clearly the single group hardest hit by the depression. The National Resources Committee on Consumer Incomes calculated that for 1935 and 1936 the mean annual family income of Negroes living in large North Central cities was $1,227; of those living in Southern towns and cities, $634; of those living in Southern rural areas, $566. In each case, these figures represented between roughly one-third and one-half of the comparable incomes for whites. (There was a small Negro middle and professional class, but since it existed chiefly to serve poverty-stricken Negroes, even its members usually had pitifully low incomes.) And the Negro's plague was that old handmaiden of poverty, tuberculosis. In the quarter-century before 1939 the national tuberculosis death rate, all races included, had been cut to one-third of what it had been; for Negroes, over the same period, it had remained almost exactly the same.

In such straits, did the Negroes look to the great and growing American labor movement that was vowing to improve the lot of the working man, and did the labor movement welcome them? The answers, it would seem, are yes and no. In 1936 the NAACP urged Negroes to join the unions of the CIO because "if they fight now, side by side with their fellow workers, when the time comes to divide up the benefits they can demand their share." By 1939, there were not yet many benefits to be shared; nevertheless, many Negro workers had applied to CIO unions and been welcomed as members, and most such unions were exemplars of "integration" far ahead of their time, their white members not only calling the Negroes "brother" on the job and in the union hall, but generally treating them as such, too. This was not so of AFL unions, many of which in 1939 still persisted in raising barriers to Negro membership—and even in using the new weapons put in labor's hand by New Deal reforms as a crowbar with which to pry Negroes out of their jobs. At the beginning of 1939, in Tampa, Florida, a firm called Tampa Shipbuilding and Engineering Corporation was operating with twelve hundred employees, about half of them Negroes. By winning a quite properly conducted election held under the auspices of that benevolent government agency, the National Labor Relations Board, two AFL unions succeeded in getting a closed shop and thus were enabled to decide who would work at Tampa Shipbuilding and who would not. Whereupon the unions expelled about five hundred of the six hundred Negroes from membership and thus forced them out of their jobs. The employer wanted them to work, the union said no—and so it went in more cases than that of Tampa Shipbuilding. Need any further explanation be made of the distinct reluctance of the Negro to join wholeheartedly in the great labor-union movement of the Thirties?

In the cities of the North, where many Negroes had lived for years, but where their numbers were increasing rapidly, they had other problems. The now-familiar pattern of residential segregation decreed by custom and economic status was still in the process of becoming firmly established. Harlem, where hardly anyone could resist the chance, however infinitesimal, of winning a large sum on an investment of pennies, was widely known for its gangster-controlled policy rackets (but not yet for dope addiction; the widespread resort to narcotics was to mark a step in alienation beyond the resort to alcohol and constant petty gambling). Many New York City department stores, hotels, and restaurants discouraged Negro patrons.

Harlem in the Thirties, like other Negro communities, was also noted for its jazz—as it had been, of course, in the storied Jazz Age of the Twenties—but now a new and more serious-minded generation of young white people was discovering and making a fad of Negro music. In retrospect, perhaps the archetypical jazz figure of the Thirties was Bessie Smith, whose recurrent theme was the sadness of the Negro transplanted from the South to the great city, and who died in an automobile crash outside Memphis in 1936—according to legend, bleeding to death because she was refused admission to a white hospital.

A talented and personable Negro jazzman in the North in the Thirties might, with extraordinary luck, become not only famous but rich; such an opportunity, however, scarcely existed in most fields. Mayor La Guardia of New York in 1939 appointed the first woman Negro judge ever to sit in the United States, but big-league baseball, the "national game," was firmly closed to Negro athletes, and, so far as I have been able to determine, no Negro sat as an officer or director of any large white-run business firm. Employment discrimination was practiced as a matter of course at all levels. Frequently it was practiced on the most insultingly flimsy and whimsical of excuses —as when the Newark police department, with the backing of the New Jersey Civil Service Commission, turned down three Negro applicants for jobs as patrolmen on the ground that they were flatfooted. It was in the performing arts, and to a much lesser extent in the creative arts, that Negroes could get ahead without unduly disturbing white stereotypes about them. The music played at the 1939–40 World's Fair's famous trylon and perisphere was composed by a Negro, William Grant Still. There were widely acclaimed Negro stars of stage and screen, but the catch was that they were supposed to portray Negroes, and usually stereotyped ones at that. Years earlier,

Paul Robeson had been considered fine for Othello, but inappropriate for Hamlet or Macbeth or Mark Antony; now, returning from a long stay in Europe to be in the movie version of *Showboat*, he found himself so demeaned by the role that he had made famous on the stage that he took ship for England vowing never again to appear in an American film except as a first-class citizen. "The American theatre has never given up its minstrel-show conception of the Negro," the playwright George Sklar wrote in 1935. Referring to American movies in 1939, the NAACP magazine *Crisis* wrote, "Almost without exception the Negro character is one to be laughed at or pitied. . . . A Stepin Fetchit, a tap-dancing butler, a grinning slave, or a 'yes-mam' maid remains a fixed picture." It was, we may remember, the year of the antebellum film epic, *Gone with the Wind*. It was also the decade of glory for radio's contribution to the minstrel-show tradition, written by whites for the delectation of whites, *Amos 'n Andy*—which, so *Crisis* decided, "should be nominated for the highest award of the American Society to Keep Negroes Down."

With so many doors so firmly and coolly shut to him, the Northern ghetto Negro found solace in religion, particularly in evangelical religion, and most particularly in that dispensed by the little man originally named George Baker who chose to call himself "Father Divine (God)." In 1939 Father Divine moved from his "Heaven" in Harlem to a new one, a private estate he had purchased near New Rochelle, New York, to the outraged howls of the surrounding white gentry. *Crisis* considered Father Divine a progressive social force: "The little evangelist has been impertinent enough to strike at the very roots of the color problem in America, first, by establishing a church that embraces human beings of all colors . . . second, by practicing as well as preaching about love and peace; and third, by undermining the system of residential segregation." But in retrospect it would appear that Father Divine, whatever his personal merits, was tragically doomed by his character and circumstances to be a reactionary social force; what with his claims to Godhood, the picturesque cognomens of his "angels," and his quaintly fustian rhetoric ("Relaxation of the conscious mentality is the super-mental relativeness of mankind"), he was the perfect minstrel-show figure, an embodiment of the white man's harmless joke Negro.

I have remarked previously on how extraordinary it is, looking back today, to find how little the New Deal government with its broad liberal and humanitarian thrust ever did to alleviate the plight of the Negro. As of 1939 not a single piece of federal legislation addressing itself to the problem—not a voting-rights bill, not a measure against job discrimination, not an antilynching law—had been passed since Reconstruction. And why not? The easy answer is that power and determination of the Southerners in Congress prevented any action. But the evidence is overwhelming that the liberals and New Dealers themselves were not pushing the matter very hard. A single antilynching law that he could never get through *was* President Roosevelt's civil-rights program. The South, the New Dealers assured themselves happily before each election, was "in the bag" for the Democrats, thereby putting their party in a position to pass much idealistic and forward-looking social legislation; and the reason the South was in the bag on the crucial votes in Congress was because its all-white representatives had tacitly agreed to go along with the liberals on matters not affecting the Negro question, provided the liberals did not harass them too much on that. Perhaps it is not too harsh to say, at this distance, that the liberals and the Southerners had made a deal to sweep the Negro question under the rug.

The liberals, to be sure, certainly did not think of it that way, and many probably did not realize the deal existed; flushed with their great triumphs in social legislation, they tended to be naïve about the South, to think of it simply as a political slot machine that mysteriously always paid off. As for Negroes—the liberals were kind, thoughtful, and generous to those they dealt with personally, and otherwise they pretended the problem was not there. It is startling, in scanning the liberal journals of the late 1930s, to find how seldom one encounters anything much about Negroes. In 1939 *The New Republic*, perhaps the leading liberal journal of them all, put out a special anniversary issue in which it included articles of American business, the American farm, American morals, the American character, the American economy, and a variety of other topics—but no article on the Negro.

Meanwhile the injustices and the outrages went on; and the worst of the outrages was lynching. There were seven officially recorded lynchings of Negroes in the South in 1938; one victim was accused of having raped a seventy-four-year-old woman, another of being drunk and resisting arrest; still another was killed like Cinna the poet by a mob hunting for somebody else; in no case was any action against the perpetrators taken by the state involved. In 1939 there were only three lynchings. The barbaric old custom was finally dying out, all right; at its height, in 1892, the lynching total for the year had run above 150. But the whole story of extralegal violence and intimidation against the Negro is not told by the formal figures on lynchings.

The figures suggest, for example, that such violence and intimidation took place only in the South; it did not. One night in August, 1939, at Cranbury in central New Jersey, almost directly in a line between the mighty and liberal cities of New York and Philadelphia, several Negro farm hands were roused from sleep by masked men, led at gunpoint to a clump of woods near a highway, ordered to strip themselves naked, and then made to kneel with their heads on the ground. Perhaps they were to be killed, perhaps not; at any rate, a car passed on the highway, frightening the tormentors, who allowed their victims to escape with the parting admonition, "Git on back South, you're not wanted up here." The perpetrators were brought to justice; but they had shown that unbridled terrorism was no Southern patent.

And the figures suggest that murders of Negroes by whites in the South in 1938 and 1939 could be counted on a man's fingers. In fact, the number of such murders that went unpublicized and unnoticed even locally is uncounted and uncountable by any means. Indirectly through the use of starvation and exposure, or directly through the use of a gun if he conveniently happened to have a deputy sheriff's badge, the boss of Negro farm hands in the South had the legal or nearly legal power of life and death over them—and, furthermore, he could exercise the power without stirring up any inconvenient publicity. Let us see how the exercise worked in the case of one Negro, a member of a mixed sharecroppers' union, in Mississippi in May, 1939.

In the version of one of the victim's fellow members:

Brother Jackson was killed last week. One day he had an argument, his plantation boss beat him something terrible while another white man held a gun on him. . . . He was setting on the porch with his wife in the evening when he seen some men coming to the house on horses. His wife told brother Jackson to run and hide in the woods. He couldn't run very fast cause he was sore and the boss rode up and shot him in the back. The union had his funeral. . . .

In the version, here reproduced in full, of the local newspaper:

May 14—Ed. Jackson, a huge Negro, was killed today while resisting a deputy sheriff. An attempt was made to arrest Jackson on a charge of disorderly conduct. A struggle took place, and the officer had to shoot in self defense.

2

Negroes shared fully in the country's great advance in standard of living during the war years. The reasons seem to be two: increasing insistence by Negroes on their own rights and the fact that, for a change, the country badly needed them. At the beginning of 1941 the defense boom was already on. Slightly more than 100,000 Americans were employed in the aircraft industry; just 240 of them were Negroes, most of these porters and janitors. Then a group of Negro organizations, chiefly at the urging of A. Philip Randolph and Milton Webster, began threatening to stage a march of ten thousand or more Negroes on Washington that July 1 to demand defense jobs. Government officials from the President on down were horrified; even Mrs. Roosevelt tried to explain to the leaders that the march was made impractical by the custom of segregation in Washington hotels and restaurants. On June 20, under severe pressure and with apparent reluctance, President Roosevelt capitulated; he issued his famous executive order banning discrimination on defense projects and setting up the Fair Employment Practices Commission, and the United States government had at last taken its first formal step.

Even though the FEPC had no real punitive powers over those who defied it, the results, over the next four years, were tens of thousands of good-pay jobs for Negroes in places where they worked side by side with white men, tens of thousands of Negro families better fed and housed than they had ever been before, and tens of thousands of well-to-do white people complaining with good or ill grace that they had lost their cooks, gardeners, handymen, or housemaids to the local war plant. Negro income during wartime increased 80 percent faster than white income did. These gains for social democracy, almost accidental by-products of the war situation, were not matched by comparable gains within the armed forces. All-Negro American units—the 332nd Air Force Group in Italy, the 92nd Infantry in Italy, and the 93rd Infantry in the Southwest Pacific—fought valiantly and well and were widely and justly publicized. But at no time during the war did whites serve under Negro officers; not until 1944 did a War Department order (which was not always obeyed very well, at that) forbid racial segregation in military buses and recreational facilities; not until the last weeks of the war in Europe was any effort made to include white and Negro soldiers in the same fighting units; and throughout the war the Red Cross explicitly endorsed the racist myth that Negro blood was medically different from white blood by storing "Negro plasma" in segregated blood banks!

Meanwhile, the war was bringing to a head the long-evaded question of exactly what was the Negro's status in American society. In June, 1944—the month of D-day, and perhaps the dead center of wartime for the United States—there appeared in *The New Yorker* a deceptively unpretentious little story entitled "A Short Wait Between Trains," by Robert McLaughlin. In the story, a group of Negro soldiers, stranded a few hours in a Southern railroad station, try to get a meal; they are first refused, and then are allowed, apparently by special dispensation, to eat in the kitchen of the station restaurant. As they do so, they see a contingent of German prisoners of war who, being white men, are having dinner in the regular dining room. "The prisoners sat relaxed and easy at the tables, lighting cigarettes, drinking water, taking rolls from the baskets on their tables . . . their eyes incurious, their attitudes casual." That is all. The story, little noticed at the time but much anthologized later, was simply a vignette. Its remarkable impact lay in the fact that what it described was not an aberration, an isolated example of malice or mismanagement, but a part of the whole fabric of American life at the time: what McLaughlin described might have happened over and over again, and probably did. And the vignette set forth with brutal clarity a moral issue that many of the best-intentioned Americans were simply not used to facing. A war, like a personal quarrel, can have the virtue of compelling the disputants to self-analysis. If captured Nazi soldiers could have privileges on American soil that Negro American soldiers did not have, then was a Negro American really an American at all? If not, was not America's proud talk about democracy mere empty rhetoric?

The issue was at last to be faced, little by little, in the postwar years.

3

Negro economic gains continued in the early years of peace, chiefly because the precedent of integrated factory work had been set, and because the surging demand for consumer goods kept the factories going full blast. And there were accompanying social gains. Jackie Robinson became the first Negro in big-league baseball in 1947, and partly because he was a man whose marvelous athletic ability was matched by marvelous forbearance and tact, the transition took place so smoothly and peacefully that within a few years Negroes were fully and unquestioningly accepted in baseball. (Exactly half of the eighteen starting players in the first game of the 1965 World Series were Negroes, and no sportswriter made anything of the fact—or even, so far as I know, noticed it.)

President Truman, whose contributions to Negro rights almost two decades ago do not seem to be sufficiently remembered these days, made two characteristically courageous and forthright moves. Shortly before the 1948 election he issued an executive order directing that "there shall be equality of treatment and opportunity for all persons in the armed services"—with the result that in the Korean War we fielded a military that was at least partially integrated, and was thus a good deal more consistent with American ideals than that of World War II. The same year, the Democratic Party under Truman's leadership showed a kind of political courage that it had never mustered in New Deal days, by virtually driving the Southern Dixiecrat faction out of its ranks—and then confounding everybody by winning the election anyhow. Indeed, many white Southerners, in the years of Truman's Presidency, seemed to be moving toward moderation. The mood of the most enlightened ones, perhaps best embodied in William Faulkner's 1948 novel *Intruder in the Dust,* was: Give us more time; let Southerners and Negroes work out their problem together, in good faith and at their own pace; meanwhile, Northerners and Washington, keep out!

But, of course, the Supreme Court was not disposed to keep out or to give the South much more time, and in 1954, by overthrowing *Plessy* vs. *Ferguson* once and for all in the epoch-making *Brown* case and decreeing that integration of public schools be undertaken "with all deliberate speed," it launched what a decade later is so often spoken of as "the second American revolution."

In trying to put this "revolution" in the context of national change as a whole, we may find it instructive to remember what Samuel Eliot Morison says about the first American Revolution, the War of Independence: that it was fought not to secure new rights but to regain old ones that had been taken away. The same may be said about the second one; that is, American Negroes once enjoyed integration in most aspects of life in all parts of the country, and once had full voting rights in all states. The curious thing, in retrospect, is that so many years passed between the loss of those rights late in the last century and the coming of the revolution in the 1950s. Various factors seem to have contributed to making the ground at last fertile for change: rising incomes, beginning in wartime, had widened Negroes' horizons and raised the level of their expectations; the opportunities many Negro soldiers had had in wartime to see other countries had opened their eyes to the fact that treatment of their race as inferior was not universal; and meanwhile the white majority was finally being forced to face the fact that, in the light of national ideals, the status quo was insupportable.

The very roll call of battles and skirmishes in the struggle for Negro rights during the decade after 1954 already has overtones of epic grandeur, even though some of the battles and skirmishes were in themselves more shameful than tragic. Promptly in 1954, then, there was the beginning of desegregation of schools and public facilities in the city of Washington, under the leadership of President Eisenhower —who, however cautious, legalistic, and uncommitted he may have been personally on the race question, nevertheless was vigorous in his insistence that the law as laid down by the Court be complied with. In 1955 there was the bus boycott in Montgomery, Alabama. In 1956 there was the drama of Miss Autherine Lucy's entrance into the University of Alabama, the subsequent riots, and Miss Lucy's withdrawal. In 1957 there was the terrible struggle over school integration in Little Rock, Arkansas, culminating in the dispatch of federal troops by the President; and the same year there was the passage of the first federal civil-rights law since Reconstruction.

After a slackening in the pace of advance during the tag-end years of the Fifties, there were the Freedom Rides of integrated Northern bus travelers through parts of the South in 1961; and in 1962 there was the admission, accompanied by the greatest tension up to then, of James Meredith to the University of Mississippi. After that the battles and skirmishes came thicker and faster. In May, 1963, the nation was appalled to see and read about the use of police dogs to attack civil-rights demonstrators in Birmingham, Alabama; the next month, the NAACP leader Medgar Evers became a Negro-rights martyr when he was murdered in Mississippi, and Governor George Wallace made the celebrated although futile gesture of using his person to blockade the entrance of the University of Alabama to Negro students; and that August was the month of the peaceful March on Washington, which culminated with some 200,000 Americans standing between the Lincoln Memorial and the Washington Monument to dramatize the cause.

Although 1964 was the first year when Northern students went to the Deep South in significant numbers to work for the registration of Negro voters (and three of them paid with their lives for their high-mindedness), it was also the year when the problem came, of necessity, to be recognized as a national rather than a Southern one. That year saw bitter and bloody riots in the Negro ghettos of Northern cities (Jersey City, Paterson, and Elizabeth, New Jersey; Philadelphia; Chicago; Rochester; Harlem and Bedford-Stuyvesant in New York City). It saw a Negro boycott protesting *de facto* segregation in New York City public schools. It saw the gathering signs of a minority "white backlash" against Negroes in states outside the South. Also in 1964 the states ratified Amendment 24 to the Constitution, outlawing the poll tax where federal elections are involved, and a new civil-rights law was passed that, among other things, for the first time put a federal prohibition on discrimination or refusal of service in hotels, motels, restaurants, and places of amusement that do an interstate business. As for 1965, that March found the conscience of most of white America stirred as never before in the civil-rights struggle by the Selma-to-Montgomery march for Negro voting rights; that August found Congress passing a voting-rights law with teeth in it, abolishing literacy tests in places where there was evidence of discrimination, and giving the federal government the right to assign its own voting examiners to such places; and that summer as a whole was marked by a cheering and generally unexpected decrease in the number and violence of race-connected disturbances in the non-Southern cities where most Negroes now lived—although no one could mistake the ominous significance of the riot that *did* occur in the Watts section of Los Angeles, where Negroes in huge numbers suddenly took to threatening or attacking whites in good part, it appeared, simply because they were white.

4

What have been the results up to now of all these forays and rebuttals, all these new laws? Or at any rate—since causes and effects are hard to connect—what are the changes that have accompanied them?

The Negro population has risen slightly but not tremendously faster than the general population—from just under thirteen million in 1940 to about twenty million in the mid-Sixties. Much more dramatic has been Negro migration out of the South and to cities. The percentage of all American Negroes resident in the South dropped from three-fourths in 1940 to less than half in 1965; there were less than two urban Negroes for every rural one in 1950, more than three in 1965. The number of Negro farm operators dropped over 40 percent between 1954 and 1959 alone. This exodus from the farm and from the South has obvious political implications. In 1940, out of a total population of more than two million, Mississippi had a bare 32,000 more whites than Negroes; in 1960 it had some 340,000 more—a workable population majority of 58-42 percent instead of a virtual standoff. In 1940 Alabama had a white majority of 870,000; in 1960, of 1,300,000. And the trend is continuing. In 1940, then, if Negroes had had full voting rights and had exercised them *en bloc* they would have been within striking distance of control in several Southern states; now they are not numerically even close to such a position in any state. As the South gains Negro voters through registration, it loses them through emigration. Ironically enough, by the time most Negroes in the Deep South are voters, there may well be too few of them there to constitute more than a powerful minority bloc.

The numerical and proportionate increase in Negroes in the North, Midwest, and even West has been equally dramatic. Between 1940 and 1960 the statewide Negro population of New York went from 4 percent of the total to almost 9 percent; of Illinois, from under 5 percent to over 10 percent; of Michigan, from under 4 percent to over 10 percent; of California, from under 2 percent to well over 5 percent. Even Nevada, where 664 Negroes were counted in the 1940 census, contained 13,484, or almost 5 percent, in 1960. Among cities, Washington, D.C., and Newark, N.J., now have clear Negro majorities, while Detroit, Baltimore, Cleveland, and St. Louis are more than one-third Negro, although none of these had anything like proportionate Negro representation in its municipal government. Nevertheless, Negroes have recently begun to capture elective offices in significant numbers, and to make their weight felt in national politics. By 1965 there were six Negro Congressmen in office, as well as about ninety state legislators. That fall a Negro missed by a whisker being elected mayor of Cleveland. Analyses of the 1964 Presidential election show conclusively that the Negro vote carried Virginia, Florida, Tennessee, and Arkansas for the Democrats, and strongly suggest that it was the decisive factor in North Carolina. And that, it should be noted, was *before* the enactment of the voting-rights law.

Other figures point to improvement in the quality of Negro life. By April, 1964, more than a quarter of Negro children went to integrated schools in Oklahoma and Missouri, not quite half in Maryland, more than half in Delaware and West Virginia—as against none in any of those states in 1939; there were, however, still seven states in 1964 in which the figure was under 1 percent. The gap between average Negro income and average white income closed substantially between 1940 and 1960. The number of Negro business and professional men remains pathetically low—Charles Silberman has concluded that Negro business is relatively less important now than at the turn of the century, and has pointed out the startling and almost unaccountable fact that there were only six hundred more Negro doctors in 1950 than there had been in 1910—but in recent years certain forward-looking companies like Chock Full O'Nuts have vigorously sought Negroes to fill executive positions, and many others have thrown open their executive ranks to qualified Negro applicants. Largely because of a belated and dramatic drop in the Negro tuberculosis death rate, the life span of the American Negro had increased markedly more rapidly than that of the white. In 1940 average life expectancy at birth was 64.2 years for a white, 53.1 for a nonwhite; in 1962 the figures were 70.9 years and 64.1 years, meaning that the nonwhite could expect to live eleven years longer than in 1939 and that the gap between his life expectancy and the white man's had been narrowed from 11.1 years to 6.8 years.

The changed attitudes that have come along with these changed facts and conditions are less calculable but not less real.

Quite evidently, Negroes as a group have gained a new view of themselves and of what their role in American life ought to be. Freed, at least in part, of the old sense of oppression that often made it impossible for them even to *conceive* of first-class citizenship—or to see themselves except through white men's eyes—they have found their sense of possibility widening, and as a result they have shed a good deal of their old apathy and passivity to become more assertive and more militant. The much-discussed "search for identity" by Negro intellectuals in the postwar years would have been impossible in 1939; then they knew all too well what their identity was—it was the one invented for them by the white man, except perhaps for a private core of individuality kept prudently hidden in the white man's presence. So far from remaining in their 1939 condition of not expecting or hoping for integration, they have come to look upon universal integration as not only desirable but certain to come; and a disturbing, often highly intelligent faction of them has gone on from there to the opinion that integration may not be desirable, after all, on the ground that white society is rotten and therefore unworthy of their participation. A Paul Robeson may have objected to being typed in demeaning roles on stage and screen in the 1930s; *any* Negro actor would make such an objection in the 1960s. One may surmise that a Father Divine used quaintly polysyllabic language in the 1930s to establish his erudition and to avoid saying what he had to say too directly; Negro leaders in the 1960s speak very much to the point. Negro leaders of 1939 were glad of whatever help they could get from white liberals (and, as we have seen, they usually got little enough); now, in the time of their growing self-confidence, they tend more and more to be leery of white liberals, to look for suspect motives in them, to feel for them the faint scorn of the front-line soldier for the headquarters desk man.

That a revolution has occurred in the mind of the black man seems unmistakable. The change in the mind of the white man has been less dramatic, more in the nature of evolution; and to distinguish the stages in the evolution, we may well look to his popular art of musical comedy. We start with the minstrel-show characters in their quaint Catfish Row in the 1930s. George Gershwin's *Porgy and Bess* could be (and was) successfully revived in the 1950s, but only as a period piece; its conception of Negro life was even then hopelessly dated, and the current conception was changing fast. As the professor of psychology Bruno Bettelheim and the professor of sociology Morris Janowitz have pointed out, there is a small study of changing American attitudes toward ethnic and racial prejudice to be found in a comparison and contrast of *South Pacific* (1950) and *West Side Story* (1957)— two musicals in which, it's worth noting, although both deal with American prejudice, the group toward which prejudice is directed is not Negro, but rather Polynesian in one case and Puerto Rican in the other. In *South Pacific,* the professors declare, race prejudice figures as a mere personal matter—an impediment (and an incidental one, at that) to the love of two white persons; while the cause of such prejudice is explicitly described, in a famous song, as being deliberate evil conditioning: "You've got to be taught to hate and fear." In *West Side Story,* on the other hand, a love affair fails to solve the problem of prejudice as a social condition, and that prejudice is shown, more pessimistically, not as an effect of evil "teaching" but as the inevitable outcome of human cussedness and modern urban conditions. The professors conclude that American society, to whatever extent its views were expressed in these examples of a popular art form, had proceeded in seven years from "naïve ignorance about the real causes of ethnic hostility" to "an impressive degree of sophistication." And maybe the professors have a point. Just as most white Americans were a good deal more aware of the existence of a Negro problem in 1950 than they had been in 1940, so in the following decade their ideas on the problem's nature and possible solution were certainly to become a good deal tougher, less sentimental, and more realistic.

In the 1960s their thinking was to advance further, and the change was to affect people in more parts of the country; it was to be symbolized perhaps most dramatically in the case of President Johnson himself, whose conversion to unstinting support of the Negro cause, acknowledged as a conversion in a public statement of stunning candor, will surely be remembered as a key moment in our history. "As a man whose roots go deeply into Southern soil, I know how agonizing racial feelings are," he told the Congress in joint session on March 15, 1965. He did not need to remind the members that in the late Thirties he had been a fairly typical New Deal Southern Congressman, voting with the liberals most of the time but lining up regularly with the opposition when it came to matters of Negro rights; or that as late as the early Fifties he had categorically opposed school integration. But now, asking Congress for legislation that was to become the new Voting Rights Act, he said, "There is no Negro problem. There is no Southern problem. There is no Northern problem. There is only an American problem. . . . [The Negroes'] cause must be our cause too. Because it's not just Negroes, but really it's all of us who must overcome the crippling legacy of bigotry and injustice. And we shall overcome." Thus the very slogan of the Negro-rights movement became the slogan of the President, of the nation itself; none of his predecessors in office, whether they came from North or South, had ever made anything like so unequivocal a commitment to the cause.

5

Negroes fighting for their cause, and their country's cause too, with courage, intransigence, and above all a degree of nonviolence surely unprecedented in the annals of social protest; a compliant Congress, led by a President who inspires them with the zeal of a convert, doing its long-deferred duty; the conscience of a white nation at last stirred to action—all this makes a pleasant story. But it is, of course, only half the story.

The process of *de facto* school and residential segregation outside the South, a function of economic disparities and of the flight of the white middle class to the suburbs, has gone on inexorably over the past quarter-century; as a result, so eminent an historian as C. Vann Woodward could write in 1965 that "Negroes now have less contact with whites in schools than they did a generation ago" and that segregated housing "is still spreading and seems destined to remain with us for the foreseeable future." As I've already noted, the old process of obstruction and intimidation continued to the extent that in a few parts of the South a smaller proportion of eligible

Negroes were voters in the early 1960s than had been in 1939. In integrated schools, as Charles Silberman has eloquently shown, Negro children often slip year by year further into apathy and despair because they cannot learn (or are not taught) to read properly in the lower grades, and thus are hopelessly unable to keep up with the white children in their classes later on.

Economically, the progress of Negroes relative to whites seems to have peaked in the early 1950s, and then, in a particularly bitter paradox, turned downward during the very decade of "the second American revolution." During the Fifties Negro income increased less than white income in every part of the country; between 1952 and 1963 the median income of Negro families nationally in relation to white ones was reduced from 57 percent to 53 percent; between 1947 and 1965 officially classified white "poverty" went down by 27 percent, Negro only 3 percent. And even over the quarter-century as a whole, certain statistics show a net loss for the Negro. Negro unemployment is one: from a rate nearly equal to that for whites during the early years of the depression, it has gone to almost twice as high. Infant mortality is another: it was 70 percent higher for Negroes than for whites in 1940, 90 percent higher in 1960.

Furthermore, painfully close present-day parallels to the 1939 incidents that I have described are all too easily found. In Birmingham in October, 1965, a Negro whose legs had been severed in an automobile accident had no better luck than Bessie Smith; he bled to death, it was reported, after a white ambulance driver had refused to take him to a hospital. And that same month in Lakewood, New Jersey—only twenty miles or so from Cranbury where the migrant farmers had been terrorized in 1939—two houses being built for Negro families in an all-white section burned mysteriously to the ground by night. It should be added, in fairness to Lakewood, that the local government and people reacted instantly with both anger and determination.

A by-product of the Negro revolution, perhaps an inevitable and some say (though I certainly don't) a desirable one, has been a clear-cut deterioration of relations between the races. Although this has been evident in many different places and circumstances, it is most clearly shown in the rise of extremist and overtly racist attitudes on both sides. The unreconstructed white Southerner's vaunted feelings of "friendship" for the Negro were always suspect because they were based on mastery; nonetheless, it can hardly be denied that they were often expressed as kindliness of a sort. A Negro druggist in Clarksdale, Mississippi, talking to a reporter for a Northern weekly in 1964, struck a note of bitter nostalgia in speaking of his lost white friends. As a boy, he said, he had known whites well: "I did the things Negro boys did, shined their shoes, got them women." But interracial friendships had ended with the 1954 Supreme Court decision. The druggist, Aaron Henry by name, became the militant state president of the NAACP. As for the white friends, one can only note, with sadness and trepidation, that the Ku Klux Klan apparently made its greatest membership gains ever between mid-1964 and mid-1965; that the three Klansmen accused of murdering the civil-rights worker Mrs. Viola Liuzzo near Montgomery in March, 1965, were given a standing ovation by a crowd when they appeared publicly in nearby Anniston two months later; and that in August a solid businessman in another Alabama town said calmly to a *New York Times* reporter, "The niggers are going to be in trouble around here when this is all over."

Perhaps it is understandable, then, that Negro leadership has tended to react by turning to "the Left." Generally in moderate hands in the Thirties, as we have seen, it remained there through the Forties and Fifties, when men like Martin Luther King, James Farmer, and Roy Wilkins came to the fore. By the mid-Sixties a whole political spectrum is discernible among Negro civil-rights leaders, from a cautious "Right" to an increasingly militant "Left"—and it is the latter that seem to be in the ascendancy. For the most part, this new Left, except for a noisy few Maoists and Castroists, is as resistant to the blandishments of Communism as most Negro leaders were back in the Thirties; it tends to extend to Communists the distrust it feels toward white men whatever their politics. The Negro Left sets itself no such abstruse and theoretical objectives as Marxism preaches; its goals are simple: it wants justice for the American Negro, and wants it right away.

In its growing militancy, the Negro Left shows signs of gradually abandoning nonviolence as a principle of the movement. In 1965 the Congress on Racial Equality, after having heroically maintained a nonviolent stance through years of the most extreme provocation, formed a liaison with the Deacons, a disciplined and armed Negro defense organization formed explicitly to combat the Ku Klux Klan, with force if necessary. As CORE's president, the moderate James Farmer, explained, "One thing is apparent in the year of our Lord 1965—Negroes in this nation are down to about their last ounce of patience. For all the hoopla and the speech-making and legislation, very little has changed in the reality of Negro life in this country. . . . Now if you accept that as fact, then it's clear that violence may be on the horizon." And far, far beyond Farmer, Negro extremists with growing influence were proclaiming outright black racism. "The majority of American white men are evil," wrote the Negro poet and playwright LeRoi Jones. "There is no sense in your praying-in, or laying-in, or standing-in, or sitting-in. . . . If America is not stopped in its tracks it will destroy the world."

I confess that I cannot see whether the accomplishments of the past quarter-century, as regards the Negro question, should be described metaphorically as the successful lancing of an old boil that now needs only time painfully to heal, or an unsuccessful operation that has released poison into the national bloodstream; whether we are heading toward racial peace and justice or racial war. What does seem clear is that, as Woodward wrote in 1965, "insofar as federal laws are capable of coping with [racial discrimination], Congress has just about fulfilled its role." What chiefly remains is to find an answer to the huge and in some ways still growing economic disparity between whites and blacks.

One federal approach—epitomized in the 1965 Moynihan Report, which met with instant rejection by Negro leaders but seemed likely to make a comeback eventually—is to search for ways of strengthening the ego of the Negro man and the structure of the Negro family, both of which seem to have been crippled by centuries of slavery (under which family life was actually forbidden) and a century of postslavery oppression directed far more at Negro men than at Negro women. Over the past quarter-century, says the Moynihan Report, the Negro community has split in half between those who are going up to comfort, distinction, and leadership and those who are going down to degradation. "It might be estimated," the report says, "that as much as half of the Negro community falls into the middle class." Yet in the urban centers that are now the principal home of the Negro family, that family has measurably disintegrated: almost a quarter of Negro births are now illegitimate, as against 17 percent in 1940; since 1940 the Negro divorce rate has gone from 2.2 percent, the same as that for whites, to 5.1 percent, 40 percent higher than that for whites; twice as many Negro as white families are now headed by females; one-third of Negro children now live in broken homes. Out of this unplanned matriarchy, ill-suited to the white culture within which it exists, come increases in Negro welfare dependency, juvenile delinquency, adult crime, illiteracy, unemployment—or so the argument goes.

There has come to be talk of tackling this huge sociological problem, and human tragedy, through the spending of heretofore undreamed-of sums—of treating American Negroes almost as if they were a separate nation receiving "foreign aid" in the billions or tens of billions. Can billions or tens of billions make whites and blacks into one people at last? No one knows, but either way, as Professor Morison says, it is certain that "the grapes of wrath have not yet yielded all their bitter vintage."

6

And now, by way of cheering contrast, for some unequivocal good news.

The late Thirties and early Forties saw an alarming increase in American anti-Semitism. Feeling against Jews had existed almost since the moment of their arrival here in huge numbers from Europe, before and just after the turn of the century; as early as 1913 Jewish leaders had taken anti-Semitism seriously enough to form an organization, the Anti-Defamation League of B'nai B'rith, specifically to combat it. Over the following two decades, as a new generation of American-born Jews had appeared, had left the Yiddish-speaking ghettos to make their way in business, the arts, and the professions, and to become increasingly assimilated into American life, anti-Semitism, if it had not actually decreased, had at least become less respectable; many Jews who grew up in urban areas during the Twenties say they recall few instances of overt prejudice against them then. But the Thirties brought an ominous upsurge. Partly it was caused by the fact that Jews were now competing all too successfully with their Gentile neighbors. The Jew as proletarian was being replaced by the Jew as solid, or distinguished, citizen; for the first time in American life, the complaint could plausibly be raised that the Jews "get into everything" and "are taking over."

And partly it was an ill wind blowing from across the Atlantic. Hitler's increasingly venemous campaign against the Jews in Germany provided Americans who had previously kept their anti-Semitism latent with a sanction of sorts, by elevating what they had previously thought of as a none too creditable self-indulgence to the status of the official policy of an important nation that had blood ties with whole sections of America. This campaign, at least as far as the prewar period is concerned, reached its climax with the Nazi-sponsored *Kristallnacht* of November, 1938, when 75,000 German-Jewish shop windows were broken, all synagogues in Germany were burned, and twenty thousand German-Jewish men were taken off to concentration camps. Here was an end of civilized inhibition; here was bestiality enshrined as policy; and it has to be recorded that to judge from the press of the time most Americans reacted with indifference, a few with approval.

"Need I state that in recent years there has been a marked increase in anti-Semitism in America?" asked Alvin Johnson of New York's New School for Social Research that same December. "Everyone knows that this is true." Early in 1939 research done under Dr. Johnson's direction showed that there were in the country at least eight hundred openly anti-Semitic organizations with a membership of three million, among the organizations being the Silver Shirts, the Defenders of the Christian Faith, the Industrial Defense Association, the Knights of the White Camellia, and, of course, the

German-American Bund. Father Coughlin, the "radio priest," weekly poured anti-Semitic poison out over the airwaves. Largely thanks to Hitler, anti-Semitism had become an accepted staple of the political Right; religious organizations like the Federal Council of Churches of Christ in America were thought to be daring when they denounced it.

Through an irony that holds a certain ghastly comedy, anti-Semitic rabble-rousing of the Coughlin sort slacked off abruptly after the announcement of the Nazi-Soviet pact that August; the standard line had been to link "Jews" with "Moscow," and now that the Right was temporarily friendly with "Moscow," the standard line had suddenly become an embarrassment. But such political-diplomatic twists and turns could have little effect on the subtler, more middle-class, more "gentlemanly" forms of anti-Semitism with which American life in the late Thirties was shot through. "Restricted"—which everyone recognized as meaning "anti-Semitic"—suburban and vacation communities and resort hotels were common; leading colleges and universities apparently maintained quotas for Jewish students and apparently did so with public approval; most country clubs excluded Jews as a matter of course; and rare was the Jewish name to be found among the officers, directors, or partners of a business or professional firm run predominantly by Christians. Jews ran the movies, yet the stories and the stars put on the screen were aggressively Anglo-Saxon. One reason the Jewish name on the corporate letterhead was so rare—and one index of the time's anti-Semitism—was that so many ambitious Jews changed their names to bland English-sounding ones; to get ahead, in short, meant to climb out of one's skin and into someone else's. The verb "to pass"—meaning to appear to be Gentile although one was Jewish—sounds almost obscene now, but in the Thirties it was common currency. Even in the enlightened literary life, anti-Semitism and its effects were common. We have given some attention to the naïve version of it found in Thomas Wolfe's *The Web and the Rock*. Further light, oblique and telling, is thrown on the literary scene of the Thirties by Alfred Kazin's story of his friend, the critic V. F. Calverton (who had long previously abandoned his real name, George Goetz). When asked point-blank if he was Jewish, Kazin says, Calverton would merely smile. "There was so much anti-

Semitism in the air, he once said to me, that he could not bear to add to it."

The course of anti-Semitic attitudes in America since 1940 can be recorded with considerable confidence in the accuracy of one's data, inasmuch as scientific polls on the subject have been made regularly and systematically under the auspices of a highly competent and generally quite objective organization, the American Jewish Committee. The key question asked at intervals of a nationwide sampling of non-Jews—a question cleverly calculated to sense the amount of anti-Semitism in the air, regardless of the particular respondent's views—was: "Have you heard any criticism or talk against the Jews in the last six months?" In 1940, 46 percent answered yes; in 1942, 52 percent; in 1944, 60 percent; in 1946, 64 percent; in 1950, 24 percent; and in 1956, 11 percent. The conformation we see, then, is a steady rise in anti-Semitism through the war years—strangely enough, during the struggle against Hitler it was a good deal better to be a German than a Jew in America—on to a very high peak in 1946, and then, over the following decade, a drop so dramatic as to amount to a collapse. The credentials of 1946 as a peak year are strengthened by the results of a *Fortune* poll published that year, which reached the conclusion that 8.8 percent of the nation's population then was "strongly anti-Semitic," as indicated by the fact that that percentage of those polled spontaneously made strong anti-Jewish declarations in answer to questions in which the word "Jew" was not even mentioned. So almost one in ten of non-Jewish Americans was apparently an unmistakable anti-Semite in 1946.

The rapid change for the better that occurred after that year is confirmed by many polls other than the one I have mentioned, and by the everyday observations of both Jews and non-Jews. Indeed, anti-Semitism in the United States in the 1960s is not a serious problem. To the extent that it is a problem at all, it is a rather musty, moss-backed one; at least in cities, a man announcing himself as anti-Semitic these days would be considered not so much sinister as eccentric—as if he had proclaimed himself a Know-Nothing. (Note that the American Right has flatly abandoned anti-Semitism as a plank in its platform; McCarthy did not espouse it, nor does the John

Birch Society.) True, there are still a few communities that go to elaborate lengths to exclude Jews if they can. There are still many large corporations, banks, professional schools, law schools, even medical schools that, all other things being equal, accept Christians over Jews. Jewish college presidents are still all but nonexistent. There are still many clubs that exclude Jews entirely (but clubs don't count for what they used to, and some of them seem to have lost prestige just *because* they commit the anachronism of being anti-Semitic). There was even a small rash of old-time swastika daubings on synagogues and Jewish gravestones during the winter of 1959–60.

So the virus still exists in our blood, but all the evidence indicates that it has been reduced to dormancy. A Rutgers sociologist reporting to the American Jewish Committee's national executive board in 1964 said that the old "negative stereotypes" against Jews—that they are clannish, dishonest, unscrupulous, or excessively powerful in business and finance—had "very nearly disappeared." The Anti-Defamation League itself—which by the 1960's had taken to devoting much of its time to opposing slurs on Negroes rather than Jews, just as the March of Dimes had turned its chief attention to other diseases after virtual conquest of polio—reported in 1965 that a survey it had sponsored showed three-quarters of Americans thinking of Jews as warm and friendly, more than four out of five declaring that it would make no difference to them if they had Jewish neighbors, and almost nine out of ten expressing the view that companies should hire the best people available whether Jewish or not. Even the old prejudice, long operative on both sides, against Jewish-Christian intermarriage was breaking down. No statistics are needed here; a better barometer is at hand. In 1955 Emily Post in her newspaper column had prescribed the correct form for a Protestant-Jewish wedding:

at ten o'clock
Trinity Church
and a second service
at eleven o'clock
Temple Emanuel

When the formidable Mrs. Post was explaining *how* to do it, surely there could no longer be any question about the social correctness of doing it at all!

Small wonder that David Ben-Gurion, long the premier of a country hungry for Jewish immigrants from America, had certain mixed feelings about all this. "American Jews," he said in 1965, "don't need to emigrate to Israel any more."

And along with all this "assimilation" of American Jews went something else, the rise of what has been called a Jewish-American consciousness, a certain reactive assimilation of Jewishness by America that is making a permanent and creative change in American life and thought. The American popular mind for generations had thought of Jews (at best) as "exotic" and "interesting" with their candles and rituals and tales of old Europe; in the past fifteen years or so the stereotyped view—at least its more favorable part—has changed to something quite different, involving intellectuality, civic responsibility, devotion to justice, and love of the arts. In sum, an American cult of Jewishness—quite possibly an excessive one that will lead eventually to a reaction—had developed. We see this in the appointment of a distinguished American of Jewish extraction, Arthur Goldberg, to represent us before the world in the United Nations. We see it in the fact that the New York cultural scene is now overwhelmingly a Jewish scene, and in the widespread and probably justified belief, expressed, for example, by Alvin Toffler in *The Culture Consumers,* that others have generally followed a Jewish lead in the nationwide expansion of interest in culture. We see it in the critical and popular acclaim accorded so many recent novels about Jewish life and containing a Jewish point of view, like Bellow's *Herzog* and *The Adventures of Augie March,* Philip Roth's *Good-bye, Columbus,* Herman Wouk's *Marjorie Morningstar,* Bernard Malamud's *The Assistant,* and a whole parcel of books exploiting Jewish "black humor." We see it in the vogue of that Jewish Will Rogers, Harry Golden. We see it in the fact that a Jewish actress now can become not just a comedienne but a national romantic heroine without pretending not to be Jewish. It might not be a bad idea to compare different times by comparing their dream girls; if so, it's a long way from Shirley Temple, or even Joan Fontaine, to Barbra Streisand.

7

How did this abrupt and yet apparently deep-running change in the American psyche come about? One may postulate that Jews caused it by being such useful and attractive citizens, relatively speaking, that anti-Semitism fell of its own weight; or that the change was long overdue anyway, and high time; or that the revelations in 1945 of the systematic Nazi murder of five or six million Jews demolished anti-Semitism in America by demonstrating its ultimate consequences.

The last postulate is the most interesting to examine. On the face of the matter, it seems to be wrong in view of the apparent fact that the peak of American anti-Semitism occurred *after* the revelations were made. But perhaps the face of the matter does not show the truth; perhaps Americans, as so often in the past, were slow to grasp the meaning of events outside their borders. A chilling little study in how we avert our eyes from distant horrors may be found in a couple of clippings from our most exemplary newspaper, the *New York Times,* in the spring and summer of 1944, when Hitler's death camps were going full blast. That May a small article datelined Istanbul appeared on an inside page saying that eighty thousand Hungarian Jews were reported to be doomed to death. That July an even smaller item out of Jerusalem said that 350,000 Jews had been reported rounded up for deportation to places of execution in Poland. And that November an item of only a few lines, telling of a clandestine booklet by a camp survivor that had been smuggled out to the West, appeared on page 3 under the caption in tiny type, "3,000,000 Jews Executed." Except for the fact that the figures were too low in each case, all the items were true—but no one, including by implication the *Times*, believed them then. The tiny items simply went unnoticed in a nation—despite repeated warnings by Jewish leaders, culminating in a rally of over 20,000 persons in Madison Square Garden on March 1, 1943–that was ideologically unreceptive to them. So, in a way, it may have been still in 1945 and 1946. Even the eyewitness reports by American soldiers of what they found at Dachau and Buchenwald seemed for a time to be disbelieved, or disregarded, or dismissed as propaganda–until at last their truths and their meaning sank in.

I believe that America did slowly grasp Nazi genocide, and by some quality of the country's that gives it the power to cure itself, always late and sometimes too late, of its worst cruelties and follies, as it cured itself eventually, to the surprise of many shrewd observers here and abroad, of McCarthyism. And it is this elusive quality that makes it possible to go on hoping that things will turn out better for the country than logic or experience gives us the right to expect.

XI. JOINING THE WORLD

1

In June, 1940, in the dark week when the French surrender to the Nazis was signed at Compiègne, the Republican Party convened at Philadelphia to choose a candidate for that autumn's Presidential contest. The leading contenders for the nomination came there heralded by the usual carefully concocted hullabaloo. Senator Robert Taft, who had been campaigning for several months out of a headquarters with the downright telephone number ME-1940, called attention to his candidacy by posting in the streets several near-life-sized papier-mâché elephants bearing his name; Thomas E. Dewey countered by establishing as his Philadelphia command post a $20,000 "highway pullman," a huge van containing, among other appointments, a kitchenette and bathroom; a third contender, the publisher Frank Gannett, topped Taft by fielding three *live* elephants; while a fourth—Wendell L. Willkie, the politically inexperienced Hoosier businessman, ex-Democrat and apple of Wall Street's eye—was getting a lot of political mileage out of not campaigning at all. Dewey's name was put in nomination first, then Taft's; and when Representative Charles Halleck nominated Willkie, a nationwide radio audience numbering tens of millions were treated to the sound of (and a television audience numbering a few hundreds, to the sight of) one of the wildest "demonstrations" in political memory. On the convention floor there were as many boos as cheers, but in the balconies (which, if later accusations were true, had been systematically packed with Willkie supporters) the cheers had it by a landslide. "Order! Order!" Chairman Joseph Martin called over and over again; "We want Willkie!" responded the balconies with matching repetitiousness; so it went on for many minutes. The following day Willkie was nominated on the sixth ballot. The day after that, his campaign song was introduced: "Heigh-ho, heigh-ho, it's back to work we go," to the tune of a popular ditty from Walt Disney's *Snow White and the Seven Dwarfs.*

The following month, the Democrats met in Chicago and quickly nominated Franklin Roosevelt to run for an unprecedented third term in what was announced as a "draft," but was certainly about as unconvincing a draft as possible. Roosevelt had elaborately refrained from announcing his availability, but he had made no protest when, contrary to precedent and what had previously been assumed to be law, his name had been entered without his public consent in the Illinois primaries; and, in fact, the big-city machines and the New Deal inner circle had quietly been at work lining up delegate strength for him for more than a year. Now, renominated, he announced in a lordly way that his White House duties would make it impossible for him to waste time on "purely political debate." And, indeed, in the weeks that followed—weeks that saw the Battle of Britain gradually rising toward a crescendo—he did very little campaigning; the whistle stops were largely left to Willkie, who shouted hoarse entreaties to the crowds from his train's observation platform, and was greeted by not only cheers but, on several occasions, showers of eggs and rocks. Joe Louis, heavyweight champion of the world, came out for Willkie, but Tony Galento, a less efficacious but not less crowd-pleasing fistic contender, came out for Roosevelt. Once, campaigning in the street in Rushville, Indiana, Willkie, absent-mindedly shook hands with his own wife, and when she protested, he apologized: "Gosh, Billie. Excuse me, I was thinking." (Another kind of handshaking mix-up brightened the 1964 Presidential campaign. In Los Angeles, a pickpocket in a crowd groped inexpertly for someone's wallet, and got, instead, the hand of the President of the United States.)

On election day Roosevelt won with a popular vote of 27 million to Willkie's 22 million, and an electoral vote of 449 to 82. In Washington that December, the electoral college went through its time-honored charade, with the expected results attended by the expected confusion: some electors failed to appear because of storms in the Midwest and had to be replaced with quickly recruited substitutes, and one Willkie elector inadvertently cast his ballot for Roosevelt.

Does it all sound rather familiar? If so, no wonder; the outward forms and organization of our national politics have remained remarkably static over a period during which, in so many other ways, the country has transformed itself. (The wonder is not that television has changed campaigning so much, but rather that it has not changed it more.) On the other hand, certain aspects of the 1940 election have a far less routine ring to the ears of the middle 1960s. May some of us not be surprised to learn, or to recall, that in 1940 the Socialist Party's Presidential ticket, led by the redoubtable Norman Thomas and running on a platform calling for immediate socialization of the railroad, oil, coal, timber, steel, aluminum, insurance, and investment-banking industries, polled a respectable 116,796 votes? Or that the Communist Party that year held regular state conventions and a national convention whose proceedings were carried on many radio stations, and that its Presidential and Vice Presidential candidates, Earl Browder and James W. Ford, wound up with almost fifty thousand votes? Or that the Communists' platform that year was far milder on domestic matters than the Socialists', and, apart from asserting opposition to Roosevelt's armaments program and support for the "peace policy" (a highly temporary one, it turned out) of the Soviet Union, expressed views almost identical with those of the more radical New Dealers? Indeed, in most ways the Communist Party in 1940 was treated by the nation about like any other splinter party; the chief exception seems to have occured when a considerable outcry arose against a huge Communist campaign poster painted on a wall of the Hotel Claridge right in Times Square, the vaunted "crossroads of the world." The hotel's manager asserted that he had had nothing to do with the deal—the poster had been arranged, he said in gloriously incongruous explanation, through an advertising agency—and had it painted out.

The decline of the radical parties in American politics since then is a subject on which I mean to say something more; right here I'll confine myself to noting that in 1940 the Cold War had obviously not yet begun in earnest. A comparison of the Republican and Democratic platforms of 1940 and 1964 will show us, further, that hardly any of the major preoccupations and pet causes of the two major parties in those days bore more than a tangential relationship to those of today.

Party platforms are, of course, partisan political documents full of rabbit punches on transient issues, rather than elevated statements of principle; nevertheless they reflect the climate of their parties and of the country. In 1940, then, both parties were concerned about staying out of foreign military entanglements: "We will not participate in foreign wars," said the Democrats; "No foreign war," pledged the Republicans. Both were concerned about unemployment: the Democratic Party "wages war on unemployment," announced the Democrats; "Idle men, idle capital, and idle farms will be put to work," promised the Republicans. Both were concerned about the status of labor: "We will continue to recognize the obligation of government to provide work for deserving workers," said the Democrats, and the Republicans spoke of "teamwork between employer and employee and protection of the rights of labor." Both were for expansion of Social Security coverage, the Republicans somewhat more vaguely. Both promised to continue parity and soil-conservation payments to farmers. Both paid lip service to Negro equality. "We shall continue to strive for complete legislative safeguards against discrimination in government service . . . and in the national defense forces," pledged the Democrats, in a statement that now seems remarkable both for the narrowness of the objective and for the brash use of the word "continue"; while the Republicans, who were not even hopeful of getting many Southern votes, went a bit further, including clauses attacking "mob violence" (meaning lynching) and promising "effective universal suffrage."

The main difference was in tone and emphasis, in the Republican tendency to come down hard on "economy in governmental expenditures without sacrificing the needs of the people." In effect, the Republicans were promising to continue the New Deal but do it for less money. Beyond that, there was a portent of things to come in the Republican pledge to root out "borers from within" (presumably meaning Fascists and Communists in government); and there was, needless to say, the ringing Republican slogan "No third term for any President"—a declaration of principle to which, in the circumstances, the Democrats could hardly subscribe.

It is interesting to see how much better Johnson's beloved term "consensus" applies to the 1940 platforms than to those of 1964—a difference surely attributable to the capture of the Republican Party in 1964 by the forces of Senator Goldwater, who was determined to offer "a choice, not an echo." Yet echoes of a sort were still there. The Democrats declared in their 1964 platform, "As citizens of the United States, we are determined that it shall be the most powerful nation on earth"; the Republicans of 1964 pressed the matter a bit further, pledging themselves to "the preservation and expansion of freedom—ultimately its victory—everyplace [*sic*] on earth." The Republicans, true to their party tradition, promised reduced expenditures and taxes, while the Democrats, instead, promised prosperity for all through continuing economic expansion. Both parties promised full implementation and faithful execution of the recently passed Civil Rights Act; the Democrats went on to oppose "lawless disregard for the rights of others" in the conduct of efforts both for and against Negro rights (a statement, incidentally, far more equivocal than the civil-rights policy that the Johnson Administration was to pursue after its victory), while the Republicans promised "improvements in civil rights statutes adequate to the changing needs of our times." The Democrats were for Medicare under Social Security, and the Republicans against it.

So it went: not a word in either 1964 platform about avoiding foreign entanglements; hardly more than a word about unemployment or the situation of organized labor; above all, nothing whatever to imply the existence in America of a class struggle, which was the very core topic of American politics through the 1930s and even as late as 1940.

2

In twenty-five years the entire *content* of our national government and politics has been transformed, in necessary response to the transformation in our national life.

In foreign affairs, both parties finally abandoned, almost certainly once and for all time, George Washington's notion that we could hold ourselves aloof from the rest of the world, and accepted the fact that we are a part of the world whether we like it or not. The word "isolationism," which described the position of not much less than half the nation during the great European-war debate of 1940 and 1941, has all but vanished from our political life. The radical Right fulminates against our participation in the United Nations not because it thinks we should withdraw into our national shell but because it thinks the UN is too greatly influenced by Communists and their allies. The right wing of the Republican Party, which used to be the natural home of isolationist sentiment, is so no longer; its 1964 representative, Senator Goldwater, favored more aggressive participation by the United States in NATO and the Vietnam war. The debate now is not about whether we should be part of the world, but how.

In economics, I have already described how we have changed our very skin. Walter Lippmann summarized the change well in 1964:

> Since the New Deal and the 1930s there has been . . . a revolutionary development in the technology of industry and in the fiscal policy and social doctrine of governments. . . . The assumption of reformers . . . from Theodore Roosevelt through Woodrow Wilson to Franklin Roosevelt was that the poor could be raised up only by a redistribution of wealth. . . . The basic assumption of the pre-war reformers is being dissolved. . . . We have come into an era when the class struggle, as Marx described it a hundred years ago, has been overtaken by events.

We formerly assumed that capital and labor were on a seesaw—if one went up the other went down, and government could tip the balance either way; to change the metaphor, now we have found that capital and labor are together in one boat, for which government serves as steersman.

The more than tenfold increase in annual federal government expenditures since before the war, and the fact that half of our present outlays (and five times *all* our outlays for 1940) are military, constitutes a change in the content of our government so profound as to make comparison almost irrelevant. Who in 1939 could have imagined a peacetime military budget of more than fifty billion dollars, dozens of whole communities from Long Island to the suburbs of Los Angeles wholly dependent for their existence on producing military supplies for the government, and a roll of four million private industrial employees who must have security clearance because of the confidential military nature of their work, or the existence of a network of federal military-and-diplomatic information-gathering agencies that are said to employ 200,000 people and spend about seven billion dollars a year? Who can wonder that this national response to the Cold War has raised problems undreamed of in 1939 or 1940? Not just radicals have expressed fears about the implications of "the warfare state"; General Eisenhower himself, in his last month in office as President, said boldly and forthrightly, "We must guard against the acquisition of unwarranted influence, whether sought or unsought, by the military-industrial complex. The potential for the disastrous rise of misplaced power exists and will persist."

So, say many economists, does the potential for economic collapse if we suddenly disarm, raising the disturbing question: Even if we can end the Cold War, can we afford to do so? Professor Emile Benoit, who headed a commission studying the question, concluded that we can—provided that we invest the funds saved by disarmament in such things as urban transportation and medical research. Apart from defense, government expenditures have risen remarkably little over the quarter-century; Benoit insisted in 1963 that "on a real basis—allowing for price increases—federal expenditures for goods and services other than defense have *declined*. . . . On a per capita basis, they are now only about half what they were back in 1939." And Congressman Morris K. Udall has pointed out that based on the 1939 dollar, between that date and 1962 federal welfare expenditures shrank from $30 to $16 per citizen.

Such a bizarre governmental dilemma could not have been imagined in prewar days. Indeed, most of the pages of this book have been devoted to the postwar emergence in American life of entirely new issues and problems vitally affecting government and politics. The problems of the cities, and those of health, education, welfare, have increased in importance and complexity to the extent that new Cabinet posts have been created to deal with them. The far-reaching developments in weaponry and rocketry have necessitated the creation of enormous and crucial new arms of government, the Atomic Energy Commission and the National Aeronautics and Space Administration. The existence of nuclear bombs in our own hands and in those of others has forced government to be preoccupied with still other issues undreamed of in 1940: in the late 1950s and early 1960s, the potential fatal poisoning of the air around us by fallout from nuclear tests, and, in the middle 1960s, the danger of greatly increased menace to world peace, and even human survival, through the spreading of the capacity to produce nuclear weapons to more and more countries. Name almost any branch of federal government and one can instantly mention entirely new issues that are its concern. The Department of Agriculture worries about the misuse of insecticides (nearly all of them developed since 1940) that are fabulously successful in increasing crop yields but, we now know, are potentially lethal to men and wildlife. The Department of Labor worries about the effects of automation (a word uncoined in the Thirties, although "technocracy" was much in vogue). The Department of the Interior worries about national beauty and the Department of Justice about Negro rights (matters by common consent left largely unconsidered in 1940). Even the Post Office Department has a good deal more to concern it now than dispensing political patronage and delivering the mail; changing times have thrust it into the thick of the fight over censorship.

We are a different country, yet we govern ourselves in very

much the old way; while the content of government has been transformed, the form has remained much the same. Washington is still very much the city it always was, its style and pace varying to a remarkable degree in conformity to the personality of the incumbent President, but its underlying tone remaining the same. A new wing, new decorations, and a hugely increased staff have not altered the White House so very much. The ultimate judicial authority is still a court of nine men, even though the country has increased its population by about half; and the senior legislative body still upholds an otherwise fictitious equality among the various states by comprising two members from each. We have added only three amendments to our Constitution since the years before the war. Two of the amendments—one limiting Presidential terms of office to two and one giving the vote in Presidential elections to the District of Columbia—are relatively trivial; only one, barring poll taxes in federal elections, deals with a matter of great substance.

One can only marvel again at the dazzling genius of those men of the late eighteenth century who set up a form of government that worked—with all its failings, better than most for all the people—in 1789 when the Constitution went into effect, and, essentially unchanged, still did in 1939 and 1965.

3

Of course, the processes of government have not remained static over the past quarter-century, and certainly the loci of government power have not. The one great federal legislative reform of the postwar period, the Legislative Reorganization Act of 1946, drastically reduced the number of Congressional committees—from forty-eight to nineteen in the House, from thirty-three to fifteen in the Senate—and carefully staked out their jurisdictions. In theory, this limited the arbitrary power of committee chairmen to sidetrack or bottle up legislation, but in practice, in the opinion of such a recognized authority on government as Douglass Cater, the increased rigidity of the new setup actually tended to enhance the chairmen's power to frustrate the will of the elected majorities. Nor did the reform even achieve a permanent simplification of the legislative structure, since it was powerless to prevent the spawning of *sub*committees; in fact, it made the subcommittee the characteristic seat of Congressional power in the postwar period. There were 180 subcommittees before the 1946 reform, over 250 in the early 1960s; and the notorious "McCarthy Committee" of the 1950s was, of course, really a subcommittee.

Essentially, only the names of things had been changed. All through the Eisenhower and Kennedy administrations the disproportionate power of committee chairmen—many of them conservative Southern Democrats, since the long-standing habit of the South of automatically electing Democrats tended to put Southern legislators in positions of seniority—continued largely unchecked, and, as a result, bills favored by a majority of Congressmen or Senators, and undoubtedly by a majority of citizens as well, were again and again prevented from coming to a vote. Even so, Congress was destined to change at last, and the agent of its change was to be not a legislative reorganization but an electoral landslide. It took Lyndon Johnson's overwhelming victory in 1964 to sweep into the Senate and House so many men so strongly opposed to the old Congressional oligarchy that it was overwhelmed by sheer numbers—perhaps once and for all.

The sweep produced a Senate, Tom Wicker of the *New York Times* wrote, "in which the old South has lost its grip, in which junior members are playing increasingly important roles, in which the fabled power of the committee of chairmen has been scattered." Even Harry Byrd of Virginia, for years the ultraconservative watchdog of the federal treasury, could not any longer control the Senate Finance Committee, although he held its chairmanship until his retirement late in 1965; as Wicker said, the only remaining really powerful Southern chairman in the Senate in 1965 was Richard Russell of Georgia, boss of the Armed Services Committee. The result was the flood of liberal legislation passed by the first session of the Eighty-ninth Congress. Medicare under Social Security; the strongest voting-rights law ever; school aid at all levels; immigration reform; relief for the depressed areas of Appalachia; federal rent subsidies for the poor; establishment of a Department of Housing and Urban Affairs—one by one, pieces of legislation previously blocked by Congressional minorities flowed to the President's desk for signature. The log jam had turned to a torrent, and Wicker felt constrained to comment that the change might not be all for the good; with so much emphasis on fast action, might not the Senate's traditional function of slow, careful, often painful deliberation be compromised?

Meanwhile, at another level, the seeds of a far-reaching change in the direction of more representative government were being sown. The long, inexorable shift of the nation's population from farm to industry, from country to city, had been unmatched by appropriate shifts in the apportionment of seats in the state legislatures—for the very human reason that reapportionment was left up to the legislatures themselves, and legislators from rural areas of declining population were reluctant to vote themselves out of office. So it came about in the late Fifties that, to take a single example, one member of the Minnesota legislature representing seven thousand country people could cancel out the vote of another member speaking for 107,000 city people. (To put it another way, one Minnesota farmer had the political power of fifteen urbanites.) And it was much the same in all other states where the industrializing process had been equally dramatic over the years. Clearly enough, this was not democracy, and some states, Minnesota among them, took a stab at putting their legislative houses in better order during the 1950s and early 1960s.

Then the Supreme Court stepped in. Since 1946 it had been largely standing on Justice Frankfurter's pronouncement that federal courts "ought not to enter [the] political thicket" of state reapportionment. But as the pace of social change had accelerated in the following years, the inequities in the legislatures had become so pronounced that the Court, if it was to stand for democracy, could no longer afford such Olympian detachment. In 1962 it opened the way for change by deciding that federal district courts had not only the power but the duty to hear cases involving inequitable districting. In 1964 came the thunderclap: that June, the Court, by a vote of six to three, decided simply and unequivocally that the districts of all state legislatures must, without delay, be made to be "substantially equal" in population.

In the whole Union, only a handful of states came close to meeting that requirement: there were exactly twelve in which it took more than 40 percent of the voters to elect a majority of legislators. The decision was staggering in the breadth of its force. "It is doubtful," Richard Rovere wrote that November, "whether anything else that happens in this decade will have as great an impact on American political life as the fulfillment of this court order." The nature of the impact, obviously, would be a radical reshuffling of political power in the states in the direction of more for the bursting cities and less for the depopulated rural areas. Washington itself was stunned by the decision. So, needless to say, were the state legislatures, which thereupon set about, often in harum-scarum fashion and almost always to an accompaniment of political infighting and skulduggery, accomplishing the job of reapportioning themselves more equitably.

All these changes in the direction of government more truly "by the people" cannot, with absolute confidence, be regarded as irreversible. The possibility can't be ruled out that Congress might sooner or later move backward in the direction of control by committee chairmen, either by outright changes in its rules or by an imperceptible process of backsliding. An influential independent private advisory group, the American Assembly, concluded as late as 1964 that eighteen specific Congressional reforms were still needed to prevent stalemates between the legislative and the executive branches, and to remove the inequities of the seniority system; the key proposal, that the Senate Majority Leader be enabled to lift any bill from committee simply by designating it a "major bill," would all but end the bottling-up power of committees—if it were ever adopted. Even the Supreme Court's reapportionment decision might at some time be reversed; there are those who feel that in simple justice it *should* be reversed, on the ground that it will tend to take the last vestiges of political power away from rural areas that are already impoverished and bypassed by the upheaval of urbanization, leaving such areas virtually at the mercy of charity from city people. Is it possible, then, that "one man, one vote" is not always the fairest principle of government, after all? Such are the paradoxes of modern America that in some cases it may be possible.

Whatever the future, it can hardly be denied that our government in the mid-1960s is more responsive to the will of the people than was that of twenty-five years ago. In those days the consensus of scholars was that the Constitution itself was at fault in being, at heart, an antidemocratic document; now it appears that the fault lay not in the blueprint but in the men who interpreted and executed it.

4

What has happened to the political parties? More paradox. The pollster George Gallup has estimated that between 1939 and 1964 the Republican Party lost one-third of its national following; yet in 1939 the Democrats were riding on the greatest national landslide in modern history, while for eight years in the 1950s, Republican Eisenhower was to maintain a firm hold on the job for which, in 1936, Republican Landon had been able to win only eight electoral votes. The death of the Republican Party, and of the two-party system, and even of democratic government, was proclaimed again and again after Roosevelt had won a third term in 1940; obviously, the obituaries were premature. The first two demises were being announced again after the 1964 Johnson landslide. Certainly, the Goldwater candidacy turned many things topsy-turvy, notably the South, which, after a century of being the region the Republicans habitually wrote off as hopeless, suddenly became just about their only stronghold.

But the two-party system has an almost mystical resilience; like the "fabulous invalid," the Broadway theater, the more it is dead, the more it comes to life again. Never, apparently, does it come to life more vigorously than when it is subjected to what ought logically to be the *coup de grâce* by the appearance of third parties representing widely held dissenting views. In 1948 the Democratic Party split into a left wing of Wallace Progressives and a right wing of Dixiecrats, a disintegration that by all rights should have rendered it helpless; yet somehow the remaining center rose up to smite not only the Progressives and Dixiecrats but the Republicans as well. In 1965 the chances for Republican John Lindsay to win the mayoralty election in New York City, always a Democratic stronghold, were apparently ruined when Conservative William Buckley set about very effectively siphoning off part of the normal Republican vote; yet somehow Lindsay won anyhow. The two-party system is most magnificent when its situation is most hopeless.

American voters have a taste for paradox; they like to do the unexpected—sometimes, it seems, at the sacrifice of their personal interests or even of some of their long-held principles—and their tendency to act unpredictably seems to me to be on the rise. Television and vastly increased education have made them far more knowledgeable in their voting, more likely to base their decisions on what a trusted commentator or the candidate himself says than on the entreaties and promises of the precinct leader down the block. These changes have made for less party regularity and more independence, and also for a certain whimsicality and personal approach—a tendency to vote for a candidate on approximately the same basis that one used to vote for Miss Rheingold in the local tavern. Whatever else television has done to politics, it has made it a national entertainment to a far greater extent than it ever was before.

Thus has arisen the emphasis of candidates on their "image." Borrowed from advertising, where it had sprung out of the unholy postwar liaison between promotion and psychology, the word "image" invaded American politics about the time Eisenhower came to the White House; and by the 1960 campaign, as Karl E. Meyer has pointed out, it had become so indispensable that Eisenhower felt obliged to accuse Kennedy of having "cruelly distorted the image of America," Kennedy to retort that as a result of a Republican Administration "no longer do we give an image of vitality," and the Governor of West Virginia to endow Abe Lincoln himself with "the image of freedom."

The intrusion of out-and-out advertising and sales-promotion methods into politics and the enormously increased costs of national campaigning brought about by the emergence of the television screen as the chief political hustings seem to me to be the two main factors determining the great recent change in the kind of man America votes into national office. Formerly we generally liked him to be wise-looking, past middle age, not too smooth or sophisticated, not too bright, and not much richer than ourselves. Now we want him to be young, vigorous, dynamic, smart as a whip, conspicuously handsome —and rich; in fact, if he does not appear to be at least well-to-do, we tend to suspect that he can't be honest or he wouldn't have the money needed for his campaign. Richard Nixon, although he qualified as to youth, stubbed his toe badly on two of the requirements; a man of modest means, he barely escaped disaster in 1952 in connection with a political fund he had accepted from businessmen, and many observers feel that the unfavorable "image" of his badly made-up face in a TV debate was the chief thing that lost him the Presidency in 1960. Kennedy, of course, fitted the new requirements to perfection, and set the new national style in American politics. Remember the wry and daring joke he made in 1958, pretending to quote his millionaire father as having warned him during his Senatorial campaign not to buy one more vote than was necessary—"I'll be damned if I'm going to pay for a landslide!" Try to imagine any prewar (or pre-Kennedy) President—even the suave and self-assured Franklin Roosevelt—coming quite so close to the bone at his own expense as that!

In the Senate the change has been particularly marked; fast disappearing are the old-guard types epitomized in Fred Allen's Senator Claghorn, with their white manes, string ties, windy rhetoric, dubious syntax, and whiff of the cornfields; and fast taking their places are the younger, smoother, harder-driving urban intellectuals, of whom Wicker has written, "They are men of postwar America, impatient with the old and eager to get on with what they see as the new business of a new day." If the transformation of our political style has meant that we now tend to vote not so much on issues as on impressions gained from the television screen, the change does not seem to have been all bad. In the first place, in this bewildering nation and world many of the issues have simply become too complex for the average man to cope with. Furthermore, perhaps we have been lucky, but up to now very few political phonies have succeeded in using television to fool us; the candidates who have looked so vigorous, intelligent, and honest have mostly turned out, once elected, to *be* all of those things. The electronic screen, it appears, is a remarkably reliable detector of charlatanism.

Those of the old guard who have survived have changed, too. Among the most interesting, and entertaining, figures in the Senate in the 1950s and early 1960s was Everett McKinley Dirksen, Republican Minority Leader, the very Platonic type of the old-style agrarian legislator, with his great forelock, his ponderously condescending manner, and his slightly malapropos polysyllables flowing as if from a bottomless well in his unctuous, funeral director's whisper. I wish someone would assemble an anthology of Dirksen's *mots* on various subjects through the years, because many of them are genuinely funny—as nobody knows better than Dirksen. For years he has flourished chiefly on his style, which combines in delicately balanced parts embodiment and conscious parody of the typical old-time senator. As for his principles and his stands, until 1961 they were as predictably conservative as was perhaps fitting for a man who bears the name of McKinley. But since then Dirksen has bent with the wind; finding himself increasingly in trouble with the voters at home in Illinois, he first showed a marked disposition to cooperate with Kennedy on various pieces of liberal legislation and then, in 1964, temporarily became a liberal firebrand, leading the Senate toward passage of the Civil Rights Act so vigorously that he was cited by President Johnson himself as representative of "all that is best," not just in the Republican Party, but in the United States!

Born too late, but no fool, Dirksen is a paradigm of what has happened in our government and major-party politics: the utter change in the content, the relative stability of the forms.

The decline of what was then the country's largest minor party, the Socialists, was already well under way by 1940, when Thomas' 117,000-odd votes for the Presidency represented only a little over 60 percent of the number he'd received in 1932. Over the intervening period Socialist strength had been leached off from both left and right. On one side, the softening of the Communist line during the Popular Front period had attracted many former Socialists to that banner; on the other side, the New Deal domestic policies had made the Democratic Party far more palatable to Socialists than it had ever been before, and furthermore many Socialists, particularly those in the labor-union movement, now found it expedient to vote Democratic in order to safeguard the New Deal social gains against modification or abandonment by a Republican Administration. But now the war in Europe brought ideological disaster to the American Socialist Party. Which was more important, to maintain its traditional stance of high-minded pacifism or to take arms against Hitlerian barbarity? On this agonizing issue the Socialist Party broke itself; by adopting a series of compromises that were intended to please everybody, it lost much of its old vitality—and most of its members. In 1948 many Democrats and even some Republicans announced themselves as intending to vote for Thomas as a "plague-on-both-your-houses" protest against the major-party candidates; but they evidently changed their minds at the last minute, for Thomas' vote was small. It was the last time he ran, and the last time, up to now, that Socialism has figured in a Presidential election.

Yet, in an odd way, the Socialist Party was killed, if killed it was, by success as much as by failure. As I've had occasion to point out before, the history of domestic legislation over the past twenty-five years has been a history of the adoption of measures not too different from those advocated by the Socialists in the 1930s. True enough, the basic Socialist plank—public ownership of the key industries—has not been adopted and has surely never been further from adoption than it is now. What we have found is that most Socialist objectives—high wages, relatively full employment, public help for the poor, the infirm, and the old—can be achieved under controlled capitalism. Republicans and Democrats alike have made this remarkable discovery. The conservative Eisenhower Administration adopted Henry Wallace's soil bank to combat farm surpluses, raised minimum wages, and enlarged Social Security. As for the Democrats, Murray Kempton tells of sitting in the press room at their 1952 national convention with Norman Thomas himself, watching the old Socialist leader read the platform of "this party which had all but destroyed him as a politician." "It was a platform fitted with planks from the Socialist program of twenty years earlier," Kempton writes. "Thomas said that night that he could feel a certain pride of authorship now: these things, now taken for granted, had seemed so wild when he began. America was, he decided, an extraordinary country, if it could change like this and remain so much the same. He seemed then to understand that his life had not been a failure."

The American Communist Party, about which we were to hear so disproportionately much in the postwar period, was in fact quite powerful in American life in 1939 and 1940, when comparatively little was heard about it. Besides (as it now appears) having a few representatives at the middle and upper-middle levels of government, it held most of the major staff positions in the national CIO, ran the CIO councils in several key states, including New York, Illinois, and California, and had wide acceptance in cultural and intellectual circles. That was—one may recall now, certainly with surprise and perhaps with a certain nostalgia—the day of the cozy ideological marriage of Marx and Freud (the devotees of whom were, within ten years, to be at each other's throats). If someone ventured the view that the labor movement was going too far, the cocktail-party social analysts would explain that he was simply at the mercy of his bourgeois hostilities—unconsciously, of couse. It was an era when it was thought possible to be at the barricades and on the couch at the same time. True enough, the flirtations of intellectuals with Communism were usually brief ones, but this very fact emphasizes the huge number of people who at one time or another indulged in such flirtations: although the Party's membership was always under 100,000, Communists claim that over the past forty years something like two million Americans passed through their ranks.

What has happened to the American Communist Party since 1940 is, in a mechanical way, obvious: with the coming of the Cold War, public and official opinion turned against it so strongly that every attempt was made to turn it into an outlaw band. Even before that, the Nazi-Soviet pact of 1939 had dealt it a body blow by appalling many of its members, most particularly the large number of romantic idealists in its ranks who had believed that Communism had meant what it said when it had bitterly condemned Nazism. The Smith Act of 1940, which made it a crime to teach or advocate the overthrow of the government by force or violence, and the McCarran Act of 1950, which required individual and organizational agents of any foreign power to register as such, together constituted a mousetrap; that is, if a Communist complied with the latter he apparently thereby became subject to prosecution under the former. Thus driven underground for cover, the Communists stopped holding national conventions or running candidates for public office in 1950, and by the mid-Sixties, after McCarthy had waxed and waned, their numbers were down to somewhere between five and eight thousand. In 1965 the Supreme Court decided what many people had thought all along—that the mousetrap violated the Constitutional provision against self-incrimination—and the Communist Party jubilantly announced that it planned to run candidates again. In such an event, however, they did not seem likely to get very many votes.

Because, the Cold War and the witch hunts aside, Communism has lost its appeal for Americans. If any broad view of human society for any particular time and place has ever been "proved wrong," then the Marxist-Leninist view has been so proved for the United States in the postwar period. The postwar Communist line held quite specifically that the American economy was on the verge of collapse into depression and chaos; in fact, of course, it was on the verge of relatively orderly expansion into unprecedented plenty. In the years after 1945 Soviet economists used to predict such a collapse season after season, with monotonous regularity. What's more, these predictions were occasionally listened to by a few clearly non-Communist Americans. I recall hearing about a couple of alert and ambitious young Ivy League investment men who decided, in the late 1940s, that the Communists had the true word on the American economy. Accordingly, they hied themselves one evening, all gray-flanneled and buttoned-down as usual, to the Communist-run Jefferson School in New York City to get the lowdown.

If they had acted in the stock market on the advice they got at the Jefferson School, they would have lost their shirts. By the same token, Communism in America has lost its shirt since 1945, and can scarcely hope to get it back short of a crash and a depression. When all is said and done, I can't help feeling that continuing prosperity combined with continuing social concern on the part of government has done far more to bankrupt American Communism than intimidation, police penetration, and repressive laws.

So the radical splinter parties have all but disappeared, and with them has gone much of the predilection for Utopian dreams and aspirations that has always in the past played such an important part in American life. The United States itself was conceived in a Utopian dream—and paradoxically, as the dream in many ways comes closer to realization, the faith that it can ever be wholly realized becomes less and less tenable. The complexity of the age of nuclear bombs and mass society has made all such dreams seem naïve. "Socialism in our time" was Norman Thomas' cry in the 1930s—Utopia, that is, seemed to him and his followers to be within grasp, and their aim was to live to see it. Such visions have lost much of their power to inspire us.

Then is American radicalism dead? Assuredly not. Moribund as it may have seemed at the turn of the last decade, it has made a strong recovery in the 1960s—but with some differences. Its leadership seems to come from two groups that are often called the outcasts of modern industrial society, the very young and the very old. It has completely dropped the "class struggle" as an issue—even in fighting poverty, it treats the poor not as a social class but simply as a number of people who have less money than everyone else—and has adopted as its chief causes the civil-rights movement and opposition to American military preparations and operations, particularly in Vietnam. For the most part it is emphatically home-grown, its kinetic force deriving not from Moscow or Peking but from the outraged consciences or sensibilities of its members—and for this reason it has been called the "spontaneous Left." It tends not to form new political parties or even to identify with old ones, but to operate in a wildly (and perhaps characteristically) disorganized way, with each adherent acting as a free-lance. Moderate opponents of the new radicalism condemn it, particularly for its bellicose attacks on American foreign policy, as ill-considered, uninformed, impudent, and in its effects subversive of the national interest—but they seldom suspect its motives, as most Americans routinely suspected the motives of *all* radicals in the Thirties, Forties, and Fifties. Above all, its members apparently feel freer than did their predecessors; as Harvey Swados writes, "The fear of being labeled radical, leftist, or subversive seems to have all but disappeared." As long as things stay that way, there will be reason to hope that the radical movement will be a helpful agent of further change rather than a disruptive force.

5

"With God's help," Senator Kenneth Wherry told a cheering audience in 1940, "we will lift Shanghai up and up, ever up, until it is just like Kansas City!"

In exaggerated form, that pronouncement pretty well caught the spirit of America's approach to Asia—and to a certain extent, to the rest of the world beyond our own borders. The approach was that of a missionary who possessed the one true gospel condescending to enlighten the benighted. Out of the conviction of our Puritan forebears and the fact of our geographical isolation on what had been a new continent, we had built up an almost touching certainty that our way of doing things was the standard to which the whole world aspired—or ought to. As we have seen, even in Great Britain, our acknowledged Mother Country, our ambassador was trying to lift up the backward locals by teaching them not to commit the gaucherie of putting such long tails on their shirts.

Over the past twenty-five years we have come a long way toward learning that we are not necessarily the center of the universe but part of a community of nations (and that may be the single most important thing that has happened to us). Yet meanwhile, in terms of economic and military power, we have moved a long way toward actually *becoming* the center of the universe. With new power, as always, has come new responsibilities. John Adams doubted in 1776 that the country had "public virtue enough to support a republic." It turned out that it had, but if Adams could have lived into the modern era he might well have had doubts on a new question: Have we public virtue enough to be responsibly the most powerful nation on earth?

The record is unclear on the matter.

It is clear enough as to wartime: we saw the national interest and the moral imperative, and acted on them. The questions of whether we should have demanded unconditional surrender of the Axis powers, whether we should have fire-bombed German and Japanese cities, whether we should have dropped two atomic bombs, are still debated and will continue to be; the fact remains that by subsequent standards our wartime foreign policy was almost as simple and straightforward as the theology of Cal Coolidge's preacher who was against sin.

The old spirit of isolationism, still so strong in the 1940 party platforms, finally went through its death throes in the early postwar years, and the death throes were perhaps most dramatically signaled by the conversion to internationalism of Senator Arthur Vandenberg, chairman of the Senate Committee on Foreign Relations. A new issue—a hard or soft line toward Russia?—swiftly replaced the old one; the debate that raged all through 1946 resulted in victory for the hard-liners and in the firing from Truman's Cabinet of Henry Wallace, the leader of the soft-liners and the man who, but for a few quirks of fate, might have been President instead of Truman. The basic shape of what has been our foreign policy ever since—in a word, anti-Communism—was laid down in the few memorable weeks in the spring of 1947 out of which came first the Truman Doctrine to shore up Greece and Turkey, and then the Marshall Plan to shore up Western Europe. Three years later the basic shape was hardened when we, with the help of other forces from the United Nations, took up arms against Communism in Korea.

All through the Eisenhower years, as the Iron Curtain drew down tighter and the arms race built up, the single idea of opposing Communism dominated our foreign policy, whether the catch-phrase of the movement was "roll-back," "massive retaliation," or "brinkmanship." Perhaps, in the circumstances, we had no alternative to this policy; in any event, the effect was to give our stance toward the world a certain limiting, even demeaning inflexibility that it had lacked in the prewar years when we were far less powerful and less concerned about our neighbor nations. True enough, during the 1950s we took notice of what now seems to have been the greatest development of that decade, the end of colonial rule and the emergence of dozens of new nations in Africa, with the progressively expanded foreign-aid program that had grown out of President Truman's "Point Four." But even in helping poor countries we too often seemed to be merely implementing our anti-Communism, buying them away from the other side; and the stupidity, tactlessness, ignorance, and arrogance of some of our aid-program representatives showed that we needed changed attitudes as well as changed policies to measure up to our new role in the world. (The vast success at home of the 1958 novel *The Ugly American,* incidentally and interestingly, seemed to show that our capacity for savage self-criticism was growing in direct proportion to our national role in the world.)

As the Fifties dragged to their end, the United States was not doing well in the world—seemed, indeed, to be paying the deferred bill for its excesses earlier in the decade. With the Korean War at last safely behind us in 1953, and with our development of the hydrogen bomb in 1953 and 1954 giving us a new sense of security from our enemies, we had gone on a national binge, glutting ourselves with automobiles and TV sets and stock-market profits. Now the account was being rendered. Its first installment had been the Sputnik in October, 1957, destroying our bland confidence in our technological pre-eminence. Hard on the heels of that came the serious recession of 1957–58—a consequence, many economists said, of previous overexuberance combined with a continuing reluctance, based on reverently held economic principle, of government to intervene decisively enough. Then we began to discover that the gold backing up our currency was flowing out of our treasury and into the treasuries of European countries at a rate so alarming as to raise the specter of devaluation of the dollar, with consequent reduction in our vaunted standard of living. The European Common Market, which we had energetically sponsored on both political and economic grounds, showed signs of growing up to be an all too mettlesome economic competitor, threatening our leadership in world trade. The final installment of the accounting—this time in the military-diplomatic sphere—was to be the most sobering, even humiliating. It would come in May of 1960, when the Russians would shoot down Francis Gary Powers' U-2 high-altitude photographic plane of the U.S. Air Force some twelve hundred miles inside Russia, and Khrushchev would deftly trick the United States into a denial, later reversed, that such a flight had been authorized. For a brief time after that, we were a laughing stock even to our allies.

Sometimes one man sums up the state of his country at a certain moment, and in late 1958 and early 1959, when foreign affairs had come so recently to loom so large in the American cosmos, it seems to me that such a man was John Foster Dulles, at the time our Secretary of State and perhaps the most powerful man in the nation. Dulles was the quintessential traditional American, with the Puritan virtues of energy, drive, ambition, love of work, indifference to personal comfort, and the Puritan shortcomings of stubborn self-righteousness and inflexibility. He epitomized a declining breed that was far more in charge of things in America even seven or eight years ago than it is in the mid-1960s.

In the fall of 1958 Dulles was a dying man, a fact of which he was unaware, as apparently his doctors were, too. He was suffering much discomfort, keeping it to himself, since he believed his troubles were relatively minor. On doctors' orders he had restricted his diet and given up smoking, and the latter deprivation, his sister Eleanor Lansing Dulles has quoted him as telling her, had resulted in a recurring and revealing nightmare: He would be sitting with a group of men with a brandy in one hand, and a butler or a friend would pass a box of cigars. He would feel his hand go out to choose one, and then he would wake up bathed in sweat.

At all events, he was of no mind to slow up on the job. Always a frequent traveler by plane, he now seemed to become an obsessive one. In October, when the long crisis over the Chinese offshore islands of Quemoy and Matsu took a turn for the worse, he resolved to go to Taipei to see Chiang Kai-shek; then when Pope Pius XII died and Eisenhower designated him to go to the funeral, Dulles decided to combine the trips, flying from Washington to Rome and then back, via England, the great-circle route over the North Polar region and Alaska, to Taipei. "Problems with France, Cyprus, Panama, Guinea, Indonesia . . . and nuclear testing had to wait," his sister has written.

The plane—an Air Force jet tanker, the only kind of passenger jet then available—was hardly calculated to make a sick man comfortable; it had a dark, windowless interior, bucket seats, and bunks hung like hammocks for sleeping. Nevertheless, late in the afternoon of October 17 Dulles set out in it for Rome, accompanied by his wife and a party of government officials. Out over the Atlantic, sometime after midnight, one of the straps holding Dulles' bunk broke, and he fell to the bottom of the compartment, wrenching his back. Without waking anyone up, he managed to straighten out his mattress and lie down on it on the floor, where he was found in the morning by his security aide, to whose alarmed questions as to why he had told no one of his accident, he replied, "You were all sleeping so nicely. I know it's hard to get to sleep again on a plane."

Despite the new agony from the back injury, Dulles went through two days of conferences, as well as the Pope's funeral, in Rome; then (still in the same dreadful aircraft) moved on to a brief stop at Brize-Norton in England and an airport conference with Foreign Minister Selwyn Lloyd; then on over the Pole to Alaska, where he learned that the Quemoy-Matsu situation had worsened further, talked to Eisenhower by phone, and decided to go on; then at last across the Pacific to Taipei for two solid days of discussions. Finally, he flew back halfway around the world to Washington, where a few days later he found a note from Selwyn Lloyd about their brief airport meeting: "May I tell you in a very personal note of the admiration I felt when I saw you at Brize-Norton, going off in that very uncomfortable aeroplane after a brief period of so much work on a long and tiring journey." Long and tiring journey indeed—and Selwyn Lloyd presumably thought he was speaking of a well man!

On and on Dulles went, over the following months, as his pain waxed and his strength waned, doggedly, indomitably, perhaps pointlessly dragging himself on to do what he thought he had to do. In mid-November he was off to Duck Island, his St. Lawrence River hideaway, for a week's vacation—to be greeted on his return to Washington by Khrushchev's famous six-month ultimatum on Berlin. Later in November—in constant pain now, his sister says—he flew from Washington to Georgia to see Eisenhower, thence to Mexico City for the inauguration of Mexico's new President, thence to Palm Springs, California, for a few hours' rest, thence to San Francisco for a speaking engagement, thence back to Washington. In mid-December he went straight from Walter Reed Hospital (where he had had a checkup that produced no definite diagnosis) to the airport and a flight to Paris for a two-day NATO foreign ministers' meeting. From Paris he went to Jamaica, where he rested for a week; but less than a month later, at the end of January, he was off to London, Paris, and Bonn for eight days of conferences on the Berlin situation. This trip must have been a nightmare awake. As Miss Dulles learned later, "He had been able to eat almost nothing but raw eggs and gruel and the like. . . . He had not been able to bathe or dress himself alone." In any case, it was his last official ordeal. A week after his return an operation disclosed he had advanced cancer, in April he resigned as Secretary of State, and in May he died.

Poor John Foster Dulles! Poor America at the end of the Fifties! Both, it may seem to the reasonable observer, had brought many of their troubles on themselves, and both dealt with the troubles with more motion than effect, more stubborn courage than vision. But maybe the case calls as much for compassion as for reason.

6

Thus tiredly, doggedly, painfully, gallantly, the country survived the hangover period that followed the binge of the 1950s. The new decade, while it did not find us with a greatly or even a significantly different foreign policy, saw us approaching the rest of the world with a new vigor and hope. The Kennedy Administration, once past the Cuban Bay of Pigs disaster in its third month in office, when our prestige around the world may have hit its all-time low, began getting across the idea that the interest of the United States abroad was essentially in peace and goodwill, but not surrender. The emphasis on conciliation may well have been a factor in influencing the Russians to implant nuclear-tipped rockets in Cuba and thus precipitate the hair-raising missile crisis of October, 1962, in which the country's lost prestige was largely recouped, and out of which, almost miraculously, Kennedy emerged as the symbol of cool-headed world leadership, not only in the United States but even in many Communist and uncommitted nations. "Massive retaliation" had given way to "flexible response"—a substantive change, all right, but even more a stylistic one.

But the changes that had taken place were by no means limited to the White House and its appurtenances. In September, 1963, when the Senate voted, 80–19, to ratify the treaty with Russia banning nuclear tests in the atmosphere, it was hardly the same Senate many of whose leading members had regularly attacked the very notion of such a treaty only four or five years earlier. The Presidential election of 1964 showed, perhaps as clearly as any election can show anything, that support for a certain change in emphasis in our foreign relations went down to the grass roots. Senator Goldwater's foreign-policy proposals—that we look more skeptically on the United Nations, that we consider giving control of the use of nuclear weapons to field commanders, that we generally toughen our military and diplomatic stance—were widely interpreted as being a major factor in bringing about the great Johnson landslide. A large majority of Americans appeared to have decided that caution and moderation rather than "toughness" should be our watchwords in foreign policy. In overwhelmingly electing a man who had been accused of following a "no-win" policy toward world Communism, and who never explicitly denied it, they gave the President such a mandate for the principle of collective security, and against the principle of indiscriminate musket-rattling, as would have been impossible twenty-five or even ten years before.

Yet to many the Johnson foreign policy in the first year after his election seemed inadequate or worse. Particularly as regards the Dominican Republic and Vietnam, his policy of "measured" response to Communist aggression or the threat of it seemed to the critics from the Left to boil down to committing American men and weapons to the shoring up of *any* anti-Communist regime, no matter how weak, corrupt, or oppressive. Meanwhile critics from the Right, including many Republican leaders, attacked him for not doing enough, for dealing too gingerly with Communist insurgency. (As to the civil liberties of dissenters in the mid-1960s, they had not only made a gratifying comeback from the McCarthy period but were almost certainly in healthier shape than they had been twenty-five years earlier —as evidenced by the fact that, when some twenty thousand people marched on the White House in November, 1965, to protest the Vietnam war, only fifteen were arrested on the minor charge of disorderly conduct.) Johnson, threading his way with immense political dexterity between these two points of view, seemed to be bent on finding the dead center of national opinion so precisely that the weight of it could balance on his policy as if on a seesaw. But the questions could still be asked, by persons from neither the Left nor the Right: Was this the way foreign policy ought to be made? Didn't the needs of the most dangerous times ever require of the world's most powerful nation that it have a more resourceful and inventive foreign policy than one based simply on the polarized proposition of military resistance to Communism?

That question was to remain unanswered through a long and agonizing period.

7

How well, then, have we met our new responsibilities as a world power? Better, it seems pretty safe to say, than we have met some of our internal problems, such as the defacing of our countryside and the physical and social degradation of our cities. But beyond that, it is probably best to keep our own counsel, and to conclude this cursory review of postwar foreign policy by tracing briefly the changing mirror image of Americans in the changing opinions of others.

Certainly the world view of us in the years just before the war had little relation to the present one. World relations then, not to mention communications, were so different! Europeans, of whom none but a tiny handful had ever seen our shores, flocked to American movies and, accepting them more or less at face value, formed a dream image of us as the land of plenty and nonsense, envying us the former and laughing at us for the latter; and while they accepted this picture in their hearts, they knew in their minds that we were going through a terrible depression, that their cousins in Chicago or Pittsburgh or St. Paul did not really live like Cary Grant. Latin America was our economic client to so great an extent that where anti-American sentiment existed it was generally kept well suppressed by vigilant local governments. Russia was too busy with its own and Europe's affairs to give us much thought other than to encourage American Communists. Colonial Africa and Asia, except for the limited regions where there were American industrial holdings, had no relation to us at all—except to think of us in vaguely friendly terms as a former colony ourselves. Our future enemies, the Axis powers, underestimated our strength and wildly misunderstood everything about us. Japan considered us a paper tiger, as its action at Pearl Harbor was soon to make clear. Even Hitler and Mussolini, while they denounced us ritually from time to time, seldom seemed to have their hearts in it, nor to have the remotest notion of whom they were denouncing. William L. Shirer has given, from captured German documents, a spectacular example of the weird Nazi views of us as of March, 1939. At that time Hitler conferred with a leading German "expert" on the United States who informed the Fuehrer that Roosevelt was his enemy solely for reasons of personal jealousy and lust for power; the "expert" also mentioned an "imperialist tendency" in America, whereupon Hitler suggested that this tendency might "strengthen the desire for *Anschluss* of Canada to the United States, and thus produce an anti-English attitude"! It is recorded that the Fuehrer considered the conference a most enlightening and helpful one.

Ignorance, confusion, and indifference—but little real hatred; savage, deeply felt anti-Americanism was to come later. And not with the clash of arms either. At this distance, German and Japanese hatred of America and Americans in wartime appears to have been shallow and concocted; what was affected more profoundly was our relations with our friends. Our necessary but often heedless bombing of friendly cities, and their subsequent occupation by war-weary and homesick troops, inevitably made many anti-Americans, particularly in France and Holland. Things worked out best in the places where our troops remained longest; at American air bases in Britain, as I saw myself, relations between the townspeople and the Yanks would be hostile for a year or so, and would finally thaw out to warm friendship as the two sides came to understand each other a little. And then, at the very end of the war, we dropped the atomic bombs on Japan. Whether, as human beings, we were justified in doing so is not the simple question that it seems to be, and it is a question that remains moot; but, in any event, it was a propaganda disaster, giving anti-Americans of every shade and stripe a weapon against us that they are not likely soon to lay aside.

In the postwar world, as everyone knows, Communist voices have consistently described us as villains and anti-Communist voices have with equal repetitiousness described us as knights in shining armor. But in fact the new polarity in opinions of America appears to lie elsewhere. Europeans, on whichever side of the Iron Curtain, clearly want to think well of us; on the other hand, Africans, Asians, and Latin Americans like us, to put it mildly, a good deal less now than they did before.

Commerce and tourism have replaced the exigencies of war as a means of throwing together Americans and Europeans. First the rise of international business and general affluence here resulted in a hugely increased flow of Americans to Europe; then the spectacular recovery of Europe began to make the flow of business people and tourists across the Atlantic a two-way affair. The annual number of European travelers to the United States tripled between 1955 and 1963. Meanwhile, for those who stayed at home in Europe, magazines, newspapers, even live television by relay satellite were bringing ever more information about America. In 1962 Benjamin Appel, an American novelist, made a tour of Europe East and West asking people in streets and cafés for their ideas about America. A sampling of the replies he got makes a striking little study in how outmoded the old stereotypes about Americans have become in the countries of Western Europe, and at the same time how ambivalent the people in the Communist countries feel about us.

From a Frenchman: "France is too *sérieuse*. In America sport is the life."

From a British intellectual: "Mostly I see America as a country of transit and travel. The idea of America is the idea of movement, the rediscovery of yourself by travel over long journeys."

From a Polish coal mine leader: "There are two Americas, the people and the Pentagon." (A *little* truer to life than Hitler's 1939 version, but, after all, not so very much so.)

From a Soviet woman: "We think of Americans with a sincere heart."

And from an Italian painter: "In America you are really alone, completely alone. . . . In America I had a sensation of a civilization without consolation."

Life, movement, enthusiasm, naïveté, loneliness, restlessness, competitiveness, sincerity—such are the characteristics making up the composite portrait that emerges out of Appel's researches, and not such a bad likeness it is. One way and another, Europeans have come to know us a little, and thus, at the level of private citizens, to forgive us a little. Only in France, our oldest friend in Europe and the famous home away from home of our writers and artists in the 1920s, do private relations seem to have deteriorated since before the war. The old, basically sound Franco-American relationship—a joshing alliance between mock-libertine and mock-Puritan—was beautifully caught in the mid-1930s by Henry Miller in *Black Spring*: "I do not find it strange that America placed a urinal in the center of the Paris exhibit at Chicago [in 1933]. I think it belongs there. . . . True, there was no need to fly the tricolor above it. *Un peu trop fort, ça!* And yet . . . one of the first things which strikes the eye of the American visitor, which thrills him, warms him to the very gizzard, is this ubiquitous urinal." Now all that spirit is gone; as America's power in the world has gone up and France's down, the old relationship has been disturbed, the old joke has gone dead, and, in consequence, the Frenchman has become ruder and more condescending, the American in France more blatant and boorish.

On the official level, of course, Europeans still do not forgive us. "From 1945 to 1962 mistrust, if not of American motives, then of American wisdom, was a prominent theme of British public utterance," says *The Economist*. "In Europe today there is a swelling tide of dissent and doubt and anxiety about the wisdom and competence with which United States foreign policy is being conducted," Walter Lippmann wrote in June, 1965. And so on. But European opinion of American policy fluctuates wildly and swiftly with new events; our prestige there went from a very low point after the Bay of Pigs to a high point after the Cuba missile crisis just a year and a half later, and it rose sharply again in the six months following Lippmann's comment. One begins to hear not-so-grudging praise, particularly for our domestic economic and social accomplishments, from strange quarters—for example, from a prominent Swedish sociologist, Stevan Dedijer, who was a Communist planner for years and now describes himself as "neither a Communist nor an anti-Communist." The New Deal, the New Frontier, and the Great Society, Dedijer wrote late in 1965, "are not simply 'vote-getting gimmicks,' but seem to be all a part of an increasing, conscious effort . . . attempting to rationalize human society into a stable, evolving, creative and innovative social system based on an enlarged complex of social values." Not for a long time—perhaps, indeed, not since the days of brave promise when the republic was new—had America heard talk of that sort from uncommitted Europeans.

But with much of the rest of the world it is very different. Except in a very few cases, we have made bad friends or even outright enemies of both the people and the governments of the new countries, the poor countries, and the nonwhite countries. The facts and figures on small, symbolic insults to America—insults of a sort that, so far as I know, did not exist in modern relations between nations before the Second World War—are dishearteningly impressive. In 1958 Vice President Nixon was spat on in Peru and stoned in Venezuela; in 1959 President Eisenhower was jeered at and pelted with water balloons in Uruguay; in 1960 Presidential aide James Haggerty's car was mobbed in Japan; and in 1965 both Robert F. Kennedy and Dean Rusk were spat upon and otherwise abused on Latin-American trips. Meanwhile, stonings and smashings of American embassies and libraries had become commonplace all around the world. From 1953 through 1964 U.S. Information Center libraries and cultural centers sustained forty major attacks, many of them triggered by no discernible cause other than general hostility. Indonesia apparently led the field with a record of five such incidents; they occurred without apparent discrimination in countries that are our allies (Taiwan, Greece, Brazil, Panama, South Vietnam), in countries that are ostensibly neutral (Egypt, Algeria, and the Sudan), and in Communist countries. As to our embassies, they were stoned so often and in so many different places that in 1965 Secretary of State Rusk proposed that the glass in their windows be replaced with shatterproof substitute material.

Scarcely the imperial style! That the world's greatest power is regularly the victim of this sort of schoolboy bullying around most of the world is a comment on both the world's greatest power and on the times. Giving America full marks for forbearance, as I think we can, the country would do well to ask itself why it is so hated. Partly, one assumes, as an effect of Communist propaganda (and it is impossible to say how many of the incidents of vandalism were Communist-staged and how many were not); partly because of greatly increased publicity about mistreatment of Negroes within the United States; partly because of the age-old hostility and suspicion on the part of the poor toward the rich, the mendicant toward the philanthropist; and partly because our representatives abroad are sometimes truly ugly Americans. I'd like to think, too, that part of the trouble results from an element of plain inexperience on both sides. Twenty-five years ago not only did our foreign-aid program not exist, but the idea of it would have been dismissed as hopelessly Utopian by liberals and wantonly profligate by conservatives. We are, remember, almost as new to the role of world's greatest power as the new nations are to nationhood.

XII. DIFFERENT AND OLDER

1

Two formidably perceptive cultural anthropologists, the American Margaret Mead and the Briton Geoffrey Gorer, set themselves the task of analyzing the American national character as it was before, during, and immediately after the Second World War. Miss Mead in her book *And Keep Your Powder Dry,* written in 1942, and Gorer in *The American People,* written in 1947, came to strikingly similar conclusions. Miss Mead put particular emphasis on the well-known American urge to "succeed," along with its psychological roots and social implications, while Gorer bore down heavily on American suspicion of authority in any form, and especially as embodied in government. But both writers made much of the influence of immigrants in American life and of the universal wish that children should "rise above" their European parents or grandparents. Both made much of the American need for approval and love. Both played on such familiar themes as the all-powerful role of the mother in the American family, the permissive American style of bringing up children, the famous chip on the American shoulder, the American male's excessive fear of being considered a sissy. Both saw Americans as being preoccupied with ethical principles, and yet leaving ethical considerations largely out of their conduct of politics and business. And both made it explicit that most of their generalizations were intended to apply only to the regions of the United States known as the North, the Middle West, and the West. By doing so the two writers admitted that they found it impossible to draw a composite portrait of the American except by limiting it to the white American living outside the South. And they were careful to include the qualification that a good many specimens of even *that* kind of American did not conform to the portrait very well.

In short, they found that generalizing about Americans in the 1940s was a chancy business. It still is in the 1960s. But since they were in exactly that business, it is interesting now to note that—apart from Gorer's passing references to that old chestnut of a theme, American "keeping up with the Joneses"—they had scarcely anything to say about conformity; indeed, I have recently reread both books without being able to find the word in either. A possible explanation presents itself. Miss Mead and Gorer made their researches in a time when the menace of Hitler was in one case very much present and in the other case so recently past that its shadow still blighted much of the world. Perhaps in their concern about the threatened loss of the physical freedom to be an individual—the threat of the coming of some form of totalitarian government to America—they neglected the whole question of the threatened loss of psychic freedom through ability to *feel* like an individual.

I need scarcely say that this problem has not been neglected in more recent analyses of American character. Out of the writings of (among others) Erich Fromm, David Riesman, and William H. Whyte, Jr. has emerged a composite American who is quite a different chap from the one discerned by Miss Mead and Gorer. Fromm sees him as possessing "the marketing orientation"; Riesman says his personality is "other-directed"; Whyte sees him as a follower of "the social ethic" rather than the "Protestant ethic." It seems to me that they are all talking about pretty much the same man, and he certainly has an advantage over many composite portraits in his lifelike quality; he is a fellow everyone knows at firsthand. He believes that success in life depends on "how well a person sells himself on the market, how well he gets his personality across, how nice a 'package' he is" (Fromm). His moral responses are based not on a fixed internal code of any sort, but on what is expected of him by others (Riesman). He believes in "the group as the source of creativity," " 'belongingness' as the ultimate need of the individual," and "the application of science to achieve belongingness" (Whyte). In sum, he is the perfect conformer. It was Whyte who finally gave him his name once and for all—Organization Man—as sharply different from "the men who built this country up" as those sour old pioneers and robber barons were different from Neanderthal Man. Furthermore, in the clearly implied view of his synthesizers, Fromm, Riesman, and Whyte, he was not the sort of man they considered likely to build the country up much in the future.

By about 1960 the vision of our national character as descried both at home and in Western Europe seemed to have come into its clearest focus in perhaps a century; it was a vision of the organization man. But was the vision the true one? And if so, was it new? Various commentators have answered the second question emphatically in the negative. Seymour M. Lipset has had fun dredging up quotations from nineteenth-century British writers about American life in which they expressed views that might almost be lifted out of Riesman or Whyte. "The worship of Opinion is, at this day, the established religion in the United States," he points out that Harriet Martineau wrote in 1837. "The very children," she went on, "beware of getting into scrapes, and talk of the effect of actions upon people's minds . . . it is a settled matter that it is unsafe to commit oneself on paper. . . . There is a fear of vulgarity, fear of responsibility; and above all, fear of singularity." Nor was Miss Martineau alone in her views; a summary of the writings of a whole slew of English visitors to America between 1785 and 1835 shows that an American characteristic mentioned over and over again was a startlingly acute sensitiveness to the opinion of others. The tendency to universal "status-seeking" that so many commentators of the 1950s saw as an important concomitant of the "new conformity" was likewise noticed by a remarkable number of the British visitors more than a century earlier. (Incidentally, even permissive American child-rearing, that favorite target of modern critics, got its lumps from the novelist Anthony Trollope. "I must protest," he wrote after visiting America in 1860, "that American babies . . . eat and drink as they please; they are never punished; they are never banished, snubbed, and kept in the background as children are kept with us.")

How marketing-directed, other-directed, social-ethic-dominated can a people get? Not much more so, it would seem, than Americans of the nineteenth century appeared to British tourists to be. Lipset's conclusion is that our national character has not really changed much, even from the nation's earliest days; that we have always contained two conflicting strains, one of individuality and self-reliance and the other of conformity and reliance on others; and that the apparent drastic turn in the latter direction over the past quarter-century or so is a superficial and perhaps temporary turn brought about by changed economic conditions. As we have grown fat and as corporations have expanded so enormously in wealth and size, these conditions have provided fertile ground for the conformist strain, just as the lean times of the 1930s provided fertile ground for the individualist strain. The apparent change in our character is thus taken to be largely an illusion.

It is an intriguing thesis—and, of course, an unprovable one. There is at least one firm fact we can seize upon: between the 1940 census and the 1960 one, self-employed persons as percentage of the total labor force went down from 26 percent—more than one worker in four—to 16 percent. If the self-employed person is the literal antithesis of the organization man, he has certainly become scarcer, whether because of changed conditions or a changed national character. No one can doubt, in a time when almost seven-eighths of all Americans who work at all work for somebody else, that the organization man in the literal sense is the characteristic working American. And probably no one can doubt that many people are worried about the consequences; the historian Richard Hofstadter, for example, sees the 1964 Goldwater candidacy, with its loud overtones of old-time rugged individualism, as an expression of "national anxiety" that "the decline of entrepreneurial competition will destroy our national character."

But, statistics notwithstanding, has entrepreneurial competition really declined all that much, or is it perhaps merely in the process of taking new shapes? Is the rat race to get ahead in a big corporation really so much less individualistic than the nineteenth century free-for-all struggle among individual economic competitors (or, as I am tempted to put it, the cat race to build a better mousetrap)? In a series of articles published in 1964, *Fortune* took a hard second look at the organization man, and found—what? He seemed to have undergone a change in the decade or so since his existence had been discovered. Now he seemed to be less of a yes-man, less concerned about the opinions of his fellows, more daring and innovative, more dependent on his own inner resources. His aim seemed to be to get ahead not by fitting in but by standing out. The organization for which he worked had become so gigantic that it was now a field of action *within* which there was plenty of room for individual initiative. The rat race showed signs of reverting to the cat race.

The suggestion is unmistakable that the ascendancy of the "marketing orientation," "other-directedness," and the "social ethic" may eventually turn out to have been a passing phase in the evolution of mass industrial society. If the typical American of the 1970s does not seem likely to be much like either Commodore Vanderbilt or Longfellow's village blacksmith, he promises to be different from the organization man of the 1950s, too. No doubt he will be something entirely new, combining elements of those various characters with other ones that can't be foreseen.

2

He—and she. In the foregoing chapters I have consciously avoided dealing with women as a group apart, on the ground that almost everything I have said applies to them as well as to men; but here goes for a few facts and impressions as to how their particular situation in America has changed, and how their attitude to it has.

To the extent that popular attitudes may be deduced from popular books, we find over the postwar era a complete reversal on the famous American woman question, home vs. career. In 1939, as we saw, the choice scarcely existed; there were far too few jobs to go around, and such jobs as there were, except those for which women were considered better adapted, such as nursing and secretarial work, almost invariably went to men. Nor was the choice a free one in wartime, when the fact of a husband overseas on low military pay and the vital need for war workers at home made it a practical necessity, not to mention a patriotic duty, for millions of American wives to take the first jobs of their lives. It was in the postwar period that women, particularly married ones, began in great numbers to have to face the dilemma: given the opportunity to take jobs not out of necessity or patriotism but just because they might feel like it, should they do it or not?

Ferdinand Lundberg and Marynia Farnham, in their influential book *Modern Woman: The Lost Sex,* published in 1947, answered the question with a resounding no. Arguing from the premises of Freudian psychology, they insisted that happiness and fulfillment for modern American women was to be found in the home and nowhere else. The notion took hold or perhaps was in the air already; in either case, the generation of young women who married in the decade following the end of the war tended for a time to cleave to the hearth and the nursery with an almost fanatical devotion—although often with resentment—and to regard the office as the habitat of the Devil. One recalls that Whyte's organization man had his counterpart in his wife, the organization woman: she was socially affable and accessible to neighbors; she was never strident or argumentative; and certainly —God forbid!—she didn't have a job of her own that would expose her to the charge of trying to compete with her husband and thus destroy him, in response to disreputable unconscious drives. But somehow, sometime around 1960, a mysterious underground change in attitude seems to have taken place. *The Feminine Mystique,* by Betty Friedan, argued that happiness and fulfillment for the modern American woman are to be found *not* in the home, but only in a career outside it—and *The Feminine Mystique* is said to have been the most popular paperback from coast to coast in 1964. Here, then, over the course of less than twenty years, is as neat an ideological flip-flop as can be readily imagined.

So much for ideology; now facts and figures. Millions of American women, and especially married women, have actually taken up jobs and careers during the postwar period. In 1940 there were under fourteen million women in the labor force—either holding jobs or actively seeking them—constituting just over a quarter of the female population above the age of fourteen; in 1963 there were almost 25 million women in the labor force, or 36 percent of the female population above fourteen. Much less than half of the female workers of 1940 were married and had husbands living; over 60 percent of them in 1963 were in that condition, and, moreover, roughly one in five of employed women in the 1960s had at least one child less than six years old. Clearly, the office life for the American mother has been making spectacular gains, and I can't help wondering whether the statistical change is the effect or the cause of the ideological one. The fact that the female labor force has been creeping up steadily—both in gross numbers and in percentage of the adult female population—since about 1950, when the stay-at-home "mystique" was still the officially accepted one, suggests strongly that the action came first; that is, all through the 1950s the girls seem to have been sneaking away from diapers and pacifiers to nice, calm, stimulating offices, even though the popular books and magazines of the time did everything possible to make them feel guilty about it. And if this suggestion is right, the vast popularity of *The Feminine Mystique* might be accounted for by the circumstance that it provided millions of women with sorely needed philosophical justification for what they had already done anyway.

Doubtless this increased and still increasing tendency to mix motherhood and a career is the greatest recent change in the estate of the American woman. But there are other changes, and important ones. In sheer numbers, for one thing, the balance has shifted. The 1940 census counted some half a million more men than women; sometime between then and 1950 the nation came for the first time in its history to contain more women than men; while the 1960 count found women in the lead by more than two and a half million, meaning that there were now 100 women for every 97 men. Even allowing for the probability that substantially more men (particularly Negro men) than women went accidentally uncounted in 1960, this is an historic shift, the explanation of which appears to be medical. How odd it is to recall now that one of the great practical problems in the early colonizing of this continent was that of keeping fragile white women alive long enough in the wilderness for them to have babies and thus insure the colonies' survival! The medical advances of recent years have been of strikingly more benefit to women than to men. "It is within our power today," a leading gynecologist said in 1965, "to delay aging in women so that they can lead good, healthy lives. We have *nothing* for men."

Exaggerated, perhaps; but several of the unconquered killers like coronary thrombosis and lung cancer do show an unmistakable predilection for men as their victims, and the effects are clear enough in longevity figures. Between 1939 and 1962 the life expectancy of American men increased 4.7 years, or 7.5 percent; of American women, eight years, or more than 12 percent. An American boy at birth can now expect to live about sixty-seven years, an American girl baby six and a half years longer—and the gap is increasing year by year.

Does this new numerical superiority of women mean more spinsters? By no means; such is the rising popularity of marriage in this lonely land that spinsterhood is actually a vanishing phenomenon. There were three million fewer single women aged fourteen and over in 1955 than in 1940, and between 1940 and 1960 the percentage of women aged thirty-five to forty-four who were married rose from 81 to 87 percent. (Happily for the credibility of the statistics, a similar trend appears for men; bachelors are down, and declining.)

Does the longer survival of women mean that money power increasingly falls into their hands? Indeed it does, and much has been written on the subject in recent years. But I am convinced that the social importance of this phenomenon has been exaggerated. Most women with money instinctively entrust it to men for management and disposition. There is a striking paradox in the contrast between the ability and inclination of American women to exercise enormous social power in the family and in the community, and their distaste for wielding economic power. Even when, through inheritance, a woman finds herself sitting on the board of an important corporation, she is inclined to show up for meetings dressed to the nines but innocent of the state of the balance sheet. Enthusiasm for a "career" notwithstanding, having "a head for business" is a trait that American women value no more now than they did twenty-five years ago—and if my impression is right, less than they did fifty or a hundred years ago.

Not the money power that widowhood sometimes brings but the emotional deprivation that it almost always brings is surely the most important effect of increased longevity on women. The middle-aged or youngish widow is becoming a more and more common American. In 1940 we had 5,700,000 widowed women and somewhat over two million widowed men; in 1963, 8,388,000 widowed women and, again, somewhat over two million widowed men. The chances of widowhood are now more than four times greater for a married woman than for a married man, and that gap is increasing rapidly. Too often, the American widow finds herself trapped in a kind of enforced uselessness. Her children are grown up and on their own; she is a little too old to be readily employable, at least in the kind of work she would like to do; and even if she has enough money, years of the frantic round of activities that being a wife and mother implies have singularly unprepared her for a life of leisure. Perhaps worst of all, her lot in life is apt to look easy when it is not—especially to her children and their husbands and wives. And her ranks include, when you stop to figure it out, approximately one in seven of all American women over twenty-one.

Some other random notions about American changes peculiar to woman: She is no longer spoken of or written of nearly so often as the smothering "Mom"—perhaps because the idea has become an unbearable cliché, or perhaps because she has outgrown the role. Nor does she appear so often in the guise of the amiably fatuous clubwoman in a funny hat; Helen Hokinson's cartoons seem now to belong to a time past. She has become more politically activist, *as* a woman, than at any time since the suffrage movement; witness the edifying spectacle of the highly non-Beatnik, in fact rather suburban-looking, women of Women Strike for Peace making monkeys of the Congressional investigators who sought to smear them as subversive in 1962. Endless discussions of her and her lot as a "problem" (possibly including this one) may well be coming to infuriate her and strain her sense of humor. Finally, since a quarter-century ago she has become infinitely more resourceful in making the best of her physical assets, whether for the sake of advantage in the mating game or merely for the hell of it. To take just one example, but not a trivial one: as Dorothy Parker noted in a famous couplet, girls who needed spectacles used to be thereby threatened with the alternatives of becoming wallflowers or else stumbling around in partial blindness; now, to leave aside entirely the matter of contact lenses, many girls manage to wear conventional glasses with so much flair that they appear a chosen adornment rather than a cross.

3

In what other respects, and to what extent, has the national character changed? Gorer, in a postscript to his earlier work written in 1965, notes as a major change in the American character over the preceding two decades a tendency he discerns in the typical American to become more compatible with authority, and especially with the authority of our own government, which, he feels, is no longer automatically assumed to be obsessed with the lust for power, but is now thought to be genuinely concerned about the general welfare. But could not this be as much a reflection of the governmental improvements we have already looked at as of any change in national character? Conveniently enough for my present purpose, Miss Mead brought *her* book up to date in 1965, too. She now finds more Americans than ever in the past turning aside from the unalloyed search for success to other, and generally less selfish, goals; she finds the need for clarity of moral purpose more pressing on the national conscience than formerly; and, in particular, she finds our attitude toward our place in the world changed in that instead of seeing ourselves as a new nation—"poorly established, uncertain, and striving"—as she says we did in the 1940s, "we now know that we are, in fact, one of the most stable, traditional-minded peoples on earth"; and with this self-confidence, Miss Mead believes, has come a new generosity of heart in which she sees great possibilities.

Others discern recent changes in other aspects of our national character. Students of American religion—of which I don't claim to be one—maintain that the quality of our religious faith has altered for the worse. Note that I say quality rather than quantity. The question of whether or not there has been a "religious revival" (or in cruder language, a "religion boom") during the postwar period has been argued back and forth. Formal church membership is up startlingly, all right (49 percent of the total population in 1940 to 63 percent in 1962), but the fact remains that the number of clergymen per population remains almost exactly what it was in 1940, and that the abandoned or converted church is in the 1960s about as familiar an American sight as the new church. But, meanwhile, the argument runs, the nature of our religion has changed in a manner apparently related to the swing toward "other-directedness"; that is, it has become vaguer, less denominational, less doctrinal, more secular, more shallow, less likely to influence people in the conduct of their lives. Will Herberg maintains that since the 1930s Protestantism, always up to then the quasi-official national religion, has been supplanted in that role by "the church of your choice"—meaning, indiscriminately, Protestantism, Catholicism, or Judaism. President Eisenhower, so often the halting but sentient oracle of the country's mood, articulated what Herberg describes as the new attitude over and over again. In 1952 he said, "Our government makes no sense unless it is founded in a deeply felt religious faith, *and I don't care what it is*." "I am the most intensely religious man I know," he declared on another occasion, prudently adding that *"that does not mean I adhere to any sect."* And, finally: "The spiritual meaning of American democracy is realized *in its three great faiths*." (Italics inserted in each case.)

Three great faiths—the doctrinal differences between which have been the cause of more bloodshed than probably anything else throughout the Western world's history, and yet among which modern America is apparently coming to feel that the choice is of little importance! Of course, it would be rash indeed to state that we are dealing here with something entirely new, or that Eisenhower's words can be taken quite at face value; there has been a strong strain of blandness in our attitude to religion for at least two generations—particularly, and for good practical reason, in the utterances of politicians. But it does seem as if a tepidly pious approval of any church, of religion in general as a "good thing"—a spirit that could hardly be more in contrast to fiery, bigoted, traditional, American evangelism—is far more general now than it was even a quarter-century ago. "Ninety-six percent say they believe in God," says the MIT philosophy professor Huston Smith, "but on examination it turns out that most people believe in believing in Him." And it does seem unmistakable that American religion has tended to secularize itself in response to an increasingly secular-minded society; Peter De Vries was not entirely joking when he wrote in *The Mackerel Plaza* about a split-level suburban church whose affable young pastor makes his congregation feel at home by delivering harmless oaths from the pulpit.

In conquering religious bigotry, then, in "liberalizing" our religion, in carrying the principle of interfaith toleration almost to the point of indifference, have we reduced our religion to bland gruel? Surely not entirely, and surely the recently increased national exposure to organized worship, like the increased national exposure to "culture," has been helpful to many. But it would be hard to deny that many church members of the 1960s join churches in search of an acceptable identity rather than in search or in expression of faith. "What are we?" the small children of agnostic parents insistently demand. The answer they want is "Protestant," "Catholic," or "Jewish," they don't care which; and they will not be put off by the evasion that they can decide for themselves when they are older; they want an assignment rather than a choice. "You have to be something," they declare with assurance. Bruce Bliven wrote in 1939 that the typical American would tolerate almost any faith but atheism; oddly enough, in the vastly more secular America of the mid-1960s that may be truer than ever.

If adherence to such amiably homogenized "religion" could hardly be given the harsh name of hypocrisy by any but the sternest of moralists, there are other things in our present national life that can. Puritanism, of course, has always been accused of having hypocrisy built into it, and America grew up as a Puritan nation; but as Puritanism has receded so dramatically in our national life during the postwar period, the hypocrisy of our official attitude toward sex, as reflected in our laws, has become more and more glaring.

"A studious, earnest, and reverent concern for sex is . . . developing in the mental habits" of the educated American citizen, Jacques Maritain decided in 1965, and the evidence in support of his thesis was to be found on every hand: uncensored literature, unprecedentedly frank and open discussion of sex in families and social groups of all kinds, the withering away during the Forties and Fifties of that concomitant of Puritanism, organized prostitution. Yet many of our laws, and the men who enforce them, too, continue to pretend that we still live in a society in which the consensus of belief is that sex outside marriage is a crime and that marriage may be dissolved only because of the grievous fault of one party to them.

This gap between practice and law becomes increasingly ludicrous—and disturbing. In 1964 a Midwestern woman was sentenced to a fine and jail term for impairing the morals of a minor; the offense was advising the minor to use contraceptives, and the minor was her sixteen-year-old daughter who had borne three illegitimate children. In Connecticut the use of contraceptives by anyone, even married persons, was still a crime in 1964. The lawyer Harriet Pilpel writes: "Fornication—that is, sexual intercourse between unmarried partners—is a crime of which, according to all relevant studies, at least half of our population is guilty." Because of the universally rigid laws restricting legal abortion (in most states, to cases in which the life of the mother is at stake), probably more than a million American women each year undergo illegal abortions often performed in unsanitary circumstances by incompetent persons—and somewhere between one and ten thousand of these women die; yet trained and skillful illegal abortionists go untouched by the law in many communities precisely because their services are so valued. The anomalies of divorce, American style, are notorious. No state allows divorce by mutual consent of a married couple; New York until 1966 allowed only adultery as grounds; the result was the fraudulently staged charade of adultery to provide the acceptable grounds, or the fraudulently established residence in some other jurisdiction—Reno or Alabama or Mexico—where more convenient grounds are recognized. Yet the unrealistic laws remain on the books; better, America would seem to be saying, to force people into fraud and to make a mockery of the courts than to write plainly into the statutes the ethic our society tacitly accepts—that a marriage may be dissolved by mutual consent of the partners provided they can afford the travel and legal fees.

Hypocrisy continues to flourish in other areas of our life, too. In business affairs we still like to make laws setting forth the boundaries of ethical practice, and then wink at violations of those laws. We are proud of the egalitarian, soak-the-rich rate schedule on which our income-tax law is theoretically based; and yet we are unwilling to repeal the many blatant loopholes that enable various categories of the rich (oil investors, top corporation executives, holders of municipal bonds, capital-gains operators) to be anything but soaked, with the result that a disproportionately heavy tax burden is borne by the middle and lower-middle class. We are invariably pious in speaking of our good intentions toward the American Indian, and to a certain degree we give concrete evidence of good intentions (the budget of the government's Bureau of Indian affairs almost tripled between 1940 and 1960 while the Indian population was increasing from 334,000 to about 525,000); but over the past quarter-century we have continued the long-established practice of breaking our treaty commitments with the Indians when we have found it convenient to do so. The list could be extended. There were a few signs in the early Sixties that the country was wearying of some of these hypocrisies enough to give up its complacency and act. New York and other states began talking about divorce-law reform. Grand and petit juries began to balk at bringing indictments in abortion cases. Even broad-scale federal tax reform appeared in prospect during Kennedy's first two years, only to see Kennedy back away from it and Johnson subsequently drop it like a hot potato.

Puritanism, while largely disappearing from our generally accepted mores, has remained enshrined in our official code of morality. Another Puritan characteristic that survives—and that continues to set us apart from other countries so sharply that they often ridicule us for it—is our strong, at times almost obsessively strong, national conscience. Like Puritan consciences both personal and national in the past, ours sometimes drives us to cruel and wrong actions; nonetheless, its existence is a fact of life. From Lexington and Concord to the war in Vietnam, we have always felt a particular and specific need to justify what we do as a nation on moral grounds. Two great acts of national violence during the past quarter-century, both of which I have mentioned earlier in different contexts, seem to me to have resulted in permanent changes in the national character through the struggle of our national conscience to deal with them.

One, of course, is the decision to use the atomic bomb in 1945. Whether a wiser nation would have decided otherwise is not the point here; the point is that both the decision and its aftereffects were characteristically American. The agonizing backs and forths during the five months when the decision was being secretly made have now been described many times—most memorably, perhaps, by Len Giovannitti and Fred Freed in *The Decision to Drop the Bomb.* From that admirable account I particularly remember the picture of Henry L. Stimson, the seventy-eight-year-old Secretary of War and key figure in the decision-making process, fighting off weariness, lying awake at night, desperately trying to clear his desk of routine decisions attendant on conducting a world war, in order to spend a single uninterrupted day weighing the one big question. For all the emphasis in his published papers on the practical considerations, he was wrestling with his angel like Jacob. After the deed, the American mood was struck off by Harry Truman, who manfully insisted that in the end the decision was his and his alone, and that he had no doubts that he had done the right thing. Behind Truman's cocky certainty, one felt, there lurked (and lurks) a certain suppressed doubt; and so with the American people. (Our half-suppressed national guilt is beautifully expressed in the fact that we have woven a legend, and even embodied it in a movie, around the figure of a major who was supposed to have participated in the Hiroshima raid and subsequently been driven by his nightmares into a life of drink and petty crime—although in cold fact the real major had not been on the

Hiroshima raid at all, but had merely flown a weather-reconnaissance mission in preparation for it.) Whether or not we were justified in what we did, in what was done in our behalf, we now walk under the burden of being the nation that dropped the bomb, and in consequence our tread is less blithe.

The other event is the Nazi slaughter of the Jews. True enough, this was done by our enemies almost entirely without our knowledge, and only by the most extreme torturing of logic can we accuse ourselves of complicity. But the American reaction to the revelations of 1945 was not the smug outrage of the innocent; indeed, the long delay before our reaction became fully apparent, on which I have commented, suggests that what we felt at first was the numbing shock that comes with the naked revelation of a terrible and hidden side of one's own nature. If the sharp reversal of national attitude that followed was partly the result of a compensation compelled by an aching Puritan conscience, that compensation was not the only effect; full apprehension of the European tragedy has left us feeling a little more part of a species rather than an isolated nation, and a little slower to hate.

In sum, the American has not changed so very much. He is the same man, but the same man many strange experiences later. Like Ulysses, he is part of all that he has met, and he has met much since 1939.

4

What could one say to the shade of a friend who died in the Thirties, to bring him quickly up to date? Wallace Markfield has a try at it in his novel *To an Early Grave*:

> What do I know? Your certainty, my problems. We got over the depression, we got over Hitler. Skeezix is married and has hands full with the kids. My life isn't really connected to anything. Discount houses are very big lately. Likewise tolerance, brotherhood, human relations, intergroup harmony. . . . I get very little personal mail. Either people are more nervous lately or there is more to get on their nerves. . . .

Everybody seems to have good taste. Bus drivers are becoming more vicious. Macy's has gone downhill. Likewise the big movie houses, the Modern Library series, wrapping paper, pencil sharpeners, kitchen matches, Nedick's orange drink. . . . Somewhere I read that it costs $3,500 a year to be poor. Comedians are very sad and keep breaking in with "Seriously, though, folks, seriously. . . ." Smilin' Jack is married. Warner Baxter, Richard Dix and Warren William died. Jack Benny is still big. No one talks anymore about Winchell. I don't think you missed too much.

Markfield's character was speaking in the context of New York. In the broader American context, but still in the same vein, he might have said that now you stay home to go to the movies, the train doesn't run to Lone Pine Junction any more, a man in the top brackets can sometimes make a profit on a gift to charity, a Catholic has been the most admired President of the century, truck drivers often go to museums, ministers are telling us that God is dead, people stand in line seven hours to get in the Music Hall at Christmastime, in a decade or two the moon looks to be subdivided like the neighbor's farm and cancer cured, and—to leave out Markfield's irony entirely—you missed plenty.

But for better or for worse? Or, to put the question another way, as we have become physically richer have we become spiritually poorer, in obedience to a fixed inverse proportion as if in a law of physics? Sociologists, perhaps trying too hard to make their study a science, seem to have promulgated such a law and adduced American experience as its proof. Edward Shils has summed up the alleged characteristics of "the new America," "America as a mass society," in a passage that resounds like a sociological litany: "Alienation, belieflessness, atomization, amorality, conformity, rootless homogeneity, moral emptiness, facelessness, egotism . . . a frivolous hedonism and a joyless vulgarity." "There is a little truth in these assertions but not very much," Shils, who is no man to suffer a cliché gladly, comments. But it is not only sociologists who are convinced of the inverse relationship. A 1939 graduate of Princeton—a member, that is, of the privileged social group that has reaped the greatest material profits from the affluent years—wrote bitterly or ruefully to the editor of his twenty-five-year classbook in 1964, "We have sold our souls for mediocrity." Among his classmates, his point of view was that of a sizable minority.

But the matter is not so simple; the moral loss is less clear-cut than the material gain. Let us see how our moral and spiritual condition stacks up with the moral prospects for America as seen by the prophets of the 1940s. Geoffrey Gorer wrote: "The time is not foreseeable when most white Americans will not feel frightened and humiliated at having Negroes as immediate neighbors, even in a restaurant." Bearing in the mind the words "frightened and humiliated," I feel safe in saying that the unforeseeable time is here. Margaret Mead, deploring the gap between life and art in America, wrote: "Out of the grandiose and beautiful and pathetic drawings of the nursery school, no new art develops." Out of what else did Abstract Expressionism develop? And Harold Laski wrote in 1947 that American industrialism was "growing oligarchical in character"; that our "historic drive toward the egalitarian society" had "failed"; and the spirit then prevalent of "anti-Semitism and of bitter hostility to the Negro advance" must give any honest observer "some hesitation about its outcome." To say now that material plenty had resulted in national moral and spiritual loss over the intervening years in the particular areas singled out by Laski would seem to me to be merely absurd.

And a reader who has gone this far will have no trouble recalling other areas—a few, at least—where, if my conclusions are right, our moral and spiritual accounts are in distinctly better order now than twenty or twenty-five years ago. Then big business was reluctantly giving ground to the public interest under strong duress; now, from however unelevated motives, it often seeks out the public interest on its own. Then Wall Street was a raw frontier town recently hacked by the New Deal out of the economic jungle; now, considering that it exists for money and nothing else, it is a relatively civilized place. Then beauty and grace of rural or urban surroundings was something taken for granted if considered at all; now they have become an active cause, at least for a vigorous minority. Culture that is more democratic, education that is more general, government that is more representative, politics that seems to be less corrupt—all these changes, most of us would probably agree, are by-products or at least concomitants of national affluence that fit the inverse-proportion notion rather badly.

And yet only the shallowest optimist would deny that something has been lost—not the simplicity and clarity of depression-time poverty; not the old-time American individualism that never quite existed, although it became the issue of the 1964 Presidential campaign; and not even personal privacy, though God knows that has become increasingly hard to come by in the age of publicity; not those things, but something less definable. I cannot define it precisely, but I have a notion that may point in the direction of a definition. My notion is that many, perhaps most, of America's current confusions and troubles stem from what might be called a widening ideological lag. Europeans like to contrast Europe with the United States by saying that the former is convinced only by facts, while the latter has a romantic New World receptivity to ideas. If so, recent social and technological changes have rushed on too fast for our ideological receptivity. In economics, politics, the treatment of minorities, and sexual mores, we cling too long and too tenaciously to ideas that have become obsolete—that is, we do not let ourselves be convinced even by facts, and the result is confusion. Long ago in America, ideas ran far ahead of realities; twenty-five years ago, on most subjects the two were pretty much neck and neck; now the fast-moving realities are opening a gap that will be hard to close.

Gertrude Stein said of writers, and might have said it of countries, "One does not get better but different and older and that is always a pleasure."

America has an old habit of regretting a dream just lost, and resolving to capture it next time. It was so in the war-haunted Thirties: "Too *bad*!" cries Fox Edwards in Thomas Wolfe's *You Can't Go Home Again*. "We should have had it! We were just beginning—we should have had it fifty years ago. . . . But all this turmoil came too soon!" It is so in the bewildering Sixties: "If ten thousand people in all walks of life will stand up on their two feet and talk out and insist," says Paul Goodman in *Growing Up Absurd,* "we shall get back our country." And it is so in the American books that are for all times: "Gatsby believed in the green light, the . . . future that year by year recedes before us," F. Scott Fitzgerald wrote at the end of his masterwork on the American theme; "It eluded us then, but that's no matter—tomorrow we will run faster, stretch out our arms farther. . . . And one fine morning—"

What is the lost thing, or the thing imagined to be lost, that animates these passages? Perhaps it is something never yet achieved, in America or elsewhere, though repeatedly achieved in the American imagination: the state of being truly free at the expense of no one else's subjection. After two hundred years it still eludes us, but there are fine mornings ahead.

NOTES ON OBLIGATIONS AND SOURCES

Rather than encumber my text with footnotes (which in some parts might have been attached to each sentence for pages at a time) or with attributions in subordinate clauses, I have decided in general to ask for the reader's confidence in the authority of my statistical sources as well as in my judgment of the figures' meaning. I can say, though, that all but a handful of the statistics are to be found in one or the other of two volumes prepared by the Bureau of the Census and published by the Government Printing Office: *The Statistical Abstract of the United States, 1964, 85th Annual Edition,* and *Historical Statistics of the United States, Colonial Times to 1957.* A selective list of sources of facts and quotations is given below, chiefly to provide suggestions for further reading.

The kind and generous persons who have helped me in one way or another are far too numerous to list in full here. I do want, though, to express my particular thanks to a few of them: Berton Roueché, Spencer Klaw, John Leggett, Elizabeth L. Eisenstein, Richard H. Rovere, Walter Lord, Bernard Taper, Harmon H. Ashley, Eric Larrabee, George A. W. Boehm, Harding Mason, Dexter Masters, Elizabeth B. Berg, and my wife Rae Brooks, who suggested sources, or gave me the benefit of their own ideas on recent change in the United States, or listened more or less patiently to mine, or read and criticized parts of the manuscript; Whitney Balliett and Dr. Lewis Thomas, who supplied facts and perspective on particular topics; Evan W. Thomas of Harper & Row, who supplied valuable advice, encouragement, and guidance at all stages of the project; and Cass Canfield, of the same firm, who not only performed those offices but conceived the idea upon which this book is based.

I. BEFORE AND AFTER

Principal Sources on the Year 1939 and Its Times:

1940 Britannica Book of the Year, a Record of the March of Events of 1939 (Chicago, London, Toronto, 1940)

1940 National Year Book Covering the Events of the Year 1939 (New York, 1940)

The *New York Times;* the New York *Herald Tribune; The Nation; The New Yorker; The New Republic*: issues of 1939

Lynd, Robert S. and H. M., *Middletown in Transition* (New York, 1937)

1939 catalogue of Sears, Roebuck and Co. (spring and summer edition)

Press releases of General Motors Corporation concerning the General Motors exhibit at the New York World's Fair of 1939–40, and "ride script" of the Futurama: supplied to me by General Motors Corporation

Smyth, Henry DeWolf, *Atomic Energy for Military Purposes* (Princeton, N.J., 1945)

Principal Sources on Concepts of Change:

Boulding, Kenneth, *The Meaning of the Twentieth Century* (New York, 1964)

Bell, Daniel, *The End of Ideology* (revised paperback edition, New York, 1962)

Eisenstein, Elizabeth L., "Rapid Change in Retrospect: Comments on the Recent Acceleration of History-Book Time" (unpublished paper)

Kristol, Irving, "The Twentieth Century Began in 1945," the *New York Times Magazine*, May 2, 1965

Allen, Frederick L., *The Big Change* (New York, 1952)

II. BIG BEYOND IMAGINING

Annual reports of U.S. Steel Corporation, General Electric Company, General Motors Corporation, and E. I. du Pont de Nemours & Company: 1939 and 1964

Brooks, John, "From Dance Cards to the Ivy-League Look," *The New Yorker*, May 18, 1957

Hacker, Andrew, editor, *The Corporation Takeover* (New York, 1964)

Bell, *The End of Ideology*

A. A. Berle, Jr., "Economic Power and the Free Society" (in *The Corporation Takeover*)

Whyte, William H., Jr., *The Organization Man* (New York, 1956)

Parkes, Henry Bamford, "The Growth of Industrialism" (in *America as a Mass Society*, edited by Philip Olson, Glencoe, Ill., 1963)

Nossiter, Bernard D., *The Mythmakers* (Boston, 1964)

Warner, W. Lloyd, and Abegglen, James, *Big Business Leaders in America* (New York, 1955)

Ferry, W. H., "Caught on the Horn of Plenty" (in *The Corporation Takeover*)

Galbraith, John Kenneth, *American Capitalism* (New York, 1951)

Brooks, John, editor, *The One and the Many* (New York, 1962)

Heilbroner, Robert L., *The Worldly Philosophers* (New York, 1953)

Keynes, John Maynard, *The General Theory of Employment, Interest, and Money* (paperback edition, New York, 1964)

Harris, Seymour E., *Economics of the Kennedy Years* (New York, 1964)

Lilienthal, David E., *Big Business: A New Era* (New York, 1953)

Harvard University Class of 1939 Twenty-Fifth Anniversary Report

III. MONEYMEN, SALESMEN, AND PHILANTHROPISTS

Foundations:

The *New York Times*, January 3, 1964, p. 1
Newsweek, August 6, 1962
Mayer, Martin, "The Leisure of the Theory Class," *Esquire*, March, 1963
Macdonald, Dwight, *The Ford Foundation* (New York, 1956)
The Ford Foundation Annual Report, 1963 and 1964

Wall Street:

Weissman, Rudolph L., *The New Wall Street* (New York, 1939)
The *New York Times*, September 25, 1964, p. 1
Brooks, John, "Making the Customers Whole," *The New Yorker*, November 14, 1964

Advertising and Public Relations:

Behrman, S. N., "The Advertising Man" (in *Faces of Five Decades*, edited by Robert B. Luce, New York, 1964)
Arnold, Thurman, *The Folklore of Capitalism* (New York, 1937)
Turner, E. S., *The Shocking History of Advertising!* (New York, 1953)

Mrs. Esther Peterson Controversy:

The New York *Herald Tribune*, October 16 and 19, 1964

IV. THE LAND'S CHANGING FACE

Smart, Charles Allen, *R.F.D.* (New York, 1938)
Kains, M. G., *Five Acres and Independence* (paperback edition, New York, 1948)
Cowley, Malcolm, *Exile's Return* (New York, 1951)
Torrence, Ridgely, *Poems* (New York, 1952)
West, James, *Plainville, U.S.A.* (New York, 1945)
Handlin, Oscar, *The American People in the Twentieth Century* (Cambridge, Mass., 1954)

Gallaher, Art, Jr., *Plainville Fifteen Years Later* (New York, 1960)
McKain, Walter C., Jr., "The Exurbanite: Why He Moved" (in *A Place to Live: The Yearbook of Agriculture 1963*, U.S. Department of Agriculture, Washington, D.C., 1963)
Blake, Peter, *God's Own Junkyard* (New York, 1964)
Faltermayer, Edmund K., "The Half-Finished Society," *Fortune*, March, 1965
Nairn, Ian, *The American Landscape: A Critical View* (New York, 1965)

Urban Renewal:

"Rebuilder of Cities—or a New Pork Barrel?" *Business Week*, December 7, 1963
Gruen, Victor, *The Heart of Our Cities* (New York, 1964)
Slayton, William L., "How to Cure a Blight in Cities" (in *A Place to Live*)

Traffic Jams:

Brecher, Ruth and Edward, "Getting to Work and Back," *Consumer Reports*, February-March, 1965

New Towns:

Von Eckardt, Wolf, "Could This Be Our Town?," *The New Republic*, 50th anniversary issue, Fall, 1964
Huxtable, Ada Louise, " 'Clusters' Instead of 'Slurbs,' " the *New York Times*, February 9 and 17, 1964

Landmark Preservation:

Ennis, Thomas W., the *New York Times*, October 19, 1964 (a useful summary of this subject)

V. WHEN EVERYONE IS SOMEBODY

U.S. Treasury Department, Internal Revenue Service, *Statistics of Income: Individual Income Tax Returns*, 1939 and 1960

Mills, C. Wright, *The Power Elite* (New York, 1956)
Kolko, Gabriel, "The American 'Income Revolution' " (in *America as a Mass Society*)

Poverty:

Harrington, Michael, *The Other America* (New York, 1962)
Nossiter, Bernard D., "It Will Be a Long War," *The Reporter*, March 26, 1964
"These Are the American Poor," *Business Week*, February 1, 1964

Bettelheim, Bruno, and Janowitz, Morris, *Social Change and Prejudice* (Glencoe, Ill., 1964)
Harvard University Class of 1939 Twenty-Fifth Anniversary Report
Spectorsky, A. C. *The Exurbanites* (Philadelphia, 1955)
Day, Lincoln and Alice, *Too Many Americans* (Boston, 1964)
Wright, Sylvia, "Do We Sit? No, We Collapse," the *New York Times Magazine*, April 19, 1964
Wiley, Bell, *So You're Going to Get Married!* (Philadelphia, 1938)

Teen-age Codes:

Eliasberg, Ann P., the *New York Times Magazine*, April 26, 1964, and November 21, 1965. Also Hechinger, Fred M., *ibid.*, December 12, 1964

Lynes, Russell, *A Surfeit of Honey* (New York, 1957)
Komarovsky, Mirra, "Blue-Collar Families," *Columbia University Forum*, Fall, 1964
Harris, Herbert, "Why Labor Lost the Intellectuals," *Harper's*, June, 1964
Stetson, Damon, the *New York Times*, February 22, 1965, p. 1
Barkin, Solomon, "The Decline of the Labor Movement" (in *The Corporation Takeover*)
Chinoy, Ely, "The Tradition of Opportunity and the Aspirations of Automobile Workers" (in *America as a Mass Society*)

VI. "PLEASURES OF A KIND"

Rosten, Leo C., *Hollywood: The Movie Colony* (New York, 1941)

Goodman, Ezra, *The Fifty Year Decline and Fall of Hollywood* (New York, 1961)

Adler, Renata, "The New Sound," *The New Yorker*, February 13, 1965

Liebling, A. J., *The Press* (New York, 1961)

An interview with Igor Stravinsky, *The New York Review of Books*, June 3, 1965

Macdonald, Dwight, "Masscult and Midcult" (in his book, *Against the American Grain*, New York, 1962)

Kronenberger, Louis, *The Cart and the Horse* (New York, 1964)

Toffler, Alvin, *The Culture Consumers* (New York, 1964)

Larrabee, Eric, *The Self-Conscious Society* (New York, 1960)

Rosenberg, Harold, "Psychoanalysis Americanized," *Commentary*, April, 1965

Swados, Harvey, "Popular Taste and the Agonies of the Young" (in *Voices of Dissent: A Collection of Articles from Dissent Magazine*, New York, 1958)

Ernst, Morris L., and Schwartz, Alan U., *Censorship: The Search for the Obscene* (New York, 1964)

Miller, Henry, "Another Open Letter," *The New Republic*, December 6, 1943 (reprinted in *Faces of Five Decades*)

VII. MIRRORS UP TO NATURE

Cowley, Malcolm, *The Literary Situation* (New York, 1954)

Hicks, Granville, "The Fighting Decade," *Saturday Review of Literature*, July 6, 1940

Jazz:

On this subject I am deeply indebted to Whitney Balliett, jazz critic for *The New Yorker*, who was most generous of his encyclopedic knowledge and sensitive appreciation, but who, of course, bears no responsibility for my statements.

Williams, Martin, "Jazz Since 1938" (in *International Cyclopedia of Music and Musicians*, New York, 1964)

Balliett, Whitney, "Comes the Revolution," *The New Yorker*, February 27, 1965

Painting:

The Nation, December 11, 1939 (a comprehensive account of the American art scene of the time)

Barr, Alfred H., Jr., editor, *Fantastic Art, Dada, Surrealism* (revised edition, New York, 1946)

Cahill, Holger, "American Painting and Sculpture in the Twentieth Century." Introduction to the catalogue of an exhibition of painting and sculpture presented at the Museum of Modern Art in New York City in February, 1955. For calling my attention to this excellent essay, and lending me a copy of it, I am indebted to Alfonso Ossorio.

Baur, John I. H., *Between the Fairs: 25 Years of American Art, 1939–1964* (New York, 1964)

The New American Painting. Catalogue of a showing in eight European countries 1958–59. The Museum of Modern Art, New York, 1959

Blesh, Rudi, *Modern Art USA* (New York, 1956)

Rosenberg, Harold, *The Tradition of the New* (New York, 1959)

VIII. FROM PARADISE TO BERKELEY

Schuyler, William M., editor, *The American Year Book: A Record of Events and Progress, Year 1938* (New York, 1939). The section on education provides a broad view of the U.S. educational situation at the end of the 1930s.

Education's "Industrial Revolution":

Gross, Ronald, and Murphy, Judith, *The Revolution in the Schools* (New York, 1964)

Berkeley:

Goodman, Paul, "Thoughts on Berkeley," *The New York Review of Books*, January 14, 1965

Stern, Sol, "A Deeper Disenchantment," *Liberation*, February, 1965

Hook, Sidney, "Second Thoughts on Berkeley," *Teachers College Record*, October, 1965

Youth in the Depression:

Chamberlain, John, *The American Stakes* (New York, 1940)

Lynd, *Middletown in Transition*

"The $25 Billion-a-Year Accent on Youth," *Newsweek*, November 30, 1964

"On the Fringe of a Golden Era," *Time*, January 29, 1965

Greene, Gael, *Sex and the College Girl* (New York, 1964)

Bromley, Dorothy D., and Britten, Florence H., *Youth and Sex* (New York, 1938)

Coles, Robert, "Opportunity to Be What?," *The New Republic*, 50th anniversary, Fall, 1964

Goodman, Paul, *Growing Up Absurd* (New York, 1960)

Rioting:

The *New York Times*, July 5, 1965, p. 1

Student Left:

Powledge, Fred, the *New York Times*, March 15, 1965

Gibson, Walker, "How Different We Were!," the *New York Times Magazine*, June 13, 1965

The Princeton Alumni Weekly, October 20, 1964

The remarks of William C. De Vane that I have quoted are from a private talk.

IX. THE RISE OF THE SORCERERS

Smyth, *Atomic Energy for Military Purposes*

Lapp, Ralph E., *The New Priesthood* (New York, 1965)

Masters, Dexter, *The Accident* (new edition, New York, 1965)
Clark, Marguerite, *Medicine Today* (New York, 1960)
Dubos, René, *Mirage of Health* (New York, 1959)
I owe thanks to Dr. Lewis Thomas, Professor and Chairmen of the Department of Medicine of the New York University School of Medicine, for a lucid and engaging briefing on the state of his art and its prospects.
Miller, Helen Hill, "Beyond the Merely Bearable," *The New Republic*, 50th anniversary issue, Fall, 1964
Handlin, *The American People in the Twentieth Century*

Automation:

"Triple Revolution: Cybernation, Weaponry, Human Rights," *Liberation*, April, 1964
Silberman, Charles E., "The Real News about Automation," *Fortune*, January, 1965
Drucker, Peter F., "Automation Is Not the Villain," the *New York Times Magazine*, January 10, 1965

The Consumers Union Report on Smoking and the Public Interest (Mount Vernon, N.Y., 1963)

X. SOME MORE EQUAL THAN OTHERS

The Crisis, official publication of the NAACP, issues of 1939
Kempton, Murray, *Part of Our Time* (New York, 1955)
Roche, John P., *The Quest for the Dream* (New York, 1963)
Cash, W. J., *The Mind of the South* (New York, 1941)
McLaughlin, Robert, "A Short Wait Between Trains," *The New Yorker*, June 17, 1944
Lewis, Anthony, editor, *Portrait of a Decade* (New York, 1964)
Silberman, Charles E., *Crisis in Black and White* (New York, 1964)
Bettelheim and Janowitz, *Social Change and Prejudice*
Birmingham anecdote, p. 296. I heard this story over radio station WBAI in New York City on October 8, 1965. I later learned

that it had been carried by the regular A.P. news wires but had, curiously, appeared in hardly any newspapers anywhere.

Woodward, C. Vann, "After Watts—Where Is the Negro Revolution Headed?," the *New York Times Magazine*, August 29, 1965

The Negro Family: The Case for National Action (Moynihan Report), Office of Policy Planning and Research, U.S. Department of Labor, March, 1965

Fortune, February, 1946 (anti-Semitism survey)

Kazin, Alfred, *Starting Out in the Thirties* (Boston, 1965)

The *New York Times* items on extermination camps referred to on p. 305 appeared in the issues of May 19, July 3, and November 14, 1944.

XI. JOINING THE WORLD

Cater, Douglass, *Power in Washington* (New York, 1964)

Wicker, Tom, "Winds of Change in the Senate," the *New York Times Magazine*, September 12, 1965

Swados, Harvey, "What's Left of the Left?," *The Nation*, anniversary issue, 1965

Dulles, Eleanor Lansing, *John Foster Dulles: The Last Year* (New York, 1963)

Meyer, Karl E., *The New America* (New York, 1961)

Raymond, Jack, *Power at the Pentagon* (New York, 1964)

Appel, Benjamin, *With Many Voices: Europe Talks about America* (New York, 1963)

Remarks of Stevan Dedijer:

Sulzberger, C. L., the *New York Times*, November 3, 1965

XII. DIFFERENT AND OLDER

Mead, Margaret, *And Keep Your Powder Dry!* (revised paperback edition, New York, 1965)

Gorer, Geoffrey, *The American People* (revised paperback edition, New York, 1965)

Fromm, Erich, *Man for Himself* (New York, 1947)

Riesman, David, with Reuel Denney and Nathan Glazer, *The Lonely Crowd: Study of the Changing American Character* (New Haven, Conn., 1950)

Lipset, Seymour M., *The First New Nation* (New York, 1963)

Guzzardi, Walter, Jr., "The Young Executives," *Fortune*, June, 1964; and subsequent articles by Guzzardi in July, September, and October, 1964

Herberg, Will, "Religion and Culture in Present-Day America" (in *America as a Mass Society*)

Martineau, Harriet, *Society in America*, abridged (paperback, New York, 1965)

Maritain, Jacques, *Reflections on America* (paperback, New York, 1965)

Pilpel, Harriet F., "Sex vs. the Law," *Harper's*, January, 1965

Lader, Lawrence, "The Scandal of Abortion—Laws," the *New York Times Magazine*, April 25, 1965

Giovannitti, Len, and Freed, Fred, *The Decision to Drop the Bomb* (New York, 1965)

Shils, Edward, "The Theory of Mass Society" (in *America as a Mass Society*)

GENERAL

Lerner, Max, *America as a Civilization* (New York, 1957)

Goldman, Eric F., *The Crucial Decade—and After* (paperback, New York, 1960)

Wattenberg, Ben J. and Scammon, Richard M., *This U.S.A.: An Unexpected Family Portrait of 194,067,296 Americans* (New York, 1965)

Morison, Samuel E., *The Oxford History of the American People* (New York, 1965)

INDEX

70 71 72 73 12 11 10 9 8 7 6 5 4 3